MIGRATION, DISPLACEMENT AND DIVERSITY

MIGRATION, DISPLACEMENT AND DIVERSITY

The IRiS anthology

Edited by

LAURENCE LESSARD-PHILLIPS
ANNA PAPOUTSI
NANDO SIGONA
PALADIA ZISS

UNIVERSITY OF BIRMINGHAM | IRiS
Institute for Research into Superdiversity

Published in 2023 by

Oxford Publishing Services
34 Warnborough Road
Oxford, OX2 6JA
www.oxfordpublishingservices.com

on behalf of the Institute for Research into Superdiversity (IRiS),
University of Birmingham, UK.

ISBN: 978 1 7397846 4 5 (hardback)
       978 1 7397846 2 1 (paperback)

Typeset in Garamond by Oxford Publishing Services.

Contents

CONTENTS

PART TWO:
LENSES, PRISMS AND METHODS

CONTENTS

CONTENTS

CONTENTS

CONTENTS

Contributor Biographies

Adejoh, Samuel Ojima – senior lecturer, Faculty of Social Sciences, University of Lagos and Research Fellow, Department of Social Work, University of Free State, South Africa. A sociologist and social work educator interested in using sociological methods to identify the probable causes and effects of social problems in society. His areas of interest are the social determinants of human health and illness and psychosocial factors in the management of diseases.

Afridi, Asif – deputy CEO at brap, a UK-based equality and human rights charity (www.brap.org.uk), a trustee of the Lankelly Chase and Baring Foundations, and a panel member on the independent Inquiry into the Future of Civil Society in England.

Allen, Chris – associate professor, School of Criminology, University of Leicester and leader of the 'Extremism Hub' based in the Centre for Hate Studies at the same university.

Allsopp, Jennifer – Birmingham fellow, School of Social Policy, University of Birmingham and visiting professor at Trinity College Rome Campus. Her research explores how people move and mobilize to pursue what they see as viable futures for themselves and their families in contexts of protracted displacement. She is a regular consultant to the European Parliament and the Council of Europe and a keen advocate for co-production in migration research.

Anderson, Bridget – professor of Migration, Mobilities and Citizenship, and director of Migration Mobilities Bristol (MMB), University of Bristol.

Antonsich, Marco – senior lecturer in human geography at Loughborough University in the UK. He is also the convenor of the Loughborough University Nationalism Network (LUNN).

CONTRIBUTOR BIOGRAPHIES

Ayrton, Rachel – Leverhulme early career fellow (2022–27) at IRiS, School of Social Policy, University of Birmingham, specializing in qualitative methodologies and epistemologies, and currently working on conviviality and grassroots peacebuilding among the South Sudanese diaspora in the UK.

Bhambra, Gurminder K. – professor of postcolonial and decolonial studies in the School of Global Studies at the University of Sussex. She is also a fellow of the British Academy and president of the British Sociological Association.

Bica, Mihai Calin – policy and campaigns coordinator at the Roma Support Group in London. The focus of his work is on the migrant rights and lives of the Roma communities in the UK.

Black, Richard – pro vice-chancellor and head of the College of Social Sciences at the University of Birmingham. He has been engaged in research on migration, refugees and development for more than thirty years.

Blackledge, Adrian – professor of sociolinguistics at the University of Stirling. He is a fellow of the Academy of Social Sciences, a distinguished visiting fellow at the Advanced Research Collaborative, The Graduate Centre, City University New York, and former Birmingham poet laureate.

Bloom, Tendayi – lecturer in politics and international studies at the University of Birmingham in the UK where she teaches political theory. She is interested in the relationship between noncitizens and states and between noncitizens and the multistate system.

Boccagni, Paolo – professor of sociology at the University of Trento in Italy. He was principal investigator of the ERC HOMInG project, funded by HORIZON 2020, which is, in effect, a multiscale comparative investigation into the nexus between home and migration.

Bonfanti, Sara – is a social anthropologist in the Department of Culture, Politics and Society at the University of Torino. She specializes in gender studies and is an expert on South Asian diasporas. She has collaborated in the ERC HOMInG project doing ethnographic research and oral history with migrants across Europe.

Burge, Amy – senior lecturer in popular fiction, University of Birmingham. Her interest is in popular genres, especially romance, with a focus on intersectional readings and approaches.

Canning, Victoria – associate professor of criminology, University of Bristol; associate director, Border Criminologies, Oxford University; head of the Centre for the Study of Poverty and Social Justice; and trustee at Statewatch EU. Her research is into the harms inflicted by asylum systems in northern Europe, and their impact on women and survivors of conflict and torture.

Cochrane, Allan – emeritus professor of urban studies at the Open University in Milton Keynes. His research is focused on the politics of, and life in, cities and regions.

Cohen, Robin – professor emeritus at the University of Oxford. He writes on social identities, migration, diasporas and creolization. A list of his publications can be found at https://oxford.academia.edu/RobinCohen.

Cole, Matthew – professor of environmental economics, University of Birmingham. His research is on the relationships between economic development and the natural environment, with a particular focus on international trade, air pollution, health and biodiversity.

Craven, Catherine – research fellow at IRiS at the University of Birmingham. The focus of her current research is on the politics of diaspora governance, and its global and historical entanglements.

Creese, Angela – professor of linguistic ethnography at University of Stirling. She is a fellow of the Academy of Social Sciences, and a distinguished visiting fellow at the Advanced Research Collaborative, The Graduate Centre, City University New York.

Dhesi, Surindar – associate professor in environmental health and risk management at the University of Birmingham. The focus of her research is on the living and working conditions of displaced and vulnerable people.

Elgenius, Gabriella – professor of sociology, Department of Sociology and Work Science, University of Gothenburg. She is an associate member of the University of Oxford and a member of the Royal Society of Arts. The focus of her research is civil society and inclusion in conditions of socio-economic vulnerability, and the nostalgia and ethnic nationalism of the radical right.

Favell, Adrian – professor of social and political theory, and founding director of the Radical Humanities Laboratory at University College, Cork.

He is the author of *The Integration Nation: Immigration and Colonial Power in Liberal Democracies* (Polity 2022).

Geldof, Dirk – professor of sociology at the Faculty of Design Sciences (University of Antwerp) and senior researcher at the Centre of Family Studies (Odisee University of Applied Sciences, Brussels).

Gilardoni, Guia – lecturer in the sociology of education, Catholic University of Sacred Heart, Brescia, Italy. Over the last decade, she has been committed to supporting knowledge exchanges between scholars, practitioners, and policymakers. She is a member on the Board of Directors of the International Migration Research Network (IMISCOE).

Godin, Marie – postdoctoral fellow, Refugee Studies Centre, and research associate, Centre on Migration, Policy and Society (University of Oxford). Her broad research interests are migration and technologies, with a focus on diasporic engagement and second-generation diasporic activism, development, and transnational social protection.

Goodson, Lisa – associate professor, IRiS Community and Practitioner Research (CPRP) lead and founding member, School of Social Policy, University of Birmingham. Lisa's research specialisms are displacement and sexual and gender based violence (SGBV); forced migration and integration; poverty, social exclusion and place based interventions; community engaged research co-production.

Griffiths, Melanie – Birmingham fellow, School of Geography and Environmental Sciences, University of Birmingham. She is a social scientist working on asylum, mobility and immigration enforcement in the UK, with a particular interest in time, emotions, rights to family life, and masculinity.

Grzymala-Kazlowska, Aleksandra – professor in the Faculty of Sociology and at the Centre of Migration Research at the University of Warsaw, particularly interested in migrant adaptation, inclusion, community sponsorship, and discourses on immigration. She is also editor-in-chief of the *Central and Eastern European Migration Review*.

Inda, Jonathan Xavier – professor and director of Latin American and Latino Studies at the University of Illinois, Chicago. He has written about anthropology and globalization, Foucauldian social theory, the geneticization of race, and the government of immigration.

Jablonowski, Kuba – research fellow, Department of Geography, University of Exeter. He is currently investigating the politics of data and automation in border-control regimes. He has also conducted research on political action generated by free movement before and after the 2016 EU referendum.

Jolly, Andy – is a lecturer in social work at the University of Plymouth. His research focuses on migration, household food security, and child welfare.

Kuznetsova, Irina – associate professor, School of Geography, Earth and Environmental Sciences, and member of IRiS, University of Birmingham. Her recent projects focus on the social consequences of population displacement from Ukraine's war-torn territories, including internal and international displacement since 2014, issues of citizenship and belonging, mental health, and gender-based violence. Dr Kuznetsova also works on the impact of migration on rural communities in LMI countries and migration and refugee policy in Russia.

Lessard-Phillips, Laurence – associate professor, IRiS, Department of Social Policy, Sociology and Criminology, University of Birmingham, and senior research fellow, IRiS. She is interested in social inequalities, as well as definitional, conceptual and methodological dilemmas, linked to migration.

Lind, Jacob – migration researcher at Malmö University, and visiting post-doctoral fellow at Copenhagen University. The focus of his research is on the effects of illegality on childhood, youth, and family life, and the vulnerabilities that states create through implementing increasingly hostile policies.

Liu-Farrer, Gracia – professor of sociology, Graduate School of Asia-Pacific Studies, and director of Institute of Asian Migrations at Waseda University. Her research focuses on immigration and immigrants in Japan and student and labour mobilities in Asia and Europe.

Martin-Jones, Marilyn – emeritus professor, School of Education, University of Birmingham. In 2008, she founded the MOSAIC Centre for Research on Multilingualism and has been conducting research into bilingualism and multilingualism in different regions of Britain for thirty years.

Martins Jr, Angelo – assistant professor in sociology, Department of Social Policy, Sociology and Criminology, University of Birmingham. He engages in ethnographic research on difference, intersectionality, social inequalities, and decolonial sociological approaches, to has participated in debates on migration and 'modern slavery'.

Meer, Nasar– professor of sociology, School of Social and Political Sciences, founding director of RACE.ED, University of Edinburgh. Co-investigator into the impacts of the pandemic on ethnic and racialized groups in the UK (UKRI 2021–23), and principal investigator for GLIMER (Governance and the Local Integration of Migrants and Europe's Refugees) (JPI ERA Net/Horizon-2020).

Menjívar, Cecilia – holds the Dorothy L. Meier Chair in Social Equities and is Professor of Sociology at UCLA. She has researched the effects of immigration laws, immigration enforcement, and legal statuses on various aspects of immigrants' lives.

Moreno-Amador, Gracia – lecturer in social work and sociology at Pablo de Olavide University, Seville. She teaches international migration at the University Institute of Studies on Migration at Comillas University. Her research is on refugee policies, migration and asylum rights, mobility, and borders.

Neal, Sarah – professor of sociology, University of Sheffield. Her work explores the situated politics of belonging and everyday multiculture in urban and rural social life. Sarah's current research focuses on three areas – rural migration and Brexit; informal sport and urban social participation; and children's citizenship in multifaith societies.

Nicholls, Natasha – doctoral student in social policy, University of Birmingham. Her work focuses on the UK Community Sponsorship scheme, specifically the temporality of hospitality and the power dynamics between volunteers and refugees.

Nowicka, Magdalena – sociologist and professor, Institute of Social Sciences, Humboldt-Universität zu Berlin, and head of Department Integration, German Centre for Integration and Migration Research DeZIM, Berlin. Her research focuses on the transnational aspects of migration and integration, including transformations of racism.

Ögtem-Young, Özlem – specializes in politics of migration, belonging, socio-economic inequality and financial precarity, and is a research fellow at the Centre on Household Assets and Savings Management (CHASM) in the Department of Social Policy, Sociology and Criminology at the University of Birmingham.

Ozgen, Ceren – economist working at the intersection of labour and urban economics. She has written on the impact of cultural diversity, international migration and firm innovation. Her recent research is on the civic and economic integration of refugees in host country labour markets.

Papoutsi, Anna – Leverhulme early career fellow (2022–25) in IRiS, School of Social Policy, Sociology and Criminology. Her work focuses on the temporalities of border control and the politics of time involved in migration governance.

Parzniewski, Szymon – research associate, Alliance Manchester Business School (AMBS), University of Manchester. He researches social complexity in disaster contexts with a specific focus on how socially disadvantaged groups cope with environmental, political, and social challenges.

Pennant, April-Louise – sociologist and Leverhulme early career fellow, Cardiff University. She researches and centres alternative narratives in her work to 'speak back' and facilitate better understandings in areas shrouded in whiteness by spotlighting Blackness, specifically the experiences of Black girls, women, and enslaved Africans.

Pertek, Sandra Iman – ESRC postdoctoral fellow, University of Birmingham, with a special interest in violence against women and faith. Her research integrates intersectional and socioecological approaches, and religious engagement in humanitarian protection from gendered violence.

Phillimore, Jenny – founding director of IRiS; interested in the relationship between violence, trauma and refugee integration. She is currently using evidence from the SEREDA project to push for migrant women to get access to the provisions of the Victims' Bill.

Piemontese, Stefano – social anthropologist and former Marie Skłodowska-Curie research fellow at IRiS. He uses ethnographic, collaborative and audiovisual methods to conduct research on migration and social inequalities among young people.

Pignolo, Loïc – acquired a PhD in sociology from the University of Geneva in 2022 and is currently working as a postdoctoral researcher at the University of Geneva. The main focus of his work is on irregular migration and informal economies.

Ram, Monder – professor of small businesses and director of the Centre for Research in Ethnic Minority Entrepreneurship. His research is on ethnic-minority entrepreneurship, and on employment relations within and the policies of small firms.

Ramadan, Nazek – executive director of Migrant Voice with long experience of working with migrants, refugees, asylum seekers and ethnic minorities in the UK. She is interested in promoting their voice, representation and participation in the media and policy platforms.

Reyes, Marisol – research fellow at the University of Birmingham. Her research focuses on the kinds of hospitality provided by the Community Sponsorship Scheme in the UK and Europe and, more recently, by the Homes for Ukraine scheme to resettle newly arrived refugees.

Rolfe, Heather – director of research and relationships at British Future. She previously led social research at the National Institute of Economic and Social Research. Her research interests are in immigration and integration, in particular within the labour market and education. She leads the analysis and interpretation of the Immigration Tracker Survey carried out for British Future by Ipsos.

Sarli, Annavittoria – gained a PhD in anthropology in 2011, then undertook research in migration at the ISMU Foundation (Milan). In 2020–22, she was a Marie Sklodowska Curie research fellow at IRiS, where she studied the intercultural competence of second-generation individuals. In 2022 she joined the University of Palma (Italy) as an assistant professor.

Schiller, Maria – assistant professor of public policy, migration and diversity, Erasmus University, Rotterdam, theme lead on diverse and inclusive cities, Vital Cities and Citizens Initiative, and managing coordinator of the Leiden-Delft-Erasmus (LDE) Master program 'Governance of Migration and Diversity'.

Scholten, Peter – professor of public administration, Erasmus University, Rotterdam, director of the collaborative Leiden–Delft–Erasmus (LDE) Research Center on the Governance of Migration and Diversity (GMD), as well as of the International Migration Research Network (IMISCOE).

Sigona, Nando – professor of international migration and forced displacement and director of the Institute for Research into Superdiversity (IRiS) at the University of Birmingham. He is also research associate at the University of Oxford's Refugee Studies Centre, and at the ODI think tank.

Sime, Daniela – professor of youth, migration and social justice, University of Strathclyde. Her work focuses on the impact of migration on young people's sense of identity and belonging, education and transitions, access to services and opportunities for civic participation.

Stonebridge, Lyndsey – professor of humanities and human rights, University of Birmingham. Her work relates to refugee studies, human rights, and the effects of violence on the mind in the twentieth and twenty-first centuries.

Taal, Sarah – director and policy advocate at the Baobab Women's Project, a Birmingham-based community organization dedicated to assisting and empowering refugee and migrant women through what are often difficult asylum applications.

Tonkiss, Katie – senior lecturer in sociology and policy, School of Social Sciences and Humanities, Aston University, Birmingham, UK. Her research mainly addresses questions that are related to noncitizenship, statelessness and belonging.

Vargas-Silva, Carlos – professor in migration studies, University of Oxford, director of Centre on Migration, Policy and Society (COMPAS), and fellow of Kellogg College. He holds a joint appointment between COMPAS, at the School of Anthropology & Museum Ethnography, and the Oxford Department of International Development.

Vertovec, Steven – founding director of the Max Planck Institute for the Study of Religious and Ethnic Diversity, Göttingen, Germany, and former founding director of Centre on Migration, Policy and Society (COMPAS) at the University of Oxford.

Wemyss, Georgie – senior lecturer and co-director of the Centre for Research on Migration, Refugees and Belonging (CMRB) at the University of East London, UK. Among other publications, she is a co-author of *Bordering* (2019).

Yeo, Colin – barrister, writer, campaigner and consultant specializing in immigration law at Garden Court Chambers, Lincoln's Inn Fields, London, and founder and editor of the website freemovement.org.uk. Also author of *Refugee Law* (2022).

Yumoto, Hiromi – PhD candidate in management at the University of Birmingham. The focus of her thesis is on the economic and legal integration of refugees in the Netherlands, especially on the determinants of gaining citizenship and assimilation in the labour market.

Yuval-Davis, Nira – professor emerita, founder and honorary director of the Centre for Research on Migration, Refugees and Belonging (CMRB) at the University of East London. Among other publications she is co-author of *Bordering* (2019).

Zanna, Jamila Wakawa – PhD candidate, School of Geography, Earth and Environmental Sciences, University of Birmingham. She works on forced internal displacement, environmental health, and social conditions of internally displaced women in the informal settlements of Abuja, Nigeria.

Zazai, Sabir – OBE, CEO of Scottish Refugee Council and a former refugee from Afghanistan. He is a fellow of the Royal Society of Edinburgh, visiting practice fellow at the Centre for Trust Peace and Social Relations, Coventry University, and has honorary doctorates from the University of Glasgow and the Open University.

Ziss, Paladia – PhD candidate in sociology, University of Birmingham. She studies social relationships and the politics of time in protracted displacement in Germany and Turkey. Broadly, she is interested in temporalities, forced displacement, bordering and belonging.

Introduction:
The Prism of Migration

The Editors

This anthology marks the tenth anniversary of the University of Birmingham's Institute for Research into Superdiversity (IRiS). A decade is an important milestone for a research centre. We want to take this opportunity to think collectively about past, present and future directions of research on migration and diversity. The contributors are current and former IRiS staff members and affiliates, researchers, practitioners and activists we have encountered, and with whom we have worked and engaged at different times and places over the years. They come from a range of disciplines and professions, work on different aspects, spaces and times of the migration phenomenon, and express a variety of scientific and political approaches. As a result, our anthology accommodates different opinions and diverse perspectives.

The chapters offer unique and concise insights into a decade of political, social and economic transformations. This has been a time when multiple interlocked crises have shaken the world and taken-for-granted alliances, when public awareness of the climate and environmental crisis has grown (although there is still plenty to do), and when wars, human rights violations, and poverty have driven millions of people to move both internally and across international borders. Responses to these movements have been mixed, polarized, and in some cases violent. Pursuing different political projects and agendas, political actors, aided by the media, have fed and mobilized anti-immigration sentiments. In the USA, for example, the criminalization of Mexican migrants and migrant caravans from central America, the promise to expand the border wall between the USA and Mexico, the commitment to produce in America and prioritize Americans in the job market, and the travel bans on citizens from majority Muslim countries, have been central factors in Donald Trump's electoral success.

Our contributors were given a loose brief: drawing on their own research or practice, they were to write a short piece focusing on the past decade or with an eye on emerging trends and future directions of migration studies and governance. In some cases, we suggested themes we thought would contribute to the overall picture, in others we left it to the contributors to come up with ideas and provided guidance and feedback on early drafts to ensure consistency. The collection you have in front of you covers a range of disciplinary traditions including social anthropology, sociology, human geography, politics, social policy, economics, international relations, development studies and humanities. It also covers a range of writing styles, methodological approaches, thematic interests and political standpoints. This includes different uses of capitalizations or inverted commas when referring to labels that describe political and social identities. The style of contributions varies from ethnographic vignettes to theoretical ruminations, from poetic contemplations to detailed accounts of research encounters, and from methodological reflections to political and policy interventions. Collectively, they evoke a world increasingly, but unevenly, interconnected through migration, layered with, and shaped by, the sediments of previous and current encounters (not necessarily peaceful ones).

We have grouped the contributions into four loosely defined sections inspired by a set of visual images, from visions to gazes, from bird's-eye views to close-up portraits, from spotlights to blind spots.

Visions and concepts

The first section considers old and new conceptualizations of, theoretical approaches to, and potential directions in the study of migration, displacement and diversity. *Sigona* opens this section with a piece looking back to the geopolitical changes that migration and diversity have undergone in the past decade and considers the implications for the future of the sector and migration itself. *Phillimore* gives an overview of how IRiS's research on migration and superdiversity has affected policy and made a difference to the people with whom we work. Subsequently, *Anderson* lays out the fundamentals of migration, citizenship, and labour relations, briefly outlining how the interplay of the border and labour regimes produces migrants and citizens alike, as well as different types of workers and labour relations. *Meer* then zooms in on the race–migration nexus to consider the institutional, historical, and political reasons why this distinction persists, despite the governance of the two issues becoming increasingly intertwined as a result of everyday bordering practices. *Yuval-Davis* and *Wemyss* further elaborate on some key transformations that brought this re-localization of border control into the everyday. They revisit their seminal work on 'everyday bordering' to consider the rescaling and rebordering caused by Covid, Brexit, offshoring practices and other developments.

The focus then turns to the concept of superdiversity and *Favell* brings us back to its origins, reminding us of its politico-conceptual trajectory: from the 1990s' optimism and utopian globalisms, the rise of the 'age of migration', all the way to the emergence of identity politics and the woke generation. He draws our attention to how (super)diversity, routed in neoliberalism and individualism, was an attempt to accommodate the complexity and hybridity of the post-colonial world, flattening the thornier issues of cultural incommensurability to celebrate (individual) difference. *Bhambra*, in turn, zooms in on the emergence of 'superdiversity' within the context of UK multiculturalism, arising out of the political mobilization and demands of Commonwealth migrants. She highlights the urgent need to reckon with the colonial histories and legacies, and the ensuing racial hierarchies involved in the British citizenship regime. *Tonkiss* and *Bloom*, looking at the UK's superdiverse context, consider the concept and existential condition of noncitizenship as a particular and substantive relation to the state and not merely as the absence of a relationship. Such a conceptual shift allows us to appreciate the condition and experience of being forced to live a life 'despite the state'. To break away from the ethno-national state, *Antonsich* highlights the political imperative to focus on the socio-spatial register of the nation-state, rather than solely on the city, as a site in which to research superdiversity. *Craven* thinks about the world-making and transformative potential of diaspora communities, both at the local level and for global politics, while at the same time shedding light on the complexities and interplays between the local and the global.

A cluster of contributions on the time and temporality of migration is opened by *Griffiths*, who provides an insightful and accessible initiation to the role that time plays in migration and how to begin thinking about it in the context of migration and border studies. *Stonebridge* turns to Behrouz Boochani's book *No friend but the Mountains*, and the temporalities of refugeedom, statelessness and imprisonment, where life is dedicated to survival; where waiting is the only way of 'being-in-the-camp'; where time is eternal and is administered in ways that make one's existence intolerable. Faced with the 'extermination of human time', the mountains become Boochani's only friends, a temporal touchpoint linking past and present, the camp and the outside world. *Papoutsi* considers the temporalities of forced immobility in Athens (Greece), how state and border violence is inflicted through time, and how affective technologies, precarity and unlivability deplete migrant bodies and their labour.

Turning to the everyday, *Grzymala-Kazlowska*'s contribution interrogates how anchoring processes may relate to the experiences of Polish migrants in the UK and considers the concept's analytical potential in comparison with 'integration'. *Nowicka* thinks about the challenges and shortcomings of superdiversity, and the basis of everyday conviviality, as well as the banalities of multiculturalism, in an effort to go beyond ethno-nationalism and ethnic diversity. *Bonfanti* and *Boccagni* reflect on the role of home and homemaking in diverse European neighbourhoods. They focus on everyday conviviality in Italy and offer their take on how difference plays out at the level of the condo, and provide fascinating examples to illustrate their argument. Looking in particular at young migrants, *Ögtem-Young* adopts a rhizomatic lens through which to look at the displacement and belonging of unaccompanied asylum seekers in the UK. Seeking to capture the messiness of belonging in multiple places at once, her root-less belonging is fleeting, ephemeral and fluctuating, a way to resist the subjugation and othering of the state. *Sime* focuses on the experiences of young migrants, the particular challenges they face in their endeavours and how they are treated by state policies and protection regimes. *Vargas-Silva* provides an invaluable sneak peek at the opaque (to most of us) world and inner workings of publishing, identifying potential future patterns and trends. The section closes with *Vertovec*'s beautiful homage to the work of the late Jan Blommaert on sociolinguistics and superdiversity, which offers an accessible insight into the paradigmatic transformations brought about by Blommaert's perspective on the concept of super-diversity.

Lenses, prisms and methods

How does the lens we apply shape our understanding of migration and diversity? Entries in the second section offer insights into different methodological and epistemological approaches, spanning disciplines and writing registers. With the poem 'Eel', *Blackledge* and *Creese* let the reader meander through the superdiverse halls of the Bull Ring market in Birmingham, thus providing a unique approach to representing ethnographic research and superdiversity. *Allsopp* links Dante's *Divine Comedy* as an allegory for researching forced migration journeys and the methodological opportunities and challenges that arise from it, using her own research experience. Continuing along this 'literary' theme, we then move to the entry by *Martin-Jones*, who demonstrates the complementarity between research on language, literature and contemporary diversities with that of superdiversity, through an exploration of the extensive collaboration between the MOSAIC Research Group and IRiS over the past decade. As a good example of this complementarity, the entry from *Burge* explores how popular fiction, and in particular the genres of crime, fantasy, and romance, engage with the topic of forced migration as a unique gauge of public attitudes. We then embed ourselves in a story of the complex experiences and identities of young Italians of migrant descent in the UK, as told by *Piemontese*, surrounding the jubilant celebration of Italy's victory in the 2020 European football championship. We then carry on exploring research-based storytelling, this time focused on the 'work twice as hard for half as much' mentality embedded in the educational pathways of Black British girls and women, through the stories penned by *Pennant* from her PhD work. The next two entries focus on more biographical accounts of superdiversity and forced migration. *Cohen*'s biographical entry on the multifaceted life of Lafcadio Hearn (1850–1904) as an epitome of both creolization and superdiversity steps into the past to show how one's life and engagement with the world can help us better understand our current (and potentially future) context. The entry from *Lind* takes an autobiographical turn to explore the way in which his experience of conducting his doctoral research in Birmingham and Malmö shaped his learning about comparative ethnographic research. Learning experience is also at the core of *Lessard-Phillips*'s entry. Using the anthology's visual metaphor, she explores the challenges, that taking a multidimensional perspective to the (quantitative) study of superdiversity and integration generate. *Goodson* shares what she learnt as part of her vast experience with the IRiS Community Practitioner Research Programme (CPRP), focusing on the advantages, challenges, and possibilities of conducting community research in the context of forced migration. Finally, in the last entry in this section by *Ayrton*, we engage in reflections on how to conduct inclusive and collaborative research while being in a position of privilege, with a particular focus on involving advisory board members who have experienced, or been affected by, conflict. The varied perspectives presented in this section only scratch the surface of the multiple, complex, and novel ways in which one can conduct research into, and write about, migration and superdiversity.

Spotlights, blindspots and case studies

The third section includes a series of case studies that shine a light on particular geographies, relations, communities, standpoints and themes in migration studies. *Black* offers a critical perspective on the idea that development 'interventions' reduce the need or propensity to migrate from Africa. The plight of internally-displaced people and the longing for home in Ukraine is the focus of *Kuznetsova*'s contribution. The refugee crisis in Ukraine is also the focus of *Pertek*'s contribution, which looks at the situation of Ukranian women in Poland. Using rich administrative data on all refugees in the Netherlands, *Ozgen, Cole* and *Yumoto* reflect on the challenges refugees face to legal and economic integration. *Parzniewski* examines the role that 'othering' plays in disaster responses and argues that we need a better understanding of disaster responses under conditions of superdiversity. *Zanna, Adejoh* and *Dhesi* bring to the fore the dynamic of displacement and coping strategies of internally displaced people in Nigeria. The issue of legal integration returns in *Ziss*'s piece, which focuses on citizenship and naturalization for Syrians in Turkey. In their contributions, *Nicholls* and *Reyes* offer complementary perspectives on community involvement in refugee resettlement in the UK. *Ram* points to the challenges that refugee entrepreneurs have to overcome to set up and run their businesses, which incidentally generate significant economic and social value. While *Allen* shows how Islamophobia becomes normalized and unquestioned in a city like Birmingham, which hosts one of the largest and most diverse Muslim population in the UK, *Martins* looks at how colonial legacies continue to shape the lives of Brazilian migrants in London. Food insecurity is the lens through which *Jolly* looks at the impact of a hostile environment on migrants with a precarious legal status. *Pignolo*'s contribution turns to the experiences of undocumented migrants looking at the moral capital and agency of undocumented domestic workers in Geneva. The spread, speed and scale of the superdiversification in Flanders is explored in *Geldof*'s piece. *Sarli* looks at the challenges that the children of migrants who act as mediators of cultural plurality face. Finally, *Neal* and *Cochrane*'s piece examines the interplay between superdiversity and the everyday politics of living together, of negotiating spaces, and of the politics of Brexit, all of which have sharpened divisions, racialization and anti-migrant hostilities.

Gazes, perspectives and interventions

In the fourth and final section, authors turn their attention to the state as an institution that imposes its intrusive and often harmful gaze on migrants, and how migrants and their allies resist by prioritizing different perspectives and intervening in dominant policies and practices. A key theme of the contributions is how nation-states respond to changing populations and how these responses can reinforce ethno-nationalist or racist boundaries. *Schiller* and *Scholten* argue that superdiversity, understood as migration-related social complexity, poses challenges to governance, as in group categorization. *Gilardoni* traces the racist roots of the Italian nation-building project, from the colonial era via Mussolini's fascism to today, which first excluded Sicilians and now criminalizes migrants and Black Italians. Japan, as *Liu Farrer* demonstrates, has liberalized migration policy for labour migrants, students and those considered of Japanese heritage since the 1980s. However, the state still insists on maintaining its ethno-nationalist identity, thus excluding and alienating immigrants. *Moreno-Amador* outlines recent changes in the Spanish asylum system: an expansion in the number of asylum applications has not been accompanied by higher refugee acceptance rates, leaving rejected asylum seekers unregularized and destitute. In the UK, according to *Yeo*, the migration policies of successive governments have failed both to attract skilled migrants and to improve working conditions for British workers. Instead, policies respond to political expediency and temporary lobbying rather than actually managing migration flows.

Several contributions show the negative impacts of governmental practices on migrants and racialized citizens. In the US context, *Menjívar* discusses how the expansion in precarious legal statuses is leaving not only temporary migrants, but also permanent residents and naturalized citizens at risk of socio-economic precarity, detention and deportation. *Inda* describes how the 'necropolitical' US immigration system routinely mistreats, harms or kills migrants at borders and in detention. As *Canning* shows, the states in Britain, Denmark and Sweden also harm the autonomy, dignity, relationships, and emotional and physical wellbeing of asylum seekers – and this is done deliberately through existing structures of racist exclusion and privatization.

In our increasingly digital age, the state expands its gaze to the digital sphere, seeking to control and discipline migrants as well as citizens. As *Godin* and *Bica* show, the digital-only immigration status for EU citizens following Brexit, compounds the existing digital and offline exclusion of Roma people. In a nod to Foucault's panopticon, *Jablonowski* demonstrates that the UK state has subtly extended its disciplinary control of migrants to 'status checkers', namely employers, universities or service providers.

As pressure on migrants mounts, so too does resistance, activism and solidarity. Several of our contributors show that the state's often racist gaze is always incomplete and contested. Civil society organizations working directly with asylum seekers and migrants are documenting harm and prioritizing different perspectives. Thus, *Taal* of the Baobab Women's Project highlights the gender-specific harm inflicted on female asylum seekers and trafficking survivors in the UK during the asylum procedure. She argues that a more trauma-sensitive approach could address some of these issues. Migrant-led, anti-racist organizations gaze back at the state and intervene to demand accountability from governments, as well as equity and the unconditional right to belong. *Zazai* of the Scottish Refugee Council elaborates on the deteriorating legal provisions for refugees in the UK, calling for mobilization against harmful legislation. *Ramadan* offers insights into how Migrant Voice counters negative media representations by placing migrant and refugee voices and actions centre stage. *Rolfe* of British Future shows that public attitudes towards immigration have in fact become more positive over the past ten years, and this could be harnessed for positive change. *Elgenius* argues that neighbourhood-based organizations play a crucial role in supporting the integration of migrants through informal networks and connecting them to state services. To make their dream of an anti-racist city of Birmingham come true, *Afridi* and the organization brap have developed concrete place-based methods and a roadmap with which to address the systemic roots of racism, build the power of traditionally marginalized groups, and foster accountability by governance actors.

Acknowledgements

We would like to thank our contributors for generously sharing their ideas, analytical insights and observations with us in this collection and over many conversations, roundtables, panels, and seminars during our first decade as IRiS.

We are most grateful to Paladia Ziss for having shepherded a very busy and dispersed motley crew of editors and contributors through most of the editorial process, and to Jason and Selina Cohen at Oxford Publishing Services for their expert editorial support for this project.

A special thank you to IRiS's founding director Jenny Phillimore, without whom we would not be here writing this anniversary anthology, and to our administrator Ann Bolstridge for her precious support, kindness and expertise in all things to do with the University of Birmingham.

PART ONE:
VISIONS AND CONCEPTS

The Decade that Changed the Geopolitics of Migration and Diversity

Nando Sigona

In 2022, we celebrated the tenth anniversary of the University of Birmingham's Institute for Research into Superdiversity. Ten years is a long time in our fast-moving academic world – for UK readers, it is almost two full REF[1] cycles. It is a long time also in the lives of the people with whom we work. It is also a long time in the world in which we all– researchers and researched – live, and the boundaries between these groupings are far from clear cut. What a decade!

In 2012, *superdiversity* as a term was only five years old. It was debated, contested, appropriated, refined, and sometimes rejected.[2] A growing number of scholars from a range of disciplines began to adopt it and to use it to reflect on what many saw as a rapidly-changing and increasingly complex society stemming from population movements triggered by the end of the cold war and post-cold war geopolitical realignment. The 'triumph' of neoliberal globalization was such to determine the 'end of history' (Fukuyama 1992). From the early 1990s, the world accelerated. It changed at a faster pace producing the phenomenon of overheating (Eriksen 2016) and complex socio-economic transformations came with it, along with a series of systemic crises, including what it is now universally recognized as perhaps the greatest one, the climate and environmental crisis. Mobility and migration sparked in many places – for example in the global

---

1. The REF is a process of expert review carried out on behalf of the four UK research councils by expert panels made up of senior academics, international members, and research users. The evaluation of research outputs affects the allocation of research funding quotas to universities.
2. For a review of the debate, see Vertovec (2019).

3

cities that Saskia Sassen (2001) so eloquently discussed in her seminal work – the process of the diversification of diversity. Vertovec (2007) aptly gave a word to this phenomenon, namely superdiversity and, over the years researchers have discussed whether this is a concept, a method, a descriptor, or, for that matter all three (Hall 2017; Vertovec 2019). However, one concern to have resurfaced a number of times over the years is that migration and diversity are not new, they existed before (Schrover 2022). Some have pointed out how imperial metropoles – places like Rome, Paris, Constantinople, London, Vienna, and Moscow – have always attracted people from elsewhere. This of course is true, and not only of the metropoles. Archaeological evidence shows that, among the 30,000 or so Roman troops who invaded Britain three times some 2000 years ago, there were soldiers from North Africa and elsewhere in the vast Roman Empire (Olusoga 2017). Vast and yet territorially bounded, this is an important aspect that often gets overlooked. As Abel and Sander (2014) so brilliantly captured in their visualizations of global migration over time, who goes where is not an independent variable.

There are reasons why a North African, as opposed to a Chinese or Japanese, soldier should have been in Britain 2000 years ago. Geopolitical and economic forces define and shape the realm of the possible with respect to mobility and migration, and create the opportunity structure within which a particular mobility may occur. Immigration and citizenship laws, passports, borders (digital or otherwise) are the instruments, the technologies of power, that nation-states, and before them empires, have used to discipline, manage and regulate the mobilities and lives of those who move. In other words, those who went to Rome 2000 years ago, or who went to work in Paris, London or Liverpool in the age of empires, were moved by forces that differed from those that move people now and their conditions were obviously different (even if people may nominally come from the same city, village or country). Thus, insofar as neoliberal globalization is different from the political economy of the *ancien régime*, so too are the (geo)politics of migration and diversity that stem from it.

And if, as some suggest, neoliberal globalization is in retreat – for some since the financial crisis in the late 2000s, for others since Trump, Brexit and the affirmation of nationalist and protectionist governments in many countries (Bello 2007; Jacques 2016) – then we should start to think how and in what ways the new political and economic reality may affect migration and diversity in the years to come. From this perspective, the emergence of superdiversity is a phenomenon rooted in a specific historical conjuncture – the era of globalization, interconnectedness and interdependency. If this is the case, we can expect events like the global Covid-19 pandemic, the call to renationalize strategic assets in response to the current energy crisis, or calls to move industrial production back to one's core market and to put national workers first, also to affect migration governance and flows.

Of course, those who migrated due to previous historical circumstances and conditions, do not disappear, which is why our societies become increasingly layered, stratified and complex, with their very presence becoming a force and driver for social, political and economic change. Our research on EU families in the UK after Brexit (Lessard-Phillips and Sigona 2018; Sigona 2019; Sigona and Godin 2019) shows how, despite Brexit, London remains one of the capitals of the EU, home to well over a million EU citizens, including a large number of families and children. This makes London by far the largest conglomerate of non-native EU citizens in a European city. They come from each and every one of the 27 EU member states and can be found in every sector of the labour market – from museum curators to aristocrats, from professors to hospital nurses, from stay-at-home parents to baristas, from LGTBQ+ activists to retired grandparents. London remains a unique and yet fragile laboratory of a possible 'Europolitanism', despite the UK's geopolitical and ideological repositioning following Brexit – the so-called *Global Britain* project – is already reshaping the politics of migration in the UK (Sigona and Benson 2022).

By looking at the quarterly immigration statistics of the UK Office for National Statistics (Home Office 2022), it is easy to see how an event like Brexit might create a new politics of immigration, emigration and diversity. One just needs to walk around the neighbourhoods of Birmingham to see how different generations of migrants and their descendants shape and share the city. There are those, for example, who came before or after the Second World War, others are from the British Empire and later the Commonwealth; there are the 'new' Europeans who moved in with the various rounds of EU enlargement, the asylum seekers and refugees of the cold war and post-cold war eras, as well as the refugees from the more recent and current conflicts in Afghanistan, Syria, and Ukraine.

Just a few headlines serve to remind us of what we have been going through in the past decade – for ten years really is a long time during which major international events have shaped migration and how we understand, debate and frame it. In 2012, the Olympic Games in London highlighted Britain's diversity and made it a distinct feature of what modern Britain wanted to look like in the eyes of the world. In the same year, for some people Barack Obama embodied the dream (which later proved an illusion) of a post-racial society in the USA. From 2013 to 2016, the so-called 'refugee crisis' brought millions of refugees and migrants to Europe, which, according to some observers, posed a threat to the 'EU project' as a whole. In 2016, we had Brexit and then came Trump. In 2020 and 2021, the global pandemic, which brought international and national travel to an almost complete halt, greatly affected our experiences and perceptions of an 'interconnected' world, which many in the West suddenly saw as more vulnerable and fragile than most had assumed. In May 2020, the murder of George Floyd gave new impetus to the Black Lives Matter movement in the USA and globally (but tragically did not end police brutality against Black and Brown people, as the murder of unarmed Chris Kaba shot by a police officer in south London a few months ago demonstrates).

What a decade for migration and for migrants and citizens alike! What a decade for migration research and researchers, with many new and old questions that need answering, including how can we make research on migration and diversity relevant to a rapidly changing society and to ensure that it benefits the people with whom we work and about whom we care.

References

Abel, G. and N. Sander (2014) 'Quantifying global international migration flows', *Science*, 43 (6178): 1520–2, doi: 10.1126/science.1248676.

Bello, W. (2007) 'Globalization in retreat', *New Labor Forum*, 16 (3/4): 109–15.

Eriksen, T. H. (2016) *Overheating: an anthropology of accelerated change*, Pluto Press.

Fukuyama, F. (1992) *The end of history and the last man*, Free Press.

Hall, S. M. (2017) 'Mooring "super-diversity" to a brutal migration milieu', *Ethnic and Racial Studies*, 40 (9): 1562–73, doi: 10.1080/01419870.2017.1300296.

Home Office (2022) 'Immigration statistics bulletin', available at: www.gov.uk/government/statistics/immigration-statistics-year-ending-june-2022.

Jacques, M. (2016) 'The death of neoliberalism and the crisis in western politics', *The Observer*, 21 August, available at: https://www.theguardian.com/commentisfree/2016/aug/21/death-of-neoliberalism-crisis-in-western-politics.

Lessard-Phillips, L. and N. Sigona (2018) 'Mapping EU citizens in the UK: a changing profile? From 1980s to the EU referendum', Eurochildren research brief series, no. 3, doi: 10.5281/zenodo.6620991.

Olusoga, D. (2016) *Black and British: a forgotten history*, Macmillan.

Sassen, S. (2001) *The global city*, Princeton University Press.

Schrover, M. (2022) 'Superdiversity from a historical perspective', F. Meissner, N. Sigona and S. Vertovec (eds) *The Oxford handbook of superdiversity*, (online edition), Oxford University Press, doi: 10.1093/oxfordhb/9780197544938.013.4.

Sigona, N. (2019) 'London is the EU's most "Europolitan" capital – what its EU families feel about Brexit', *The Conversation*, 5 December, available at: https://theconversation.com/london-is-the-eus-most-europolitan-capital-what-its-eu-families-feel-about-brexit-127630.

Sigona, N. and M. Benson (2022) 'The UK's refugee "invasion" is a Brexit-made policy failure', *The Political Quarterly*, 10 November, available at: https://politicalquarterly.org.uk/blog/the-uks-refugee-invasion-is-a-brexit-made-policy-failure/.

Sigona, N. and M. Godin (2019) 'Naturalisation and (dis)integration', Eurochildren brief series, no. 6, doi: 10.5281/zenodo.6620906.

Vertovec, S. (2007) 'Super-diversity and its implications', *Ethnic and Racial Studies*, 30 (6): 1024–54, doi: 10.1080/01419870701599465.

Vertovec, S. (2019) 'Talking around super-diversity', *Ethnic and Racial Studies*, 42 (1): 125–39, doi: 10.1080/01419870.2017.1406128.

Making a Difference with Superdiversity

Jenny Phillimore

It has been a real struggle to decide what to write about for this anthology. Having established IRiS just over a decade ago, I feel a degree of pressure to reflect on our achievements and our legacy. There is much to talk about but I want to reflect on one of the key drivers for the establishment of IRiS – policy impact. In this piece I focus on our work seeking to identify the differences that make a difference to people's lives and to influence policies for the benefit of communities. I start by describing how this came about.

Lisa Goodson and I were commissioned in 2006 to run the 'Making a Difference' project. We trained the leaders of eighteen community organizations in accredited research skills, and worked with migrant and refugee community groups to identify a research agenda that would cover the areas they considered most important. Under the supervision of mentors, the community researchers collected qualitative data on refugee mental health and access to language training. Once the data were analysed, the research team worked with a new community group to use this evidence in such a way as to make a difference to regional and local refugee integration policy. Our data highlighted how structural problems generate barriers to access to services for refugees, which related more to their experiences of forced migration and of the UK asylum system than to their ethno-national identities. When presented to local policymakers, this was seen as powerful evidence of the need for change.

In 2008, Lisa Goodson and I joined the School of Social Policy at the University of Birmingham and engaged in policy-focused research looking at the housing, health and broader welfare needs of extremely diverse communities in inner-city Birmingham and the Black Country. Funders were keen that we identify the main ethnic 'groups' in our proposals. Yet, experience in the field and from the Making a Difference project showed that enormous demographic change was underway following the accession of CEE countries to the EU and the arrival of asylum seekers from many countries. Identifying ethno-national groups made little sense when some neighbourhoods contained people from more than 150 such groups and whose experiences of accessing services appeared to relate more to their immigration status and to how long they had lived in the neighbourhood.

Reading Vertovec's (2007) paper was a real Eureka moment for me. His description of new patterns of superdiversity connected so well with our experiences of engaging in social-policy research in diverse parts of Birmingham, and underlined the importance of moving beyond simple group categories. Furthermore, we appeared to be well placed, in fact had already started, to address Vertovec's concerns about the research-policy nexus and to help address the policy challenges he outlined on the role of community organizations and the design and delivery of public services.

Vertovec's paper prompted me to focus my research on the relationship between superdiversity and access to social welfare. I met local policymakers to talk about the need to shift from using an ethno-national lens in research to thinking more across factors such as place, gender, recency of arrival and immigration status. This research was not intended to displace that of the well-established groups that had in the last two decades been the focus of service provision, but rather to look at differences within those groups and the long-established indigenous populations. Over the next few years, I led several projects on the health and housing needs of people living in some of the most diverse neighbourhoods in the region. We were able to persuade what were then called primary care trusts, which were responsible for designing local-level healthcare services, to work together to combine their datasets of Flag 4 data, which recorded who from overseas was registering for the first time to access the National Health Service in Birmingham. Analysis of the data identified the destinations of numerous newcomers and showed that, in the previous five years, they had come from more than 170 different countries. These findings were instrumental in convincing the local authorities of the need to broaden the services they were offering.

Our work on housing showed that residents in areas earmarked for regeneration tended to identify with their neighbours beyond their ethno-national groupings, and would develop affinities based on class or recency of arrival. This information provided a rationale for wider consultation on the proposed changes to the new housing being planned to ensure that they met everyone's needs. Finally, we were able to work on the provision of migrant maternity services in the West Midlands; we used a combination of interview and peri-natal mortality data to identify common factors shaping access to antenatal and postnatal maternity care and the health of women and their babies. This was influential in securing a new pathway for migrant women, in the development of NHS–NGO relations, and in funding a doula service, which provides professional assistance to migrant women during labour. Meanwhile, Lisa Goodson's work on community research continued (and continues) in new communities. It also followed up on some of the themes from Making a Difference, including working to develop a new route through which forced migrants can access mental health services.

My early academic work on superdiversity used data from this policy research to reflect on what factors make a difference to people's access to welfare services. In 'Approaches to health provision in the age of super-diversity' (Phillimore 2011), I reflected on the barriers to accessing health-care; and, in 'Delivering maternity services in an era of superdiversity' (Phillimore 2015), identified novelty and newness as the two main factors that differentiated new migrants' experiences of maternity services from those of the established population; then, in 'Housing, home and neigh-bourhood renewal in the era of superdiversity' (Phillimore 2013), I looked at the ways in which shared understandings of home and home-making can shape regeneration practices.

The wish to expand our research agenda, work across disciplines and use our evidence to make a difference to policy and practice shaped our decision to apply to the University of Birmingham to establish the Institute for Research into Superdiversity. The focus of our launch event, which more than a hundred policymakers, practitioners and community activists attended, and with many of whom we continue to work, was on policy and practice. Some community researchers we trained in Making a Difference, and others whom Lisa subsequently trained, have gone on to lead large organizations, or take on roles in migration governance, and many remain collaborators. Our approach continues to prioritize attempts to influence policy and practice to ensure we make a difference to people's lives.

Some recent work has adopted a more international and comparative stance. For example, the UPWEB (Understanding the practice and develop-ing the concept of welfare bricolage) project used what Berg et al. (2019)

described as a 'methodologically neighbourhoodist' approach to see how *all* residents living in superdiverse neighbourhoods, not only migrants, address their health concerns. By establishing when and why people engage in welfare bricolage to ameliorate their health concerns, we were able to demonstrate how austerity, managerialism and racism shaped access and constrained the ability of service providers to meet diverse needs. A maximum diversity sampling approach allowed us to identify commonalities like communication problems faced by elderly residents and new arrivals alike, and the poverty endured by many, especially post-austerity. While this project yielded many academic outputs (for example, Phillimore et al. 2021), including an article sent to all public health professionals in the UK, it did not have the policy impact of previous projects. Although the concept of welfare bricolage shed light on the complexity of the actions undertaken by residents in superdiverse areas, this complexity was not readily understood by policymakers. It was evident that more work was needed to disseminate the idea beyond academic circles, but as IRiS director I did not have the time. However, UPWEB has led to collaboration with colleagues in Sweden on a new project (Rethinking and Localities) looking at the role of civil society organizations in superdiverse neighbourhoods, and its findings are being fed directly into Swedish policy agendas.

In 2020 I stepped down as IRiS director to focus on shaping policy and practice. Using the findings of the international SEREDA project, undertaken in partnership with several NGOs and universities in Sweden, Turkey and Australia, I wanted to try to influence the UK government's asylum and immigration policy, which is taking an increasingly hostile turn, to improve the lives of forced migrant survivors of sexual and gender-based violence (SGBV). We also wanted to influence international humanitarian policy so that it protects forced migrants in transit and after they have reached supposed refuge. I learned from UPWEB that change at national or international level would take a great deal of time and effort. With the support of many colleagues in professional services at the University of Birmingham, the Helen Bamber Foundation, Doctors of the World and Refugee Women Connect and working with PhD student-turned-colleague Dr Sandra Pertek and the Women's Refugee Commission, we are seeking to increase funding for mobile SGBV services and to change asylum interview practice and to write migrant women into the UK's new Victims Bill.

We have used many approaches to make our evidence accessible and to try to generate a sense of outrage at how existing structures generate and intensify suffering. So far, we have made videos, appeared on prime time news, generated media coverage in more than forty outlets, blogged, held events at the House of Lords, Welsh Parliament and the International Red Cross Museum in Geneva, run workshops with policymakers and practitioners, written policy reports and policy briefs, held multiple meetings with civil servants in several government departments, provided advice and guidance on SGBV and the Ukraine crisis, developed and run an Unfiltered Lives photography campaign and commissioned some graphics illustrating the continuum of violence experienced by SGBV survivors. We have negotiated a secondment at the International Federation of Red Cross and Red Crescent to prepare some new guidelines on SGBV in forced migration. We have met ministers, shadow ministers, MPs and countless members of the House of Lords to evidence the harm occasioned by hostile immigration policy and to advocate for new more humane approaches.

There is, however, much more work to be done. Evidence alone is not enough. The experience we gained over a decade of working with IRiS to influence policy and engaging in research have placed us in a strong position. We recognize the importance of working with communities to help them articulate their policy concerns and develop mechanisms for telling their stories to those in power. We have learnt how important it is to keep our messages simple and streamlined; and, we have learnt the importance of persistence. This means attending policy events, building networks, responding to relevant consultations, generating policy briefs, and reaching out to politicians and policymakers when we have something to say. We find that eventually, after several e-mails, most will talk to us although this does not guarantee a willingness to make changes.

References

Berg, M. L., B. Gidley and A. Krausova (2019) 'Welfare micropublics and inequality: urban super-diversity in a time of austerity', *Ethnic and Racial Studies*, 42 (15): 2723–42.

Phillimore, J. (2011) 'Approaches to health provision in the age of super-diversity: accessing the NHS in Britain's most diverse city', *Critical Social Policy*, 31 (1): 5–29.

Phillimore, J. (2013) 'Housing, home and neighbourhood renewal in the era of superdiversity: some lessons from the West Midlands', *Housing Studies*, 28 (5): 682–700.

Phillimore, J. (2015) 'Delivering maternity services in an era of superdiversity: the challenges of novelty and newness', *Ethnic and Racial Studies*, 38 (4): 568–82.

Phillimore, J., H. Bradby, T. Brand, B. Padilla and S. Pemberton (2021) *Exploring welfare bricolage in Europe's superdiverse neighbourhoods*, Routledge.

Vertovec, S. (2007) 'Super-diversity and its implications', *Ethnic and Racial Studies*, 30 (6): 1024–54.

The Politics of Us and Them

Bridget Anderson

Migration is a class issue. Politicians across the world make efforts to mobilize support from low-waged, precarious and otherwise marginalized workers, by claiming that they will protect them from the depredations of 'migrants', foreigners (often racialized) who take resources from citizens. This mobilizes an old fear: that there is not enough to go around. But this response assumes what is bad for migrants is good for citizens. In practice, this is far from always the case.

Take, for example, the claim that migrants take jobs from citizens and tough immigration controls are needed to protect national workers from unfair competition. This rests on the so-called 'lump of labour fallacy' that imagines there is a fixed number of jobs in a national economy and that migrants (or women, young people or whatever group is the object of concern) simply substitute for citizens (or men or older workers) and vice versa. Neither of these assumptions is correct. An economy is never a fixed size and workers, whatever their skill levels, are not simply substitutable: logical or not, many households would not see a female live-in care worker as simply substitutable for a male live-in care worker. But there is a further issue to consider in the case of migrant workers: immigration controls do not simply facilitate a flow of labour to particular countries and jobs, but they are highly productive, making 'foreigners' and creating particular kinds of workers and types of employment relations. This is sometimes acknowledged in the case of undocumented people, who are recognized as more vulnerable to abuse, exploitation, and poor labour conditions because of their fear of deportation. But less attention is given to the ways in which legally working migrants are heavily constrained by immigration controls.

In most countries of the world people who work on migrant worker visas are subject to conditions that, if imposed on citizens would be considered a significant infringement of their rights. Migrants may be tied to their employer, prohibited from claiming social assistance or healthcare, forbidden to join trades unions, required to take health and pregnancy tests, and required to live on site. Many find that they cannot access the limited rights they do have because of racism and xenophobia, language barriers, administrative complexity, or lack of knowledge. These restrictions, combined with sponsorship requirements that mean that low waged migrants typically depend on their employer for their (often highly temporary) right to stay in a state gives employers mechanisms of control over their legal as well as undocumented migrant workforce. Far from 'protecting' the labour market for citizens, immigration restrictions can mean employers actively seek to employ migrants (Anderson 2013).

Those who are deemed 'low skilled' are particularly vulnerable to these restrictions. Skill is a key factor in labour migration regimes, with entrance facilitated for the high skilled and restricted for the low skilled. Migrants or not, those who can turn their hand to everything, construction workers who dig and plaster today, and tomorrow lay foundations, bricks and tiles, and domestic workers who clean and cook at the same time as caring for an elderly person, are 'unskilled'. These are typically the most marginalized workers – often women, migrants, minoritized people, or disabled people. While unskilled work is depicted as work that anybody can do, not any *body* is regarded as suitable for any job (Iskander 2021). Working together, immigration and skills' regimes internationalize class distinctions, and at the same time naturalize national divisions between workers. This is evident in the claims about the natural abilities of particular nationalities that are a feature of employer demand for migrant workers across the world. Employers are often open about wanting nationalities associated with certain physical and personal characteristics. Different nationalities are ranked against each other, designated as better or worse depending on what jobs are to be done where. At the same time this means people's aptitudes can be characterized as natural rather than demonstrating skill. To designate such physical and behavioural characteristics as 'racial' would be unacceptable, and rightly so, but describing them as 'national' can be presented as simple common sense.

Categories like 'migrant', 'citizen' and 'skill' are represented as technical, but in practice are highly politicized. The Australian backpacker working in a bar in Thailand, the US financier living in Hamburg, may be subject to immigration controls, but they are rarely regarded as 'migrants'. In contrast, the woman cleaning the banker's flat may be so regarded even if she has

15

never crossed an international border in her life. Putting it crudely, the 'migrant' is imagined as poor and often negatively racialized or otherwise associated with backwardness. This is how some people who have the legal status of citizens can nevertheless be described as 'migrants'. Think of India's 54 million internal migrants whose vulnerabilities were so starkly exposed by the Covid-19 pandemic. Or the descriptor 'second/third generation migrant' or 'person of migration background', a synonym for Black and ethnic minority citizens in Europe.

The distinction between the migrant and citizen is, in practice, not clear cut and racism and xenophobia are key to the production of us and them. In many states, these framings have been profoundly shaped by colonial histories. Colonialism entrenched and codified differences between people across continents with continuing consequences for groups who may be born in a country but are nevertheless imagined as 'out of place'. Infamously, in 2013, the Dominican Republic's constitutional court removed citizenship from anyone who could not prove that their parents were legal residents when they were born. As a result, 70,000–80,000 people were deported to Haiti over three years, and unknown numbers moved 'voluntarily'. In India, the implementation of strict requirements for documenting citizenship and the publication of the National Register of Citizens in 2019 removed citizenship from 1.9 million people in Assam. People without documents, or whose documents contained 'discrepancies', were declared stateless, removed from voting registers and rendered liable to imprisonment as foreigners, even if they had never moved from the village in which they had been born. In both countries, the vast majority of those affected were impoverished and marginalized. The mobilization of ethnicity and ancestry to strip or otherwise undermine citizenship is, like migration, a class issue.

Taken together, immigration/skills regimes on the one hand, and citizenship stripping on the other, expose how the ambiguity of the term 'national' is politically utilized. 'National' can signify a legal relation with, or recognition by, the state – as in 'national territory' or 'national citizenship'. But 'national' can also mean belonging to the nation, with the nation understood very loosely as referring to culture/cultures, languages and a people that stretches back in time. Membership in the nation is claimed through ancestry and often imagined as independent of and predating the state. The ambiguity of 'national' means that it is possible to be a legal citizen, yet not be considered as belonging to the nation (Mongia 2018). History teaches us that neither citizenship nor membership of the nation are stable statuses, and this is not only because of ethnicity: those who are homeless, who are disabled, who have criminal records, who do not conform, who depend on social assistance, or who are queer, can be rendered vulnerable to state violence and exclusion (Anderson 2021).

Ideas of migration, belonging and the nation mobilize race, labour, migration, gender and citizenship to divide and hierarchize. Making connections, alliances and solidarities between marginalized citizens, people whose presence is only tolerated, and migrants is vital for social justice. In a world in which increasing and grotesque inequalities are manifest between and across state borders, what is bad for migrants is not good for citizens. In fact, in the final analysis, it is bad for citizens too.

An earlier version of this piece appeared in *Amandla* no. 82, https://amandla.org.za/.

References

Anderson, B. (2013) *Us and them? The dangerous politics of immigration controls*, Oxford University Press.

Anderson, B. (2021) 'Methodological de-nationalism: de-exceptionalizing displacement, re-exceptionalizing citizenship', *Humanity*, 12 (3): 300–11.

Iskander, N. (2021) *Does skill make us human? Migrant workers in 21st-century Qatar and beyond*, Princeton University Press.

Mongia, R. (2018) *Indian migration and empire: a colonial genealogy of the modern state*, Duke University Press.

The Race–Migration Nexus

Nasar Meer

How can we understand the nexus between race and migration governance? One answer is that 'anyone concerned with questions of race and racism today must readily recognize that they present themselves in a particularly acute way in the European migration context' (De Genova 2017: 1768). To establish why this may be so requires both historical and contemporary insights, which begin by recognizing the role of imperial systems reliant on racism having produced the social, political or economic legacies that underlie the very formation of most European nation-states. Other vestiges besides national symbols bear the imprint of imperialism: economic assets, built environments, the laws that govern our societies and, chief among these, our very criteria of citizenship (Bhambra 2015).

Drawing on the experience of Britain, the recent Nationality and Borders Act (2022) provides for circumstances in which the British citizenship of some individuals can be revoked, but only if that person is able to obtain another nationality. As detailed below, citizenship deprivation has been used disproportionately against British citizens who are not white, with one analysis maintaining that non-white British citizens are eight times more likely to be eligible for deprivation of citizenship than white residents of all backgrounds (van der Merwe 2021).

Yet typically, especially in high-level policy discourses and practices, a sustained effort is made to maintain the distinction between how categories of race and migration are adopted, and in ways that sit uncomfortably with a significant portion of the social scientific analysis of migration and nearly all the scholarship on race.

One reason why the distinction endures is because each is said to refer to the governance of separate policy domains. This is especially apparent with respect to what rights are conferred on those deemed members of either a racial or migrant group, and equally what responsibilities are expected of the state's actions towards them.

The meaning of governance here is key. In the migration literature, governance can often refer to the role of dispersed networks based on partnerships and the blurring of boundaries of the state, consistent with how governance can refer to 'less emphasis on hierarchy and the state, and more on networks and markets' (Bevir 2011: 1). Yet, governance can also mean something more squarely associated with forms of centralized state regulation in which racial inequalities, in the application of migration criteria, can be seen to operate in ways that are systemic.

It is in the latter usage that we can observe how the race–migration nexus can be mutually sustaining, and in ways that could not be more important to our understanding of a number of matters that cut across each siloed domain, including the very laws that govern our societies. We can illustrate this point by observing how only a generation after its height, when it claimed jurisdiction over a quarter of the planet's population, Britain would become a nation-state with the introduction of the British Nationality Act of 1948. Henceforth, colonial 'British subjects' became Citizens of the United Kingdom and Colonies (CUKCs).

Without wishing to detail a chronology documented elsewhere (Meer 2010), Britain's post-imperial story can partly be read through its subsequent immigration legislation in ways that make self-evident the relationships between the policy objectives of race equality and migration control, and which have remained characteristic of the race–migration nexus in Britain ever since. What is important to note is how 'colonial citizens' (under the terms of the CUKC) would become coded out of subsequent iterations of a substantive British citizenship – in other words, 'populations that would, historically, have been part of the body politic' (Bhambra 2017: 402) were placed outside it as the ground cruelly shifted under their feet.

This 'migrantization' of erstwhile British citizens became especially visible in the ongoing Windrush scandal. Here, a number of the children of Black Britons who came from the Caribbean between 1948 and 1973, and who were legally entitled to all the rights that came with full membership of the nation-state, have seen their citizenship rights rescinded. The trap was partly set in the 1971 Immigration Act, which, by introducing a 'partiality' clause, enshrined a *jus sanguinis* type of legal citizenship based on ethnic descent. Accordingly, a person seeking entry from the Commonwealth would need to demonstrate that a parent or grandparent had been born in the UK. This meant that 'new' Commonwealth citizens (from the West

Indies, South Asia and East Africa) would be less likely than 'old' Commonwealth citizens (from Australia or Canada) to qualify for entry. The 1981 Nationality Act tried to delineate this further through the creation of three categories of British citizenship – British, British Dependent Territories, or British Overseas – and ultimately withdrew a right to settlement from most Commonwealth citizens. Many of those affected had moved to the UK as CUKCs before their birth countries became independent, and thus for any number of reasons may not have applied for a British passport.

Their stories are too numerous and rich to be summarized; they included people like Paulette Wilson, who 'had been in Britain from the age of ten, worked, raised a family and should have been enjoying her retirement, but she'd had her liberty taken away and been threatened with deportation back to Jamaica – a country she hardly knew' (Vernon 2020). In her review of 'Windrush lessons learned', Wendy Williams concluded that 'these failings demonstrate an institutional ignorance and thoughtlessness towards the issue of race and the history of the Windrush generation within the department, which are consistent with some elements of the definition of institutional racism' (Williams 2020: 7).

The key point is that none of these outcomes would have been plausible without the underlying racial concept with which to rationalize that approach, and upon which a wider system to operationalize it rested. Consistent with this view, a number of scholars (El-Enany 2020; Mayblin 2017) have argued that we need to see the race–migration nexus as something that exists within a broader framework of global racial hierarchies. This framework is said to function (a) to inhibit movement from former colonies to the imperial centre, and (b) to delegitimize the claims of citizens of the ex-imperial nation-state. In the context of this framework, the emergence of 'everyday bordering' (Yuval-Davis et al. 2018) practices to which displaced migrants are subject – coerced immobility, enforced impoverishment, precarious and unsafe accommodation – should therefore further direct us to an understanding of the governance of the race-migration nexus as something deeply intertwined.

References

Bevir, M. (2011) 'Governance as theory, practice, and dilemma', in M. Bevir (ed.) *The SAGE handbook of governance*, Sage, 1–16.

Bhambra, G. K. (2015) 'Citizens and others: the constitution of citizenship through exclusion', *Alternatives*, 40 (2): 102–14.

Bhambra, G. K. (2017) 'The current crisis of Europe: refugees, colonialism, and the limits of cosmopolitanism', *European Law Journal*, 23 (5): 395–405.

De Genova, N. (ed) (2017) *The borders of 'Europe': autonomy of migration, tactics of bordering*, Duke University Press.

El-Enany, N. (2020) *(B)ordering Britain: law, race and empire*, Manchester University Press.

Mayblin, L. (2017) *Asylum after empire: colonial legacies in the politics of asylum seeking*, Rowman & Littlefield.

Meer, N. (2010) *Citizenship, identity and the politics of multiculturalism*, Palgrave.

van der Merwe, B. (2021) 'Two in five people in England and Wales from an ethnic minority background could become eligible to be deprived of their citizen status without warning', *New Statesman*, 1 December (updated 2 December).

Vernon, P. (2020) 'Paulette Wilson remembered by Patrick Vernon', *The Guardian*, 14 December, available at: https://www.theguardian.com/world/2020/dec/14/paulette-wilson-remembered-by-patrick-vernon.

Williams, W. (2020) 'Windrush lessons learned review: independent review by Wendy Williams', HMSO.

Yuval-Davis, N., G. Wemyss and K. Cassidy (2018) 'Everyday bordering, belonging and the reorientation of British immigration legislation.' *Sociology*, 52 (2): 228–44.

Everyday (Re)bordering

Nira Yuval-Davis and Georgie Wemyss

The last ten years have witnessed the rapid transformations and shifts of external and internal state borders globally. National borders have been contested since nations have existed, resulting in the rebordering of state territories. In the past decade, violent conflicts have forced changes in territorial borders, the recent invasions and claims to Ukrainian territory by Russia being only one of many examples. Brexit and the closing of national and regional borders during the Covid-19 pandemic made clear to millions that we are moving further away from the utopian vision of a borderless world. At the same time, Covid-19 shutdowns exposed how borders that appeared closed to most of the world's population were permeable for elites with private jets and multiple residences. We were definitely not 'all of us together' in this situation.

A key transformation that we have all experienced is the increased reorientation of border control from policed lines or solid barriers that bound territories, to active processes carried out not only by official border guards but also by fellow citizens, often within those territorial borders but also beyond them. In our pre-pandemic book, *Bordering* (Yuval-Davis et al. 2019) we investigated these processes historically and in the context of twenty-first century neoliberal globalization. What we named 'everyday bordering' was made an explicit strategy central to UK government immigration policies in 2012 when the UK home secretary, Theresa May announced the government's aim to create a 'hostile environment for illegal immigration'. Subsequent immigration legislation in 2014 and 2016 compelled individuals to take on the roles of border guards in their everyday lives as landlords, employers, banks; health, welfare and educational providers were tasked with checking the immigration status of their service users. It also became clear that the 'hostile environment' is having a far wider reach beyond so-called illegal migrants.

While territorial borders may officially be changed over the courses of decades through treaties and negotiations, everyday rebordering takes place through diverse encounters at different levels, in multiple contexts and involving multifarious combinations of people. Everyday rebordering processes merge government legislation with regional or local policies and practices and individual decision making, thus rendering them dynamic, unpredictable, differentially visible and violent. They affect everyone, not just the racialized migrant minorities, in that they impose new citizenship duties on people by turning them into unpaid, untrained border guards.

Since 2016, rebordering has been speeded up through increasingly radical and all-encompassing clusters of legislation that are tightening territorial borders while extending the reach of everyday bordering processes. Globally, growing numbers of people are being suspended in grey zones – spaces outside the protection of contemporary states that can be either outside or within territorial borders. The detention camp of Guantánamo Bay is the most well-known example of off-shoring used to avoid applying existing civic and human rights. However, the externalization, and hence rebordering, of asylum management to islands or third countries was expanding well before the UK government negotiated its asylum deal with Rwanda via the 2022 Nationality and Borders Act. The deterritorialization of migrant detention camps and offshore processing that brought Papua New Guinean citizens into bordering roles on behalf of Australia in 2013 are now giving Rwandan citizens the responsibility of administering Britain's borders.

The everyday rebordering various governments introduced during the Covid-19 pandemic saved many lives globally through confining people to their homes and localities. However, the lockdowns also made obvious to us how bordering processes work as computer firewalls, filtering those who are permitted to, or prevented from, crossing official borders (Rumford 2006). In the UK in March 2021, those owning holiday homes were allowed to travel abroad, supposedly to prepare the property for rent or sale, when potential holiday makers faced a £5000 fine. The 'Partygate scandal' showed how government ministers were able to flout social distancing rules while others whom neighbours reported to the police were speedily fined.

Everyday rebordering is having a violent impact on women and minoritized communities. Following the US Supreme Court overturning the Roe vs Wade ruling, it is likely that some states will seek to legislate to prosecute women who cross borders to obtain abortions, along with those who help them. When travelling, women have been deleting the apps they use to monitor their menstrual cycles for fear that their states might access and used information about missed periods against them. Their ability to travel to seek abortions may depend not only on their financial status but also on their employer's political position.

The normalization of everyday rebordering must be resisted and part of that fight involves professionals, who are not its targets, recognizing and acting when the state legislates to co-opt them into borderguarding roles. For example, in their objection to proposals in the Nationality and Borders Bill to make dentists carry out age assessments though X-rays of child migrants, the British Dental Association argued that 'dentists are health professionals, not border guards' and they 'should not be put in a position of having to make judgements that are clinically and ethically inappropriate' (BDA 2021: n. 3). However, the partial success of their submission made little difference and far more extensive interventions are needed to prevent increasingly intimate and violent (re)bordering laws.

It is therefore important to identify and understand processes of bordering wherever and whenever they take place, on different scales from the global to the local and in different technologies, from legislation and formal policies to everyday-life encounters. Most importantly, we need to deconstruct the ways in which different intersectional power dynamics operate via them and affect diverse people differently.

For this reason, in our research we have used the epistemological and methodological approach of situated intersectionality (Yuval-Davis 2015). Fundamental to our approach to situated intersectionality analysis is that it is a mode of investigation that should be applied to all people and not just to marginalized and racialized women, with whom the rise of intersectionality theory is historically linked. Only such a generic intersectional analysis could ultimately avoid the risk of exceptionalism and of reifying and essentializing social boundaries. As critical race and ethnicity studies point out, not only black people are racially constructed, and feminists remind men that they too have a gender. Moreover, limiting intersectional analysis to the racialized and marginalized might reinforce rather than decentre the surveillance culture of the vulnerable in society. When studying processes of bordering this argument is even more important.

Situated intersectionality analysis is used to examine the way different members of the society are distributed along different social divisions and axes of power; these include class (or social economic positionings), gender, race and ethnicity, stage in the life cycle, sexuality, ability, and citizenship status. However, it is important to emphasize that we do not see the different social divisions that construct power relations as additive or interlocking. Rather, we see them as mutually constituted and shaped. They form the specific nuanced and contested meanings of particular social locations in precise historical moments within particular social, economic and political contexts in which some social divisions have more saliency and effect. Although different social divisions focus on different forms of inequality, they all relate to particular dynamics of power relations of exclusion and/or exploitation. They therefore use varieties of legitimate and illegitimate technologies of inferiorization, intimidation and, sometimes, physical violence.

When we study processes of everyday bordering, we study a spectrum of official and unofficial border guards, members of communities and varied groups of border crossers, plus those who try to cross internal and external borders, but are blocked. Only by encompassing the different situated gazes of them all, in addition to more formal local, national and global legal and policy discourses on borders, can we approach a fuller understanding of what contemporary rebordering actually involves.

The ongoing conflicts over the post-Brexit Northern Ireland Protocol, now part of international law, demonstrate the multilevel complexities of territorial and everyday rebordering.[1] Traders from Great Britain are obliged to complete customs documents for goods crossing into Northern Ireland, whereas traders in Northern Ireland can trade freely with the EU. This anomaly has created checkpoints at ports and pushed bordering responsibilities and costs on to diverse individuals who had never imagined that the UK would be divided by an internal trade border. Continuing local opposition to the Protocol has implications for the future of the UK's wider relationship with the EU.

However, this example of rebordering is only one of many. The ongoing scandals affecting the Windrush generation and the Grenfell victims, for

---

1. The Northern Ireland Protocol was introduced in the 2020 EU–UK withdrawal Treaty to protect the 1998 Good Friday Agreement and prevent the historical violence associated with a hard border on the island of Ireland.

example, show that being a citizen and/or a permanent resident, and being fully engaged in British society and its economy provide no protection from the intersectional racialized effects of everyday bordering in Britain today. Let us hope that when we come to assess bordering in the UK in ten years' time, we shall have more positive observations to share.

References

BDA (British Dental Association) (2021) 'Nationality and Borders Bill: written evidence submitted for The Nationalities and Borders Bill by the British Dental Association', 21 September. UK parliament website, available at: https://publications.parliament.uk/pa/cm5802/cmpublic/NationalityBorders/memo/NBB02.htm.

Rumford, C. (2006) 'Theorizing borders', *European Journal of Social Theory*, 9 (2): 155–69.

Yuval-Davis, N. (2015) 'Situated intersectionality and social inequality', *Raisons politiques*, 58 (2): 91–100.

Yuval-Davis, N., G. Wemyss and K. Cassidy (2019) *Bordering*, John Wiley & Sons.

Diversity

Adrian Favell

Were Raymond Williams rewriting his magisterial handbook *Keywords: A Vocabulary of Culture and Society* (Williams 1976) today, he would undoubtedly have found a place for the term diversity.[1] While we might reserve a different genealogy for the notion of bio-diversity in the natural sciences, the concept of social diversity, in the sense of referring to heterogenous societal formations, or inherent differences between people, is clearly a word that emerged to prominence as a characteristic term of the epoch of neo-liberal globalization, at its height in the optimistic 1990s.[2] Post-1989, diversity became associated with open or opening borders and free movement, with cosmopolitanism and multiculturalism, with hybridity and the rise of identity politics, and with mobilities and transnationalism. This was ironic, perhaps, given that the end of the cold war above all signalled the triumph of a more mono-cultural political economy. Talk of diversity gestured towards the supposed multiplicities of the big, flat, global world, if not always the multitudes beyond the North Atlantic West, while affirming the moral primacy of individualism, and the freedom to be, do, or (even) think differently.

We were now living, it was said, in an 'age of migration', with immigration a rising political concern well beyond those powerful nations that had learned – or tried to learn – how to absorb the consequences of the

---

1. This article was first published in German in the Zeitschrift für Ideengeschichte, based at the Wissenschaftskolleg zu Berlin: 'Diversität: Literaturbericht zu einem Gebot der Stunde', Konzept & Kritik, XVI/3 Herbst, 124–8. With thanks for advice, to the editors, Stephan Schlak and Daniel Schönpflug, and to Anthony Ossa-Richardson, Lorraine Daston, and Eva von Kuegelen.
2. A very basic indicator is a quick search on Ngram, which shows a dramatic rise for the term in English from the 1980s to a peak in the early 2000s. https://books.google.com/ngrams/graph?content=diversity&year_start=1800&year_end=2019&corpus=26&smoothing=3&direct_url=t1%3B,diversity%3B,c0 - t1%3B,diversity%3B,c0.

dissolution of their post-colonial Empires.[3] Unity from (or in) diversity became the catchword concept for such national futures, not coincidentally patterned on a classic constitutive North American self-image, now promoted globally. Demographers could speak confidently of there being a 'transition to diversity' in previously mono-cultural, European ethno-national nation-states, with growing numbers of citizens born abroad (Alba and Foner 2015) – assuming still, as ever, some sense in which European evolution (in the American mirror, at least) was at the advanced edge of civilizational forms; and that no previous pan-ethnic empires, or indeed huge and capacious present-day societies like India, Brazil or Nigeria, had achieved diversity in this way in their heterogeneity.

What was found, rather, on the streets of the new global cities of the West – archetypically, Los Angeles, Toronto, New York and, above all, London – was what was now referred to as super-diversity, measured usually in terms of the numbers of languages spoken, as well as the span and weight of countries of origin (Vertovec 2007). Superdiversity, though, was not just made up of recognized disparate racial and migrant groups, as had been mapped out in the post-colonial categories adopted to manage the substantial movements to the metropole of former empire subjects. It was now a much more complex mix, factoring in gender and sexuality, religion, age, new class formations, levels of education, and a vast new heterogeneity of global origin. Within superdiversity, protection of religious beliefs and practices, including certain issues specifically faced by minority women, exceeded the established frameworks of anti-racism, and race-based claims-making (Farris 2017; Modood et al. 1997). A racialized migrant group might also in this context be composed of 'white' workers – for example, transient Romanian agricultural crop pickers in the east of England (Fox et al. 2012). Moreover, superdiversity signalled how in major cities, the ethno-cultural 'core' population – referred to romantically by many as the 'white working class' – could in fact become a minority amidst a majority rainbow of multiple diversity (Crul et al. 2013).

A sleight of hand also transformed intersectionality – a term that Black women writers in the USA introduced to signal the accumulated disad-

---

3. The first edition of Stephen Castles and Mark J. Miller's canonical textbook in migration studies, *The Age of Migration*, dates from 1993. It is now in its sixth edition (de Haas et al. 2019).

vantages that Black, female, queer, lower-class, elderly, and/or disabled persons face in a heteronormative society (Collins 2019; Crenshaw 1989) – into an affirmative quality of diversity. In a sense, this conformed with the key point of Williams's genealogical lexicon: a keyword was not something pointing to something out there in the world in a realistic sense, but rather an evolving historical term with a materialist base that needed careful contextual understanding, its defining quality being that it had made the expression of rising new groups possible, thus leading to new social formations and social change. For Williams, for instance, culture was a master concept of the long nineteenth century, at the heart of the making of the English working class – and its political voice. Diversity surely had initially emerged as a way of signalling difference from white, racial, heteronormativity in liberal democracies. It made identities possible and, as such, opened up new positional dynamics – as a value that might need, normatively, to be recognized in assessing the outcomes of consensus, in which distinct people with different conceptions of the good come to a like-minded single conclusion on the right that can unify them – as classically in the Rawlsian framework (Rawls 1993). Diversity might in this early phase have rhetorically flagged a necessary recognition of domination or discrimination as distorting one's ability to enjoy democratic processes of overlapping consensus. This is a vital critique of the liberal Rawlsian or Habermasian imaginary of ideal communication – see, for example, the feminist multiculturalism of Iris Marion Young (1990) who speaks of the masked 'faces of oppression' in contemporary liberalism. However, race or other terms might do the same thing. In fact, neo-liberalism especially has shown itself capable of absorbing such terms of cultural critique as a fuel of its genre-crossing entrepreneurialism – indeed, this is one of its defining hallmarks (Frank 1998).

Diversity, instead, became 'a new mode of incorporation' in the words of German sociologist Thomas Faist (2009). It enabled debates on multiculturalism to slide away from difficult issues around incommensurable values – for example, issues raised about religious (in)tolerance in relation to radical Islam in the West – and to emphasize instead the more celebratory appeal of difference, or even to praise its corporate efficiency as the extension of a logic of equal opportunities for multiple diverse individuals. As diagnosed especially in the key work of Sarah Ahmed (2012), it took off especially as an organizational jargon in private and public sector alike for absorbing the challenge of racial and gender difference, within a flattening mode of recognition that could take on board identity claims, while doing little to address structural domination and its legacies. Diversity signalled in this phase a recuperation of the positives of migration-led social change and hence multi-ethnic heterogeneity, without dealing with the weight of colonial history and the irreducible scar of W. E. B. Du Bois's racial 'color line' in Western thought (Lentin 2020). The use of the supposedly analytical term ethnicity – which dates back to Robert E. Park and the Chicago School – indeed often parallels that of diversity, in its elision of race (Alba 1992). With intersectionality now also a superdiverse positive at the heart of diversity-driven urban economies and identity-entrepreneurship, the scene was set for these terms to take their place as core values within the new spirit of capitalism (Boltanski and Chiapello 1999). The appropriation was captured in the phrase 'Benetton multiculturalism' – after the fashion brand and its colourful multi-racial advertising – as wielded particularly in the cynical assessment of Slavoj Zizek (1997).

Yet, there is a sting here. More recently, this line of critique has often been used clumsily to tie together the utopian globalisms of the post-1989 era with later post-Millennial 'woke' generation sensibilities – in other words, dismissing as 'cancel culture' the anger of younger generations very conscious of the legacies of race and colonialism (such as the Black Lives Matter movements). In this way, scepticism about the terminology of diversity rapidly becomes a classic tool of neo-conservative reaction (see Hirschman 1991); even when it is dressed, as it sometimes is, in pseudo-Marxist critique (Grau 2021 is a good example, riffing on *New York Times* columnist Ross Douthat; see also Michaels 2007). Diversity may have sunk as a hooray word in the emotivist evaluation of critical terminology, and rightly so. However, we should not doubt for a moment that there are real political issues at stake with the questions of race, difference, or even multiculturalism, as it used to be termed before neo-conservatives effected their critical demolition (Joppke 2004; see Lentin and Titley 2011).

We might then seek to take a different line with diversity. In some nominalist sense, to see the world as composed of diversity, is simply to say that diversity signals all that is the case. The world is infinitely diverse – as diverse as the entities that make it up and the categories we use to capture that diversity. The key question here, then, is political. States and their institutions may talk about promoting or protecting diversity, but they are in fact constitutively in the business of reducing the diversity of the world. Most obviously, what nation-states try to do is differentiate themselves from the rest of the world by projecting a singular bounded unity – something in which all members share what is distinct from everybody else in the world. Nations are a strange case in which a universalizing sub-system emerges as a totality in its own right – a political system, usually accompanied in its ideal type by a bounded notion of language, history, heritage and the institutional systems that maintain this, such as education or the media, as opposed to wider world systems, such as the economy or culture as such (see Joppke 2011 on Luhmann). The integration this implies then has to approach the internal population – itself potentially infinitely diverse, in theory – to process this diversity as unity. Successful imposition and assertion of political sovereignty hinges on this political operation.[4] As diversity came to be recognized within liberal democracies, it usually took the shape of imposing formally in legal and institutionalized terms particular ethno-racial categories as a way of recognizing and protecting (or promoting) diversity equally across individuals and groups. So all diversity-related laws and organizational practices require in some sense a finite notion of identity categories in order for discrimination or domination to be operationally recognized and treated, while also reifying distinctions that may reproduce existing racial hierarchies. A politics emerges around the mobilizations and contestations that these categories engender.

Diversity then keeps moving. Categorization produces political incentives for recognition by making claims that can then lead to the recognition of further categories. A classic case of this is the mixed–other category in surveys, which, with high rates of intermarriage, is currently breaking down established race categories and hierarchies in the USA. For some commentators, this has produced the possibility of not only transcending ethnicity – which was always implicit in classic assimilatory modes recognizing racial difference as hyphenized ethnic-American, linked to migrant/national origins – but also, in tandem with 'white' majorities becoming a minority majority, of a movement towards a supposedly post-race society (Alba 2020). This builds on the well-known class-based arguments about the declining significance of race as a middle-class African-American

---

4. I develop this argument at length in Favell (2022), The Integration Nation: Immigration and Colonial Power in Liberal Democracies (Polity).

population moved away from a truly disadvantaged underclass (Wilson 1980). Diversity, too, seems to be going with the demographics, towards a *caffe latte*-coloured vision of future 'whiteness'. Diversity here becomes the equivalent of intense individualization – with individuals no longer recognized for the positions their imputed racial categorization might have imposed, or reflected. In a society with racism still present, and indeed endemic, this slide towards non-recognition of race is hugely problematic. Similar problems follow from all existing post-race ideologies, such as republican citizenship in France.

There are no golden rules for recognizing claims of diversity. There are very lively debates among critical scholars on how to go beyond existing clumsy ethno-racial check boxes, recognizing intersectionality and complex positionality without it collapsing into a nominalist individualization of positively chosen 'identity options'. In Europe, continental population systems that have hitherto rigorously refused to recognize race-based classification because of the legacy of Nazism, have over time pragmatically recognized the need for survey data and group categories in order to ground meaningful anti-racist action (Simon et al. 2015). Yet, one of the great points of interest here is the intense diversity between otherwise relatively similar North Atlantic Western societies in terms of wrestling with these post-colonial questions – the USA, Canada, the UK, France, the Netherlands, Germany and Sweden all have distinctive ways of formally recognizing ethno-racial diversity as constitutive of their national populations.

Ultimately, we may wish to be agnostic about whether diversity is a good thing. There are specific colonial and racial legacies that have been poorly addressed by past attempts to formulate multiculturalism as a progressive philosophy, and that have been significantly rolled over by the turn towards more nationally-oriented ideas of integration that came with its critique (see Favell 2022). At the same time, mobilization around race, post- and de-colonial issues in recent years has shifted the ground of the politics of difference considerably, at ground level at least, if not always in legal or state-institutional contexts. Diversity as a progressive term, though, is well past its sell by date. While it gestures towards something that needs terminology to generate the kind of transformative politics that Williams endorsed, the search for a renewed keyword in this conceptual space continues.

References

Ahmed, S. (2012) *On being included: racism and diversity in institutional life*, Duke University Press.

Alba, R. (1992) *Ethnic identity: the transformation of white America*, Yale University Press.

Alba, R. (2020) *The great demographic illusion: majority, minority, and the expanding American mainstream*, Princeton University Press.

Alba, R. and N. Foner (2015) *Strangers no more: immigration and the challenges of integration in North America and Western Europe*, Princeton University Press.

Boltanski, L. and E. Chiapello (1999) *Le nouvel esprit du capitalisme*, Gallimard.

Castles, S. and M. J. Miller (1993) *The age of migration: international population movements in the modern world*, first edition, Macmillan.

Collins, P. H. (2019) *Intersectionality as critical social theory*, Duke University Press.

Crenshaw, K. (1989) 'Demarginalizing the intersection of race and sex: a Black feminist critique of antidiscrimination doctrine, feminist theory and antiracist politics', *University of Chicago Legal Forum*, 1 (8): 139–67.

Crul, M., J. Schneider and F. Lelie (2013) *Super-diversity: a new perspective on integration*, University of Amsterdam Press.

de Haas, H., S. Castles and M. J. Miller (2019) (6th ed.) *The age of migration: international population movements in the modern world*, sixth edition, Macmillan.

Faist, T. (2009) 'Diversity – a new mode of incorporation', *Ethnic and Racial Studies*, 32 (1): 170–91.

Farris, S. (2017) *In the name of women's rights: the rise of femonationalism*, Duke University Press.

Favell, A. (2022) *The integration nation: immigration and colonial power in liberal democracies*, Polity.

Fox, J., L. Morosanu and E. Szilassy (2012) 'The racialization of the new European migration to the UK', *Sociology*, 46 (4): 680–95.

Frank, T. (1998) *The conquest of cool: business culture, counter culture and rise of hip consumerism*, Chicago University Press.

Grau, A. (2021) 'Woke Kapitalismus: es wächst zusammen, was schon immer zusammengehörte', *Der Spiegel*, 48, 27 November.

Hirschman, A. O. (1991) *The rhetoric of reaction*, Harvard University Press.

Joppke, C. (2004) 'The retreat of multiculturalism in the liberal state: theory and policy', *British Journal of Sociology*, 55 (2): 237–57.

Joppke, C. (2011) 'Immigration, citizenship and the need for integration', in R. Smith (ed.) *Citizenship, borders and human need*, University of Pennsylvania Press, 157–76.

Lentin, A. (2020) *Why race still matters*, Polity.

Lentin, A. and G. Titley (2011) *The crisis of multiculturalism: racism in a neoliberal era*, Zed Books.

Michaels, W. B. (2007) *The trouble with diversity: how we learned to love diversity and ignore inequality*, Holt McDougal.

Modood, T., R. Berthoud, J. Lakey, J. Nazroo, P. Smith, S. Virdee and S. Beishon (1997) *Ethnic minorities in Britain: diversity and disadvantage*, Policy Studies Institute.

Rawls, J. (1993) *Political liberalism*, Princeton University Press.

Simon, P., V. Piché and A. A. Gagnon (eds) (2015) *Social statistics and ethnic diversity: cross-national perspectives in classification and identity politics*, Springer.

Vertovec, S. (2007) 'Super-diversity and its implications', *Ethnic and Racial Studies*, 30 (6): 1024–54.

Young, I. M. (1990) *Justice and the politics of difference*, Princeton University Press.

Williams, R. (1976) *Keywords: a vocabulary of society and culture*, Fontana.

Wilson, W. J. (1980) *The declining significance of race*, University of Chicago Press.

Zizek, S. (1997) 'Multiculturalism, or the cultural logic of multinational capitalism', *New Left Review*, 225: 28–51.

Superdiversity:
On the Need for History

Gurminder K. Bhambra

Political debate frequently operates through performative constructions of 'them' and 'us', the 'nation' and 'our' past. These constructions highlight some histories and silence others. They matter because, in the process, people are represented as in, or out, of place and their movements facilitated (as citizens, or as tourists) or constrained (as migrants, or refugees). The idea of a common past, and who is part of it, is bound to the politics of the present.

Similar constructions also operate within social science. The racialized discourses at work in the 'Brexit debates', for example, were not only evident in the politics of the event, but they were also implicit in much social scientific analysis as well (Bhambra 2017a, 2017b). Populist political claims of who belongs are mirrored by an equivalent social scientific 'presentism' that also elides proper historical context. Here, I discuss the emergence of the term 'superdiversity' in the context of broader debates on multiculturalism within the UK and discuss the importance of a more expansive understanding of history as the basis for our social science concepts.

'Multiculturalism', as public policy and normative claim, came about as a consequence of the collective mobilization of political demands being made by migrants and minorities predominantly from the Commonwealth. It was, as Ipek Demir (2017: 122) argues, a conceptual frame that enabled scholars 'to think through ways in which diverse societies can live together, accommodate diversity, tackle racism and exclusion, and aid justice'. It was regarded as a successful frame, although some concerns were raised about the challenge to the liberal conception of individual rights that was entailed in the calls for 'group' rights with which it was associated by its critics. In the early twenty-first century, arguments for needing to go beyond multiculturalism were given a particular boost by the emergence of the idea of 'superdiversity', an idea that was more amenable to the discourse of individual rights.

'Superdiversity' was coined by Stephen Vertovec in a 2007 article in which he argued that the demographic diversity of Britain had changed dramatically in the preceding thirty years (that is, broadly coterminous with EU membership, though he did not note the connection) and that policy frameworks and public understanding had not yet caught up with the new social patterns. His claims were largely asserted, rather than demonstrated or analysed, but the frame of superdiversity has come to predominate in ethnographic research interested in issues of difference. In his own words, reflecting on the popularity of 'superdiversity' less than a decade later, Vertovec (2014: 92) suggested that its key concern 'was intended to address the changing nature of global migration that, over the past thirty years or so, has brought with it a transformative 'diversification of diversity''.

Vertovec accepts that 'diverse' people have lived in Britain since at least Roman times, but suggests that it was 'the post-war large-scale immigration of African-Caribbean and South Asian (i.e. non-White) peoples which particularly prompted a set of changes in public policy' in Britain (Vertovec 2007: 1027). While the 'Windrush moment'[1] – of post-Second World War migration from the West Indies – had been central to earlier work on migration, diversity, and multiculturalism, Vertovec saw these concepts as inadequate for dealing with the new migrations and new migrants since the 1970s. Superdiversity has thus been heralded as a concept that could address these new populations and the new social and political landscapes they constituted.

In particular, Vertovec argued that diversity should not be understood simply in terms of race or ethnicity, but the conjunction of a variety of factors, including 'differential immigration statuses and their concomitant entitlements and restrictions of rights, divergent labour market experiences, discrete gender and age profiles, [and] patterns of spatial distribution' (Vertovec 2007: 1025). In this way, superdiversity gathers within a single frame multiple possible differences as features of a complex present – this is

---

1. On 22 June 1948, the *Empire Windrush* entered the Thames and close on 500 West Indians, with British citizenship, disembarked at Tilbury Dock. This rather mundane event – of Commonwealth citizens moving within the bounds of the Commonwealth – has, subsequently, become foundational to mythologies of the changing nature of Britain. See Bhambra (2017b).

what the 'diversification of diversity' points to. What seems to be of primary concern is the description of new migrants and a detailing of their characteristics and the conditions within which they live.

For example, Vertovec (2007: 1029) argues that the decades since the 1970s 'have seen fairly dramatic change' in terms of the countries of origin from which migrants come, but there is little by way of explanation for those changes. There is no accounting, for example, of the Commonwealth Immigration Acts of 1962, 1968, and 1971 restricting the rights of those from New Commonwealth countries on the basis of race; nor was there any discussion of accession to the European Community in 1973, as broader political contexts for these changing patterns (and, indeed, for the very restrictive new immigration acts themselves as European membership was under negotiation). By abstracting differences from the different histories of their constitution, however, the concept of superdiversity renders issues of domination and political exclusion 'attitudinal' rather than 'structural' – it becomes more about how people feel about things, rather than about examining the social and political structures that create hierarchies and inequalities.

When Vertovec suggests that social scientists need to come up with more innovative theories and methods to study migrants and diverse places with a view to informing public policy better, the one thing – and, I would suggest, the most important thing – that is not addressed is the way in which public policy has already set the frame through its understanding of who is entitled to citizenship. The standard accounts of political citizenship, for example, align it with the contours of the nation-state where non-citizens are (or can be) admitted to citizenship (see Baubock 1994).

In the British context, however, the defining of British citizenship has been predicated on the basis of turning some citizens into immigrants through an explicit racial hierarchy associated with colonial histories (Karatani 2003). Indeed, as Hampshire (2005: 77) has comprehensively demonstrated, 'the development of immigration controls in post-war Britain was governed by a racial demographic logic' (see also Dummett and Nichol 1990). This points to the current British polity as deeply structured by race such that the state itself – and all associated concepts, such as citizenship – are themselves racialized as a consequence of their colonial histories.

The usefulness of concepts such as superdiversity would have to be assessed in terms of their efficacy in the light of a consideration of this history. Not to engage with this history locates superdiversity as a concept that simply skates on the surface of perceived differences and, in focusing on difference rather than historically structured inequality, erases race and the colonial histories that ultimately configure the present debates on policy, citizenship, and rights.

In this way, superdiversity continues a problematic critique of multi-culturalism that rested on the idea that the demands made by migrants and minorities for 'cultural' rights challenged 'the conception of a unified, undifferentiated citizenship' (Koopmans and Statham 1999: 658). What this critique failed to address, however, was that these demands were made in the context of the establishment of a dual system of citizenship differen-tiated by race and colonial histories. The demands for cultural rights would better have been understood as demands for social, political, and economic inclusion on the basis of equality within a racialized and post-colonial state.

Given that the concept of superdiversity rests on the notion of the immi-grant, as distinguished from the citizen, the inadequate conceptualization of these terms within the literature also misrepresents and misunderstands the contemporary social and political landscape. Specifically, the failure to reckon with colonial histories means that ethnic minority members are misdescribed as immigrants and are not understood as citizens with attend-ant rights. It is this that has enabled the stripping of citizenship (mostly from ethnic minority members) through the hostile environment, some-thing that is also present in the political issues associated with Brexit.[2] The standard historiography of British citizenship is complicit to the extent that it similarly turns some (darker) citizens into immigrants and thereby enables the disavowal of their rights in the present. These histories and their ongoing legacies in the present need to be addressed more explicitly within scholarship on superdiversity.

References

Baubock, R. (ed.) (1994) *From aliens to citizens: redefining the status of immigrants in Europe*, Avebury.

Bhambra, G. K. (2017a) 'Brexit, Trump, and "methodological whiteness": on the misrecognition of race and class', *British Journal of Sociology*, 68 (S1): S214–32.

---

2. For further details, see: https://novaramedia.com/2021/12/15/first-citizens-were-turned-into-immigrants-now-were-being-stripped-of-political-rights/.

Bhambra, G. K. (2017b) 'Locating Brexit in the pragmatics of race, citizenship and empire', in W. Outhwaite (ed.) *Brexit: sociological responses*, Anthem Press, 91–9.

Demir, I. (2017) 'Rethinking cosmopolitanism, multiculturalism and diaspora via the diasporic cosmopolitanism of Europe's Kurds', in G. K. Bhambra and J. Narayan (eds) *European cosmopolitanisms: colonial histories and postcolonial societies*, Routledge, 121–35.

Dummett, A. and A. Nicol (1990) *Subjects, citizens, aliens, and others: nationality and immigration law*, Weidenfeld & Nicolson.

Hampshire, J. (2005) *Citizenship and belonging: immigration and the politics of demographic governance in postwar Britain*, Palgrave.

Karatani, R. (2003) *Defining British citizenship: empire, commonwealth and modern Britain*, Frank Cass.

Koopmans, R. and P. Statham (1999) 'Challenging the liberal nation-state? Postnationalism, multiculturalism, and the collective claims making of migrants and ethnic minorities in Britain and Germany,' *American Journal of Sociology*, 105 (3): 652–96.

Vertovec, S. (2007) 'Super-diversity and its implications', *Ethnic and Racial Studies*, 30 (6): 1024–54.

Vertovec, S. (2014) 'Reading super-diversity' in M. Keith and B. Anderson (eds) *Migration: a COMPAS anthology*, Centre on Migration, Policy and Society, 86–8.

Noncitizenship and Superdiversity

Katie Tonkiss and Tendayi Bloom

A person is considered in a 'noncitizen' relationship with a state (or multi-state system) if they have to live out their life and perform their politics despite that system (Bloom 2021: 168), a terminology that goes beyond the traditional citizen/non-citizen binary (Bloom 2018: 2). Rather than being merely the absence of citizenship, in this context noncitizenship (without a hyphen) denotes a relationship between an individual and a state (or between an individual and the multi-state system) in its own right. In this short essay, we examine some ways to think about how noncitizenship is enacted and experienced in what has been referred to as a 'superdiverse' UK (using the terminology of Vertovec 2007). The language of noncitizenship, we suggest, enables us to talk about a substantive relationship beyond citizenship, which may function and be experienced in complex ways. Through this terminology, noncitizen relationships can also be accessible to those theorizing our political world and informing social scientific study.

In a 2015 special issue of *Citizenship Studies*, we issued a collective call for noncitizenship to be considered a foundational concept in political theory and other disciplines, alongside – rather than as a derivative from – citizenship (Tonkiss and Bloom 2015). We noted that, while for some time important work has been interrogating more deeply the complex relationships that people have with states beyond citizenship, there is still a strong tradition that presumes and privileges citizenship, whether implicitly or explicitly. As a result, state citizenship often remains the core principle on which to build theory. The central argument of that special issue was that it is too simplistic to understand noncitizenship merely as a derivative of citizenship. Rather, theorizing from the perspective of noncitizenship as a core principle sitting alongside citizenship enables us to examine, understand and theorize from the diverse ways in which noncitizenship is itself enacted.

This work both adds to and reframes some important developments in critical citizenship studies. There is a large body of work showing that state-bestowed legal citizenship is not the only form of political relationship a person can have with a state. For example, scholars have talked about a different sort of citizen politics that is claimed from below through the performance of 'acts of citizenship' (Isin and Nyers 2008). In Isin's approach, people do not wait to be claimed by a state. Instead, they seize citizenship for themselves. However, retaining the language of citizenship can still leave it difficult to frame the burden that the realities of state-bestowed and state-withheld citizenships can place on people. The language of noncitizenship makes it possible to describe a separate and independent set of relationships that can be claimed and enacted, while at the same time making it possible to describe the very real implications of citizenships bestowed and withheld (Bloom 2022).

The proposal here is to demonstrate how a noncitizen-type approach could be used in sociological analysis, including that of what has been referred to as 'superdiversity'. In his account, Vertovec (2007) defines 'superdiversity' as a diversification of diversity, and points to the growing complexity of diversities to be found in many countries around the world, including the UK. The language of noncitizenship could provide a lens through which to explore how this is experienced politically. This includes examining the complex diversity of ways in which people must live and act despite the institutions of the state. That is, the diversity of ways in which people experience noncitizenship. We will show this through three sets of reflections from the UK, highlighting three important issues – connections abroad, racism at home, and legal status.

Consider two recent UK government policies. First, the implementation of the Immigration and Borders Act (which became law in the UK in April 2022) introduced, among other measures, the UK–Rwanda Migration and Economic Development Partnership. As part of this new partnership, the government of Rwanda would receive those who have applied for asylum in the UK while their claim is being processed. This would not affect asylum seekers and those connected to asylum seekers equally. That this is the case can be seen from a second policy launched around the same time. In March 2022, the UK government launched its 'Homes for Ukraine' scheme. According to this initiative, UK individuals, charities, community groups and businesses could volunteer to support and to host people fleeing the Russian invasion of Ukraine. While the idea behind the UK–Rwanda partnership would forcibly relocate some people seeking sanctuary in the UK outside the country, the idea behind the Homes for Ukraine scheme would actively bring people to the UK for protection. For those directly affected, there are symbolic and practical implications of the different framings of these two schemes. While the UK–Rwanda partnership would force some to live out their lives despite, and indeed outside, the British state, others, according to the Homes for Ukraine scheme (at least in its ideal form) would live out their lives thanks to a relationship with the state. There are also specific implications for those who may function mostly as citizens, but are also put into a noncitizen relationship with the state because they have family members or friends whom they would like to support.

Recent history in the UK indicates that noncitizenship can also be produced by policies couched in the language of 'migration control' that, in a context of racialized discrimination, affects people in different ways. In 2017 and 2018, the British public was made aware through newspaper reports that people who had lived in the country for half a century were being asked to prove their right to remain and to participate in its political, social and economic life, part of a reality that was not new and has not stopped (de Noronha 2020), but that became known through what would be called the 'Windrush scandal. This arose from the implementation of a series of policies that required people to prove their eligibility for rights in ways that had not previously been required. This was framed as being about controlling migration but it affected people who were not migrating. This meant that people who had been living as citizens, and who were entitled to citizenship, were suddenly put into a strongly noncitizen relationship with the British state. That is, they had to live and act despite the state. As most of the news stories referred to people with roots in the Caribbean, it was framed as part of the logic of the *Empire Windrush*, a ship that had brought workers from Jamaica to the UK to help rebuild the country after the Second World War, and there was public outcry.

This policy can be understood as racialized in two major ways. First, in practice, not everyone has been asked to prove their eligibility to work, to claim benefits, or to access healthcare. Instead, those affected had heritage in former British colonies and may also have experienced discrimination in other ways (de Noronha 2020). Second, disregard for the potential impacts on those who were affected meant that there was a failure to recognize the urgency of what was happening, and to address it. British people were suddenly put into a position of having to live out their lives despite the British state. This illustrates what Bhambra (2018) called a racialized conditionality of citizenship, which sees some citizens turned into noncitizens on the basis of race, and how such individuals must navigate their lives and act politically despite the actions of the state. In this way, we can see how citizenship and noncitizenship are not mutually exclusive, but are different modes of thinking about a person's relationship with the state. Talking about noncitizenship in this way makes it possible simultaneously to advocate recognition of citizenship and acknowledge the experience of noncitizenship. This case also highlights how a person's relationship with the state can change over time. This was not an isolated occurrence. Those caught up in the Windrush scandal had been subject to shifting dimensions of racialized exclusion for decades (see also Tonkiss 2013; Tonkiss and Bloom 2013).

Finally, an increasing range and complexity of quasi-citizenship statuses characterize contexts Vertovec describes as 'superdiverse'. That is, while it can be tempting to see work visas, humanitarian visas, refugee papers, and so forth as relating to noncitizenship statuses, the relevance of these statuses depends on how much citizen-like membership a state is willing to grant, along with factors such as income (Bloom 2018: 11, 19). Someone with a quasi-citizen status is also likely to be affected by noncitizenship in relation to the state in which they hold that quasi-citizenship. However, the form of citizenship or quasi-citizenship granted in relation to the state will affect the extent to which that person also experiences noncitizenship. For example, the right to a family life in the UK is relatively easily accessible for a comfortable citizen or someone on a highly skilled migrant visa. The same is not true for a migrant entering the country into low-paid, precarious employment, someone who may not meet the UK's income requirements for family reunification and find themselves living in a separate country from their closest family. As such, a noncitizen relationship with the state can also be shaped by a quasi-citizen status and income, and the noncitizen lens provides a way in which to understand this.

As we have shown in this essay, the scholarship around 'superdiversity' demands that the social sciences embrace and engage with the complexities arising from all the diversities of diversities that coexist in contemporary societies. Noncitizenism requires that the starting point and focus of this work must be those who live out their lives and their politics despite the states with most power over their lives, often driven by a range of socially contingent factors.

References

Bhambra, G. (2018) 'Turning citizens into migrants', *Red Pepper*, 19 April, available at: https://www.redpepper.org.uk/talking-about-migrants-is-a-dogwhistle-way-of-talking-about-race/.

Bloom, T. (2018) *Noncitizenism*, Routledge.

Bloom, T. (2021) 'Human rights are not enough: understanding noncitizenship and noncitizens in their own right', in M. Land, K. Libal and J. Chambers (eds) *Beyond borders: the human rights of non-citizens at home and abroad*, Cambridge University Press, 167–82.

Bloom, T. (2022) 'Can citizenship studies escape citizenism?', *Citizenship Studies*, 26 (4–5): 372–81.

de Noronha, L. (2020) *Deporting Black Britons: portraits of deportation to Jamaica*, Manchester University Press.

Isin, E. and P. Nyers (eds) (2008) *Acts of citizenship*, Zed.

Tonkiss, K. (2013) *Migration and Identity in a Post-National World*, Palgrave Macmillan

Tonkiss, K. and T. Bloom (2013) 'European Union and Commonwealth free movement: a historical-comparative perspective', *Journal of Ethnic and Migration Studies*, 39 (7): 1067–85.

Tonkiss, K. and T. Bloom (2015) 'Theorising noncitizenship: concepts, debates and challenges', *Citizenship Studies*, 19 (8): 837–52.

Vertovec, S. (2007) 'Superdiversity and its implications', *Ethnic and Racial Studies*, 30 (6): 1025–54.

The Superdiverse Nation

Marco Antonsich

Looking at recent media coverage, it is clear that nationalism is on the rise, particularly in its most odious nativist and xenophobic forms. Yet, this coverage often tends to obliterate the one thing that nationalism has to offer many people, namely a sense of stability, an anchor when everything around them – people, goods, money, and information – is moving. Holding onto the nation might give to many a sense of security, as the nation is assumed to be stable, fixed: it was here yesterday, it is here today, and it will be here tomorrow. One can trust the nation. The nation is what holds things together in a globalized world in which people can feel lost due to the fast pace at which it moves. This is what scholars call 'ontological security' (Kinnvall 2004) and what the nation might offer people (Skey 2011). Or at least this is what some people think the nation might offer them.

Fantasy or reality? There is no doubt that what often matters in the social sciences is not necessarily how things are, but how people perceive them to be. For instance, the question of 'when' a nation was born can certainly be a key one for historians, but from a more sociological view-point, what matters is that, in the perception of many of its members, the nation is 'timeless' and 'eternal', irrespectively of what historians might say. This is an important point because, as Walker Connor (2004) rightly observes, 'it is not facts but perceptions of facts that shape attitudes and behaviour.'

When it comes to ethno-racial diversity, perceptions matter too. Various demographic projections point, for instance, to a continuous decline of white majorities in western Europe and elsewhere, with different scholars discussing when a majority–minority scenario will feature in country X or Y. If we were to move from the national to the local scale, majority–minority societies are already a fact in some major European cities (such as Amsterdam, Vienna and Frankfurt). Similarly, if we were to consider age groups, this demographic shift is also true in many other cities, as the

45

younger the cohort, the higher the share of people with an immigrant background. Yet, despite this fact (or because of the way it is amplified in people's minds), the fantasy of a fixed, stable, immutable nation is widespread among the public, particularly among its white population.

Whiteness is clearly an unstable signifier, which varies in relation to different spatio-temporal contexts. Yet, in recent times, some commentators have found it a useful label for capturing how political actors capitalize on people's fears about the demographic changes wrought by international migration. From this perspective, the nation becomes exclusively associated with its white ethno-racial core. White people feel that only they are entitled to speak legitimately about the nation. The nation is 'theirs' and others who do not belong to this ethno-racial core do not fully belong to the nation. As such, a conceptual overlapping is generated for which the boundaries of the ethno-racial core coincide with the boundaries of the nation.

It is not surprising that over the last two decades or so, many scholars interested in diversity or superdiversity have often ignored the nation as a site of investigation or, when present, they often treat it as a locus of discrimination, oppression and marginalization. The city, with its forms of cosmopolitan conviviality, has instead received growing interest, and is often heralded as a progressive, inclusive and empowering site where diversity is 'in place' rather than 'out of place'. My argument is that, besides acknowledging that there is nothing inherently progressive or regressive about any given spatial scale, the obliteration of the nation in favour of the city (and in other studies of the transnational scale too) unwittingly reinforces the very nationalist narrative that this scholarship aims to dispel. This is because it leaves the nation in the exclusive hands of white xenophobic nationalists who can then claim a monopoly over 'what' and 'who' is the nation.

To be clear, I do not contest that the nation, like any socio-spatial register, can be activated in exclusive and discriminatory terms. Yet, I argue that it would be analytically unwise to stop here. There is more nation beyond the (white) exclusivist one that awaits to be studied. In my research, which focuses on the case of Italy (www.newitalians.eu/en), I have tried to attend to other narratives of nation as they emerge from the discourses and practices of young Italian adults with foreign backgrounds. Listening to the voices of people who speak like 'us' but do not look like 'us' (Antonsich 2018) allows to move away from the white nationalist narrative of a nation exclusively associated with a given ethno-racial group.

From a normative perspective, various attempts have been made to theorize how to reconcile nation with diversity. Most noteworthy in this respect are studies in liberal nationalism (for example Will Kymlicka, Yael Tamir, and David Miller) and multicultural nationalism (Bhikhu Parekh, Tariq Modood, and Varun Uberoi), which set out the ideal characteristics of a nation in the age of (super)diversity. Politicians on the left or centre-left of the political spectrum have also elaborated ideas on inclusive nations, in which they often espouse notions of civic nationalism (for the case of the UK, see John Denham's idea of progressive patriotism). These noteworthy attempts all aim to unite a diverse national society. However, they are mainly normative: they tell us what a nation should look like rather than how it actually looks. How nation and diversity meet (rather than merely clash) on the ground is still in need of additional empirical research. Thus, my invitation here to students of superdiversity is to bring the nation back into the picture and to explore when, where and how the nation is embraced by a superdiverse population and what people do with it.

This engagement with the nation by ordinary people is what goes under the label 'everyday nationhood' (also called everyday nationalism or everyday nation) – a field that has seen a growing number of scholarly publications in recent years. The everyday is also at the centre of many studies of superdiversity presented under the label 'everyday multiculturalism'. Strangely, despite paying the same attention to the everyday, no attempts have been made to bridge the two fields, that is to close the gap between the former's focus on the nation and the latter's attention to the locale. In both cases, the focus is on how both 'isms' (nationalism and multiculturalism) are the lived, embodied experiences of ordinary people, and not the product of top-down discourses. Bridging the two would reveal important intersections between the local and the national registers.

In the case of everyday nationalism, laying emphasis on a nation composed of a (super)diverse public sharing a culture – ways of doing things in everyday life like talking, eating, and interacting – rather than ethno-racial origins, helps to construct a sense of familiarity, if not necessarily sameness, among a people otherwise unalike in many respects. This point highlights the enduring unifying character of the nation, even in times of demographic change. A (super)diverse public need not reject the nation in favour of local or transnational forms of social identification. Even when a nation is contested for its exclusivist thrust, for instance in some forms of rap music in

Italy and elsewhere, this very contestation is not a rejection of the nation *tout court*, but the demand for a different nation, one that includes all its diverse members.

This last point matters because paying attention to how its ethno-racially diverse members describe and imagine the nation challenges the structural nexus between race(racism) and nation(nationalism), which scholars like Stuart Hall, Paul Gilroy, and Etienne Balibar have at times theorized. As I noted elsewhere (Antonsich 2018: 458), equating race with nation, and thus conflating nationalism with racism, not only frustrates the aspiration of many ethno-racially diverse people to be regarded as full members of the nation, but also denies them the agency they need to redraw the symbolic boundaries of the nation beyond its racial borders.

Nations might remain sites of 'ontological security' for many, but these people might not always be aware of how a nation articulated along racial lines might become a source of insecurity for racialized others. Yet, rather than wishing the nation away, scholars should investigate how the demographic change brought about by international migration transforms the meanings and symbolic boundaries of national belonging. What a super-diverse nation looks like still remains unchartered territory.

References

Antonsich, M. (2018) 'The face of the nation: troubling the sameness–strangeness divide in the age of migration', *Transactions of the Institute of British Geographers*, 43 (3): 449–61.

Connor, W. (2004) 'The timelessness of nations', *Nations and Nationalism*, 10 (1-2): 35–47.

Kinnvall, C. (2004) 'Globalization and religious nationalism: self, identity, and the search for ontological security', *Political Psychology*, 25 (5): 741–67.

Skey, M. (2011) *National belonging and everyday life. The significance of nationhood in an uncertain world*. Palgrave Macmillan.

A Diasporic Perspective on Global/Local Political Change

Catherine Ruth Craven

In recent years, the term 'diaspora' – dispersed populations of migrants who maintain a connection to their homeland – has become the talk of the town among policy-makers. At a global level, there is discussion of their impact on international politics, how they influence states and shape global governance agendas, help eradicate poverty through their remittances and development initiatives, or fight and fund wars thousands of miles away in their home-lands. At a national or local level, diasporic communities and organizations have been lauded for solving the problems of 'superdiverse' communities by supporting initiatives to help people integrate (such as language learning), thereby fostering social cohesion in the host state. Thus, in a world riddled with rising nationalism and isolationist tendencies, they serve as global and local beacons of hope in a complex interconnected world.

Often, what such policy debates miss is the deeply political nature of diasporic mobilization, and the pressures individuals and groups face when they engage at both global and local levels. The same communities that are expected to support the UN's Sustainable Development Goals and their host state's integration efforts are also securitized and marginalized, accused of infighting and state subversion, and roped into community policing and surveillance programmes. The space in which diasporic communities can act in ways that are truly transformative is narrow and rife with oppor-tunities for co-optation. Furthermore, the explanatory value of the concept remains hotly contested by scholars.

Nevertheless, I want to show that the term 'diaspora' has transformative potential, not for what it is (in essence) but for what it can help us see. A diasporic perspective is important because it can illuminate often obscured relations between the global and the local. A better understanding of this entanglement is essential for galvanizing political and social change.

Towards a diasporic perspective

There is an age-old debate about what the concept of a diaspora means. Early usage of the term referred to displaced people bound together by collective trauma and genocide, as in the case of the Jewish and Armenian diaspora. The concept has also been used to describe the descendants of slaves, violently forced from Africa to the Caribbean and now dispersed across the 'black Atlantic' (Gilroy 1993). Others speak of a diasporic consciousness reliant on a myth of return to the ancestral homeland.

From the 1990s onwards, the focus in the discipline of International Relations moved more and more towards theorizing the power of non-state actors in global politics. From this perspective, because they were seen to prolong conflicts through their long-distance nationalism (Anderson 1992), fundraising activities, or lobbying the host-country governments, diasporas were increasingly being depicted as exerting a negative impact on global political processes. While such accounts gradually gave way to more positive conceptualizations of diasporic agency (they could also be peace-makers or development entrepreneurs), approaches remained essentialist and normatively biased towards a liberal-peace paradigm. Even today, a lot of the literature seeks to understand the essential or underlying nature of diasporas. One reason for this is that 'liberal' Western-centric understand-ings of diaspora and diasporic power fit well with the agenda of policy-makers to 'engage' diaspora at the global, national or local levels.

Critics of such 'engagement' policies argue that they construct or position diaspora to become extensions or pawns of powerful states, co-opted by capitalism. This is a convincing but ultimately damning indict-ment of the potential of diasporas to contribute to the transformation of global politics. According to this argument, diasporas remain eternally constrained by the powers that be, but is this actually the case? Truthfully, this question can only be answered in context. Diaspora are not by default or essence radical or transformative actors. Rather, I suggest that a diasporic perspective has potential because it allows us to see how the global and the local are connected. This opens space for imagining global/local justice.

If we assume that a diaspora is not a 'thing' out there in the world but a meaningful relational category that changes in context, then we need to pay attention to how (and where) the concept is used and to what end. Such a relational conceptualization of the term (Brubaker 2005) – one in which we look closely at how and where diasporic social formations emerge and are sustained – will allow us to see how global and local politics become interconnected, sometimes in emancipatory ways. The following anecdotes from my research and involvement in community organizing illustrate how a diasporic perspective can reveal links between global and local, and what happens when either is neglected.

The global and the local through a diasporic lens

Between the summers of 2016 and 2017, a number of diaspora-led civil-society organizations based in Toronto formed a (net)working group around shared attempts to engage in development processes in their respective homelands. The network was initiated and overseen by the Ontario Council for International Cooperation, an organization that receives funding from the Canadian federal and provincial governments. The understanding was that organizations would adhere to and promote the UN's Agenda for Sustainable Development. Only by pledging this, were they able to access support for their activities. Consequently, most groups enthusiastically endorsed these 'global' development norms, discourses, and practices, but often experienced difficulties translating them to the diasporic communities they represented and in which they were embedded. In meetings, they often lamented the short-termism and unsustainable nature of the practices in which their co-ethnics engaged, which they saw as too 'local', for example sending sewing machines to, or building a house in, a single village in north-east Sri Lanka. The narrative was that 'local' engagement in the diaspora went against 'global' development perspectives.

Ironically, or perhaps tragically, what was rarely discussed at these meetings were the 'local' day-to-day struggles these diasporic organizations faced inside their host countries when trying to do their 'global' development work. Something that emerged quickly from my research was that a key barrier to receiving funding for their activities, either from international organizations, or Canadian federal, provincial or municipal agencies, related to their being a registered charity, something that came at considerable cost and much bureaucratic manoeuvring. Another factor was that maintaining links to powerful global actors in the development sector, or even attending the specialized networking meetings, required people to travel vast distances across Toronto during lunch breaks or at the end of long working hours in their day-jobs. These 'localized' struggles over navigating bureaucracies and urban infrastructures played a huge role in determining which organizations could attend and influence spaces of 'global' governance and decision making in the development field. This ties in with the ways in which spaces of 'global' governance and decision-making tend to obscure bureaucratic proceedings and material infra-structures, thus leading to the reproduction of existing power relations, with little space for small diaspora-led organizations to make a difference. In this vignette, we therefore see the detrimental effect of ignoring the 'local' for the sake of the 'global'. But it does not have to be this way. Let us skip ahead a few years.

In March 2020, the world ground to a halt in the wake of the emerging Coronavirus pandemic. As densely populated cities across the globe went into lockdown, political and economic elites were touting the pandemic as the 'great leveller'. It very quickly became clear that the opposite was the case. Existing socio-economic divisions were brought into sharp focus, exacerbated by vaccine nationalism on both a global scale and more locally. People who were already marginalized, especially the poor, racial minorities, and migrants living in crowded, multi-generational housing, were dying at alarmingly higher rates than others. Vulnerable people were confined to their homes, unable to procure food or medicine.

But this unfolding crisis also triggered the increased visibility of so-called mutual aid networks. These were highly localized networks of neighbours who organized via social media to help each other out, doing shopping or taking care of children and pets. These 'local' networks were not without their political struggles. For example, as UK councils caught on to their existence they sought to co-opt them into their public service delivery. In my borough in North East London, this began to cause tensions, between those who thought that state resources should go to the most needy versus those for whom this spelt the death of 'local' neighbourhood endeavours in the true spirit of mutual aid.

What this debate on the correct way to do 'local' community organiz-ing obscured was the real politics and history of these mutual-aid networks in the Global North and West, most of which were built through the hard graft of diaspora communities. Indeed, it was a local Islamic association that prepared thousands of free meals a week to feed people across the region in which I was living. Likewise, Kurdish diaspora groups in north London were at the forefront of leveraging their networks to gather and distribute donations for food banks. Most of these organization were not vocal about the fact that part of the reason why they had the capacity to feed so many people in the first place – or why they could reach out to vast networks of donors – was because that was what they had been forced to do in their places of settlement; the very 'global' processes of displacement from their home countries through colonialism and wars, and subsequent neglect by the receiving states (often themselves implicated in the displacement) were decisive reasons for the existence of these solidarity networks.

Importantly, some groups and individuals engaged in explicit action to correct this political amnesia. In other words, they linked the 'local' practice of mutual aid to its 'global' roots by emphasizing how the practice emerged in Black communities in North America and Britain from the mid-twentieth century onwards, as these faced intense deprivation, state-racism, and violence. Such diasporic collectives held workshops, and distributed educational resources (on and offline) that told the story of mutual aid from a global historical and anti-colonial perspective. These often emphasized that, in the absence of a state that acts as protector/provider, radical forms of community care could emerge and thrive.

In the diaspora the local is always already global

The two anecdotes illustrate the different strategies and politics that characterize diverse diaspora groups and community engagement. They show how important it is to remember that diaspora politics (like all politics) is always both global and local. While diaspora groups that states 'engage' (either for foreign-policy purposes or to provide domestic services) are often reproducers of global power inequalities and caught in systems of capitalist extraction, it does not have to be that way. Many groups and individuals are already engaged in world-making beyond the nation-state, outside presently dominant systems.

Diasporas are not just significant for global political change because of how they influence inter-state relations or contribute to governance, but because they force us to think across scales and beyond borders, both theoretically and politically.

Resources centring the global roots of radical community organizing and redistributive justice:

Galdem Magazine – https://gal-dem.com/weve-been-organising-like-this-since-day-why-we-must-remember-the-black-roots-of-mutual-aid-groups/

Maynmai – www.instagram.com/maynmai/_

Decolonising Economics – https://decolonisingeconomics.org/

The Indigenous Kindship Collective (US) – https://www.instagram.com/indigenouskinshipcollective/

Our Migration Story – https://www.ourmigrationstory.org.uk/oms/transcontinental-activism-in-inter-war-britain

The Black Curriculum – https://www.instagram.com/theblackcurriculum/

References

Anderson, B. (1992) *Long-distance nationalism: world capitalism and the rise of identity politics*, Center for Asian Studies Amsterdam.

Brubaker, R. (2005) 'The "diaspora" diaspora', *Ethnic and Racial Studies*, 28 (1): 1–19.

Gilroy, P. (1993) *The black Atlantic: modernity and double consciousness*, Harvard University Press.

The Times of Migration

Melanie Griffiths

Migration has long been considered a primarily spatial phenomenon, in which people move from one place to another. A recent 'temporal turn' in migration studies has changed the landscape, heralding an appreciation of the many ways in which *time* arises within the experience and management of mobility. At the beginning of the twenty-first century, social scientist Saulo Cwerner called for exploration of 'the complex temporal dimensions of the migration process' (Cwerner 2001). A decade later, Bridget Anderson, Ali Rogers and I reviewed the burgeoning work on time and migration (Griffiths et al. 2013). Since then, migration scholars have begun exploring the times of migration in diverse and rapidly expanding ways.

Time is a complex and slippery concept, one that has long captivated and alluded scientists and philosophers alike. It is humanly universal, yet culturally informed and context dependent, with enough faces to mean everything and nothing. It can be considered measurable and precise, or phenomenological and embodied. Time is individual and personal, but also collective and institutional, and embedded in legal, political, financial and social institutions (Adam 1995). State power itself is operationalized through temporal devices and controls, or what Cwerner calls 'time politics'.

Time imbues the subjectivities, journeys and strategies of migration, and is written into the categories, legislation and decision-making of immigration systems. There is the timing, flows and orderings of journeys, moments of haste, deceleration and limbo. Movements may be temporary or long-lasting, hang on intended futures or hark back to ancestral pasts. Immigration policies are infused with temporal safeguards, conditionalities, barriers and punishments: qualifying periods, notice periods, protections for minors, sanctioned pockets of time-space in a territory, and an array of complex temporal requirements. Here I shall consider some of the ways in which we can think about the temporal dimensions of migration and the insights this provides into understanding migration and the production of borders.

Rhythms

There are rhythms to both the experiences and management of mobility. Attempts to govern migration often focus on anticipating or managing 'flows' of people into particular time-space configurations, such as the periodized, time-limited durations of visas. Both policymakers and migrants may expect movements to be circular; tied to agricultural seasons, financial cycles, political terms, academic semesters or life stages. Often policymakers imagine immigration journeys – through both space and law – to be linear and progressive, whether endlessly and unstoppably flowing, or episodic and halting. The journey is simplified as a mechanical forward-facing sequential march from A to B, or across legal categories – arrival, settlement, integration and eventual naturalization or its demonized opposite: illegal entry, illegitimate residence and eventual detection, detention and deportation.

In practice, migration journeys are more often ones of diversions, delays, queues, repetition, reversals, stasis and liminality. Temporary periods and transit countries may drag on for years. Supposedly temporally-secure immigration statuses and citizenships may be lost or revoked. The anticipated eventual return 'home' may be endlessly delayed or take the form of repeated short visits rather than the expected single, final move.

Tempos

The tempos of migration may be complex and contradictory. I have described this as torturous 'dual temporal uncertainty' (Griffiths 2014). For some, mobility is fast and efficient, for many it entails suspended limbos or uncontrollable frenzies. Migration journeys may take years, decades or even generations, as people wait for opportunities to travel, court hearings, letters, documents, reunions and decisions. Irregular and precarious migrants are especially likely to face little change over long, indeterminate periods, with immigration detainees and asylum seekers invariably describing time as slowed or stopped. Immigration governance is often focused on slowing movements – from detaining people at the border, to excessive delays and red tape 'wasting' people's time. And yet, migrants' experiences are also often ones of destabilizing rushes, in which little can be anticipated or planned: sudden decision-making that is too quick for support to be mobilized and time frames that require urgency.

Durability

Whether intended or not, migration experiences are frequently impermanent. Immigration categories are often time-limited, movements may be seasonal, involve in-transit pauses or alter with changing life stages. Impermanence might reflect ambiguity towards host countries, a desire for different destinations, or an eventual return 'home'. It is also produced by immigration policies, with visas enshrining transience and conditionality. Many countries recognize that time accrued in a place should contribute to rights to remain. This is reflected in longstanding practices of amnesties and of according increased rights to long-term residents, including those who are present illegally. Some immigration statuses, however, entail chronic liminality – an 'enduring temporariness' (Nyers 2013). Indeed, irregular and forced migrants – and sometimes even their children – may never have the opportunity to acquire a secure legal status. Imposing or implying people's chronic transcience is a technology of power and process of othering, reflected in calls for ethnic minorities to 'go home'.

Tenses

The past, present and future are embedded in migratory experiences in myriad ways. 'Return' migrants and diasporic and transnational communities may look 'backwards', appealing to roots, genealogy and ancestral languages and places. Decisions to migrate and acts of crossing borders can be considered future-facing; they are built on potentialities and becoming, and are infused with a 'future-driven emotion' such as aspiration (Griffiths et al. 2013). Mobility may be experienced as a way of creating new futures, accessing 'modernity' or escaping uncertain futures and leaving behind 'traditional' places. Hopes for a better future can provide people with reasons to move or the resilience to withstand arduous migratory presents. For some migrants, however, the future is so beyond one's control or anticipation, that only the nearest temporal horizon is visible, trapping people in an overly-powerful and prolonged present.

(A)synchronicity

Communities, be they diasporas or nations, build collective identities and cohesion through temporal harmony, such as synchronized presents, shared pasts and common imaginings of the future. With temporal dissonance often framed as cultural conflict (Bastian 2014), temporal disjuncture can work to marginalize. Indeed, migration may be characterized by temporal disconnection, be it from local time practices, one's planned personal time-line or the temporalities of countries of origin or separated family. Temporal discord is also a feature of immigration management, reflected in disputes over the length or value of people's time, from ages to the durations of relationships and periods of residence. Policies prohibiting immigrants from working or studying prevent them from sharing local schedules and 'normal' busy life, what Saulo Cwerner (2001: 23) describes as exclusion from the 'meanwhile' (a sense of sharing the same time as others). Immigration enforcement measures, like detention and deportation, are particularly powerful in reconfiguring people's time and violently rupturing their presents and anticipated futures (Khosravi 2018).

Conclusion

Through discussion of time and its rhythms, tenses, speeds, tensions and (im)permanence, this contribution has explored how temporalities frame, constrain and offer opportunity for movement and settlement, and in so doing help produce borders and nations. Time is bound up in the exercise of authority and relationships of power, and is also embodied, psychological and affective. We have seen how time is integral to immigration systems: written into immigration bureaucracies, categories and legislation, and the complex webs of temporal conditions, restrictions, stipulations and deadlines. We have also seen that time underpins people's experiences of moving and settling, illuminating subjective experiences, agency and tactics of mobility. Considering the conceptualizations, regulation and experiences of time by institutions and individuals, provides new insights into Cwerner's 'time politics' and the ways power, borders and the state are operationalized and negotiated. This temporally-infused approach offers new insights into and ways of understanding and theorizing migration and diversity in the twenty-first century.

References

Adam, B. (1995) *Timewatch: the social analysis of time*, Polity.

Bastian, M. (2014) 'Time and community: a scoping study', *Time & Society*, 23 (2): 137–66.

Cwerner, S. (2001) 'The times of migration', *Journal of Ethnic and Migration Studies*, 27 (1): 7–36.

Griffiths, M. (2014) 'Out of Time: the Temporal Uncertainties of Refused Asylum Seekers and Immigration Detainees', *Journal of Ethnic and Migration Studies*, 40 (12): 1991–2009.

Griffiths, M., A. Rogers and B. Anderson (2013) *Migration, time and temporalities: review and prospect*, COMPAS research paper, available at: www.compas.ox.ac.uk/wp-content/uploads/RR-2013-Migration_Time_Tem poralities.pdf.

Khosravi, S. (2018) 'Stolen time', *Radical Philosophy*, 203: 38–41.

Nyers, P. (2013) 'Liberating irregularity: no borders, temporality, citizenship', in X. Guillaume and J. Huysmans (eds) *Citizenship and security: the constitution of political being*, Routledge.

Survival Time/Human Time: Behrouz Boochani's *No Friend but the Mountains*

Lyndsey Stonebridge

In this piece, I turn to Behrouz Boochani's extraordinary book *No Friend but the Mountains*, first published in 2018. Written on Manus Island, it is a text distinguished by – among very many things – its determination to keep human time going in the face of its systematic destruction by the Australian state, and the recognition that the persistence of totalitarian forms in modern history requires the development of counter-temporal and historical forms of agency through the acts of thinking and writing.[1]

Half-way through her essay, 'The Modern Concept of History' (published in the same year as *The Human Condition*), Hannah Arendt (1958: n. 285) quotes four lines from Rainer Maria Rilke's tenth poem in the cycle, *From the Remains of Count C. W.* Denver Lindley's translation of these lines reads:

> Here even the mountains only seem to rest under the light of the stars; they are slowly, secretly devoured by time; nothing is forever, immortality has fled the world to find an uncertain abode in darkness of the human heart that still has the capacity to remember and to say: forever.

Nothing is forever. Even the mountains seem temporary. Human time now resides only in the human heart. Arendt, as she well knew, was writing under the shadow of an already failing European cosmopolitanism.

---

1. A longer version of this piece has been previously published as Chapter 6: 'Survival time/human time' in my book, *Writing and Righting* (Stonebridge 2021).

Statelessness, with its grammar of immobility, imprisonment, and stasis, had already begun to undermine the poetics of exile offered by Rilke. Today, the 'soft exile' of the cosmopolitan writer is embarrassingly inadequate to the realities of mass displacement, deportation, and imprisonment. By contrast, Behrouz Boochani's writing comes directly (literally) from the histories of statelessness and colonial and postcolonial appropriation that Arendt was beginning to analyse. Like Arendt and Rilke, Boochani finds a temporal touchpoint in the vulnerable but seeming permanence of the mountains – they are his only friends, linking the past to the present, the outside to the inside of the camp. Boochani's mountains are the ones he grew up on in Kurdistan – the nation that is not allowed to be a state – and that he remembers; the mountain on Manus Island, which offers both a refuge and viewpoint from which, with patient precision, he documents and analyses the slow sovereign violence of what he describes, after the work of the feminist theologian Elisabeth Schüssler Fiorenza, as the 'kyriarchy system'.

Arendt predicted that forms of totalitarianism would persist in the world long after the demise of totalitarian states. Boochani and his translator and collaborator Omid Tofighian demonstrate how totalitarian thinking has migrated from the inside of the twentieth-century state to provide the logic of contemporary border controls in the twenty-first century. As with its twentieth-century variants, a mix of totalitarian ideology and terror work both the system of the detention camp and the politics that enables the citizens of Western democracies to stomach what is being done in their name. Arendt argued that one of the characteristic features of modern totalitarianism was the 'boomeranging' back to the European nation-state of colonial administrative practices of brutal dehumanization. Boochani reveals that it is precisely the colonial aspects of totalitarianism that have endured into the twenty-first century.

The racist legacies of Australian settler colonialism proved to be a fertile seedbed for the early experiments in border control; they were begun there in the 1990s and have since been rolled out to Europe and the USA. Under colonial rule, it was labour, resources and capital, now it is the political economy of refugees and migrants that is outsourced overseas in dodgy trade-offs based on implicit and increasingly explicit racist thinking. Whereas in the twentieth century the point of the totalitarian camp was to eliminate those deemed enemies of the state, the point of the kyriarchy system is *refoulement* – 'returning the refugee prisoners to the land from which they came.' Not since Primo Levi's accounts of how the Nazi *Lager* was designed to create the terror necessary for prisoners to collude in their own dehumanization has the organization of violence been described with such controlled, and devastating, accuracy. 'Hatred runs through every prisoner. In the prison hatred makes prisoners more insular. The weight of hared is so intense that the prisoners will suddenly collapse on a dark night and give up resisting ... surrender to a system that induces and amplifies hatred ... and accept refoulement' (Boochani 2018: 165). The obscenity of industrial genocide has been replaced with the illegality of *refoulement*, a practice that the 1951 Refugee Convention prohibited.

The suppression of human time is intrinsic to the aims of the refugee regime in Manus prison. Life is reduced to the labour of survival. The endless queues; the waiting lists for specialist medical attention when all that is ever available is paracetamol; the appointment with the Godot-like dentist who never arrives (and whose absence means that Boochani seeks relief in the excruciating, but effective, cauterizing methods of the Manus islanders); the tobacco trade likewise designed to create need, not relief; the rationing of phone calls home: all these are 'mad' in the sense that Arendt would have recognized. It is a madness administered with the goal of making it so intolerable to exist in this timeless zone of never-ending affliction that the refugees will willingly spring back 'to where they came from' if only to re-enter some kind of temporal existence. And if they go back, or at least so goes the fantasy, so too might the familiar temporalities of the nation-state be restored.

In Baucom's terms, we could say that the Australian state, like the USA, the UK, and most of the nations that make up the European Union, is attempting to restore its temporal equilibrium. As this involves constantly recreating its own 'non-time' in the present – that is, reconstructing versions of the very past and future it was supposed to banish in the field of reality – this, as is rapidly becoming apparent, is something of a self-defeating strategy.

Even to write, in this context, is to seize back work – and so human time – from the dead-time of labouring-to-survive. Boochani wrote his book in the form of texts and WhatsApp messages. This is no agentless refugee testimony, nor is it fiction. Those yet to read *No Friend but the Mountains* usually refer to is as either a 'memoir' or a 'novel'. In reality, Boochani, like

Arendt, is inventing a new genre of writing – out of historical, political, and existential necessity. From its opening descriptions of the terror of crossing from Indonesia to Australian waters, two things are made clear in his text: first, that human time will not be surrendered, and second, that the act of keeping time in play depends not on the heroism of the individual author – there is no triumphing over adversity, no bright new future forged from toil and suffering, absolutely no redemption here – but on the creation of a temporal agency that is at once collective and contingent. 'All our hopes are focused on one tiny luminous point in the distance,' Boochani writes of the refugees' journey in the too-small, too-rickety boat: 'a common will takes form in solidarity and struggle. What is the connection between our survival and reaching that insignificant bright spot?' he asks (Boochani 2018: 27).

It is precisely any connection to the future that the Australian state is denying. Survival time, not human time, comes to define solidarity and struggle. Even so, from the start, Boochani's writing claims time for those on the boat, for refugees, for those about to be imprisoned, and for himself. 'The path of death and the flow of life are both made manifest in our bodies,' he writes. It is the 'empty vessel' that is 'subject to destruction' not the flow of human time. 'I imagine myself looking back from an unknown place beyond' he continues – 'myself looking back at me. I see a dead body, but with eyes still alert, struggling to survive' (Boochani 2018: 38). I see myself surviving. Might it not be, recalling Ricœur's reading of Arendt, that to survive is also to actualize yourself in narrative time?

It both is and is not. Like Arendt, Boochani refuses to validate either statelessness or stateless time. As with *The Human Condition*, perhaps the most unaccommodating writing in her oeuvre, *No Friend but the Mountain* consciously pushes against a language that might naturalize the political and historical conditions of its telling.

Boochani's collaborator and translator, Omid Tofighian (2018: 366–7) has written of the 'horrific surrealism' of his writing. I think this is right, and that the otherworldliness of this text is partly where the originality of its politics is located. Nothing and nobody on Manus can ever be quite itself – the flowers on the island, for example, only 'resemble chamomile', the mountains are both those of Boochani's Kurdish home and those of the island, his fellow prisoners are recognizable only by their traits – 'Maysam the Whore', 'The Gentle Giant', 'Father-of-the-Months-Old-Child'. This writing does not so much stutter arrested in time and space, to go back to Abani, it shimmers between realities.

Boochani imagines himself looking back 'from an unknown place beyond'. Edward Said wrote of Conrad's prose that its elaborate strangeness communicated the twentieth-century exile's sense of never being able to convey his existence to an uncomprehending and hostile world (Said 2001: 180). Boochani's 'horrific surrealism' likewise speaks from 'an unknown place beyond' the time-space of the Western nation-state. However, there is an important difference too. Whereas Conrad's encounter with the destructive element brought him face to face with human solitude, Boochani writes not (or at least not only) to a hostile world, but from Kurdistan, Iran, from the sea, from the Manus prison, from Manus Island and its people, and from networks of transnational activism. In Arendtian terms, we could say that the actions and encounters recorded in his book reveal a kind of agency, but it is not only the agency of Boochani as the author and producer of his book.

This book is not only about the extermination of human time, but also about what Elena Fiddian-Qasmiyeh (2019) described as the 'poetics of undisclosed care' between those trapped in the grey zones of contemporary statelessness. At every move, other lives and life forms connect. In a shared glance at a child across the refugee boat, for example: 'my eyes follow the child – my eyes, the eyes of a foreigner, together with the loving eyes of the mother, both stitched to this infant's little body. Our concerned gazes are transfixed by this child' (Boochani 2018: 36). In an obscure moaning that at once comes from the mountain and Behrouz's mouth: 'maybe we share the same affliction?' (Boochani 2018: 247). In the prison, Boochani discovers that a woman and her daughters there before him have left poems to mark their presence on the walls and ceiling (Boochani 2018: 112):

> I don't know why I feel the presence of that family when I read the
> poetry/
> I don't know why I feel the presence of the wife and her daughters
> when I read the poetry/
> I feel their presence and their beauty/
> They were lively and active/
> They were living life.

It is not just with a human presence that Boochani is connecting here, but with human time. The family has left him its story, which he, in turn, is telling. This storytelling – between authors and sufferers – claims the right of biography from within the deadtime of the Manus prison. To keep the narrative threads between birth and death, past, present, and future connected is to defy the non-time of the camp. This is also why, in another scene, Boochani carefully describes how the prisoners attempt to ensure that the 'Father-of-the-Months-Old-Child' can defeat the endless waiting in the telephone queue to speak to his own dying father. They fail, but the point is that by trying (by acting as Arendt would say), the possibility of a human world in which men and women are born and die – in which biography is possible – endures.

Boochani is giving us more than the Hobbesian fantasy that haunts the ever-more murderous politics of contemporary border controls. Like Arendt, he is allowing us to glimpse another kind of time. His book ends with a staging of tragedy that Arendt, I think, would have appreciated. The prisoners riot. Suddenly, we glimpse a world in which the men can assume their roles, to be seen, heard, to act: '*The Comedian embodied an actor on stage/The Comedian embodied a poet/*'; '*The Hero ... and his roar*'. Like the Greek poets whom Arendt loved because of the way in which they recorded the spontaneous acts that made freedom possible, Boochani captures the moment for prosperity – for, exactly, another time.

When inevitably the lights go down – the prison authorities kill the generator and quash the rebellion – amid all the noise, one sound distinguishes itself from the chaos (Boochani 2018: 347):

A familiar sound from a forlorn point/
The sound pierced my ear like the wind/
It rested on my heart/
It rested on my heart/
It was the sound of someone who uttered in Kurdish 'dālega!/
It was the sound of someone who cried 'Mother!'

A footnote informs us that *dālega* is the 'word for mother in the Kurdish Feyli dialect'. Whereas in strict legal terms most of the refugees on Manus, as elsewhere, are only potentially stateless, the Feyli Kurds who live on the border between Iran and Iraq are comprehensively stateless; recognized by nobody. They really do live in stateless time. But, in the end, I do not think that that cry is only a lament uttered from the deep history of statelessness – the non-time a currently out-of-control nationalism is manically, and uselessly, attempting to banish. The cry is also the sound of a voice, a child, a son, a man, with a life and a biography, inserting himself in time at the precise moment that it is human time itself he is being denied.

References

Arendt, H. (1958) 'The modern concept of history,' *The Review of Politics*, 20 (4): 570–90.

Boochani B. (2018) *No friend but the mountains*, Picador.

Fiddian-Qasmiyeh, E. (2019) 'The poetics of undisclosed care', Refugee Hosts webpage available at: https://refugeehosts.org/2019/05/21/the-poetics-of-undisclosed-care/.

Said, E. W. (2001) 'Reflections on exile', in *Reflections on exile and other essays*, Granta.

Stonebridge, L. (2021) *Writing and righting: literature in the age of human rights*, Oxford University Press.

Tofighian, O. (2019) 'No friend but the mountains: translator's reflections,' in B. Boochani *No friend but the mountains*, Picador, 366–67.

The Temporalities of Encampment: Producing Discomfort 'in Transit'

Anna Papoutsi

My friend from the Congo, let us call him André, once told me when discussing his life in Athens that 'if after three years you are not sorted in a country, then you should move on to a new place.' He told me that this was something he had heard from an older family member before he left his hometown. That was more than five years ago. It stayed with him, and he lived by this rule of thumb during his migratory project. He was slowly approaching this improvised temporal milestone for Athens: he was still – two years after arriving – living in a container home in one of the many refugee camps in Athens, along with four other asylum seekers; his asylum case, which was at the appeals stage, was pending; he could neither find nor hold a job because of the remoteness of the camp and its erratic schedules; and he was under constant threat of eviction, irrespective of whether his asylum case was approved or denied. He was definitely *not sorted* in Athens and, heeding his relative's advice, was planning to escape to Paris as soon as he could raise enough money. André's discomfort over 'not being sorted' is the result of certain temporalities, such as indefinite waiting, and asynchronicities, such as delayed, interrupted and accelerated time, which are common among immobilized migrants. By instilling uncertainty and causing protracted unlivability among different groups of migrants, these temporalities and asynchronicities produce the affective and material discomfort of 'not being sorted'. André routinely talked about the physical pain of hunger, and the bodily depletion he had experienced in Athens and during his journey, while his constant state of anxiety, of feeling humiliated and agitated, was noticeable to his interlocutors.

Behind these initial observations lies the concept of *time*, and the role it plays in shaping migratory experiences and projects. Melanie Griffiths (2021) has identified five key themes in the scholarship on the temporalities of migration – rhythms, speeds and stasis; (im)permanence; past, present and future; and temporal synchronicity and disjuncture. Furthermore, the migrant experience is one of transnationality and simultaneity, and is characterized by complicated past, present and future connections and disconnections. For example, with colleagues from the SEREDA[1] project, we discovered that forced migrant survivors of sexual and gender-based violence experience a particular kind of shame, which stems from the multiple time–spaces they occupy at once – their present material condition in a new country; being embedded in co-ethnic communities; and being closely bound to their life back home through memories, cultural practices, and social norms (Papoutsi et al. 2022). In turn, as migration is by default a forward-looking and future-oriented project, there is a tendency to project the fulfilment of migrant rights to the future (Nyers 2013), thereby neglecting the lived present and the ways in which migrants already practise their membership and politics (Pascucci 2016).

Against this backdrop, in this contribution I am interested in the experience of the present and the temporalities of forced immobility and encampment 'in transit'. I seek to lay out how André's discomfort over 'not being sorted' is produced by the affective violence of the border, through certain temporalities that deplete migrant bodies, and that devalue their time and thus their labour power. Remarkably, these discomforts are themselves productive in the sense that they often initiate migrants' onward movements. André, like many other migrants in Athens, would much rather stay and settle there, but with every passing day, month, and year it is made impossible for him to do so. Inka Stock (2019) argues, and I agree with her, that the experiences of migrants like André (in her case immobilized Africans in Morocco) is that of being forcibly immobilized, rather than of transiting, as is often said. This resonates with my research in Athens, also often considered a transit city or intermediary destination. Stock explains that the condition of forced immobility can be viewed in three insightful ways: (a) as a stage in the migratory journey, which constrains migrants' control over their trajectory and structures their journeys in particular ways; (b) as a state of rightlessness in which migrants are denied any protections; and (c) as a condition of life that shapes their experiences, identities and

---

1. https://www.birmingham.ac.uk/research/superdiversity-institute/sereda/index.aspx.

options. Understanding André's present in this way highlights his lack of control and the very limited choices he faces, which would in turn be obscured if we thought of him as transiting. André has been in Athens for two years without being able to improve his living situation or material conditions one iota. He is also unable to move forward to a new country, at least not before he raises enough funds to pay for a smuggler. This, in turn, would necessitate him finding a job and, more importantly, maintaining it. Under these crippling circumstances, he cannot possibly meet someone, get married and have a family, which is ultimately his life goal. He understandably feels uneasy and humiliated. His discomfort is a product of his protracted exposure to the affective violence of the state.

The temporalities of discomfort and the production of (im)mobilities

Forced migrants usually have little choice but to inhabit camps while in exile and during displacement. Camps and camp-like spaces are created to be temporary in two ways: on the one hand, they form (part of) a dynamic and often improvised infrastructure put in place in response to exceptional events. As such, they are intrinsically ephemeral (Siddiqi 2020), existing in a permanent temporariness (El Masri 2020). On the other hand, camp residents are rarely (or think of themselves as) permanently settled; they are either en route somewhere or waiting to return, even after decades of immobilization. Encamped migrants have to constantly negotiate the 'impasse between the political imperative to return [or to move on] (and thus remain temporary) and the material exigencies of life and the need, essentially, to build' (Abourahme 2015). The camp's paradoxical ephemerality is reflected in its materiality (think of the containers used for housing), and shapes its relationship to the surroundings, most notably to the city. The camp 'is somewhere, sometime, between temporary and permanent – it is beyond temporary but is not yet permanent' (Qasmiyeh and Fiddian-Qasmiyeh 2013: 136). As such, it becomes a space of memory, politics and action, conditioning the possibilities available to those who inhabit it. In my research, I found that camps subject migrants to the temporal violence of the border, which strips them of their temporal autonomy. Abandonment (understood as the withdrawal of care) and control (understood as the intensification of care) in the camp are produced by imposed temporal practices and mechanisms, such as routines and cycles, which have material and socio-spatial implications (Papoutsi 2021).

André has survived two entire years immobilized in the Athenian camp under a condition that echoes many immobilized migrants' feeling of 'being stuck'. This condition has a spatial element (being stuck somewhere), but its affective dimension is indeed temporal. Being stuck is experienced 'as living in liminal times where one is neither part of processes that structure time as clock time, nor embedded in times of transcendence which would make life meaningful' (Stock 2019: 85). In that sense, the asylum and border apparatus mobilizes affective technologies, such as precarity and unlivability, to deplete and cause discomfort 'in ways that make it very difficult for specific bodies to maintain mental and bodily health' (Meier 2020: 3). Feeling stuck (or not being sorted) is the result of certain temporalities and is itself productive of mobilities and of 'particular kinds of economic subjectivities, as waiting time is converted to devalued labour' (Ho 2021: 1672).

André's story, and that of so many others forcibly immobilized in places where they do not want to be and are frequently unwanted, demonstrates the (often weaponized) temporal power of states. The discomfort of 'being stuck' and 'not being sorted' is achieved through temporalities, like waiting indefinitely, which ultimately disrupt the bond and continuity between past, present, and future, essential for maintaining a sense of self. The border empties the present as the realization of rights, of life, and of happiness is always projected to and postponed for some time in the future. The past becomes a distant memory as skills, relationships, and socio-economic statuses become lost in the material condition of deprivation and degradation of the present. The future, onto which the fulfilment of a meaningful life is projected, is characterized by such levels of uncertainty and unpredictability that is almost impossible to imagine.

References

Abourahme, N. (2015) 'Assembling and spilling-over: towards an "ethnography of cement" in a Palestinian refugee camp', *International Journal of Urban and Regional Research*, 39 (2): 200–17, doi: 10.1111/1468-2427.12155.

El Masri, Y. (2020) '72 years of homemaking in waiting zones: Lebanon's "permanently temporary" Palestinian refugee camps', *Frontiers in Sociology*, 5, doi: 10.3389/fsoc.2020.587063.

Griffiths, M. (2021) 'Interrogating time and temporality in migration governance', in E. Carmel, K. Lenner and R. Paul (eds) *Handbook on the governance and politics of migration*, 316–28.

Ho, E. L.-E. (2021) 'Social geography I: time and temporality', *Progress in Human Geography*, 45 (6): 1668–77, doi: 10.1177/03091325211009304.

Meier, I. (2020) 'Affective border violence: mapping everyday asylum precarities across different spaces and temporalities', *Emotion, Space and Society*, 37: 100702, doi: 10.1016/j.emospa.2020.100702.

Nyers, P. (2013) 'Liberating irregularity: no borders, temporality, citizenship', in X. Guillaume and J. Huysmans (eds) *Citizenship and security*, Routledge, 37–52.

Papoutsi, A. (2021) 'Temporal bordering in the space of the camp: producing and contesting abandonment in Skaramagas and Elaionas camps in Athens', *Political Geography*, 89: 102423, doi: 10.1016/j.polgeo.2021.102423.

Papoutsi, A., J. Phillimore, S. Akyüz, H. Bradby, L. Goodson and C. Vaughan (2022) 'Geographies of shame: diachronic and transnational shame in forced migrants with experiences of sexual and gender-based violence', *Journal of Refugee Studies*, 35 (3): 1221–49, doi: 10.1093/jrs/feac036.

Pascucci, E. (2016) 'Transnational disruptions: materialities and temporalities of transnational citizenship among Somali refugees in Cairo', *Global Networks*, 16 (3), 326–43, doi: 10.1111/glob.12115.

Qasmiyeh, Y. M. and E. Fiddian-Qasmiyeh (2013) 'Refugee camps and cities in conversation', in J. Garnett and A. Harris (eds) *Rescripting religion in the city*, Routledge, 131–43.

Siddiqi, A. (2020) 'Ephemerality', *Comparative Studies of South Asia, Africa and the Middle East*, 40 (1), 24–34, doi: 10.1215/1089201X-8186005.

Stock, I. (2019) *Time, migration and forced immobility: sub-Saharan African migrants in Morocco*, Bristol University Press. Available at https://bristol universitypress.co.uk/time-migration-and-forced-immobility.

Applying the Concept of Anchoring to the Adaptation and Settling of Migrants

Aleksandra Grzymala-Kazlowska

The life of present-day migrants is often characterized by its temporariness. Migrants consider returning to a country, or changing the one they are in for another; they look for new opportunities, are open to various possibilities, and maintain multiple social relations across state borders. The established concepts in migration studies, such as adaptation, integration or settlement, seem insufficient to capture the complexities and dynamism of the migrants' experiences. We need new tools to understand the dynamic and complex processes associated with how migrants adapt and settle down.

The concept of anchoring, which I developed over years of conducting research with migrants from Poland in the UK, may provide a framework for analysis (Grzymala-Kazlowska 2013, 2020). Anchoring can be defined as the process of establishing footholds and reference points that allow migrants to achieve relative psycho-social stability and a sense of security, and to function effectively in a new environment.

My starting point in developing the concept of anchoring was my growing awareness of the limitations of and insufficient links between central notions in migration studies, such as integration, adaptation, and settlement. Although the idea of integration remains central to migration studies, it is increasingly being questioned for the following reasons:

- it remains under-theorized because of the domination of a practical over an analytical approach, and its concentration on measurable outcomes;
- its approach is too unidirectional (linear) or binary, selective and over-simplistic;

- it is too politicized and contains too many normative aspects (such as placing overstated expectations on migrants, which, for example, are apparent in the citizenship tests);
- it is inadequate for contemporary societies where social cohesion and internal integration are questioned because the receiving societies are becoming increasingly interconnected, fluid and diverse; and
- it fails to include the new types of migration, social ties and settling processes that are observable in cases of transnational, liquid and multiple migration.

The integration paradigm also pays insufficient attention to the migrants' sense of stability and safety, which, according to Maslow's hierarchy, constitutes a basic need almost as important as the physiological ones. The research into identity and integration is also inadequately merged. In an increasingly complex, changing, diverse and unpredictable world, identity may become the main point of reference for individuals trying to find relatively stable footholds for themselves. The important inspiration has come from the metaphor of anchoring, which is surprisingly rare in the social studies literature, and the work of Little and collaborators (2002), who evoked the use of anchors in helping cancer patients overcome their identity crises and restore their sense of continuity. This differs from the cognitive approach found in neuro-linguistic programming or in negotiation studies.

What are the benefits of using the concept of anchoring? First, it allows one to overcome the limitations of well-established yet increasingly debatable concepts such as identity and integration, and it gives researchers an opportunity to analyse and relate to the issues that lie behind the concepts.

Second, anchoring highlights the importance of a sense of security and stability, which has been underrated in migration studies. Meanwhile, the spontaneous narratives of migrants collected in my research, for example their frequent references to 'security', 'peace', and 'stability' are evidence of their importance. For instance, one of my interviewees, Renata, used the metaphor of being 'a drifting raft' to describe her unsettled position in the UK and her continuous struggle to find stability and security: 'so far I have been like a drifting raft, since I spend my time searching for work to make a living, to survive. Costs are much higher here than, for example, in Poland, and I have nobody here I can rely on' (UK17/w/single/2y6m).

Third, the concept captures the multidimensionality and unevenness of anchoring. An analysis of interviews with Polish migrants in the UK revealed the key importance of dimensions such as close family; a Polish identity, language and culture; and work, whether current or in terms of future employment opportunities. Other dimensions of anchoring that served to strengthen the interviewees' sense of ethnicity included an ability to (re)construct a home and everyday practices, which included being able to affirm their own values and beliefs, among which family and gender roles were of vital significance.

It was also important to be anchored in a circle of social support consisting of family and friends, Polish acquaintances and, more broadly, the Polish community and institutions. Religious practices and leisure activities were other spheres in which strengthening a sense of being Polish coexisted with getting closer to British society by, for example, participating in the life of the Polish church, and affiliating to religious schools and local parishes. Factors that stimulate mixing include anchoring in the neighbourhood and local community, engaging one's children in school and out-of-school activities, and enrolling in language courses for adults. British governmental and non-governmental institutions only played a prominent role in the lives of migrants requiring special assistance in the event of serious illness or the threat of homelessness. Others could be perceived as independent individuals, relying on their work and support within networks of family and friends.

Anchoring can be characterized differently in different spheres, for example as shallow in some while deep in others. It can be also viewed from the perspective of layers: the outermost one is related to work and relations with institutions; the middle one is composed of the social sphere and everyday practices; and the innermost one relates to one's spiritual or cognitive world. As one Polish migrant being filmed as part of a Polish Expats Association project put it:

I forgot about my profession. I forgot who I was. I forgot what I wanted. I started looking for a job. I knew it would not be easy, but I found it within three days. I found a job through the Job Centre. It had nothing to do with my profession – a factory job, a beautiful job. I worked there for precisely six months. Owing to this, I got the NI number. I got a bank account. I could start planning. I moved to a different house on my own. I began organizing myself internally.

Even my wife came to visit. ... And then I bought a car. I got a contract for a mobile phone and started reading newspapers. And I bumped into the ad of a company looking for someone of my profession.

After setting up external footholds, that is establishing himself in a job, finding a house and accessing formal institutions, the abovementioned migrant brought his wife and children to Birmingham where, despite his strong Polish identity, over the years he began to feel at home, settled in his social network and anchored in the surrounding diversity.

Fourth, the concept of anchoring emphasizes the agency of migrants and their attempts to achieve a sense of security and stability. However, it also embraces the structural constraints, unequal opportunities, and the barriers that migrants face.

Fifth, anchors signifying specific points of reference and support might be analytically distinguished and these identifiable footholds, to which one might be pointed, provide an especially useful tool for analysis.

Sixth, this concept captures the transnational nature of anchoring. While looking for new footholds in the host country, migrants may still have anchors in their home country (for example, in the form of relatives, property or civic privileges). Individuals can also anchor in other countries, and thus establish footholds for future migration or anchoring in geographically undefined spaces (such as virtual communities). Transnational anchoring can be parallel or complementary.

And seventh, the concept displays flexibility, dynamism and a possible two-way direction, for we can talk about anchoring, unanchoring, and reanchoring. The case of Maria illustrating uneasiness, unevenness and changeability after Brexit – evoking the reversibility of anchoring following an unsettling event (Kilkey and Ryan 2020) – is a good example of this point. When interviewed in 2014, this single female migrant with no children, living in the UK for more than ten years, presented herself as somebody whose major anchors in England were in her work, social life, volunteering, and artistic activity. In an interview five years later, her anchoring seemed shallower and diminished than before and, when reinterviewed, appeared even more unsettled and displayed even higher levels of uncertainty. Her temporary work contract had been terminated and, despite her considerable job experience and high proficiency in English, she struggled to secure a permanent or long-term job. Her circle of acquaintances shrank, partly because she withdrew from some relations to 'save energy' for her new short-term contract, but also because of her expressed preference for in-depth and more intimate relationships, which she, however, failed to sustain. Not only did she have fewer friends, but her closest social relationships also became weaker than in 2014. In 2019 Maria no longer felt that she belonged in her neighbourhood and, apart from one Polish friend, had no substantial anchors in the local community.

The repeated interview with Maria demonstrated fewer and weaker anchors in the UK and related high levels of temporariness and disconnection; hence, her uneven settling could be noted in some spheres, especially in British culture and the surrounding superdiversity as well as limited and dispersed social relations, not very strong but emotionally significant. Feeling hurt by the Brexit vote, Maria at first attempted to counteract her increased sense of insecurity by establishing a stronger anchor in the UK by applying for permanent residency. Despite having relatively strong family and friendship anchors in Poland, she was unwilling to return there, but fantasized about moving to a third country in which she had started to establish footholds by securing herself a social insurance number and several friends. However, with the heightened stress brought about by the pandemic, she eventually sought her security and stability in Poland.

The above material shows that the concept of anchoring may be particularly useful for studying the processes of adaptation and settling in the face of destabilizing events such as Brexit. Likewise, the concept may be relevant for research into how migrants have adapted to the Coronavirus pandemic and the ongoing war in Ukraine.

References

Grzymala-Kazlowska, A. (2013) 'Zarys koncepcji społecznego zakotwiczenia. Inne spojrzenie na tożsamość, adaptację i integrację imigrantów', *Kultura i Społeczeństwo*, 57(3): 45–60.

Grzymala-Kazlowska, A. (2020) *Rethinking settlement and integration. Migrants' anchoring in an age of insecurity*, Manchester University Press

Kilkey, M. and R. Louise (2020) 'Unsettling events: understanding migrants' responses to geopolitical transformative episodes through a life-course lens', *International Migration Review*, 55 (1): 227–53, doi: 10.1177/019791832 0905507.

Little, M., K. Paul, C. Jordens and E. Sayers (2002) 'Survivors and discourse of identity', *Psycho-Oncology*, 11 (2): 170–8.

Conviviality and the Banalities of Multicultural Settings

Magdalena Nowicka

The great achievement of scholarship on superdiversity was to demonstrate that, in many places around the globe, diversity is not only normal but also highly complex. Yet, there are limitations to such claims, both historical and geographical. Some places were more diverse in the past than they are today and, what is more, diversity is unevenly distributed across the world (cf. Schrover 2022; Stansfeld 2022). Towns in Poland exemplify this phenomenon. Pre-Second World War Polish towns were more ethnically, linguistically and religiously diverse than they are today, and their relative homogeneity is all the more conspicuous given the diversity that shapes many contemporary cities in Germany, Britain and France. At the same time, it should not be forgotten that some places might be ethnically diverse but homogenous in terms of social origin or economic class. Nevertheless, many urban dwellers are typically confronted with a great variety of diversities among their neighbours – personal identities, faiths, cultures, languages, immigration statuses as well as economic and social positions. This experience has compelled scholars to reflect on contemporary societies as superdiverse. Alongside documenting this human, material, and symbolic variability (we can think of goods imported from abroad, cultural practices, or foreign sounding languages), researchers also ask if long-term settlers become xenophobic when they encounter people whose group identities they do not share, or if they instead become more tolerant and embrace the possibility of the cosmopolitanism that their neighbourhoods can offer (Foner et al. 2019; Oosterlynck et al. 2018).

Migration-related superdiversity is a challenge to government policies and social service practices that are framed by particular understandings of national sovereignty and welfare. When characteristics such as legal status, age, gender, language skills, religion, national origin, transnational connections, or phenotype overlap, the state is required to adapt its approaches to the specific needs of ever smaller groups. The governance of superdiversity involves mainstreaming and designing new policies towards multilingualism, rethinking the relationship between the state and religion, acknowledging multiple migration patterns and transnational biographies, reorganizing the system of political representation, and refashioning welfare services and healthcare provisions (van Breugel and Scholten 2017).

Beyond these practical issues, acknowledging such superdiversity could – and should – force us to reconsider its implications for how scholars imagine the social, for example as an entity consisting of different groups, or organized into sovereign nation-states. In revising social theory, as I shall argue below, scholars must strongly engage with the question of equality and its modern premises.

Ethno-diversity

Ethnonationalism, in which ethnic ties are core to the conception and experience of 'nation', continues to mould our thinking about sociality. Ethnic diversity is an artefact of ethnonationalism. In its implication that 'ethnicity' is an essential trait because people are naturally born into an ethnic community, diversity would refer to a variety of exclusive ethnic groups distinguished by their 'culture', religion, and language, producing an 'us and them' along ethnic lines. Acknowledging that these groups are unnatural does not mean denying the existence of cultural differences and distinct communities. However, thinking about relations between groups through an ethnic lens has two implications: first, it reframes conflicts as ethnic, even if they are waged over social and economic statuses; second, it creates a condition of quasi-equality between co-ethnics. Ethnonationalism extends the ideal of equality to all members of the nation. Modern societies are premised on the myth of egalitarian principle, which makes people aspire to any economic and social position, but ethnonationalism de facto systematically refuses equal status to those who are perceived as ethnic others inhabiting its territory. In this context, cultural, religious or linguistic difference stops being an asset and becomes a marker of distinction, according to which someone can be included or excluded from the community. It becomes politically contentious (Riggs 2002).

Courtesy and civility

Although globalization and migration have accelerated the mixing of peoples and cultures, these phenomena are not new. Navigating diversity requires rules and skills, and these were developed in the early modern era in spaces preceding urban contexts familiar to us, namely in the kings' courts. Since the Renaissance, courtesy accorded to those who are not one's kin has been the core element of modern cultural competence. The systematic treatment of 'others' as if they were equals was a cultural competence expected of elites in Europe (but not necessary outside it) in the Enlightenment period and beyond (Taylor 2004). The same kind of skills that enabled people in early modern Europe to socialize in the public arena across gender and socio-economic status, without questioning or aiming to destabilize it – speaking politely (and in a foreign language), showing respect, displaying tolerance towards other religious beliefs, knowledge of other places and cultures or easiness with and a preference for foreign tastes and foods – is now central to operating in settings differentiated along the lines of ethnicity, race or religion (Hannerz 1990).

Courtesy was an outcome of (elitist) humanistic education that was not available to all. For example, women in Europe (with few exceptions) were long excluded from university studies and were educated for silence in the public arena rather than conversation. However, those non-nationals, non-ethnics who lack intercultural skills are not only perceived as impolite, but they are also associated with incivility and placed on the lowest rung of cultural stratification. Indeed, courtesy as a paradigm of sociality operates hand in hand with racism, Islamophobia or anti-Semitism, as it masks the existence of structural inequalities.

Banal and celebratory multiculturalism

When ethnonationalism meets courtesy and civility, ethnic diversity feels banal, obvious and commonplace, but cultural difference does not necessarily become an asset. The exception might be 'celebratory multiculturalism' – essentially a way of consuming cultural difference (Davis 1996), but one that does not yet involve the equal treatment of others. Similarly, diversity as 'added value' in organizations, promising a competitive advantage, does not automatically lead to more equal treatment. Since sovereign individuals are seen as capable of collaborating with others and bridging group boundaries, cultural difference seems manageable as a feature of an individual, but a risk to the quality of groups. The attractiveness of diversity is thus linked to the idea of individuality.

In urban and other contexts shaped by migrations, ethnic differences might matter less in everyday situations in that they do not confound people. However, instead of celebrating the irrelevance of (ethnic) difference, social scientists should repoliticize it. This happens, for example, in debates on the Janus-faced management of superdiversity when comparing cosmopolitan neighbourhoods in western European cities with occurrences on the shores of Spain, Malta or Italy where the refugees arrive (Schlenker 2013). These are powerful reminders that 'colour-blind', 'raceless' and depoliticized superdiversity scholarship draws our attention away from the pertinence of inequality debates.

Convivialist epistemology

Various scholars researching superdiverse contexts started to describe them as convivial. The English term 'conviviality' etymologically stems from the Latin *convivere*, meaning to live together or cohabit. The everyday meaning of 'convivial' refers to events or relations played out in a friendly, joyful, or lively sociable atmosphere. Yet, as Arjun Appadurai (2018) reminds us, such friendly encounters mask the precarity and asymmetry involved in dialogues across class, gender, race, and ethnic boundaries. Contested or ethical conviviality, as a perspective on such relations, must thus recognize structural inequalities and how conflict is avoided and equality faked with the help of friendly gestures, courtesy, and rules of civility.

Critical convivial approaches also remind us that an individualistic approach underpins our thinking about community; in fact, we are humans and, as such, are sociable individuals. Within this vision of individuated sociality, people are capable of being liberated from the ties of their primary community and are free to choose with whom they associate (based, for example, on their interests or perceived similarities in status). This modern idea of a human as an individual, as an autonomous 'self' capable of social relations with other individuals, contradicts these convivial approaches, which stress relational identity and the sense of personhood that cannot be imagined outside relational bonds (Boisvert 2010). Conviviality as an analytical perspective might help to transform the value of interdependence towards interrelatedness, which is beyond the choice of individuals, and to reconsider equality as a start and not as the end of social relations.

To understand better the experiences of multicultural settings and their banality as a convivialist epistemology based on the irreducible sense of the 'with-ness' of existence, we need to move beyond ethnonationalism and ethnic diversity, and abandon the fantasy of individuality, which makes a sovereign individual a member of an ethnic group capable of detaching from it. That way, multicultural settings could be reframed as being populated by ethnically indifferent but inherently cultural and interrelated beings.

References

Appadurai, A. (2018) 'The risks of dialogue', Mecila: working paper series, no. 5, São Paulo.

Boisvert, R. D. (2010) 'Convivialism: a philosophical manifesto', *The Pluralist*, 5 (2): 57–68.

Davis, A. (1996) 'Gender, class, and multiculturalism: rethinking "race" politics', in G. Avery and C. Newfield (eds) *Mapping multiculturalism*, University of Minnesota Press, 40–3.

Foner, N., J. W. Duyvendak and P. Kasinitz (2019) 'Introduction: super-diversity in everyday life', *Ethnic and Racial Studies*, 42 (1): 1–16.

Hannerz, U. (1990) 'Cosmopolitans and locals in world culture', *Theory, Culture and Society*, 7 (2–3): 237–51.

Oosterlynck, S., G. Verschraegen and R. van Kempen (eds) (2018) *Divercities: understanding super-diversity in deprived and mixed neighbourhoods*, Policy.

Riggs, F. W. (2002) 'Globalization, ethnic diversity, and nationalism: the challenge for democracies', *The ANNALS of the American Academy of Political and Social Science*, 581 (1): 35–47.

Schlenker, A. (2013) 'Cosmopolitan Europeans or partisans of fortress Europe? Supranational identity patterns in the EU', *Global Society*, 27 (1): 25–51.

Schrover, M. (2022) 'Superdiversity from a historical perspective', in F. Meissner, N. Sigona and S. Vertovec (eds) *The Oxford handbook of superdiversity*, (online edition), Cambridge University Press.

Stansfeld, K. (2022) 'Mapping Superdiversity: a geographical exploration of a relational global condition', in F. Meissner, N. Sigona and S. Vertovec (eds) *The Oxford handbook of superdiversity*, (online edition), Cambridge University Press.

Taylor, C. (2004) *Modern social imaginaries*, Duke University Press.

van Breugel, I. and P. Scholten (2017) 'Mainstreaming in response to superdiversity? The governance of migration-related diversity in France, the UK and the Netherlands', *Policy & Politics*, 45 (4): 511–26.

Front Doors and Backyards of Social Difference

Sara Bonfanti and Paolo Boccagni

As a normative ideal of permanence and wellbeing, either as a place or condition, home does not resonate easily with migration and displacement. As our recent five-year ERC HOMInG project proved, the lived experience of home, its loss or pursuit, and continuous making or unmaking for people on the move, constitutes an effective tool with which to study various forms of mobility, as well as to understand the possibilities of living together with difference. This short entry builds on fresh ethnographic findings that reflect the authors' approach to understanding human movement and settlement, while assuring diversity in post-migration societies. Drawing on ordinary tussles in a superdiverse neighbourhood, we reflect on the multiscale and processual nature of home-making for a migrant household. This example, which resounds with many across our fieldwork, reveals divergent claims for spatial appropriation, alongside rampant attempts to enforce borders. As a conclusive remark, we see home not necessarily as a place of belonging and contentment, but as a trope for the unsustainable inequality we all live in this world, each with our own trajectories. As Monza from Milan put it in March 2021:

> Corinna's laundry drips down the terrace on her ground-floor neighbour: 'Terrona,[1] take you shit inside and get if off my property!', rages a white man looking up. At the next condo residents' meeting, a chorus surges loud: 'we can't allow such behaviours, filthy rags on the line all day. ... This is a place for decent families, not a campsite

---

1. Derogatory term used to address people of southern Italy who used to move to the north after searching for jobs and better life opportunities during the Second World War.

for Indian Roma who live off begging.' 'They are devaluing the price of our houses!', thunders an echo.

This may well be a scene familiar to any urban dweller in a superdiverse city today: the inadvertent ethnographer can read behind the lines of commonplace complaints for 'living together with difference'. Dwelling in times of superdiversity, or in post-migration societies, one cannot fail to consider those continuous struggles for home that unfold in the lives of people and in the spaces they inhabit every day, in that interstice between forms of sharing and thresholds of inclusion or exclusion (Bonfanti et al. 2019). If *home studies* and *housing studies* have shared out the research on people's dwelling places (either looking in at their lived experience, or looking out at the property market and underlying structures of inequality), within migration studies, the social process of making a home has been increasingly regarded as a critical source of insight on mobility, belonging, circulation, space appropriation and inter-group relations.

Corinna (a nickname adopted to interact with Italian locals) came from Pakistan 23 years ago. She then rejoined her husband, an economic migrant who had settled in Italy ten years earlier, and together they had three children. Now an adult, their elder son has moved to Britain. Their younger one, suffering from cerebral palsy, is rather homebound and their daughter has moved back home with her toddler after her divorce. When one income could not suffice to provide for a family of five, the household was allocated a flat under a social housing scheme. The property assigned to them is part of an estate in which unsold units from a bankrupt developer were handed over to the municipality. The welfare services pay the rent for a few underprivileged tenants, while most of the neighbours pay their own mortgages. As an affordable block for aspirant working-class families, house ownership status and the residents' origins (whether native or immigrant) determine how much public tolerance is granted to private home-making practices, which might deviate from local ideas about 'respectability' (Bate 2018).

Appeals to civic decorum and blatant racism are just two lenses through which to view migrant housing and inter-ethnic relations on the fringes of society, where often misrepresented cultural diversities intersect and screen socio-economic disparities. When, if ever, does one's domestic abode stop being a family haven and become the fetish of a contested neighbourhood and a metaphor for licit or illicit territorial belonging? The petty conflicts over migrants' attempts at homemaking reveal the magnitude of the issue: who has the right to a home in a place where they are perceived (and themselves might feel) as *alien*, undeserving or threatening to breach some majority's common law? Under what conditions can social reception and space domestication occur? Who welcomes the foreigners in and how do the latter appropriate the environs? Studying where and how international migrants try to make a home for themselves in a destination country allows one to go beyond the interplay of transnational dynamics and assimilation policies; it enables one to appreciate the value of locality and the lived experience of place (Boccagni and Hondagneu-Sotelo 2022). The condo residents took a cognitive shortcut to despise their Pakistani neighbours' habits, as if they were expressions of other traditionally-discriminated-against minority groups, such as southern Italian immigrants or the Roma. For a number of reasons and constraints, there is little interest in getting to know each other or meeting another halfway. So-called culturally-enriched communities – areas where diversities are valued and promoted (Hadjiyanni 2019) – are still far from sight in a northern Italian town beset by the gusts of economic stagnation and mounting right-wing politics.

With intercultural encounters just happening on people's doorsteps, and new migrants taking over places where previous waves and generations still live, the characteristics of new migrants are 'layered' on top of earlier kinds of diversity. Furthermore, superdiversification also entails growing differences among people within ethnic, religious and national categories: apart from identity tagging, their social, economic and demographic charac-teristics can be very different. In all these ways, urban populations are becoming ever more complex, and the places in which the various gener-ations of migrants dwell make such homes a meaningful focus for in-depth social analysis, as in the case we report here.

At the height of the summer, the youths living in the condo frequently hold parties in the common foyer. The handwritten advert stuck on the gate reads 'all welcome'. Corinna and her husband Reman, hoping for some friendly gestures, wonder whether they too should attend. There was no need to pretend that mutton and rice would appeal to her neighbours, so she played it safe and baked them some pizza slices, and Reman generously offered a round of *bedi* cigarettes to smoke. Their efforts were met with a mixture of blank stares, frowning foreheads and timid smiles. Inhaling the hand-rolled tobacco leaves might be haram, Reman comments, but the Prophet said, 'there is no good in the one who is not hospitable.' Hospitality is like karma – 'what goes around comes around', or at least it should be. He is keen to form acquaintances in the courtyard, believing that a weak social tie is better than being strangers to each other day in and day out. The festive night has failed to change the inbuilt wariness and intolerance of a microcosm in which diversities coexist. Social exclusion is still the order of the day because, with ethnicity and religion to start with, a well-rehearsed script grinds the many axes of difference that migrants embody.

Spatial proximity in the neighbourhood invites a topological reading of informal social relations that not only involve consideration and mutual help (Ruonavaara 2022), but that can also lay bare a 'convivial disintegration' (Meissner and Heil 2021) that gives voice to conflict and uncertainty in bridging differences. Conviviality, alongside interconnected concepts such as 'cosmopolitanism' and 'everyday multiculturalism', has emerged as an interpretative paradigm with which to explore the socio-cultural dynamics linked to migration in an urban context. Nonetheless, 'convivial situations generate nothing more than a mere impression of freedom from material or other axes of inequality between the participants' (Nowicka 2020: 22). Such differences are not necessarily limited to ethnicity, but are continuously reshuffled by the intersection between different criteria, including age and length of residence.

Fauzia, Corinna's daughter, has just brought in the laundry. The *dhurrie* (a sturdy carpet woven in Pakistan and ordered online) is still wet, but she rolls it out on the kitchen floor to prevent further ado. Her mother talks loudly on the phone, no one else in the neighbourhood would pick up words in Urdu anyway. Fauzia explains that a cousin of theirs was stopped at the Brenner Pass while trying to enter Austria. Gone are the days when leaving one's native village and taking a gamble with one's life in Europe, like her father had done, could come about through regularizing one's working papers. Once he had entered the country on a tourist visa, Reman had remained in Italy as an irregular migrant for almost two years before an amnesty extended him the right to stay, and his boss advanced him the credit he needed to turn an off-the-record job into a regular one.

Since the 2015 'refugee emergency' following the protracted economic crisis, government control of human mobility in Italy has left less space for flow decrees and amnesties.[2] In the absence of safer options, present-day migrants seeking to make their home in Europe increasingly contemplate asking for asylum. Fauzia's cousin, who is a Shia Hazara, has been transferred to an SAI[3] facility in Verona to await the processing of his file. Could being part of a beleaguered minority in one's home country be enough to secure the right to stay in a host country? A 'global time lag' and another politics of migration had come into play in the interim between the migration of Corinna's family in the 1990s and that of their newly arrived relative. The former had benefited from an easier and more inclusive admission process (amnesty followed by family reunification), whereas the latter had been subjected to lengthier and more exclusionary 'emergency reception' rules.

The man is asking his auntie Corinna for extra provisions, for he can do little other than idle away his time in the flat he shares with five other co-nationals. Corinna retorts that, after thirty years, they have barely made a home for themselves as Italo-Pakistanis: family can help, but he must learn to be patient. Fauzia suggests sending him a prayer mat, for he might fare better if he begged Allah for a place of welcome. However long one has been in the country, it is difficult to shake off one's migrant status and feel oneself on a par with the natives. As Harney (2020: 771) put it, 'migrant trajectories undermine any straightforward engagement with interculturalism and signal complex socio-political processes in hospitality or integration.'

Europe will not yet be a post-migrant society so long as social disparities are reproduced in terms of a nativist and exclusionary 'politics of home' that borders people's movement and their right to home-making at multiple scales. For much of the world population, living with or in diversity has never been more common: one need not be an ethnographer to see that home, as a place or a metaphor, has also become a trope for the obscene inequality that divides the world in which we dwell. It takes committed citizens to advocate for alternative politics and to bring about social change.

2. Flow decrees and amnesties are different legal procedures that have been issued recursively in Italy to grant otherwise irregular migrants the papers to stay (reside and work) in the country. The main difference between the two is that the former puts a cap on the number of legalized individuals entering the country; the latter aims to incorporate those who have already been in Italy for a certain length of time (possibly hired in the shadow economy, then allowed to register as resident guest workers). See Fasani et al. (2019).
3. SAI (Sistema Accoglienza e Integrazione) is the current reception system operating in Italy for asylum seekers.

Additional information

The authors report no conflict of interest. Their research was supported by ERC HOMInG (StG 678456, 2016-2021).

References

Bate, B. (2018) 'Understanding the influence tenure has on meanings of home and homemaking practices', *Geography Compass*, 12 (1): e12354.

Boccagni, P. and P. Hondagneu-Sotelo (2022) 'Integration and the struggle to turn space into "our" place: homemaking as a way beyond the stalemate of assimilationism vs transnationalism', *International Migration*, Early View article. doi: 10.1111/imig.12846.

Bonfanti, S., A. Massa and A. Miranda-Nieto (2019) 'Whiffs of home: ethnographic comparison in a collaborative research study across European cities', *Etnografia e ricerca qualitativa*, 12 (2): 153–74.

Fasani, F., G. Mastrobuoni, E. G. Owens and P. Pinotti (2019) *Does immigration increase crime?*, Cambridge University Press.

Hadjiyanni, T. (2019) *The right to home: exploring how space, culture, and identity intersect with disparities*, Springer Nature.

Harney, N. D. (2020) 'Interculturalism, inequality and hospitality in Italy', *Ethnos*, 87 (4): 771–89.

Meissner, F. and T. Heil (2021) 'Deromanticising integration: on the importance of convivial disintegration', *Migration Studies*, 9 (3): 740–58.

Nowicka, M. (2020) 'Fantasy of conviviality: banalities of multicultural settings and what we do (not) notice when we look at them', in O. Hemer, M. P. Frykman and P.-M. Ristilammi (eds), *Conviviality at the crossroads: the poetics and politics of everyday encounters*, Springer Nature, 15–42.

Ruonavaara, H. (2022) 'The anatomy of neighbour relations', *Sociological Research Online*, 27 (2), 379–95.

The Image of Root-less Belonging in the Age of Migration

Özlem Ögtem-Young

The late-twentieth-century French philosophers Deleuze and Guattari favoured the image of a rhizome – an underground plant stem with lateral shoots – over that of a tree. This was because they viewed the tree as emblematic of classical Western philosophical and political thought, which they accused of creating binaries and hierarchies of human races, societies and identities. It was this sense of vertical and rigid arrangements only allowing movement in one direction that Deleuze and Guattari opposed. I am less sure that they would still be against trees, despite their hierarchical connotations, now that deforestation and climate change haunt our contemporary times with their devastating effect on the planet and humanity.

Nevertheless, I too opted for the image of a rhizome rather than that of a 'root' or 'anchor' for my research into the displacements and attachments of unaccompanied young people seeking asylum in the UK (Ögtem-Young 2021). In 'the age of migration' (Castles et al. 2005), the stiffness of the notions of 'roots' or 'anchors', which are often used to depict our sense of belonging, fail to convey the true nature of our connectedness – our bonds, attachments and identifications with people and places. This is because these metaphors create a sense of too much certainty in an uncertain, precarious and ever-changing world. A rhizome, by contrast, with its unexpected, non-linear lines, twists and turns, implies movement, transition and rupture. For me, it neatly captures the messiness of belonging to multiple 'homes' in multiple places. It captures both the obstinacy and fragility of our sense of belonging when we desire, need or are forced to leave our homes and when we need to build new ones.

Therefore, I am proposing a rhizomatic belonging, which is root-less and resembles what Foucault (2021) described as 'counter-memory', or what Deleuze called 'nomadism' – a kind of resistance to hierarchical

Image credit: Cemal Kazankaya.

notions of representing 'the other'. In other words, it opposes the political violence of populist, nationalist discourses and their mundane narratives of origin and nativism. Rhizomatic belonging has no fixed destinations or rigid paths, only potentials and possibilities. 'A rhizome has no beginning or end', wrote Deleuze and Guattari (1987: 25):

> It is always in the middle, between things, interbeing, intermezzo. The tree is filiation, but the rhizome is alliance, uniquely alliance. The tree imposes the verb 'to be', but the fabric of the rhizome is the conjunction, 'and ... and ... and.' This conjunction carries enough force to shake and uproot the verb 'to be'.

I would add that it also uproots the notion of 'belonging'. It is in fact an expression of root-less belonging.

Just as with the rhizome, it is also the image of water that comes to mind when I think about our contemporary belonging and its nature. I think that this figure also helps to come to terms with the condition of belonging. As such, our sense of belonging sometimes temporarily seems to freeze in time and space until it melts and moves again. It also evaporates, becoming imperceptible, hence our consciousness is filled with the desire to make it more tangible and solid. However, it always changes its shape, consistency and composition – to become perceptible, liquid and to flow through the cracks of nation-states, borders, the segmented rhetoric of being and becoming. Perhaps when it wants to, or when conditions are right, it freezes again only to melt, evaporate and flow in different directions and to different lands. So, it always engages in a non-linear, cyclical process of contraction and expansion. It transitions from tangible to intangible, concrete to abstract – it is never complete, and never disappears. It is much like energy, which, as Einstein once said, 'cannot be created or destroyed, it can only be changed from one form to another'.

Consequently, a 'rhizome', 'water' or 'energy' are more helpful analogies when thinking about the complexities of our belonging in the age of migration than a tree, root or even anchor, which suggest a fixed origin, nation and identity. They are based on a sense of difference that is coupled with often hostile perceptions of the 'other'. Rhizomatic belonging is the antithesis of a hegemonic model of populist, nationalist politics – and its notions of belonging – and is also a way of preserving ideas and subjectivities that may otherwise be subjugated (Braidotti 1994). Rhizomatic belonging is the forest of conjunctions and passages that has no trees or roots but only routes!

References

Braidotti, R. (1994) Nomadic subjectivities: embodiment and sexual difference in contemporary feminist theory, Colombia University Press.

Castles, S., M. J. Miller and G. Ammendola (2005) The age of migration: international population movements in the modern world, The Guilford Press.

Deleuze, G. and F. Guattari (1987) *A thousand plateaus: capitalism and schizophrenia*, University of Minnesota.

Foucault, M. (2021) *Language, counter-memory, practice*, Cornell University Press.

Ögtem-Young, Ö. (2021) 'Molar lines, molecular flows and nomadic belongings: an examination of belonging of unaccompanied young people seeking asylum in the UK', unpublished PhD thesis, University of Birmingham.

Youth Migration

Daniela Sime

About one in four of the world's 272 million migrants are young people between the ages of fifteen and twenty-four (IOM 2020). Over the last two decades, these young migrants' lives have been affected globally by the financial crisis of 2007–9, austerity, wars, political tensions, restrictions to mobility brought about by stringent migration rules and, more recently, the Covid-19 pandemic. In this piece, in which the focus is on the young people who migrate, either alone or with their families or carers, I shall examine the extent to which state policies on integrating migrants address their needs, rights and expectations.

While most migrants tend to be relatively young, for those aged between fifteen and twenty-four, migration poses especially significant challenges, particularly in relation to their access to education and jobs (France 2016). In a context of rising inequality, researchers have documented the high risk of social exclusion facing young migrants globally. Because of their age and restricted rights, these young people are particularly vulnerable to poverty, stress, poor health, exploitation, and trafficking. Political responses to the financial crisis, and more recently to the Covid-19 pandemic, continue to produce inequalities on a global scale.

Other global crises have followed, including the wars in Syria and Ukraine, and the ongoing climate emergency. Some of these crises have had direct implications particularly for states receiving thousands of forced migrants, as extra resources have to be acquired to meet their immediate needs and support their wellbeing and integration. How governments respond to migrant arrivals, which is often in a politically-charged atmosphere, has a direct bearing on migrants' ability to access opportunities in the host country, especially in situations of increased vulnerability through restricted access to work, education, housing and public services.

91

Youth, inequality and mobility

The growth in inequality globally has been felt particularly by young people. Over the last thirty years, youth wages have continued to decline, leaving many at risk of poverty, even when working (ILO 2021). During the pandemic, young people, who were often the first to be made redundant, either moved to more insecure contracts or were forced into inactivity and isolation. In 2020, after decades of precarity and insecurity, global youth employment fell by 8.7 per cent (ILO 2021). The media used the terms 'Covid generation' or 'lockdown generation' to highlight the potentially scarring effect of the pandemic on young people, especially on their education, career opportunities and mental health. Many nation-states restricted the mobility of all citizens during the pandemic, making it more difficult for young people to seek employment in other countries. The long-term effects of the pandemic, rising inequalities and increasing political instability and wars are all factors likely to lead to a surge in youth migration in the decades to come.

These economic trends raise the question of what happens to social mobility and international migration when inequalities continue to increase. Across all countries, evidence is strong that young people of low socio-economic status have limited opportunities and lack the economic or cultural capital they need to weather these crises; also, education and employment opportunities have failed to recover globally following the financial crisis. Measures taken by states across the globe to limit the impact of Covid-19 on their economies are likely to reduce opportunities even further. While youth unemployment has remained at around 13 per cent globally, there are considerable geographical variations – it is 11 per cent in Africa and 23 per cent in the Arab states (ILO 2020). In addition, even before the pandemic, more than one-fifth of young people globally, or 267 million, were categorized as NEET (not in employment, education or training) (ILO 2020). Young women, in particular, are at additional risk of exploitation or violence if they are unable to secure work, and also are much more likely to be burdened with care commitments. When it comes to work opportunities, the groups at the bottom of the social structure are hit hardest and find it most difficult to cope. These increasing class and gender inequalities have continued to influence young people's decisions to migrate and seek opportunities abroad.

In addition to the group of young migrants seeking better employment opportunities, it is important to acknowledge that an increasing number of young people with economic resources are choosing migration as a route to personal growth. Many, with students from Asian countries at the forefront of this growth in middle-class migration, are able to study abroad, travel, or move across countries because they are highly skilled in sectors such as IT or finance. Students make up one of the biggest migration groups globally and many of them clearly see the opportunities afforded by studying abroad as a route to improving their future life chances and employment opportunities. While countries vary over according students the right to work, in recent years many governments have started to think more strategically about using migrant students to tackle the various skills shortages and the challenges of an increasingly ageing population.

Migrant rights and policies for integrating migrant youths

The last decade has seen migrant rights eroding throughout the world, along with a rise in anti-immigration agendas. The right-wing extremist groups fuelling anti-immigration sentiments globally are posing a threat to democracy in countries like the USA, Brazil, Hungary, Italy, Poland and New Zealand. A xenophobic narrative of 'taking back control' from the EU characterized the UK's 2016 Brexit referendum. Changes to the residency rights of EU nationals following Brexit made numerous EU-born people vulnerable to xenophobia and future insecurities unless they could secure a 'settled status' or British citizenship (Sime et al. 2022).

The global pandemic further eroded the rights of some young migrant workers (ILO 2021). Since not all were entitled to furlough schemes, compensation packages, investment funds, or grants, many were left vulnerable. Also, in many countries, without full citizenship or residence rights, there is no access to funded education or training, social security, or healthcare. Young people also find themselves falling between systems that target certain categories, such as migrants *or* young people, in which their age can affect their claims. For unaccompanied young people seeking asylum, turning eighteen carries the immediate risk of losing the state support given to them as children. Currently, young migrants, particularly asylum seekers, refugees, girls, women, those with disabilities, or those categorized as NEET, remain especially vulnerable to the accumulated social impacts of successive crises.

Another area of concern relates to 'the politics of belonging' (Yuval-Davis 2011), namely the discourses used to exclude particular migrant groups and how these are shaped by specific social actors. While young people's subjective sense of belonging to places has been shown to be in flux and influenced by factors such as opportunities to become involved in their communities, or perceived attitudes towards migrants, policies of inclusion and access to full citizenship can facilitate a sense of belonging and can influence the future plans of a migrant. Young migrants are often more likely to settle in countries where they feel their rights are respected and their skills recognized, and where the state facilitates access to secure citizenship. On the other hand, they are likely to move on if the country in question fails to meet their long-term expectations.

The 2007–9 economic crisis and the 2020 pandemic show how global events can rapidly jeopardize young people's opportunities and futures and subject them to forced mobility or immobility, marginalization and vulnerability. Over the last few decades, we have seen significant increases in the number of young people migrating in search of better work or education opportunities, but also because of conflict, war and threats to their safety or rights. Increasing global inequalities and the climate crisis will likely drive youth migration in the future, causing concerns about 'brain drain' in the countries young people leave behind. Developing policies that tackle youth marginalization and create fair opportunities for young people must remain a priority for all governments. The integration policies of receiving countries affect the amount of support young people can access, and create hierarchies of opportunities that depend on their age or status on arrival, for example on whether they are children, students, workers, or asylum seekers. The priority policy areas remain regularizing migrant rights, reducing risks of trafficking and exploitation, tackling social and political exclusions created by residence and citizenship restrictions, and ensuring an intersectional approach to policy making. The intersection of certain characteristics, such as migrant status, gender, age, and disability, will likely further exacerbate the vulnerability of migrant youth, unless policy measures are specifically directed at boosting their rights, protection and recognition. Young migrants should also participate in the social dialogues that inform policies and practices to ensure that inequalities exacerbated by the pandemic are tackled rather than further entrenched.

References

France, A. (2016) *Understanding youth in the global economic crisis*, Policy Press.

ILO (2020) *Global employment trends for youth 2020*, International Labour Organization.

ILO (2021) *Youth employment in times of Covid: a global review of global policy responses to tackle (un)employment and disadvantage among young people*, International Labour Organization.

IOM (International Organisation for Migration) (2022) *World migration report 2020*, IOM.

Sime, D., N. Tyrrell, E. Käkelä and M. Moskal (2022) 'Performing whiteness: central and Eastern European young people's experiences of xenophobia and racialization in the UK post-Brexit', *Journal of Ethnic and Migration Studies*, 48 (19): 4527–46.

Yuval-Davis, N. (2011) *The politics of belonging: intersectional contestations*, Sage.

Directions of and Developments in the Field of Migration Studies

Carlos Vargas-Silva

In 2019, I became editor-in-chief of the *Migration Studies* journal. One of the perks of the job is that you get interesting insights into the directions of and developments in the field. Everyone sees the published articles. Editors get to see all submissions of articles and special issue proposals, even the unsuccessful ones. We also see how colleagues evaluate articles on different topics. The discussion below highlights five tendencies I have identified during this period. While there are differences across 'migration journals', these patterns are likely to be reflective of broader trends in the field.

Further consolidation of the field

Migration studies as a field of scholarship has become consolidated and we can expect this to continue – that is, we can expect to see the development and further consolidation of core concepts that link different disciplinary perspectives related to migration. It is commonplace for presenters of sessions at migration-related conferences to come from different disciplinary backgrounds, and a similar dynamic occurs in migration journals. For instance, Table 1 shows the department and institutions of contact authors for the last issue of the *Migration Studies* journal in 2021.[1] There are, among others, authors in psychology, economics, sociology and political science.

That this diverse pool of scholars should select a 'migration journal' in which to publish their research speaks to the development of the field as one that speaks to multiple audiences. A priority for the next decade is to keep promoting the development of these core concepts to facilitate discussion and feedback across a wide range of perspectives.

---

1. https://academic.oup.com/migration/issue/9/4.

Table 1: Department and institutions of contact authors for *Migration Studies* journal Q4: 2021

Institute for Social and Political Sciences, University of Lausanne

Department of Economics, CUNY, Queens College

Department of Psychology, Université du Québec à Montréal

Department of Sociology, University of Wisconsin-Madison

Duke Center for International Development, Duke University

Department of Sociology and Human Geography, University of Oslo

Institute for Employment Research, Germany

Institute of Political Science, Goethe University Frankfurt am Main

Department of Sociology, Södertörn University

European Commission, Joint Research Centre

Department of Public Policy, Central European University

Austrian Academy of Sciences

More empirical, less conceptual

Migration studies has become more empirical, with new work intending to document empirical regularities related to migration, rather than providing new conceptual frameworks. Those of us who believe in the benefits of a strong conceptual background end up assigning students readings from the 1950s to the early 2000s. The challenge moving forward is to encourage the production of new conceptual frameworks at the same time as empirical work to show that existing ones largely lack validity in the real world.

More emphasis on migration and...

There is more emphasis on the intersectionality of migration and other factors, such as race, gender, sexual orientation, class, age, national origin and others. Overall, the idea is that migrants are a diverse group and that their outcomes, experiences and relations with others are influenced by these multiple identities. The challenge is to expand this intersectional approach to reflect broader social inequalities, while also maintaining coherence in the analysis.

More comparative

There is more emphasis on comparative research. The comparisons take place in many ways, between locations, migrant groups, and periods. Comparative research increases our understanding of questions across different contexts and facilitates the developments of different classifications. Yet, it is important, particularly for reviewers, to understand that not all interesting questions are comparative. Many studies make clear methodological and theoretical advances without a comparative dimension.

Forever stuck in the North

Migration studies has been largely developed by scholars in Europe, North America and other high-income regions of the world, and the articles in different migration journals reflect that pattern. For instance, Table 2 provides a summary of the articles submitted to *Migration Studies* by country of location of the contact author during 2016–21. For reasons of space, it only includes the top twenty countries. The USA and UK account for over a quarter of the articles submitted during this period. Some countries in the Global South account for a good share of the articles submitted, such as India (3.3 per cent) and Nigeria (1.4 per cent), but as it is clear in the second column, this is just a reflection of the large populations of those countries. Unfortunately, the knowledge publication gap is not closing. One of the biggest challenges for the field during the next decade is to find ways of reversing this trend.

Summary of challenges and priorities for the next decade

While there are plenty of challenges for scholarly activity during the next decade, including work on migration, it is possible to identify six priorities based on the discussion above:

- Promote the development of core concepts in migration studies.
- Encourage the production of new conceptual frameworks.
- Expand the intersectionality approach, while maintaining coherence in the analysis.
- Understand that not all interesting questions are comparative.
- Close the publication gap between high-income countries and the rest of the world.

Table 2: Location of contact authors of articles submitted to the *Migration Studies* journal during 2016–21 (top-20 countries)

	Share of total (%)	Per 1,000,000 population
USA	16.44	0.68
UK	11.47	2.31
Germany	6.06	0.99
Canada	5.33	1.93
Turkey	4.16	0.68
Italy	3.65	0.83
Netherlands	3.43	2.74
India	3.29	0.03
Australia	2.63	1.41
Spain	2.63	0.77
Sweden	2.48	3.37
China	2.41	0.02
Israel	1.90	3.00
Norway	1.68	4.24
Poland	1.68	0.61
Belgium	1.53	1.81
Nigeria	1.39	0.09
South Africa	1.31	0.30
Finland	1.02	2.53
Mexico	1.02	0.11
Rest of the World	23.65	–

Jan Blommaert's Inspiration

Steven Vertovec

The purpose of my short essay is to praise, honour and give thanks to Jan Blommaert, who passed away on 7 January 2021 at the age of 59. Jan was a renowned linguistic anthropologist and director of Babylon, the Center for the Study of Superdiversity at Tilburg University. By titling my piece 'Jan Blommaert's Inspiration', I wish simultaneously to stress that Jan was himself an inspired academic, he was an inspiration to a generation of scholars, and he inspired much far-reaching thinking based on the concept of superdiversity. Indeed, Jan took the concept to exciting and significant theoretical and methodological places that I never anticipated when I originally coined it.

Among other places, a good overview of Jan's work and life has been provided by his long-time friend and collaborator Ben Rampton (2021) in an article that also includes numerous quotes from students and scholars whose professional outlooks were profoundly influenced by Jan. Jan's own perspective was anchored in the realization that language and communi-cation are integral to what constitutes society. Jan's view largely drew from the interactional approaches of Erving Goffman, Dell Hymes and John Gumperz concerning ways to understand language-in-context, language contact and language change, code-switching, and semiotic variations affecting meanings, interactions and social order of a community. For Jan, the key to this approach to communication and society is the ethnographic method.

If some kind of social change is affecting any society, Jan often said, it happens in language first. In his own ongoing ethnographies, Jan noted a variety of such social changes (Blommaert 2013a). The growth of ever more complex social environments led Jan to pick up, run with and masterfully riff upon the concept of superdiversity. Describing the linguistic landscapes of his own Antwerp neighbourhood, for instance, Jan (Blommaert 2014: 431) wrote of how:

We see how the use of languages, notably of a lingua franca, 'oecumenical' variety of Dutch, contributes to the perpetual shaping and reshaping of an infrastructure for superdiversity: a space in which constant change and motion are the rule, in which complexity and unpredictability are rife, but within which important forms of conviviality are being articulated and sustained by means of language choice and language display.

Complexity and unpredictability were among the foremost reasons why, he believed, we must move away from conceptualizations of bounded categories. As he and Ad Backus (2013: 13, italics in original) suggested,

The impact of superdiversity is therefore paradigmatic: it forces us to see the new social environments in which we live as characterized by an *extremely low degree of presupposability* in terms of identities, patterns of social and cultural behavior, social and cultural structure, norms and expectations. People can no longer be straightforwardly associated with particular (national, ethnic, sociocultural) groups and identities; their meaning-making practices can no longer be presumed to 'belong' to particular languages and cultures – the empirical field has become extremely complex, and descriptive adequacy has become a challenge for the social sciences as we know them.

Always a keen mind in discerning modalities of power, inequality and social justice, Jan also insisted that 'we must realize that superdiversity has created unprecedented levels of polycentricity in social systems' (Blommaert 2013b: 3). Across a range of communicative and semiotic practices, Jan recognized how 'power and control are dispersed over different groups, located in different sites and operating with different scopes and degrees of impact. Power, like the neighbourhood, is complex and multi-scalar' (Blommaert 2013a: 129).

The advanced perspective on superdiversity that Jan Blommaert advocated included no less than a fundamental methodological reassessment of the social sciences. He underlined 'the paradigmatic impact of superdiversity: it questions the foundations of our knowledge and assumptions about societies, how they operate and function at all levels, from the lowest level of human face-to-face communication all the way up to the highest levels of structure in the world system' (Blommaert 2013a: 6). In particular, Jan called for a special reorientation of sociolinguistics in the light of superdiversity.

Pointing to contemporary disciplinary changes and beyond, Blommaert and Rampton (2011: 3). suggested that within sociolinguistics 'there has been ongoing revision of fundamental ideas (a) about languages, (b) about language groups and speakers, and (c) about communication. ... Super-diversity intensifies the relevance of these ideas,' Jan (Blommaert 2013a: 8) further underlined the call to reassess the field by writing of how:

> Superdiversity, thus, seems to add layer upon layer of complexity to sociolinguistic issues. Not much of what we were accustomed to methodologically and theoretically seems to fit the dense and highly unstable forms of hybridity and multimodality we encounter in fieldwork data nowadays. Patching up will not solve the problem; fundamental rethinking is required.

This approach has been at the core of much recent sociolinguistic work on language and linguistic change in superdiverse contexts. It includes more attention to communicative capacities within complex social environments seeking to understand how people use, create, mix and signal meanings through a variety of semiotic materials (see Arnaut and Spotti 2014). These dynamics themselves contribute to perpetually forming and constituting 'superdiverse repertoires' (Blommaert and Backus 2013). Such repertoires are not just comprised of spoken vocabu-laries, grammars, genres and registers, but also gestures, postures, written and symbolic materials and physical arrangements themselves. Such insights underpin new developments surrounding notions of languaging, polylanguaging and translanguaging; metrolingualism; multiple discur-sive practices; supervernacularization; multiple subject positions; socio-linguistic economies; and the polycentricity of semiotic resources. Indeed, in large part stimulated by the work of Jan Blommaert, an entire field or approach of 'sociolinguistic superdiversity' has emerged (Blommaert and Rampton 2011; also see Creese and Blackledge 2018). Sociolinguistic superdiversity, according to Jan, represents 'a new theoretical approach to language in society, a new key in which sociolinguistics can be played' (Blommaert 2015: 84).

Few social scientists have made such substantial contributions to their field as Jan Blommaert. Although I cooked up the concept of superdiversity and have continued to think through it over the last fifteen years, the development of many key intellectual lines is directly owed to Jan Blommaert. His thinking on social change and complex modes of communication has delivered probably the most significant insights of any scholar who has engaged the concept. It has been a great joy and privilege to have as my friend a scholar who was truly inspiring.

References

Arnaut, K. and M. Spotti (2014) 'Superdiversity discourse', Working papers in urban language and literacies, 122: 1–11.

Blommaert, J. (2013a) *Ethnography, superdiversity and linguistic landscapes: chronicles of complexity*, Multilingual Matters.

Blommaert, J. (2013b) 'Citizenship, language and superdiversity: towards complexity', Tilburg Papers in Culture Studies, 45: 1–4.

Blommaert, J. (2014) 'Infrastructures of superdiversity: conviviality and language in an Antwerp neighbourhood', *European Journal of Cultural Studies*, 17 (4): 431–51.

Blommaert, J. (2015) 'Commentary: superdiversity old and new', *Language & Communication*, 44: 82–8.

Blommaert, J. and A. Backus (2013) 'Superdiverse repertoires and the individual', in I. de Saint-Georges and J.-J. Weber (eds) *Multilingualism and multimodality*, Sense Publishers, 11–32.

Blommaert, J. and B. Rampton (2011) 'Language and superdiversity,' *Diversities*, 13 (3): 1–21.

Creese, A. and A. Blackledge (eds) (2018) *The Routledge handbook of language and superdiversity*, Routledge.

Rampton, B. (2021) 'Jan Blommaert and the use of sociolinguistics: critical, political, personal', *Language in Society*, 50 (3): 331–42.

PART TWO:
LENSES, PRISMS AND METHODS

Artistic Representation of Research on Superdiversity

Adrian Blackledge and Angela Creese

The poem 'Eel' is an outcome of linguistic ethnographic observation conducted over four months at Birmingham Bull Ring market, as part of a larger research project: *Translation and Translanguaging: Investigating Linguistic and Cultural Transformations in Superdiverse Wards in Four UK Cities.*

The project broke new ground in its detailed investigation of communicative practices in superdiverse settings in four cities. It was supported by the Arts and Humanities Research Council (1 April 2014–31 March 2018) as a Translating Cultures Large Grant (AH/L007096/1; £1,973,527). The principal investigator of the research project was Angela Creese. With Mike Baynham, Adrian Blackledge, Jessica Bradley, John Callaghan, Lisa Goodson, Ian Grosvenor, Amal Hallak, Jolana Hanusova, Rachel Hu, Li Wei, Agnieszka Lyons, Bharat Malkani, Sarah Martin, Emilee Moore De Luca, Jenny Phillimore, Mike Robinson, Frances Rock, James Simpson, Caroline Tagg, Jaspreet Kaur Takhi, Janice Thompson, Kiran Trehan, Piotr Wegorowski and Zhu Hua.

The poem comprises a set of 51 rhyming haiku, which offer an artistic representation of the voice of the market's Health and Safety Operative, uniquely placed as he circulates the market hall, mopping floors, cleaning toilets, clearing spillages, making the environment safe, and coming into contact with those who work and shop in the market. The 51 haiku articulate the sensuality of the market hall – the smells, sounds, tastes, textures, and sights of the busy commercial environment. Taken together, they make audible the music of what happens in the superdiverse spaces of the market.

Ethnographic researchers have begun to use poetry as a medium for expressing their sense of connection to their field and their subjects. The poet and social scientist share commonalities in approach: both ground their work in meticulous observation of the empirical world, and are reflexive about their experience. But the poem reaches for something more. It is in the enhancement of, and elaboration upon, social research outcomes that poetry has rich potential. Ethnographic poems rely on a belief in the ability of poetry to speak to something universal, or to clarify some part of the human condition.

'Eel' was first published in *Voices of a City Market: An Ethnography* (Multilingual Matters, 2019), by Adrian Blackledge and Angela Creese.

Eel

I

I start work at six
when souls of pigs and pixies
are up to their tricks.

II

The way people leave
the public convenience
you wouldn't believe.

III

Lesley's Take-Away.
A sausage and egg sandwich
to kick-start the day.

IV

I do have a chat
with some of the stall-holders
about this and that.

V

Throw a sprat to catch
a mackerel, mackerel
to catch yellow jack.

VI

The butcher told me
to get rid of stomach cramps
drink Chinese green tea.

VII

All bloody morning
hammering on the heat pipes
no word of warning.

VIII

Health and safety, too.
It's not all about cleaning
the disabled loo.

IX

The butchers at Chik's
do like to take the mick but
I give them some stick.

X

She was here last week
from the university
noting how we speak.

XI

I pretend to flirt
with the girl on frozen fish
in a cheesecloth shirt.

XII

So says the gaffer:
Lutjanus campechanus
is the Red Snapper.

XIII
For gratis and free
Zsuzana from Global Foods
slips me a lychee.

XIV
The pungent perfume
of pig offal calls to mind
one Leopold Bloom.

XV
They sell things in here
you've never even heard of:
beef mask, caul, ox ear.

XVI
At the hardware shop
Jeyes Fluid, carbolic soap,
my nan's old string mop.

XVII
Eels in a tank like
gym freaks going nowhere fast
on exercise bikes.

XVIII
That bag of samphire
is akin to a necklace
of sea-green sapphire.

XIX
It isn't my place
to say whether people should
stick studs in their face.

XX
Doherty's fish stall
claim to have landed the year's
biggest conger eel.

XXI
He just strokes his chin
when asked the simplest method
to cook sea urchin.

XXII
The clock they restored
with four dancing figures was
damaged in the war.

XXIII
The way they rampage
through the grafter repertoire
they should be on stage.

XXIV
It's a canny squid
peddles residual ink
for three or four quid.

XXV
How splendid is that –
an impeccably dressed pig
in a porkpie hat.

XXVI
A man from Tabuk
teaches me how to say thanks
in street Arabic.

XXVII
The story I told
of a fugitive lobster
is centuries old.

XXVIII
It's green caviar
not frogspawn in pond algae.
Eat with vinegar.

XXIX
She was so chatty
I ended up purchasing
saltfish and ackee.

XXX
You'd think the sting ray
with one flap of its wings would
be up and away.

XXXI
From eyebrows to boots
a Balkan jazz crew bedecked
in red Santa suits.

XXXII
That skinny fellah
with silver eye shadow is
the fortune teller.

XXIII
The pig's intestine
is best stuffed with chopped pork
lung hartwort, garlic leaves.

XXXIV
The cats Pantagruel
and Gargantua play me
for an ancient fool.

XXXV
The worn-out leather
of her shoes testifies – heel
toe, step, together.

XXXVI
It seems a sick note
is not a sick note these days
it's called a fit note.

XXXVII
Mrs Belkedi
on the candied fruit counter
suggests fennel tea.

XXXVIII
The couple who run
the Polish deli turn out
to hail from Bodrum.

XXXIX
I take out my book
to record an incident
with a butcher's hook.

XL
Not a methane leak
but a box of durian.
Closed for a whole week.

XLI
The German market
has come to town for Christmas.
Some traders are narked.

XLII
Something to be seen:
sardines in their very own
Busby Berkeley scene.

XLIII
Today's dilemma:
a quarter of sherbet lime
or sherbet lemon.

XLIV
It didn't take long
for that Leviathan eel
to be dubbed King Kong.

XLV
She's got my number
now I've fallen for a brace
of sea-cucumber.

XLVI
At afternoon break
it is useless to resist
home-made lardy cake.

XLVII
Artisan coffee
prepared by a full-bearded
apothecary.

XLVIII
There's no way to pick
a winkle from its shell with
a winklepicker.

XLIX
I spoke to a man
said he'd walked most of the way
from Tajikistan.

L
You wouldn't have thought
mopping floors for a living
required knee support.

LI
The end of my shift
a large tub of jellied eels
I'll take for a gift.

The Divine Comedy of Forced Migration: The Journey as Method and Beyond

Jennifer Allsopp

I first read the *Divine Comedy* in a public library in Milton Keynes when I was fifteen. Penned by the Florentine politician–poet Dante Alighieri some 700 years ago after he was exiled from his city, dispossessed, and threatened with being burnt at the stake in the event of his return, it was the first story in which I had ever engaged that had been written 'by a refugee'. Besides its stylized evocation of 1300s Florence, which transported me a million miles from the bleak concrete jungle of my own city, what so enticed me about Dante's fictional journey through the afterlife was its stark emotional realism. He had accomplished exactly what he set out to do, tricked time with words to 'render himself immortal', and he took me, the reader, on a journey. And, as I want to show in this piece, there is much in Dante's fictional account of his 'search for freedom' that speaks great truth to those of us seeking to research forced migration. Alongside its clear thematic parallels with refugee journeys, we can take the journey itself as an ethic of research, a method and an epistemology of sociological and philosophical enquiry – it is a way, to cite Dante's portrait of the border-defying trickster Ulysses, of capturing 'our zeal to explore the world, and explore the ways of life/Man's evil and his virtue.'

The *Divine Comedy* made me laugh; it made me cry and it instilled in me a deep curiosity about the world around me. I struck up an unlikely friendship with its medieval author and pledged to learn Italian so that I might one day read it in its original form. It was the makings of my evolution as both an Italianist and a social scientist, with the journey having become the central thematic concern and praxis of my research. Indeed, the journey, as exquisitely illustrated in the *Divine Comedy*, brings together themes of geographical movement and personal transformation; it is a journey of intellectual reflection in which the intertwining of the research, researcher and research participants together create a unifying force – *a will to mobility*.

Writing and the camp

The thematic integration of Dante into my worldview began when I started to study Italian at Oxford and became involved in a group called Student Action for Refugees. There, my social conscience and poetic sensibilities came together in a series of writing workshops I co-ran at Campsfield House – an immigration detention centre a short bicycle-ride away from the dreaming spires in which more than 200 people were being held for indefinite periods as they waited for their asylum or immigration claims to be resolved.

On a basic level, there was a clear parallel to be found between the stories people shared from inside detention and my studies of Dante's account of his allegorical journey through the realms of Hell, Purgatory and Paradise – their bodies bore marks in the form of fingerprints singed off from their skin for safe passage, wounds still oozing from the bites of border guard dogs, and torture scars awaiting documentation by a supplementary medic if time and resources permitted. Their tears projected the emotional turmoil of being separated from loved ones across space and time and, for those who had 'abandoned all hope' of ever exiting the icy reception system, often silence, or, on occasions, suicide. In his ethnography of Auschwitz, *If This is A Man*, Primo Levi describes how he famously ploughed his mind for lines from Dante, believing that if he could recall the humanizing words of his poem, he might retain humanity in the face of a system that arbitrarily appeared to accord people the fate of being either 'drowned or saved' in the face of impossibly hostile conditions. In telling stories, the people I have met in refugee camps and detention centres seek to do the same. The forward movement their narratives inspire in the face of stasis is what fuels my thinking of the journey as method and beyond.

In a prophesy about his exile, an ancestor, Cacciaguida, cautions Dante that he will 'come to know how salty the taste of another man's bread is/ and how hard is the way up and down another man's stairs.' Some 700 years later, in a container in Kidlington, Oxfordshire, we discussed all this and more. Later, in thousands more conversations with asylum seekers and refugees from around the world, Dante felt like an invisible presence in the room, guiding my method of enquiry and deeply human 'desire to know'.

Like his, ours was a common will 'to go beyond' the boundaries of the status quo in an effort to improve the state of the world – to address the causes of civil wars, halt corruption, and reverse the trauma of exile.

Writing self into society: the ethics of accompaniment

At 35, I am now the same age as Dante was when he started drafting the *Divine Comedy*, and I find myself reflecting on the political and personal events that shaped my own work and the kind of journey of which I am a part. I am not a refugee, but I have known many, and I am human. I have at times felt 'lost in a dark wood'.

Some of the refugees with whom I worked found ways of climbing up and beyond the Mountain of Purgatory, while others have gone on to fulfil their dreams of paradise. I have been fortunate enough to share in many moments of joy at being released from detention, not to mention from endless hours of trying to make sense of an unfathomable bureaucratic logic. Text messages still reach me years after our initial encounters to say, 'hey, Jen, look, I made it!' Sometimes, as in Dante's allegory, family members pay large sums of money to dubious guardians to help them on their way out of the dark and into the light. These connections evoke scenes of Dante as a character reflecting on the meaning of acquaintances from another period of life while on a seemingly shared journey.

By placing himself in his text as character and author, and in the playful dialectic between the two, Dante displayed a very modern sensitivity to the kind of reflexivity I regard as an ethical imperative in forced migration research. He humanizes his subjects and himself, for he is not travelling alone in the pursuit of knowledge, but is guided by, participates with, and *accompanies* others. In recent years I have been involved in the conceptualization and practice of similar research ethics based on work with indigenous migrants in central America, something Valentina Glockner referred to as the Spanish 'accompaniment' (*acompañiamiento*). It is hardly surprising, given the Catholic roots of Dante's poem, to come across similar patterns in the work of organizations such as the Jesuit Refugee Service, which recognizes the task of 'accompaniment' as central to its mission. If Dante's journey in search of meaning as an exile and philosopher is a pilgrimage in space, then 'accompaniment' encompasses the relational practices of care and connection that bond communities together over both space and time.

Flawed justice and the incomplete nature of knowledge

The logic of Dante's journey is also flawed, in that no system, not even the totalizing vision of his *Divine Comedy*, can be complete. And, indeed, Dante warns us of this totalizing impulse by sensitizing us to the complexity of his subjects as both sympathetic and villainous – a bloodthirsty tyrant and a noble patron; a scheming politician and a loving parent. Even from the fixed places assigned to them in the underworld, like any worthy ethnographic portrait, Dante's characters are three-dimensional and push at the boundaries of their classification.

For example, when Dante and his guide Virgil encounter the Roman poet Statius on their journey through Purgatory, Statius reaches out to embrace Virgil, whose work has inspired him and for whom he feels a great debt of gratitude. However, Virgil denies him the hug, for, along with other great writers and philosophers born before Christ, he has been assigned a place in Limbo – in Hell he is 'but a shade'. While the souls in Purgatory will eventually rise up to *transumanar* and surpass their human nature as they move towards salvation, those in Hell are stuck in a state of suspension where their presence is authenticated through Dante's quasi-Foucauldian invention of aerial bodies, or non-corporeal half-bodies that exist purely as a means through which the guardians of Hell and Purgatory can inflict a range of biopolitical punishments.

'Now you can grasp the greatness of the love that burns in me towards you', says Statius to Virgil, 'when I forget our emptiness, treating shades as solid things'. This scene, which still moves me profoundly, reminds me of an encounter with a friend called E from Afghanistan, who, after years of sharing aspects of our respective journeys, has come to seem like a brother to me. I was visiting him at yet another detention centre – this one at Gatwick airport from where the UK government was trying to deport him at the age of 18.

As I leant over the stainless-steel table – which, like the chairs, was bolted to the floor – a guard snapped his fingers fiercely from across the room. 'Visitors', he said, 'are not allowed to touch the detainees'. Who was I to treat 'shades as solid things?' After his aborted hug with Virgil, Statius recoils, embarrassed, perhaps perplexed, as was I, at the injustice of a system that renders one person more human than another because of circumstances beyond their control.

Conclusion: stasis and the will to mobility

We often read accounts of asylum seekers 'stuck in limbo', which is the place to which Virgil returns as Dante crosses the frontier to the Heavens willed to perpetual mobility by 'the love that moves the sun and other stars'. Here souls are punished through no fault of their own but as a matter of circumstance. There is no hug between Dante and Virgil; no goodbye. Their journeys part abruptly as a frontier is crossed between the worlds of Purgatory and Paradise, 'the drowned and the saved'.

Enforced immobility (or stasis) has come to characterize the experience of refugees today, the majority of whom live in states of protracted displacement in camps, precarious urban settlements, or immigration detention centres. For Dante, stasis, as seen in Hell, is the worst punishment imaginable – it is the very antithesis of Paradise, which is a kaleidoscopic vision of unfettered motion. In Dante's view, human beings are made to move; at the core of our humanity is a will to mobility.

Dante's *Divine Comedy* is more than an allegory of individual sufferings – it is a field guide to getting lost and finding oneself again, which can be as relevant to a researcher seeking knowledge as to a refugee seeking a sense of ontological security in a world of forever shifting borders. The goal of Dante's journey, we are told, is 'freedom he is seeking', and, despite the infernal vagaries of the asylum system, some find the liberty they seek. That narrative impulse to continue the journey is at the heart of what makes us human in the lives we project, strive for, and hope to create for ourselves.

The final word goes to all refugees who have overcome – or, like Dante, strive to overcome – overwhelming odds to break out of the cycle of Hell in which the legal system all too often places them. I am yet to give E his long overdue hug, but he managed to evade deportation. He fled to a third country where he is now safe and, after fifteen long years, is reunited with his mum, Fatima. She hugged him, he told me – a lot. And I know because in the middle of the journey of our friendship I received a photograph with a text: 'she looks at me as if I'm real. She holds me and says I can't believe this is your actual body, that you're here with me.' Through a journey spanning continents, decades and generations, E's will to mobility prevailed. His was a *Divine Comedy of Forced Migration*, of sorts.

Researching Language and Literacy Landscapes: Local and Global Perspectives

Marilyn Martin-Jones

The launch of the MOSAIC Group for Research on Multilingualism took place in 2008, with an international conference funded by the British Academy. Since its foundation, MOSAIC has been at the forefront of research and theory-building in the sociolinguistics of multilingualism, language and contemporary diversities. It is the only research group in the UK dedicated to this particular area of research on language. It is based in the School of Education, in the College of Social Sciences, so, from the outset, the MOSAIC researchers have had a primary focus on language and literacy in educational settings.

When the Institute for Research into Superdiversity (IRiS) was founded in 2012, fruitful new spaces for collaboration were opened up in the College of Social Sciences. The interdisciplinary collaboration and conversations between MOSAIC and IRiS around language and superdiversity that began in 2012 still continue today. For example, through the organization of MOSAIC-inspired panels, at the tenth anniversary conference of IRiS in September 2022, on 'Constructing Diasporic Links: Languages, Identities and Belonging', and on 'Linguistic Citizenship, State Policy and Localized Practices in Adult Migrant Language Education'.

In this contribution to IRiS's anthology, I show how our critical, socio-linguistic and ethnographic research complements the work of our colleagues in IRiS, and I give some examples of the productive ways in which we have collaborated over the last decade. I also anticipate some of the new directions that research related to language, literacy and contemporary diversities will need to take in the decade ahead.

How the research in MOSAIC complements that of IRiS

First, the research undertaken by the MOSAIC research group since 2008 has been part of a broader epistemological shift in the study of language, literacy and multilingualism towards a critical, sociolinguistic and ethnographic approach. Communicating in spoken or written language, face to face or online, is now seen as an essentially social practice (Heller 2007) and there is a commitment to investigating the specific, situated ways in which local language and literacy practices are bound up with wider social, political and ideological processes. This epistemological shift has reflected. and added to the wider turn across the social sciences towards post structuralist perspectives on social life. A new sociolinguistics of multilingualism is being forged, one that takes account of the new communicative order and the particular cultural conditions of our times, while retaining a central concern with the construction of social difference and social inequality.

Second, in critical sociolinguistic research on multilingualism, there has been an intense focus, over two decades, on the social, cultural and linguistic changes ushered in by globalization, by transnational population flows, by the advent of new communication technologies and by the changes taking place in the political and economic landscapes of different regions of the world. These changes have had major implications for the ways in which we conceptualize the relationship between language and society and the multilingual realities of the contemporary era. As with our colleagues in IRiS, a key focus for the research undertaken by the MOSAIC research group has been the far-reaching changes of a social and demographic nature taking place in contemporary social life, with the increasingly differentiated composition, trajectories and social positionings of different migrant and refugee groups – changes that Vertovec (2007) captured in the notion of superdiversity. These social and demographic changes have considerable implications for the study of language and literacy practices since, as Blackledge and Creese et al. (2018: xxviii) and others have pointed out, 'social transformations go hand in hand with sociolinguistic transformations.'

Within these new lines of sociolinguistic research, new conceptual compasses have been adopted: there is now a focus on mobilities and on trajectories (Heller 2007) There have also been calls for the development of 'a sociolinguistics of mobile resources' (Blommaert 2010). This process of formulating new conceptual compasses has also been accompanied by considerable methodological innovation. For example, the development of multi-sited ethnography and different ways of engaging in team ethnography (for example, in interdisciplinary teams involving researchers with different language and literacy resources).

Spaces for research collaboration between MOSAIC and IRiS

In 2010, MOSAIC researchers secured funding from the Economic and Social Research Council (ESRC), under its Researcher Development Initiative, for specialist research capacity-building at doctoral and early careers levels. The project, 'Researching Multilingualism, Multilingualism in Research Practice', ran from 2010 to 2013. During this period, members of the MOSAIC group ran capacity-building workshops, residential courses, master classes and a final international conference. Doctoral researchers participating in these events were encouraged to present their research. Those who were based in MOSAIC were working on a range of topics, from language policy in Global South settings, to complementary schooling, nursery education provision in a minority setting in Birmingham and the lived experience of students in adult ESOL (English for Speakers of Other Languages) programmes.

Participants in the final conference contributed to a volume published by Routledge called *Researching Multilingualism* (Martin-Jones and Martin 2017). When IRiS was founded in 2012, initial contacts were made with colleagues in IRiS, so Jenny Phillimore and Lisa Goodson were invited to contribute to this final conference. This first moment of collaboration paved the way for further joint activities.

An international consortium on language and superdiversity

In the years that followed, the MOSAIC group and IRiS became part of INCOLAS (International Consortium on Language and Superdiversity). The late Jan Blommaert (then director of the Babylon Centre, Tilburg University, Netherlands) led on the establishment of this consortium, in collaboration with Ben Rampton (Centre for Language, Discourse and Communication at Kings College, London), following their landmark publication on language and superdiversity (Blommaert and Rampton 2011). Members of this consortium went on to participate in events organized by IRiS, such as the June 2014 international conference on 'Superdiversity: Theory, Method and Practice'.

MOSAIC Research projects, publications and collaboration with IRiS

Members of the MOSAIC group have had considerable success securing external research funding. This has included a number of small-scale projects, four funded by the ESRC; one funded by HERA (Humanities in the European Research Area) and a large grant from the Arts and Humanities Research Council (AHRC), under its 'Translating Culture' programme. The three professors in the group took the lead in securing the funding. The publications that ensued covered a wide range of topics, including language and superdiversity; language practices and identities in complementary schools; linguistic diversity in higher education; bilingual literacies and learning in further education; digital literacy practices and contemporary mobilities, communicative repertoires and language resources, translanguaging, linguistic ethnography and team ethnography.

One of the most significant developments in the research collaboration with IRiS came with the successful application for the AHRC large grant to support a project called 'Translation and Translanguaging: Investigating Linguistic and Cultural Transformation in Superdiverse Wards in Four UK Cities' (2014–18). This was designed as an interdisciplinary project, involving IRiS colleagues, as well as researchers from three other universities in the UK. The IRiS researchers made contributions at each stage of the project, including publication of the *Routledge Handbook of Language and Superdiversity* (Blackledge and Creese 2018).

Another development has been the establishment of a Routledge Book Series, entitled Critical Studies in Multilingualism, which is associated with MOSAIC. It was first established in 2012, and now, in early 2023, the thirty-fourth volume has appeared. The success of this series is testament to the intense interest in the sociolinguistics of multilingualism and in the sociolinguistics of superdiversity – for details, see www.routledge.com/Routledge-Critical-Studies-in-Multilingualism/book-series/RCSM09.

Looking ahead: priorities for the decade ahead

First, we need to continue to document the specific, situated challenges that adult migrants and refugees face in educational settings in different national contexts, especially when preparing for language tests related to applications for citizenship. Despite a growing body of research on language policies, on the nature of provision for adult migrant education and on the administration of language tests in different countries, particularly in Europe, there is still a need for more research within the tradition of the ethnography of language policy on how national or regional policies are being translated into local practice and on adult learners' lived experiences of such provision and testing regimes.

Second, we need to build a fuller understanding of migrants' lived experiences of mobility and mooring in particular contexts, and into the agentive ways in which they develop and use the language and literacy resources in their communicative repertoires. As Blommaert (2010) noted, the networks of urban neighbourhoods are organized locally and face to face, whereas translocal and transnational networks are developed online. Increasingly, multilingual families are developing new diasporic lines of connectedness through the use of social media. Yet, we still know relatively little about how language, literacy and multimodal resources are used and developed as these digital practices unfold. What does 'doing family' trans-locally or transnationally entail? What values guide these practices? What digital media are used? What communicative resources are used? And how do the practices differ across generations? Addressing questions such as these will involve new ways of working ethnographically, and aiming to achieve epistemic solidarity between researchers and participants. These will be key challenges for the decade ahead.

References

Blackledge, A. and A. Creese, with Mike Baynham, Melanie Cooke, Lisa Goodson, Zhu Hua, Bharat Malkani, Jenny Phillimore, Mike Robinson, Frances Rock, James Simpson, Caroline Tagg (et al.) (2018) 'Language and superdiversity: an interdisciplinary perspective', in A. Creese and A. Blackledge (eds) *The Routledge handbook of language and superdiversity*, Routledge, xxi–xlv.

Blommaert, J. (2010) *The sociolinguistics of globalization*, Cambridge University Press.

Blommaert, J. and B. Rampton (2011) 'Language and superdiversity', *Diversities*, 13 (2): 1–22.

Heller, M. (2007) 'Bilingualism as ideology and practice', in M. Heller (ed.) *Bilingualism: a social approach*, Palgrave Macmillan, 1–22.

Martin-Jones, M. and D. Martin (eds) (2017) *Researching multilingualism: critical and ethnographic perspectives*, Routledge.

Vertovec, S. (2007) 'Superdiversity and its implications', *Ethnic and Racial Studies*, 30 (6): 1024–54.

Migration in Popular and Genre Fiction

Amy Burge

A growing number of popular and genre fiction texts published in recent years have focused on themes of migration or the experiences of seeking asylum or displacement. These texts are interested in how migration impacts on people's lives. They depict the bureaucracy of migration (paperwork, processes) and represent anxieties around state and status often felt by those who are displaced. Yet, when critics talk about 'migration literature', they do not usually mean genre texts like these. But genre fiction, with its global market and specific tropes, offers a unique and untapped resource for exploring representations of migration, displacement, and refugeedom. To illustrate this, I am going to share examples of popular fiction from three genres – crime, fantasy, and romance – to show how authors use genre tropes and motifs to explore ideas about migration, including public rhetoric around the European refugee 'crisis', anxieties of identity, 'marriage migration', and the impact of migration on intimate relationships.

Crime and detective fiction

One of the most commercially successful genres of the twentieth- and twenty-first centuries – crime or detective fiction – has shifted away from its interwar golden age (associated with the 'classic' whodunit) towards twenty-first century works that offer more diverse protagonists, and social critiques. Ausma Zehanat Khan, a Canadian author of detective fiction, is an example of a writer who uses the genre to deal directly with the theme of migration, particularly the role of NGOs and government organizations. Khan's 2018 novel *A Dangerous Crossing* describes the experiences of Syrian refugees in and around camps in Greece and Italy. An author's note and recommended reading section are clearly aimed at educating a global genre audience about the 'Syrian refugee crisis'. The novel itself contains lengthy descriptions of conflict in Syria and the 'inadequate ... facilities' of the Moria camp on Lesvos, filtered through the perspective of key protagonists – usually either Sergeant Rachel Getty, a white Canadian woman, or Inspector Esa Khattak, her Muslim Canadian boss. Readers are encouraged to reflect on their own views through identification with Rachel or Esa, learning and developing as the characters do. At one point, Rachel describes the work of the 'Hellenic Rescue Team ... during the crisis' (Khan 2018: 155). A male teenager, Ali Maydani, himself a refugee from Syria, overhears, and responds, coldly: 'You call it a crisis?', to which Khattak explains: 'Where we're from, this is how the conflict has been framed ... It's accurate as far as it goes, which is not far enough, I know.' Ali 'put his long head in his hands, his fingers buried in the curls: 'I find it hard to think of myself as the victim of a crisis. I feel like a person – do you think the war erased that?"' (Khan 2018: 155). Later, Ali intervenes in a discussion between Rachel and Esa about the Syrian conflict (Khan 2018: 209–10), stating:

> Am I allowed to speak? I know my country better than you do. Better than Interpol, better than whatever it is you represent, Inspector. ... You all do it. The UN, the volunteers, the border agents, people on the news. You make choices that affect us, you decide what our lives will be, you decide what we should think about those choices.

A Dangerous Crossing is modelling a typical response to the 'refugee crisis' that might be heard in Western public discourse and, through the voices of key characters, pointing to its limitations.

Fantasy fiction

While a notoriously difficult genre to define, fantasy is most strongly associated with 'the impossible and the unexplainable' (Mendlesohn and James 2009). Fantasy genre tropes – such as portals, quests, and magic – have been combined with accounts of migration to generate new ways of thinking about movement across space and time. Take, for example,

Mohsin Hamid's *Exit West* (2017), where a series of temporary portals allow movement across the world: 'rumours had begun to circulate of doors that could take you elsewhere, often to places far away, well removed from this death trap of a country' (Hamid 2017: 69). G. Willow Wilson's *Alif the Unseen* (2012), a fantasy novel set in a fictional Gulf city, uses portals to represent 'anxieties of identity and displacement' (Wilson 2012: 153). The novel depicts the semi-autobiographical 'convert' and her struggle to fit in; despite her efforts to 'dress respectfully, learn the language, follow all the insane rules ... even adopt your religion', she will 'always be foreign' (Wilson 2012: 151). The convert travels with Alif, the protagonist, and Vikram, a djinn, to the Immovable Alley – a parallel world reached via a portal. In fantasy, portals are often protected in some way: 'to pass through a portal is likely to pass some kind of test, to gain a new level of understanding of power, to demonstrate oneself as a chosen one, whether through birth or actions or some other merit' (Clute and Grant 2022). While Alif, who was born in the city, is able to pass through the portal and clearly observe what is on the other side, the convert 'kept swaying back and forth as though falling asleep and catching herself each time she dozed off' (Wilson 2012: 157). The explanation given is that 'She's an American ... half in, half out' (Wilson 2012: 157). The key to passing through this portal, this border, is related to identity and authenticity. Because the convert does not belong – she is perpetually 'foreign' – she is not able to access the world beyond the portal as easily as Alif.

Romance fiction

Romance is 'the most popular and bestselling genre of fiction produced and consumed in the world today' (Kamblé et al. 2021: 1). Romance, as a genre, explores the way migration affects intimate relationships between couples, friends, and family members, and is particularly interested in representing marriage migration – an area of wider concern in migration studies.

Take, for example, American author Helen Hoang's (2019) *The Bride Test*, which tells the story of Vietnamese Esme, who travels to the USA and falls in love with Khải. This novel contains two examples of potential marriage migration – Esme and Khải, and Esme's mother and estranged father. Migrant couples and families across the world are subject to damaging discourses of marriages of convenience or sham marriages (Bonjour and de Hart 2021). *The Bride Test* challenges this stigma. Esme declares that she 'can't marry [Khải] just for a green card', because he is 'a person, not a stack of paper' (Hoang 2019: chapter 1). Furthermore, while Esme does settle in the USA, she does so through naturalization via her long-lost American father, not through marriage to Khải. She repeatedly rejects Khải's marriage offers on the basis of immigration status, saying she will only marry him if he loves her. The only occasion where marriage via migration is shown to have occurred (or migrating as a result of marriage) is for Esme's parents – her mother gains immigration status through marriage to Esme's father (which is shown as a love match). It seems that marriage via migration is discussed and depicted for older characters, but explicitly rejected for a younger generation.

Romance is also concerned with the ways migration can damage existing intimate relationships. In Brigitte Bautista's *You, Me, U.S.* (2019), set in the Philippines, the protagonist Liza's overseas worker father 'justified his absence by showering Liza with gifts' (Bautista 2019: chapter 2). In turn, Liza sees herself as her family's 'ticket to a better life' and seeks an American husband (Bautista 2019: chapter 13). When Liza's family hear she is marrying Christopher, they declare that she 'did good' – Liza remarks that her father had not been 'this excited in years' (Bautista 2019: chapter 12). When Liza decides not to marry Christopher (and thus migrate to the USA), her father articulates the specific desire and duty Liza feels (Bautista 2019: chapter 16):

> What's love got to do with it? You think – you think love sends your brothers to school? Puts food on the table? You had a chance to make something of your life, Liza! You had the ticket to get us out of here, to America, like we always dreamed, and you blew it.

Yet, *You, Me, U.S.* ultimately absolves Liza of this responsibility. Liza's mother apologizes 'for putting you in a situation ... where you risked being miserable to make our lives better. I'm sorry for forcing you into that sacrifice' (Bautista 2019: chapter 16). Liza breaks off her engagement and resolves that 'she mattered. This was her life to live. She had a choice' (Bautista 2019: chapter 16). The novel emphasizes the need for Liza to choose herself and her own happiness over that of her family.

The global potential of popular and genre migration fiction

Popular and genre texts, as global products, show how views on migration can circulate transnationally, with similar attitudes towards migrants and migration expressed in different examples of genre fiction from different countries and cultures. The 'crisis' rhetoric in *A Dangerous Crossing* is visible in media across the world. Preconceptions about marriage migration are shared in texts dealing with different national and cultural contexts. And genre tropes – like the portal of fantasy fiction – are used to explore anxieties common to many who experience migration and displacement. These genre texts, like many others I have not mentioned, are produced locally, yet circulate globally. That they present similar views shows how widespread ideas about migration are in the global north (and perhaps beyond). Thinking about migration fiction in this way pushes us to go beyond the lens of nation-states, through which migration literature is usually considered, and shows how genre fiction can provide a view into the shape of this popular, global discourse on migration.

References

Popular and genre fiction texts
Bautista, B. (2019) *You, me, U.S.*, Amazon.

Hamid, M. (2017) *Exit west*, Penguin.

Hoang, H. (2019) *The bride test*, Corvus.

Khan, A. Z. (2018) *A dangerous crossing*, St Martin's Press.

Wilson, G. W. (2012) *Alif the unseen*, Corvus.

Critical texts
Bonjour, S. and B. de Hart (2021) 'Intimate citizenship: introduction to the special issue on citizenship, membership and belonging in mixed-status families', *Identities*, 28 (1): 1–17. doi: 10.1080/1070289X.2020.1737404.

Clute, J. and J. Grant (eds) (2022) 'Portals', in *The encyclopedia of science fiction*, fourth edition, online resource, first published 1997, SFE Ltd.

Kamblé, J., E. M. Selinger and H.-M. Teo (eds) (2021) 'Introduction', in *The Routledge research companion to popular romance fiction*, Routledge, 1–23.

Mendlesohn, F. and E. James (2009) *A short history of fantasy*, Middlesex University Press.

Brothers of Italy? Young Racialized Italians Living the 'British Dream'[1]

Stefano Piemontese

A customer leaves the pizzeria in the cool breeze of the evening and slips between the electrified bodies of other football supporters in search of a comfortable spot in which to relish the celebrations. He needs a breath after seven minutes and fourteen seconds spent in apnoea, between the first kick penalty scored by Berardi and the last one saved by Donnarumma, and the following twenty minutes of cheering, singing and jumping. Italy had just won the European Football Championship against England. The terrace of the pizzeria was heaving with jubilant supporters, but a question had kept buzzing in his head, ever since the first half break when he glimpsed the veins of Milton's neck popping under his dark skin to the joyful rhythm of the Italian national anthem.

The customer's flushed body slowly moves towards us and ends up sandwiched between mine and Milton's. Then, balancing one hand on his shoulder, he uses the other to get Milton's attention, taps his arm, and reaches towards him. 'Tell me, why do you support Italy? Were you born in Italy?' he asks in a hoarse voice while the wrinkles at the edges of his eyes curl into a smile that softens the acrimony of his question. When the corners of this sentence reach Milton, for a millisecond, his facial muscles reveal a distinct 'what the fuck, even tonight!' Instead, he answers with a mixture of kindness and compassion, 'I was born and raised there! In

---

1. "Brothers of Italy" (Fratelli d'Italia) is both the incipit of the Italian national anthem and the name of a national-conservative and right-wing populist Italian political party that won the 2022 Italian political elections. Fratelli d'Italia is an anti-immigration party and has hostile positions towards immigrants residing in Italy. In recent years, its representatives have energetically boycotted the approval of a citizenship reform law that would facilitate the naturalization of young people born in Italy of foreign parents.

Bologna.' And the name of his city comes out with an accent that leaves no room for doubt.

The customer nods repeatedly, then, while looking around for an appropriate answer, the high-pitched sound of a trumpet comes to his aid: 'Yes, well, no, I thought you were a sympathizer', he smiles. 'Are you kidding?' laughs Milton, vigorously shaking his fingers in the void. At this, the customer's hand joins the choreography of ancient gesticulations that shudder across the terrace. 'Italian!' he cries while, with a quick gesture, he pulls his hand down, index and thumb united to create a circle as if he wanted to string together, one after the other, all the reasons he had not grasped. 'That's right, that's right', he concludes, just before being overwhelmed by the voices of Milton and other fans singing at the tops of their lungs *Notti Magiche*, the official song of *Italia '90* World Cup.

A few steps away from us, Mourad is passionately singing along with a melody composed before he was even born, his voice hoarse from an evening spent castigating and cheering. We had come to the pizzeria in south Birmingham a few hours earlier from Small Heath, one of the city's poorest neighbourhoods, where for the last year Mourad has been renting a room in the modest male hostel of a local mosque. 'Only separated men and I live here!' he joked, as we started to walk to the pizzeria through dark corridors that smelled of aged carpets.

Mourad had arrived in Birmingham almost accidentally during the first year of the Covid-19 pandemic after the tech start-up event he had planned to attend in London had been cancelled. He came to visit Ahmet, his father's old friend who would help him find temporary accommodation and work. Since then, he has lived in the hostel and worked in various menial jobs to save money and brainpower to develop ideas for his tech start-up. Mourad acquired his entrepreneurial disposition from his father, who, in the late 1980s, along with Ahmet and other young pioneers of the Moroccan migration to Italy, opened the first halal butcher's shop in Turin, then an import–export company, and eventually the first mosque in town. From his mother, widowed when Mourad was little more than a child, he inherited the indulgent spirit with which he confronts the future.

Despite things starting to get going in Birmingham, Mourad often feels like a fish out of water in the majority Pakistani neighbourhood in which he lives. He is one of the very few Arabs attending the local mosque – and definitely the only Italian. And, while this has never been a problem for him, over time, he became increasingly aware that the uncommon overlaps of his multiple identities and origins aroused disorientation and suspicion among the people around him, who perceived him as an unidentified migrant object. It must be for this reason that I regularly met Mourad in an Italian–Moroccan café close to where I live, apparently the only place where his hyphenated identities did not have to be explained. Yet, for other White Italians, whether at home or abroad, Mourad remains a foreign body. 'If I grow a beard, they think I'm a terrorist. If I shave, I'm a drug dealer!' he told me once. And while we were on the bus heading towards the game, he sarcastically admitted, 'in Italy, they think I'm a foreigner, and instead, I'm Italian. While here, people think I am British when I am a foreigner!' Indeed, that evening, before the collective hysteria flooded the pizzeria, I could clearly read in his gestures the defensive detachment with which, every now and again, Mourad exchanged a few words with other Italian supporters. Likewise, I could witness their questioning looks, and I finally realized that being a bit naïve, clumsy and jovial for Mourad was his way of overcoming barriers erected by others. 'I laugh not to kill myself, but someone does.'

In the days leading up to the final match, the Facebook group 'Italians in Birmingham and Surroundings' was in turmoil. The international removal companies' advertisements and queries about visas and entry requirements generally populating the wall had given way to photographs of the national team, tributes to its players and caustic memes about competing teams. Then, as the final match approached, one question took over the others: where to watch the final? The main concern was finding a location safe from the provocations of the dreaded supporters of the opposing team.

On the frontline of this conversation, one could see a wide assortment of profiles. However, an eye unaccustomed to acknowledging the plurality of contemporary Italian identities – as most Italian eyes tend to be – would have noticed the vital presence of young Italians of migrant heritage, easily recognizable by their unfamiliar surnames, the colour of their skins, or both, Narinder was probably the most annoyingly enthusiastic among them, especially for a football agnostic like me. His cumbersome presence in every football-related conversation also bothered other group members, but for a different reason. When, for the umpteenth time, Narinder interacted under one of the posts addressing the most burning issue of the

Italian diaspora in England at the time, a short altercation developed, which left me helpless, unsurprised, but also with some hope. A young woman whose imagination of Italianness must have been upset by the presence in the group of people like Milton, Mourad, and Narinder asked, 'but do we have Italians in the group?'. 'Pardon me – answered irritated Narinder – but is it not enough to be born in Terni, to grow up for 27 years in Italy, and have the citizenship and everything else, to be Italian?'. 'Sorry, I didn't mean to be rude, but I rather referred to the background', added the young woman, barely realizing that she had just upheld whiteness as a prerequisite of Italianness. 'Do not worry, Madame', he closes with the false courtesy that haughty people deserve. This brief exchange was still so fresh in my mind that a few days later, during the halftime break in that crowded pizzeria, I pricked up my ears when I heard two boys speak in a strong Terni accent. I approached them with my freshly rolled cigarette to ask for a lighter and, as the south Asian-looking one hands me a lighter, I asked him, 'are you the one who responded to that stupid comment on Facebook?'. 'Oh, yeah, it's full of dickheads, even here. She deserved at least an answer', smiled Narinder.

That evening, on the terrace, everyone seemed proud to be Italian. After the game, some took courage and went to celebrate the victory in the city centre. Others lingered on the road before the pizzeria and eventually went back home. Milton, Mourad, and Narinder also walked away cheerfully, each in his own direction. However, as I watched them leave, I could not help but think about the interactions I had witnessed and how they collided with the jubilant atmosphere of the evening. I asked myself if, besides victory, they were also left with a sense of estrangement and defeat. In subsequent conversations I had with them, they admitted that growing up in Italy as the children of immigrant parents had accustomed them to facing suspicious gazes, inappropriate questions, and racist micro-aggressions on a daily basis. Those behaviours did not alter their cheerful spirit that evening either. Instead, they had sedimented at the bottom of their souls, along with the indelible marks of many other experiences of racialization, othering, and exclusion.

This was perhaps a worse prospect. In fact, the consequences of this constant emotional trickle would not have been immediately obvious, only becoming apparent in the long term, for example, in the decision not to return to Italy. Years before, it was precisely this painful process of layering

130

that had contributed to the decisions of Milton, Mourad, Narinder and many other young Italians of migrant heritage to live in the UK. After all, they had moved there for a combination of work, study and lifestyle motives, but, unlike other Italian peers, also to flee a political and public environment that was overtly racist and hostile to immigrants and their children. In Italy, they were not yet considered '*Italian* Italians', as some of them put it, although they aspired to nothing more than to be 'just Italians, and that is it!' Across the Channel, instead, they found a place that seemed more accustomed to ethnic, racial and religious diversity than their home country, a place that, perhaps somewhat naively, one of them had defined as the 'British dream'. For most of them, it remained an unfinished dream, a stage of a transformative journey one had to undertake, hoping that, in the meanwhile, Italy would also change.

Acknowledgements

This ethnographic vignette is based on research on the mobilities of young Italians of migrant heritage living in the West Midlands funded by the European Union's Horizon 2020 Research and Innovation Programme under the Marie Skłodowska-Curie Grant Agreement n° 846645.

Lafcadio Hearn: An Early Embodiment of Creolization and Superdiversity

Robin Cohen

Creolization and superdiversity are social scientific concepts and they have to work as collective terms. However, an individual can embody, refract or reflect wider forms of social action and act prismatically to illuminate them. I use the captivating life of Lafcadio Hearn (1850–1904) as an early Träger (carrier or bearer) of the social contradictions and opportunities wrought by creolization and superdiversity.

Hearn was born on the Greek island of Lefkada (a place reflected in one of his names) to a Greek mother (with Maltese, Arab and Moorish roots) and an Anglo-Irish father. He was baptized Patrikios Lefcadios Hearn in the Greek Orthodox Church and known as Patrick Lefcadio Kassimati Charles Hearn in English. His birth name has also been hispanized to Patricio Lafcadio Tessima Carlos Hearn. His father was a British army officer who, when posted to the West Indies, abandoned Lafcadio and his mother, Rosa, to his Dublin family. She was a fish out of water in Ireland and returned to Greece leaving a bewildered Lafcadio to navigate the rivalrous demands of his Irish relatives to change his religious affiliation either to Protestantism or Catholicism. He was subsidized by a rich aunt to study in France (where he was a classmate of Guy de Maupassant), but abandoned again and wandered the streets of London in penury, until he was sent to a distant relative in Cincinnati, Ohio.

To the Americas

Thus, aged 19, began his American period, where Hearn stumbled into journalism and became an accomplished reporter of murder mysteries and

132

Hearn always posed showing his right-side, though his right eye was bulbous from overuse. He was blind in his left eye following a fracas at school. In later depictions he wore Japanese robes.

Picture credit: https://eu.wikipedia.org/wiki/Lafcadio_Hearn#/media/Fitxa tegi:Portrait_of_Lafcadio_Hearn.jpg.

other exciting stories. Described now as 'an Irish journalist', he crossed the racial tracks and married a twenty-year-old African American woman, somehow escaping the anti-miscegenation laws. Finally, conservative Ohioans caught up with Hearn and he decamped, minus his wife, to New Orleans, where he plunged into Louisianian Creole culture with gusto, reactivating his French and learning Spanish and six dialects of Creole. He published a dictionary of Creole proverbs, *Ghombo Zhèbes* (Hearn 1885a) and a cookbook *La Cuisine Créole* (1885b), still in print as *The Creole Cook Book*, together with some of the 175 cartoons he drew for one of the newspapers for which he worked. He was not merely a journalist but an engaged and well-read public intellectual with a vision for the future of America. As Bronner (2005: 145) noted:

> Hearn had caused controversy in Cincinnati with journalistic essays on cultural miscegenation before he arrived in New Orleans in the 1870s, but it was in Louisiana with its combination of a diverse colonial past (i.e. French, Spanish), pronounced racial-ethnic mix (e.g., Indians, Creoles, Cajuns), southern racial attitudes, Caribbean influences, and Reconstruction-era political and economic turmoil that Hearn's persona and his thoughts on hybridization attracted broad public notice. ... Hearn caught the attention of the modernizing nation when he suggested in popular magazines that the creolization common in Louisiana could, in fact, be a metaphor for America's future.

After a decade in New Orleans (1877–87), he persuaded *Harper's Magazine* to commission a series of articles on the French West Indies, where he lived for two years. He fell head over heels in love with the landscape, the food, the flora and fauna, the way of life and the beauty of the people, describing Martinicans in a way that we would now find uncomfortable but, at that time, explicitly challenged racist characterizations. As Hearn (1890) lyricized:

> Agreeable to the eye the darker skins certainly are, and often very remarkable – all clear tones of bronze being represented; but the brighter tints are absolutely beautiful. Standing perfectly naked at doorways, or playing naked in the sun, astonishing children may sometimes be seen – banana-colored or gulf orange babies. There is one rare race-type, totally unseen like the rest: the skin has a perfect gold-tone, an exquisite metallic yellow the eyes are long, and have long silky lashes – the hair is a mass of thick, rich, glossy the curls that show blue lights in the sun. What mingling of races produced this beautiful type?

To Japan

Hearn's books and magazine articles had brought him considerable fame in the USA – to such an extent that he was bracketed with Mark Twain, Edgar

Allan Poe and Robert Louis Stevenson as a major chronicler of the emerging American zeitgeist (Codrescu 2019). He also found time to translate six French books, including one by his old classmate Guy de Maupassant, by then France's best short-story writer. He could have looked forward to a renowned literary life in the USA but, bowing to his endlessly questing spirit, he plunged into yet another alien culture, this time Japan.

Though intended as a temporary sojourn, Japan became his permanent home. There he acquired yet another name, Koizumi Yakumo, and became a Japanese citizen. He married the daughter of a samurai warrior, had four children and died in Japan, aged 54. Insofar as he continues to be read, his fifteen books on Japan have survived as an enduring legacy. He was widely regarded, inside and outside Japan, as the best Western interpreter of Japanese culture, folk tales and religion. A museum dedicated to his memory is still a tourist attraction in his home town, Matsue. Curiously, his facility for languages stalled somewhat, though he developed a comprehensible interlanguage referred to as 'Hearn-san Kotoba'. While the thrust of his work on Japanese work was mainly expository, he also depicted Japan's resistance to Western culture as a reincarnation of the noble ideals of ancient Greece, which he lionized. This turned out to be an intellectual misfire that was later used to infer that he would have favoured the nationalism and xenophobia that gripped some of the Japanese intelligentsia in the 1920s (ultimately leading to fascism).

Conclusion

For those interested in Hearn's many lives, McWilliams's (1946) comprehensive biography is unlikely to be superseded. Here my purposes are more limited. What I wish to suggest is that Hearn's life illustrates that, at least for some, one's heritage identity is not, or need not be, a prison or a final fate. For such favoured people, it is possible to surf the waves, duck under them and resurface – making and remaking their names, religions, nationalities, languages and ethnicities. In his religion, Hearn moved with various degrees of engagement through Greek Orthodoxy, Protestantism, Catholicism, pantheism, Shintoism and Buddhism. He was described by others as a Greek student, an Irish journalist, a great American writer, an accomplished French translator and a Western interpreter of Japanese culture.

However, he was not merely a chameleon, taking on the colours of the societies around him. Hearn was a doer and a thinker, well-versed in the great debates of his time. He had translated Zola, whose remorseless social realism he found 'putrid'. He read Schopenhauer and admired Herbert Spencer, with whose work he fully engaged. Rather than an excess of realism, he favoured a romantic, sensuous, idealistic world in which human potential could flourish. Thus, Hearn's recognition of diversity and creolization was not merely a passive sociological description, but an active moral philosophy. As Boynton (1927: 430–1) notices, Hearn exhibited a

> succession of infatuations with places and peoples. In this aspect his romantic impulse was of the most elemental sort. The spirit of the quest was in it, but it sprang superficially from restlessness, the feeling that beyond the horizon was something fervently, to be desired. The Creole life of the Gulf port first stirred him as woodland and stream stirred the boy Wordsworth, needing no supplement unborrowed from the eye.

There is no escaping his romanticism, which some may find naïve, but Hearn's later observations of the USA from the distance of Japan were grounded in a sober recognition that the time for a creole future for the USA had come and gone – modernity, allied to industrialization, had promoted a more undeviating nationalism as the dominant American ideology. The contemporary turn to nationalist rhetoric associated with the Trump period suggests another body blow to Hearn's ideas. However, such rhetoric should not obscure the diversification of contemporary migration flows to the USA and elsewhere. Together with the more relaxed recognition and tolerance of other religions and ethnicities, it is possible that the wheel will turn once more to Hearn's vision. In this eventuality, Hearn's life and work will be dusted off and re-examined with fresh eyes – just as his own damaged eyes observed social differences and unflinchingly saw beyond them.

References

Boynton, P. H. (1927) 'Lafcadio Hearn', *The Virginia Quarterly Review*, 3 (3): 418–34.

Bronner, S. J. (2005) '"Gombo" folkloristics: Lafcadio Hearn's creolization and hybridization in the formative period of folklore studies', *Journal of Folklore Research*, 42 (2): 141–84.

Codrescu, A. (2019) 'The many lives of Lafcadio Hearn', *The Paris Review*, 2 July, https://www.theparisreview.org/blog/2019/07/02/the-many-lives-of-lafcadio-hearn/.

Hearn, L. (1885a) *Ghombo Zhèbes*, Will H. Coleman.

Hearn, L. (1885b) *La cuisine créole*, Will H. Coleman.

Hearn, L. (1890) *Two years in the French West Indies*, Harper. Available at: https://www.gutenberg.org/files/6381/6381-h/6381-h.htm.

McWilliams, V. (1946) *Lafcadio Hearn*, Houghton Mifflin.

Rebuking the 'Work Twice as Hard for Half as Much' Mentality among Black Girls and Women

April-Louise Pennant

Throughout the ages, and out of the mouths of many before, passed down from generation to generation like quiet skilful training, lies an introduction to the main rule to follow when playing a biased game; this rule, ingrained and spoken like a mantra, guides many marginalized groups, particularly Black girls and women, in how to survive in an unfair system:

You must work twice as hard for half as much.

You must work twice as hard for half as much.

You must. WORK. Twice as hard. For half as much.

Based on my PhD research (Pennant 2020) on the educational journeys and experiences of Black British women graduates, Ṣadé and Zuri are the fictional, composite mother and daughter characters who explore the intergenerational impact and social aspects of this mentality.

For Ṣadé, a second-generation English woman of Nigerian heritage, this was the accepted norm by which she was raised, a constant reminder of what she always had to do as the minimum requirement to have any chance of gaining so-called 'success'. It became interwoven into the very fabric of her DNA. Like the mentality demanded, she worked twice as hard as her white counterparts, and grudgingly expected to receive half as much. She had studied hard, completed an undergraduate and then a master's degree in law, entered a decent profession as a solicitor, and achieved upward social mobility. However, after years of continuing professional development (CPD), jumping from company to company and incessantly networking, she was still underemployed, underpaid, stressed, and dissatisfied. Ṣadé's experiences are not uncommon. As Dey et al. (2021: 8) highlight in their report, due to structural racism and barriers compounded by sexism, 'women of colour are almost invisible from positions of power across both public and private sectors ... overrepresented in entry-level and junior positions and virtually disappear the higher up we go into management and senior leadership.' Was this really the *real* results of working twice as hard for half as much?

* * *

Zuri was just about to finish her undergraduate law degree. Against the established educational narratives of Black British student under-achievement at key stages of the education system (see Tomlin et al. 2014), she was on track to gain a first-class degree – something that Black British women are least likely to achieve compared with women from all other ethnic groups (AdvanceHE 2021: 214). She had always wanted to be educationally 'successful', but struggled to be so within an unfair education system. These struggles are identified in a series of blog posts by the charity UK Youth, in which During (2020a, 2020b) illustrates some of the 'social, economic and identity barriers facing young, Black women every day', including lack of support, adultification and trauma, and how the education system perpetuates discrimination and bias.

Achieving educational 'success' was not only for Zuri, but also for her mother, family, and community, which meant that she carried a huge weight on her shoulders, a weight that constantly reminded her that she could ill afford to fail; no matter what, she had to keep going. Zuri was taught from an early age that educational qualifications could lift some of the weight that she was born to carry. Her education would enable her to soar; her qualifications would stand the test of time and would speak for her when she was denied a voice; they would uplift her from the bottom of society's totem pole. She also felt privileged because, unlike many of her peers, she had a determined mother with the experience she needed to guide her through the education system. It was her mother's access to financial resources that helped her excel and navigate her way through to the very end, and she was nearly there. All she had to do was complete her exams and then she would have the certificate in her hand.

It was all going well until the beginning of her final year when she became uncontrollably anxious. She started experiencing panic attacks and having restless nights worrying about her upcoming exams. She even started to worry about all the assignments she had already submitted – despite knowing she had passed them with flying colours. Zuri found herself unable to concentrate and in floods of tears whenever she tried to revise as she was unable to remember the course content. She had become a hermit, refusing to go out because she did not want to waste time on anything other than preparing for her exams. She barely ate – only enough to avoid fainting – so that she could continue her attempts to revise. She did not know who to turn to because she had always been the strong one, the one her friends consulted when they needed a pep talk. She had always done well – at school, in the sixth form, and in her earlier years of university – successfully balancing her extra-curricular activities while maintaining good grades. She had a proven-track record of excellence that she could not afford to tarnish, and this put additional pressure on her to perform. However, try as she might, her mind and body were rapidly shutting down due to her crippling fear of failure, and after years of working twice as hard for half as much. She needed the kind of help that Stoll (2021) needed while navigating her way through her own mental difficulties at university, which resulted in the co-creation of Black Students Talk (BST) to support the mental health and wellbeing of other Black university students.

Ṣadé was only alerted to the severity of the situation when a close friend of Zuri's phoned her. While driving to Zuri's student house, Ṣadé could not stop wondering what had gone wrong. Perhaps, she thought, it was her fault because she had pushed her too hard, but Ṣadé had not wanted her only daughter to be denied opportunities. She had thus gone above and beyond to plough most of her finances and support into Zuri's education – both inside and outside the classroom. Ṣadé felt that her daughter's education was one of the few things she could control, one of the few things that would ensure Zuri would get all the opportunities she deserved.

* * *

Ṣadé kneeled beside her only daughter, Zuri, who was on the floor in tears. Ṣadé, cradling Zuri in her arms, pleaded with her, trying desperately to remotivate her, to ensure that she continued to follow the mantra that had been so clearly laid out for her.

'Darling, I am going to need you to get it together, you can have your cry now, but you must get it together.'

'But why?' Zuri responded between tears, 'I am TIRED!'

'I know you are, but you can't be tired! You can't stop! Keep going! This is just the way it is. As Black women, we must work twice as hard for half as much as our white counterparts!' Ṣadé replied.

'But how?' her daughter asked, 'How can I keep going when I do not have anything else to give. I have given my all to my education to make sure I succeed.'

'I know you have, and I am so proud of you, but you must continue or everything you have done up until now will be pointless.'

Ṣadé's daughter, Zuri, continued to weep loudly, releasing all the pent-up frustration, pain, and exhaustion of the injustice of a society that required her to be superhuman to succeed. All Ṣadé could do was to hold her closer, supplementing the mantra with a silent prayer, requesting additional strength, hope and a breakthrough from the Most High.

But what do you do when you feel powerless and unable to change systemic, intersectional barriers that mean you must raise your young Black daughter to give her all, for 'success' that is never guaranteed? How do you ease the pressure and pain of your only daughter when you too are still experiencing and fighting it in the workplace? How do you continue to support your daughter to work twice as hard for half as much as her white counterparts, when she has clearly reached her breaking point? What if working twice as hard for half as much is no longer a viable option?

Ṣadé decided to pack up Zuri's belongings and take her home. They contacted her tutor, accessed her university's support services and it was decided that Zuri would defer her studies for a year.

* * *

As Zuri closed the question booklet of her last exam, she smiled confidently. She was so pleased that, with the support of her mother and her university, she was able to take some time out. She had spent the year in therapy, working through her mental health problems, the internalized pressure and her heightened fear of failure, and had learned many different strategies to help her cope. Her university's support services had provided her with extra exam time, alongside other aids to assist her in completing her studies. She had even had time to reconnect with and understand her mother more.

> 'You know, your breakdown taught me so much,' Ṣadé opened up to Zuri one day, 'You taught me that we should always move at our own pace and be unafraid to rest and recover as many times as necessary! I wish I learnt that when I was younger!'

> 'Yessssssss!' Zuri agreed as she hugged Ṣadé.

*　*　*

Zuri jumped for joy while wiping away happy tears as Ṣadé beamed with pride. Zuri had received her results and was graduating with first-class honours, excited for further study. Zuri adopted a new mentality and a new mantra that could replace the one passed on over generations, and that she would pass on to others, too:

Always move at your own pace and be unafraid to rest and recover as many times as necessary.

Always move at your own pace and be unafraid to rest and recover as many times as necessary.

Always. Move at your own pace. And be unafraid. To REST and RECOVER as many times as necessary.

References

AdvanceHE (2021) *Equality in higher education: student statistical report 2021*, available at: https://www.advance-he.ac.uk/knowledge-hub/equality-higher-education-statistical-report-2021.

Dey, M., C. White and S. Kaur (2021) *The pay and progression of women of colour: a literature review*, The Fawcett Society/The Runnymede Trust. Available at: https://www.fawcettsociety.org.uk/the-pay-and-progression-of-women-of-colour-literature-review.

During, J. (2020a) *Growing up Black: being a young, Black woman in Britain – part 1*. UK Youth blog, 13 October, available at: https://www.ukyouth.org/2020/10/growing-up-black-being-a-young-black-woman-in-britain/.

During, J. (2020b) *Growing up Black: being a young, Black woman in Britain – part 2*. UK Youth blog, 20 October, available at: https://www.ukyouth.org/2020/10/growing-up-black-being-a-young-black-woman-in-britain-part-two/.

Pennant, A. (2020) '"Look, I have gone through the education system and I have tried damn hard to get to where I am, so no one is gonna stop me!": the educational journeys and experiences of Black British women graduates', unpublished PhD thesis, University of Birmingham.

Stoll, N. (2021) *Black students' mental health, wellbeing, and unbelonging in UK higher education*. AdvanceHE webpage, available at: https://www.advance-he.ac.uk/news-and-views/black-students-mental-health-wellbeing-and-unbelonging-uk-higher-education.

Tomlin, C., C. Wright and P. Mocombe (2014) 'A structural approach to understanding black British Caribbean academic underachievement in the United Kingdom', *Journal of Social Science for Policy Implications*, 2 (2): 37–58.

Comparing the Everyday Lives of Undocumented Migrants in Birmingham and Malmö

Jacob Lind

During the unexpectedly sunny winter of 2014/15, I cycled around the streets and along the canals of southern and central Birmingham, conducting ethnographic fieldwork among migrant families with precarious legal statuses. I mostly alternated between the student accommodation in Selly Oak, the shared office of the IRiS doctoral students in Muirhead Tower, and child-unfriendly, shabby hotels around town where the social services had allocated temporary housing to my research participants. In my hometown of Malmö, cycling is the preferred means of travelling in town. However, as I quickly realized, staying alive when dashing down Bristol Road was something I only shared with Critical Mass activists defending the right to the city for cyclists. The physical strain of scaling the hills of the West Midlands got me into better shape for a short while, which was something the flat fields of Malmö never achieved. However, my close encounters with stressed motorists on narrow or non-existent bike paths gave me a very corporeal sense of the space in which my participants were living. Petrol-fuming, double-decker buses were their only option for travelling around town. One participant visited a church drop-in for destitute migrants just to collect the £4 daily bus pass they handed out, which he saved for later as he already had a monthly bus pass at the time. The organizers gave out bus passes worth around £7500 a year. My participants in Malmö did not seem to struggle over affording public transport as most of them (at the time of the research) received financial support from the local authorities. In some cases, people also used bikes in Malmö, which has been named the most cycle-friendly city in Sweden for many years and has regularly ranked among the five most cycle-friendly cities in the world. However, police checks on cyclists are common and unless you are equipped with the correct lights and reflectors, you risk being asked for an identification document and being detained as a result.

In this short reflection, I discuss what I learned from comparing Birmingham and Malmö as sites of undocumented migration from three perspectives – how migration policy changes affect undocumented migrants locally; how local geography and urban spaces condition their everyday lives; and the centrality of legal status across different urban and national spaces.

Changing migration policies

I designed my PhD project (Lind 2020) around conducting ethnographic research in two relatively similar cities. Malmö and Birmingham are both the third largest urban areas in their respective countries, and they are both relatively diverse and have young populations. However, they are different in size, both in relation to population and geography, which, as described above, not least affects their public transport systems. Still, I found that the differences in the migration policies of each country had a much more important impact on the participants' everyday lives than did their geographical differences. In Birmingham, just before the 2015 'summer of migration', when a record number of people applied for asylum in Europe, the UK was busy creating an increasingly 'hostile environment' for migrants. This meant designing policies to make life as unbearable as possible for people without the correct paperwork in the UK, such as cutting off access to fundamental services like healthcare, making it illegal for them to work, and preventing landlords from renting property to them (Corporate Watch 2018). By contrast, before 2015, Sweden was known as a relatively welcoming place for migrants and refugees.

As I learnt about the impacts and everyday implications of the UK's hostile policies during my time in Birmingham, I experienced an eerie sense of what was to come in Sweden and, after a sharp U-turn in its migration policy and law following the 2015 events, my pessimistic fears came to be realized faster than I had imagined they would be. Meanwhile, UK migration policies had since become even more hostile through the Brexit spectacle (along with an increasing number of migration related deaths in the English Channel and plans to relocate asylum seekers in Rwanda). With Sweden's politicians seeing restrictive migration policies as a way of tackling the country's perceived failure to integrate its non-European migrants, its policies have also become harsher. For a while during the 'Windrush crisis', the UK slightly softened its stance to compensate for the worst effects of having suddenly deported people of Caribbean origin who had lived their whole lives in the UK because of administrative errors made decades earlier (Jolly and Lind 2021). Nonetheless, the trend in both countries is towards increasingly harsher policies. However, having first immersed myself in the UK and, during the later parts of my fieldwork there, having learnt from the migrants' own experiences, I felt better prepared to understand the developments in Sweden.

Re-experiencing the local setting

When I travelled to the UK, my knowledge of the Swedish political context in relation to migration was infinitely greater than of the same context in the UK. Nonetheless, by immersing myself in the everyday lives of migrants in precarious situations in Birmingham, I got to learn about the UK system from both those who experienced it and those who supported them – families sometimes facing the threat of imminent deportation and the NGO workers and activists helping them navigate their relationships with the different authorities. However, throughout these six months, I kept recalibrating my understanding of the Swedish situation and was continuously comparing what I was seeing in Birmingham with what I knew about Malmö and Sweden. These ongoing comparisons both helped me process what I was learning in Birmingham and renewed my interest in the local situation in Malmö. While my decision to conduct fieldwork in Birmingham was primarily a pragmatic one, I am certain that it was pivotal to my learning, since it gave me a reference point and later helped see Malmö with fresh eyes. By looking at it in the light of Birmingham, Malmö took on a new form. When I came back, I experienced the streets differently. I appreciated their flatness more. I was more attentive to the different kinds of people I met while cycling. Malmö also felt closer to the rest of the world after I learnt that the owner of the hair extension and beauty salon around the corner from my apartment in Malmö was a relative of a participant in Birmingham.

The centrality of fearing deportation

While my approach yielded fewer comparisons between the two sites than I had perhaps imagined they would, comparing Birmingham with Malmö did, however, help me see each individual site more clearly. It enabled me to identify key issues in the overall politics of controlling migrant children in northern Europe, such as the centrality of children's rights as a resource for undocumented migrant families in their everyday struggles (Lind 2019). Comparing the two cities also made me recognize the importance of other comparative measures. For example, while local factors clearly shape the experiences of precarious migrants, the threat of deportation, which Gonzales (2016) termed the 'master status', overshadowed all others. Although the regulations and practices of local authorities might differ in various ways, the threat of deportation, being forbidden to work and struggling to provide for themselves permeate every aspect of the lives of undocumented migrants. Based on my experiences in both countries, my realization that children's rights and vulnerabilities were being mobilized for the purposes of migration control (Lind 2019, 2020), is perhaps what struck me most. Although I still feel that I am yet to disentangle how these processes really work, I do know that if it were not for the welcoming and helpful staff at IRiS, I would never have been able to conduct the study to begin with.

References

Corporate Watch (2018) *UK border regime: a critical guide*, Corporate Watch.

Gonzales, R. G. (2016) *Lives in limbo: undocumented and coming of age in America*, University of California Press.

Jolly, A. and J. Lind (2021) 'Firewalls as a resource for resistance: separating border policing from social service provision in Sweden and the UK', *Nordic Social Work Research*, 11 (2): 183–196, doi: 10.1080/2156857X.2020.1862898.

Lind, J. (2019) 'Governing vulnerabilised migrant childhoods through children's rights', *Childhood*, 26 (3), 337–51, doi: 10.1177/0907568219847269.

Lind, J. (2020) *The politics of undocumented migrant childhoods: agency, rights, vulnerability*, Malmö University, doi: 10.24834/isbn.9789178770830.

Thinking Multidimensionally: Some Visual Challenges

Laurence Lessard-Phillips

Recently, a colleague and I examined the concept of multidimensionality, which we saw as 'an understanding that multiple, interactive, and interdependent dimensions are an inherent feature of specific concepts' (Lessard-Phillips and Fajth 2023: 209), one such feature being its possible application to the quantitative study of superdiversity. In superdiversity studies, multidimensionality is seen as linked to the diversification of characteristics, conditions, processes, and/or relations (Lessard-Phillips and Fajth 2023: 211), but, we argued, no explicit details have been provided on how to engage with it empirically. Our broad definition, shown above, implies that it would be difficult to capture multidimensionality via a single trait or attribute.

To carry this idea forward, we explored how the concept had been defined and empirically applied in related fields, as in research on social exclusion, 'migrant integration' and race studies. A brief review of how multidimensionality has been tackled in these fields suggests that (1) we can think about two main conceptualizations of multidimensionality, based on characteristics or outcomes; (2) there are major contrasts in thinking – and applying – a multidimensional lens in policy- and academic-based approaches (to use a crude distinction); and (3) the operationalization of a multidimensional concept and the methods of analysis that can be used to deal with this are quite specific – and get 'complicated' quite quickly, as well as being quite 'data hungry'. Despite this, however, we thought that learning from the experiences of other fields that had attempted to tackle multidimensionality in an empirical manner was nonetheless useful, if not challenging, for researching superdiversity.

This focus on multidimensionality is based on research that we (and others) have done, separately and collectively, on migrant integration.[1] The emphasis on integration as a multidimensional concept has started to gain ground in quantitative empirical research, which acknowledges it as an umbrella (or latent) concept including many dimensions (economic, political, and social to name only a few). The latter, in turn, have sub-dimensions that can be measured through specific indicators, which is relevant when we think about the operationalization of concepts (de Vaus 2001). These dimensions tend to be closely aligned with different contexts – whether economic (or structural), social, cultural or otherwise (Fajth and Lessard-Phillips 2022). And this alignment is often driven by theoretical, political or ideological positioning and/or data availability. Within these specific dimensions,[2] integration is often analysed separately by focusing on specific representative indicators. For example, in the case of economic integration, educational attainment or employment status would be used as indicators, of which there are plenty. In some cases, analysis techniques are applied to examine aggregated domains of integration (for example, aggregating various indicators of integration together, for which specific techniques such as factor analysis can be used) in a more general manner, sometimes with the idea that 'integration' in one domain may not necessarily imply 'integration' in others for the same individuals. As one workshop participant told me, 'I have a good job [economic integration], I vote [political integration], but I will never fit in [sense of belonging/discrimination].'

Our work on multidimensionality has raised interesting conceptual (and analytical) challenges, driven by reactions from and discussions with peers, reviewers, students, and broader debates in other fields, mainly about the lens that a multidimensional approach generates (or ignores). Of course, these challenges are inevitable and highlighting them does not imply that we should avoid multidimensional approaches (however conceptualized).

The first challenge we encountered was that of taking too aggregated a view. This happens when using analysis techniques that aggregate multiple indicators into fewer ones, often based on correlations between different indicators, such as factor analysis. In that instance, analyses tend to focus on

1. Here, I use this broad generic term, integration, which is widely contested (see recent debates in *Comparative Migration Studies*) but still features prominently in academic and policy work on the long-term settlement of migrants and their descendants.
2. What this means is also up for debate, but I will not go into it here.

latent variables that are deemed to represent an aggregation of indicators that 'work well together'. Of course, it makes theoretical sense to think of integration as this umbrella/generic/latent concept. When it comes to analysing it, however, while such a viewpoint allows examining integration in the broad sense of the term, it inevitably leads to losing quite a bit of detail, of refinement. Thus, focusing on the broader picture makes us lose sight of the finer details, a drawback with which one must contend.

At the other end of the continuum, a multidimensional approach may mean looking at as many indicators of integration in as many domains as possible. This can be likened to 'zooming in' on particular aspects of integration that are deemed important (or that are present in the data we are using – often an analytical limitation). A good example of such a focus can be found in the works of the OECD (OECD/EU 2018) and Home Office (Ndofor-Tah et al. 2019), which engage with multiple indicators of integration. This allows for a more fine-grained overview of integration, akin to what is known in certain fields as 'fragmentation'. As is argued in poverty research (Crossley et al. 2019), while fragmenting poverty into different types allows for an individualized focus, it risks making people lose sight of the bigger picture, as well as of the structural constraints that are present, but take responsibility away from the main actors typically involved in interventions, especially the state. The level and extent of fragmentation can also be driven by the types of indicators selected; and this selection is not necessarily data-driven and can be highly political. Thus, it can make one lose sight of the bigger picture.

Finally, a last challenge I wish to highlight is linked to the idea of focusing on the inherent multidimensionality of integration and the impli-cations of taking such an all-inclusive approach. To a certain extent, taking a multidimensional approach to integration implies taking a holistic, general perspective in understanding and analysing the concept. Whether taking a bird's eye view or spotlighting individual domains, one underlying implication can be that all dimensions/domains of integration are to be considered simultaneously, without a hierarchy of importance about which dimensions 'matter more'. Yet, this can be problematic and end up setting aside important domains that should be centre stage (such as ignoring issues linked to race and discrimination). Of course, determining what ought to be centre stage will vary depending on who looks at the issue (and can be deeply embedded in power relations). The idea here is that taking such a holistic lens to looking at integration, while providing a rounded under-standing, can have the potential perverse side-effect of setting aside or deprioritizing important dimensions that should not be ignored.

Taking a multidimensional approach to concepts such as integration has many advantages. One such advantage is that it highlights the complexity of integration as a concept, which comprises embeddedness in many spheres of life. Another is that it allows us to look at integration from different angles, thus reminding ourselves that it does not necessarily occur in a linear fashion. It does, however, also raise important challenges that ought to be considered, or at least reflected upon. This is not to say that these challenges should stop us from using a multidimensional perspective, but that we remain acutely aware of what we can gain, as well as lose, by taking such an approach.

References

Crossley, S., K. Garthwaite and R. Patrick (2019) 'The fragmentation of poverty in the UK: what's the problem? A working paper', available at: https://www.whatstheproblem.org.uk/a-working-paper.

de Vaus, D. A. (2001) 'Tools for research design', in D. A. de Vaus, *Research design in social research*, SAGE.

Fajth, V. and L. Lessard-Phillips (2022) 'Multidimensionality in the integration of first- and second-generation migrants in Europe: a conceptual and empirical investigation', *International Migration Review*, Early View, doi: 10.1177/01979183221089290.

Lessard-Phillips, L. and V. Fajth (2023) 'Multidimensionality and superdiversity: some reflections', in F. Meissner, N. Sigona and S. Vertovec (eds) *The Oxford handbook of superdiversity*, Oxford University Press, 209–24.

OECD/EU (Organisation for Economic Co-operation and Development/European Union) (2018) *Settling in 2018: indicators of immigrant integration*, OECD Publishing, doi: 10.1787/9789264307216-en.

Ndofor-Tah, C., A. Strang, J. Phillimore, L. Morrice, L. Michael, P. Wood and J. Simmons (2019) *Home Office indicators of integration framework 2019*, project report, Home Office.

Advancements in Community Research in Forced Migration

Lisa Goodson

Empowered migrant communities are a vital part of the answer to some of the biggest problems facing our failed immigration system today. What is more, to help tackle racial injustices, widening inequalities, distrust in institutions and hostility towards migration, there is a growing consensus for the need to reimagine social research and what we consider valuable in terms of knowledge production (Grzymala-Kazlowska and Goodson 2021). In writing this piece, reflecting on two decades of experience developing and delivering what is now the IRiS Community Practitioner Research Programme (CPRP), my reflections really brought home just how many people and organizations have been instrumental in the survival and development of IRiS's CPRP. The CPRP was conceived as a joint initiative with Professor Jenny Phillimore in 2002, and has been supported and nurtured over the years by IRiS's Ann Bolstridge, TSRC's Angus McCabe and more recently Dr Aleksandra Grzymala-Kazlowska, Dr Sara Hassan, Dr Marisol Reyes Soto, Sian Thomson, Alison Thompson, Debbie Kerslake and Bircan Ciytak. From Jenny's and my own humble attempt to use community research (CR) as a tool to engage young dyslexic offenders in conversations about drivers of increasing recidivism rates among BAME communities, we have seen the growth of a movement of likeminded people passionate about knowledge justice.

The CPRP, delivered in recent years in partnership with Dave Newall, Director Brushstrokes Community Project, offers accredited participatory modular training that takes trainees through research design, data collection and analysis, lobbying and commissioning. The CPRP has helped raise awareness of the potential of community and practitioner-engaged research across disciplines and has provided accredited research training opportunities to more than 250 talented individuals living or working in our local communities. Many of our trainee community and practitioner researchers (CRs) have gone on to use CPRP as a springboard to engage in further research and/or advocacy work supporting forced migrants – Marcianne Uwimaana, James Omunson, Jimmy Sydney, Roger Nyantou, Dr Andy Jolly (see Chapter 44), Sarah Taal (see Chapter 61), Razan Amoush, Hannah Weiz, Harriet Thumbe. The CR commissioning model, developed and tested within the ERDF funded Unlocking Social and Economic Innovation Together! project (USE-IT! 2017–2019), as a CPRP spin-off opens pathways to more enduring research partnerships through commissioned research. Through this commissioning model we have seen the power of connecting trained community researchers to research opportunities. Over time, this has led to sustained relationships between commissioners and community research teams that have undoubtedly enriched and increased the relevance of research by opening doors and tapping into knowledge sources not typically represented in research. These partnerships have also served to legitimize and validate community and academic research respectively, created an environment that values research co-production and provided the space for community perspectives, skills and expertise to be recognized as assets that need unlocking in the research process. The director of the Birmingham Voluntary Service Council (BVSC), Sophie Wilson, has been at the forefront of embracing the potential of the commissioning model supporting trained CRs to take lead roles in commissioned CR projects relating to serious youth violence in the city.

From the start, CPRP has been embedded in a broad spectrum of policy research projects focusing on forced migrants' experiences of resettlement, such as the welfare needs of unaccompanied minors following the closure of the 'jungle' refugee camp in Calais, refugee mental health, food poverty, housing and destitution. Over time and in different contexts, we have seen how community research has provided a vehicle to give voice to those whose skills and experience are often overlooked by mainstream research. Our experience of working with community researchers has demonstrated the crucial insights and expertise they bring to social research facilitated by the power of trusted social relationships and connections (Grzymala-Kazlowska and Goodson 2021). The CPRP has also directly influenced the research design of other large-scale grant projects led by academics from a number of disciplines with different research interests – education and applied linguistics (Professor Angela Creese, see Chapter 21), applied health and infant mortality (Professor Jo Garstang), geography and urban planning (Dr Peter Lee) and psychology and trauma informed care in Gaza, Palestine (Professor Heather Flow). Furthermore, the level of international interest sparked by (i) the call for contributions to our edited book, exactly a decade ago, entitled, Community Research for Participation (Goodson and Phillimore 2012); (ii) interest in participation in IRiS's (2017) international conference 'Global perspectives on research co-production with communities' co-hosted at UoB in partnership with Deborah Warr from the Melbourne Social Equity Institute, University of Melbourne; and (iii) the 2020 UoB organized conference 'The university as a social and public "good": creating an anchor out of community engaged research' (halted due to the pandemic), are all testimony to a growing research movement and the drive to make the aspirations and principles of the civic university a reality.

While the foundations of IRiS's CPRP were established in 2002, over time it has evolved into a multi-disciplinary research co-production methodology that has underpinned bids successfully secured from a range of national and European sponsors. The CPRP is underpinned by the principle of the university as an anchor institution – a large organization with asset and spending power that can be consciously used to benefit the communities in which they are rooted. We have indeed witnessed how this anchor role can leverage the potential of community experts, commissioners and policy stakeholders to work collaboratively to tackle pressing migrant resettlement concerns. In the early 2000s, when our CR journey was just starting, the research funding landscape looked radically different from what we see today. In the past twelve months the community research funding space has opened up and, dare I say it, on some levels become overcrowded. While securing funding for CR projects has at times been challenging, we have been lucky to cross paths with individuals who became pioneers of the CPRP approach, for they were willing to fund or support research considered in some camps as unscientific and simply too risky – namely Heather Petch, OBE, then director of the Housing Association Charitable Trust (HACT), Dipali Chandra, then at Joseph Rowntree Foundation, Dr Arten Llazari, CEO, founder of Refugee and Migrant Centre (RMC) and the dedicated team at Barrow Cadbury Trust that have kept the CPRP alive over the years through flexible core funding.

We have learnt a lot about the importance of having supportive non-academic partners in statutory positions to push through evidence-based community-led research. Working with professionals such as Birmingham City Council's Karolina Medwecka, a veteran of community research advocacy and supporter of the vision of policy integrated CR interventions. More recently, working with Dally Panaser at West Midlands Strategic Migration Partnership (WMSMP) to plan the co-production of a West Midlands integration strategy, using the CPRP model to engage stakeholders at different levels of governance across the region, has demonstrated the potential of research co-production when the political will exists. We have also seen how the work of the CPRP is only made possible through close links with CSOs that act as social anchors by supporting the development and maintenance of social capital and networks at the community level.

Findings emerging from the EMPOWER community research project, led by Professor Simon Pemberton at Keele University, show that CSROs in the UK, Germany and Sweden provide a point of connection across racial, ethnic, gender, legal and other demographic boundaries that can strengthen bonding and bridge the links that provide a social anchor for developing intersectional collective identities, a sense of belonging, pride in the area, trust and reciprocity (Pemberton et al. 2022). Brushstrokes community project, led by Dave Newall BEM and Baobab Women's Project led by Sarah Taal have a nuanced understanding of *what works* in research co-production and we have been blessed with their involvement in the CPRP journey since the inception of IRiS. Working with likeminded people passionate about advocating for the rights and inclusion of migrants at all levels, including research, has enabled what are sometimes perceived as too difficult or 'tricky' research ideas to be operationalized.

Projects involving individuals with irregular immigration status, for example, and research exploring sensitive topics such as refugee mental health, migrant maternity, and infant mortality require careful facilitation through relationships and spaces of trust. Aside from the personal edification of engagement at individual, community and practitioner-researcher levels, which should not be undervalued, we have seen how a number of CSOs involved in CPRP have been able to improve the ability of their organizations to collect and utilize evidence enabling them to improve their integration practices. The development of new datasets has been used to access funds, develop new practices and improve organizational effectiveness, thus ensuring better outcomes for forced migrants in some resettlement areas.

Despite the existence and benefits of established research co-production training programmes, such as IRiS's CPRP, CR methodologies still tend to fall on the margins of social research and are often not applied to their full potential. Instead, they tend to be limited to ad hoc projects, which has created a patchwork of CR expertise and pockets of nationally and internationally scattered excellence. For example, Professor Christiane Falge in Germany and Professor Gabriella Elgenius in Sweden have been inspirational in their approaches to co-produced research with forced migrant communities. While the value of co-producing research is now well recognized among academic and non-academic stakeholders, there is, however, a pressing need for a more joined-up approach to allow for a more strategic and sustainable way of managing and developing community research efforts and advancing theoretical and methodological thinking to inform our ontological frames of reference. New funding commitments supported by a portfolio of UK funders offer real potential to develop more robust infrastructures in the coming years to support the ability to respond to community research opportunities and to create synergies between these opportunities and progression routes to help nurture those looking to further advance their skills in community research.

We see the ongoing need for community-led research to help us better understand the lived experiences of our increasingly diverse diasporic communities, and to think through and inform resettlement policies relating to refugees and other vulnerable migrants. For example, there is a pressing need for community-led research on the immediate resettlement requirements of thousands of Afghans still in limbo in UK hotels twelve months after Operation Pitting following the 2021 Taliban offensive, and the risk of homelessness and SGBV facing thousands of Ukrainian women and children in the coming months. The question of how to move people from positions of no agency to ones in which they feel sufficiently valued and empowered to engage in research about matters that have an impact on their daily lives is often raised. Using community research initiatives to build strong and enduring partnerships between universities and communities can help bridge the gaps between communities and academic research projects in a range of different disciplinary perspectives, which will help to shift the balance of power in knowledge production and evidence-based policy making.

There is much more to be done to advance methodological thinking and practice in the field of community research to address pressing social and spatial inequalities and injustices in communities of growing diversity. Experience of working with a wide range of CPRs has revealed a number of important lessons to take with us moving forward.

These are (i) that relationships based on trust are key to community and practitioner engagement in research. As the evaluation of the USE-IT! community research illustrated:

Source: Grzymala-Kazlowska and Goodson (2021).

(ii) that engagement in research can bring about changes to an individual's sense of belonging, a collective sense of identity and pride in their resettlement neighbourhood; (iii) building capacity for the future mainstreaming of CR into different levels of governance has potential to bring about changes to policy decision making. At this moment, the future for community research certainly seems bright. There are opportunities to take CPR methodologies beyond ad-hoc initiatives to a more sustainable CRR infrastructure given the availability of current funding streams, which I think in time will make a marked impression on the future direction of research co-production. I support a vision whereby opportunities will open up to embed trained community researcher in academic and non-academic partnerships to help build the capacity of local stakeholders to co-produce research for impact and in so doing realizing the value of CPR mainstreaming. The evolving community research landscape will undoubtedly be an interesting one – preferably with more opportunities for empowerment through research – for those of us interested in exploring different frames of reference and representation in forced migration research. Let us continue our efforts to press for cultural changes in social policy research that not only recognize but actively seek to unlock the value of communities in research processes and more importantly develop an infrastructure that can sustain CR assets, beyond transactional relationships associated with funded projects, once academic research teams have stepped away.

References

Goodson, L. and J. Phillimore (2012) *Community research for participation: from theory to method*, Policy Press.

Grzymala-Kazlowska, A. and L. Goodson (2021) 'Remaking the future of local community through research co-production', British Sociological Association Annual Conference 2021: Remaking the Future.

IRiS conference (2017) 'Global perspectives on research co-production with communities: ontologies, epistemologies and methodologies', 14–15 September, University of Birmingham in partnership with University of Melbourne, Australia.

Pemberton, S., B. Ciytak, G. Elgenius, C. Falge and L. Goodson (2022) 'Place making and spatial justice in superdiverse neighbourhoods', IRiS Tenth Anniversary Conference, 14–16 September, University of Birmingham.

USE-IT! (Unlocking Social and Economic Innovation Together) (2017–19) Project website available at: https://www.uia-initiative.eu/en/uia-cities/birmingham.

In the Shadow of Conflict: Reflections of a South Sudanese Research Advisory Group

Rachel Ayrton

'Asking questions is always a position of power.'

– Linda Tuhiwai Smith (2021)

Like many researchers in the fields of migration and superdiversity, I am concerned with how inequalities show up in research relationships. Researchers are 'question-askers', a position of privilege from which to exercise power over what (or whose) knowledges count as important. There is a colonial dynamic to research relationships as they tend to be constructed in the dominant models of research emanating from the Global North. There are researchers, and there are the researched. There are subjects, and there are objects. There are narrators, and those who are represented, experts and laypeople. Some exist in the centre, others at the margins. Insofar as researchers seek social justice, we cannot help but also pursue *epistemic* justice – that is, justice in the way research knowledge is produced and represented – to turn this dynamic on its head.

Inclusive research practices are one way in which researchers can unsettle the privilege of being a question asker. According to Melanie Nind, inclusive research 'can be usefully thought of as research that changes the dynamic between research/researchers and the people who are usually researched: it is conceived as research *with*, *by*, or sometimes *for* them, and in contrast to research *on* them' (Nind 2014: 3). It includes various approaches that share the goal of achieving social change through research in which the researchers' values and personal commitments shape the way they work (Brydon-Miller et al. 2003; Nind 2014). My disposition towards inclusive research was shaped by my early career as a community development worker in an urban regeneration programme from around 2006, in particular the occupational values of participation, self-determination, social justice, and reflective practice.

Figure 1: Nind's (2014) spectrum of overlapping approaches

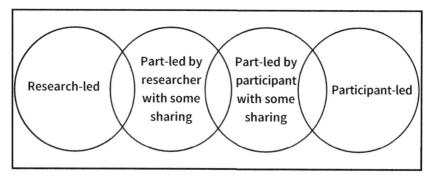

Inclusive research involves decentring the researcher and sharing power. The degree to which power is shared, which Nind depicts as a continuum of overlapping approaches (Figure 1), can vary. Much inclusive research falls in the middle two circles along this spectrum – where the lead lies with either the researcher or participant, but with power sharing between these positions. Advisory groups are one tool that can be useful to researchers and participants attempting to collaborate in these shared power spaces. They are becoming common practice in health and social care research and other spaces where funders require public involvement. As advisory groups become more commonplace, there has been a corresponding growth in critical perspectives. As Sherry Arnstein (1969) classically acknowledged, participation too easily falls into tokenism. Relinquishing a position of privilege takes more active effort than sitting tight. This is an ethical commitment and, where it is strong, I have seen advisory groups achieve genuine collaboration in the community settings in which I have worked.

'Participants', of course, have unequal access to power, particularly in populations affected by conflict. Over several years, I developed a research programme with the South Sudanese diaspora in the UK looking at national identity and belonging. South Sudan seceded from Sudan in 2011 after a decades-long struggle for independence. However, in 2013 a devastating civil war broke out in the new state, and violent oppression is still a daily reality. South Sudanese people living in the UK report that the dynamics of the conflict are mirrored in fractured relationships between groups in the diaspora. By convening the research advisory group, I hoped to create a democratic space in which governance of the research was owned by a group of which I was just one member (albeit also the facilitator), while members representing different South Sudanese ethnic groups could cooperate on a level playing field outside the conflict-induced divisions. This is an ongoing learning process for us all. I asked advisory group members to reflect on their experience of working in this way. Based on their responses,[1] I collate here four key themes that have shaped our journey so far.

Shared commitment to purpose

Collaborative research involves a three-part relationship between researcher, participants and the research topic (Ben-Ari and Enosh 2012). A shared commitment to the purpose of the research is what motivates advisory group members to commit their time, insights, organizational and relational capacities, despite the personal/emotional cost of doing so.

> Tumunit – When I was invited, my first impression was that this was an inconsequential and small academic exercise. But as the group grew larger and the scope expanded, the far-reaching potential of this study for the community became apparent.

> Liz – The research findings will help address issues and concerns within the community and that hopefully will enable the South Sudanese to develop a sense of community and embrace a spirit of togetherness, give us a deeper sense of belonging and bring a sense of security.

> Alaffi – I loved the topic of the research and I thought it touched the fundamental issues that have never been addressed by us South Sudanese.

In some cases, the participatory approach itself has potential to contribute to the peacebuilding goals of the research at individual and structural levels.

---

1. Advisory group members are identified with pseudonyms of their choosing. Some prefer anonymity, so this is to represent them equally here. The analysis and insights remain their own.

Cynthia – Our meeting was the first time I could vent all the turmoil inside me. Your initiative was the place where I could speak my experience and those who felt like me.

Nahima – I feel that the research will help the government of South Sudan to start looking at the people of the country as an asset that has to be respected and empowered for the good of the country.

Genuine interdependence and collaboration

The members' comments highlight the interdependence between me as a white British 'outsider' researcher and them as South Sudanese community representatives. Their involvement is both an ideological imperative and a practical necessity for the research to achieve its purpose.

Amos – Rachel constituted [the advisory group], not only to assist her, but also to include South Sudanese input in the work.

Alaffi – I became interested in the research and like the method used specifically the involvement of the advisory group who are members of the very community, the target of the research ... I felt I am part of the process of the research.

Liz – We advised her on the best way of doing the project and how she can approach the community members, because in 2013 South Sudan went into a conflict where some topics become sensitive.

I remember when I first discussed the role and function of the advisory group with Amos, he said, 'it is actually refreshing.' He knew about valuable research projects on the South Sudanese diaspora, but direct collaboration with the community was new.

Careful formation, composition and facilitation

This advisory group was formed by invitation – personal contacts, previous research participants, and 'snowballing' based on personal recommendations. Liz and Amos highlighted the importance of members being carefully selected and committed, as well as representing a diverse balance in terms of gender, ethnic, and regional groups. The presence and facilitation of an 'outsider' researcher were important aspects for Cynthia and Damian:

> Cynthia – The one thing I see in our group is the fact that you are neutral and un-biased provides a conducive environment for being open and non-judgmental. ... We hope that this will eventually lead to healing of the rift between us.

Damian confides that he was *'apprehensive and too scared to speak out freely'* at first. He (Damian Talanga) continues,

> It took me time and courage to finally decide to participate. I think the feeling of apprehension ran throughout all the meetings because you could see that participants usually spoke carefully and were slow to start rather than spontaneous. But, after some time, they felt a lot more comfortable because the meetings were ... skilfully moderated, which calmed the situation a great deal and everyone began to enjoy the discussions fully. I am confident that everyone did honestly say what they wanted to say.

Relationship-building for the long term

Having begun this research in 2016 as an element of my PhD, I began to develop the advisory group as part of an ESRC post-doctoral fellowship in 2019. The richness of this growing collaboration and the commitment of South Sudanese–British advisory group colleagues is what spurred me to apply for the Leverhulme Trust funding that has taken the project into a new phase based in IRiS, looking at practices of togetherness ('conviviality') as everyday peacebuilding. Advisory group members also focus on the value of building trust and jointly developing a research agenda:

> Damian Talanga – A relaxation of tensions became evident when Rachel, the moderator, informed us about more research in the pipeline, for everyone was eager to continue to work with her on the next project.

> Alaffi – For the research to be complete the second part needs to be accomplished.

Inclusive research comes in many guises along the power-sharing spectrum. My experience suggests that it is important that the form and extent of collaboration is appropriate to the project, transparent, and agreed to by all involved, rather than assuming that greater participant independence is always the 'best' model. Although I 'lead' in this research, I do so from a position of service to the advisory group. There are certainly limitations to our approach – progress comes in fits and starts, largely due to my capacity as a part-time individual researcher, pulled away by other academic and caring responsibilities. Advisory group members generously bear with me. On my working days, it is my partnership with them that causes me to leap out of bed in the mornings. Their passion is the driving force of our work.

References

Arnstein, S. (1969) 'A ladder of citizen participation', *Journal of the American Institute of Planners*, 35 (4): 216–24.

Ben-Ari, A. and G. Enosh (2012) 'Power relations and reciprocity: dialectics of knowledge construction', *Qualitative Health Research*, 23 (3): 422–29.

Brydon-Miller, M., D. Greenwood and P. Maguire (2003) 'Why action research?', *Action Research*, 1 (1): 9–28.

Nind, M. (2014) *What is inclusive research?*, Bloomsbury.

Smith, L. T. (2021) 'Decolonial research methods: resisting coloniality in academic knowledge production (webinar 2)', National Centre for Research Methods, 2 November, available at: https://eprints.ncrm.ac.uk/id/eprint/4488/1/Linda_T_Smith_Decolonial_Research_Methods.pdf.

PART THREE: SPOTLIGHTS, BLINDSPOTS AND CASE STUDIES

Migration Choices in the Context of Development

Richard Black

The notion that a lack of 'development' in Africa is the root cause of hundreds of thousands of desperate people risking their lives to cross the Mediterranean and English Channel each year as migrants is a surprisingly resilient one in policy circles and public discourse. European governments and the European Commission spend millions of euros (and pounds) each year trying to address this 'problem', not least through the EU Trust Fund for Africa. A range of development 'interventions' are designed explicitly or implicitly to reduce the need or propensity to migrate from Africa. The idea is a simple and alluring one: if support can be provided for a 'good life' back home, people will not need to migrate. Indeed, some of those who have migrated will be able to return, to benefit from, or even spearhead development efforts.

There are few working in the development industry on the ground in Africa who think such interventions work. After all, if they did, and given the amount of money spent, why would men, women and children continue to die at sea trying to reach Europe? In reality, the relationship between development interventions and migration choices is complex. Development interventions come in all shapes and sizes, from targeted training of 'potential' migrants and returnees explicitly designed to enable them not to migrate, or re-migrate, through to multi-sector, multi-year programmes designed to build a public discourse that it is 'better at home', and to kick-start the wider economic conditions in which a choice to stay makes sense. Migration choices are also multiple, rarely a single choice at one point in time, but rather a series of opportunities and constraints experienced through a significant part of the life course.

There is a wide body of academic literature that seeks to understand migration choices. This ranges from classic 'push–pull' theories of migration, which weigh up the strength of benefits and disbenefits at 'origin' and 'destination', to more recent analyses that distinguish the 'aspiration' to migrate from the 'ability' or 'capability' to do so (Aslany et al. 2021; Carling 2002). There is a growing understanding that migration choices are not simply economic; and also a realization that migration is only a 'choice' in the context of the range and quality of the alternatives available (Erdal and Oeppen 2018). Considered in this way, if development interventions were to widen the range of available choices to people, then they would at least make it more likely that any resulting migration is a choice, rather than a response to lack of choice.

Do development interventions work in this way? Recent research at the University of Birmingham involving an interdisciplinary team of geographers, anthropologists, political scientists and international relations scholars suggests they often do not. With funding from the UK's Foreign and Commonwealth Office (FCDO) and the International Organization for Migration (IOM), we followed direct outcomes from a targeted intervention in The Gambia and also explored wider patterns of engagement between communities in areas of high emigration and a range of development actors across The Gambia, Senegal and Guinea.

A specific focus of one part of the project was on tracking the changing aspiration to migrate in a sample of just under 800 young entrepreneurs eligible to take part in an IOM Youth Coaching programme, who were randomly assigned either to participate in the programme or not. Those in the programme received a targeted intervention involving one-to-one coaching and a cash grant. Initial results suggest that participation in the programme significantly reduced the aspiration to migrate, but that this was short-lived. Thus, while the programme substantially improved individuals' sense of self-sufficiency and self-efficacy, these changes did not ultimately impact on their aspiration to migrate. However, the programme also influenced their sense of place attachment, at least in the short-term, and it is this channel that temporarily reduces the desire to move abroad (Simon et al. 2022a).

More broadly, there have been numerous initiatives aimed at bolstering life 'at home' so that individuals will not 'need to move'. For example, in both Senegal and The Gambia, there have been (separate) initiatives with the name '*Tekki Fii*', which roughly translates as '(you can) make it here' in Wolof. In both countries, *Tekki Fii* also offers support to individuals who might otherwise migrate; but drawing on European funding, it also represents part of a wider campaign to persuade young people across the region that life is better in West Africa and that migration undermines this by eroding social cohesion. Our interviewees were not so sure. *Tekki Fii* was regarded with scepticism at best, and ridicule at worse. For many, it was evidence that the country's leaders are out of touch with the reality of life of ordinary people and the choices they face. Similar scepticism appears to greet a range of initiatives promoting developments in agriculture and fisheries, small business support and vocational training. These are not necessarily seen as bad things in their own right, but the very fact that they have to be backed up with calls to 'do the right thing' for the country is seen as illuminating the lack of choices that young people have in reality (Black et al. 2022).

Such scepticism is also not limited to development interventions focused on migration. Our study coincided with the onset of the Covid-19 pandemic, and a baseline survey in The Gambia showed considerable scepticism about the capacity of the government to deliver early economic recovery, in contrast to what was perceived as the situation in the Global North (Simon et al. 2022b). Interestingly, the same survey showed that having and retaining a job was the key factor most likely to be associated with a lower aspiration to migrate, and loss of employment most likely to lead to an increased aspiration to migrate. This chimes with earlier macroeconomic evidence produced by Clemens and Postel (2018) suggesting that employment is key. Against this criterion, a key measure of success of development interventions would be whether they actually *create* jobs, rather than whether they provide support *towards* job creation at an individual or collective level. And, all too often they do not.

Indeed, not only do migration-related development interventions fall short of actual job creation, even in the short term, but they also take place in the context of a loss of jobs elsewhere, whether in supposedly 'secure' government employment as states adopt austerity measures against declining revenues, or directly in response to a series of 'crises', real or otherwise, of which Covid-19 is only the most recent. This, combined with the perception that government elites talk about staying at home being the 'right thing' at the same time as sending their children abroad for education, and taking opportunities themselves to be mobile, fans a sense of double standards and insincerity.

However, it would be wrong to focus on jobs as the only thing that influences migration choices in a development context such as West Africa. Indeed, one of our key observations is that strategies of geographical mobility (rather than specific migration choices) reflect one way to maximize the benefits of *any* inflow of external resources. In part, this reflects the fact that so few people have formal jobs; in such a context, there is a need to adapt flexibly to opportunities that themselves have a spatial structure. Such flexible mobility is primarily national and regional in nature – in other words many more people migrate within and between the countries of West Africa than move to Europe or beyond – but it is a mobility that is not and probably cannot be constrained within regional boundaries once it becomes a normal feature of seeking a decent life.

Non-economic factors also weigh heavily. The illness or death of a close family member often acts as a significant constraint on mobility, while choice itself is frequently exercised within a family context. In other words, while some family members might be expected by parents or siblings to be 'mobile' to secure resources necessary for the family, others need to stay at 'home' if the value of those resources is to be maximized. Most important of all, decisions about how to deploy and mobilize resources are almost always made in the context of trying to anticipate future benefits and risks in conditions of extreme uncertainty. Development interventions seldom seek to reduce such uncertainty, even though this is one of the biggest ways in which migration choices could be made more informed and effective.

In this context, our work has suggested a 'future-orientated' lens for migration (Black et al. 2022), in which uncertainty is understood as the norm. With a future lens, we can understand migration as a set of creative projects of becoming, in which development itself is also being defined. The future has emerged as a substantive field of study in the social sciences over the last two decades, one which is seen as having a transformative dimension rather than simply being the fulfilment of aspiration. Yet, our conceptual tools with which to understand the future and how we engage with it remain weak, perhaps especially so in relation to the study of migration.

References

Aslany, M., J. Carling, M. B. Mjelva and T. Sommerfelt (2021) *Systematic review of determinants of migration aspirations*, QuantMig Deliverable 2.2., University of Southampton.

Black, R., A. Bellagamba, E. Botta, et al. (2022) 'Migration drivers and migration choice: interrogating responses to migration and development interventions in West Africa', *Comparative Migration Studies*, 10 (10), doi: 10.1186/s40878-022-00283-3.

Carling, J. (2002) 'Migration in the age of involuntary immobility: theoretical reflections and Cape Verdean experiences', *Journal of Ethnic and Migration Studies*, 28 (1): 5–42.

Erdal, M. B. and C. Oeppen (2018) 'Forced to leave? The discursive and analytical significance of describing migration as forced and voluntary', *Journal of Ethnic and Migration Studies*, 44 (6): 981–98.

Clemens, M. A. and H. M. Postel (2018) 'Deterring emigration with foreign aid: an overview of evidence from low-income countries'. Policy paper 119, Center for Global Development.

Simon, M., C. Schwartz and D. Hudson (2022a) 'Start-up or set out: experimental evidence on entrepreneurship and migration decisions', unpublished manuscript.

Simon, M., C. Schwartz and D. Hudson (2022b) 'Covid-19 insecurities and migration aspirations', *International Interactions*, 48 (2): 309–26. doi: 10.1080/03050629.2022.1991919.

'Longing for Home': Internally Displaced People in Ukraine Before 2022

Irina Kuznetsova

The 2022 phase of the war finally destroyed the hopes of many people displaced since 2014 of returning home. Russian aggression has forced one-third of Ukrainians to flee from their homes since February 2014. It is estimated that more than 7.7 million have fled Ukraine to European countries (UNHCR 2022). As of October 2022, there were 6.5 million internally displaced people in Ukraine (IOM 2022).

The following is an excerpt from a message I received from Olena (pseudonym) on 24 February 2022. 'I am not going anywhere. I have already had to flee several years ago. How many times shall I move? I will try to cope.' I first met her in 2017 in Chernihiv. She had lived there for some time after fleeing from Luhansk with her children, and before moving to Kyiv. A few weeks after our conversation in February, she would be in Poland, like millions of other Ukrainian refugees.

Olena's case, unfortunately, is very common. Since 2014, eight years before February 2022, more than 1.5 million people fled to other parts of Ukraine from eastern parts of the country (Kuznetsova and Mikheieva 2020) as the results of armed conflict and a change of regime, what the Ukrainian government defined later as a 'temporal occupation' of Donetsk and Luhansk areas (Hromadske 2018). Since that time, the war-without-declaring-war had already taken the lives of more than fourteen thousand people, including civilians, and shortened the days of those who could not cope anymore. Ukraine has been facing the most extensive population displacement in its history since the Second World War. During those eight years, some internally displaced people (IDPs) returned to their homes; some moved to EU countries as labour migrants or students, as it was not possible to receive the status of a refugee or temporary protection at that time, but most tried to cope and settle in a new place. Below, there are just a few stories collected back in 2017 that will give a sense of what people felt to leave home in 2014 in Ukraine and cope at a new place of residence. Some of those people possibly had to find a new place again in 2022. All names of interviewees have been changed to preserve their anonymity.

Olia, a 35–40-year-old woman, with her husband and three young children, moved more than five hundred miles from Luhansk to a small town in the Kyiv region. As she put it:

> Our apartment has not been destroyed, thank God, but we left because we worried about our kids; they were little at that time.
>
> You know, if someone would tell me now, that it [military aggression] has finished, and everything is back to normal, I would probably, return as my home is there. ... Here it is just impossible to buy your accommodation. So, all your life you will have to move from one rented flat to another. I do not see any future yet. I live day by day.

They had to leave their small but stable business in their home city behind and at first had to rely on charitable help. One family provided temporary shelter for them before they found a low-paid job and could provide for themselves.

Halyna fled from a village in the Luhansk area near the Russian border to Chernihiv, a city in north-eastern Ukraine in 2017. Back home, she used to work in the food industry and was studying part-time at the university. Halyna, then a 35–40-year-old woman, could not continue her studies because of the military actions in Luhansk. She had a stable income and excellent career prospects until the war started:

> There were lots of military vehicles and lots of military men. Once, there was even shelling, in May 2014. For more than a year we lived in fear. Many people started to flee, and took their children because it [military aggression] could start there any day. Of course, we all worried ... and one day I realized that I could not cope anymore with all these fears and worries. I was working 24-hour shifts, and on the nights the shelling was especially scary. I gave up everything, took my

173

son, and moved here [in summer 2015] to one random acquaintance who later became my friend. She just took pity on us and helped a lot.

Then Halyna was able to find a job and rent separate accommodation, though at the time of the interview she was thinking of going back to her home village:

Most of my university mates went back to Luhansk because here they did not have much support. There are difficulties with accommodation, and all my friends have families. It is very difficult to cope. They go back. ... Even people who were over 59 years-old, at first, they took their grandchildren and left, but then came back. Home is home. ... I am longing for my home. I think about it day and night. I quite like to live in Chernihiv, it is a nice small town, but it is challenging financially. Salaries are very low. You need to work day and night. Of course, I do not plan to stay there all my life. I want to return home. Or at least be closer to my home. Mom keeps saying: 'Move at least to Kharkiv! That would be a bit closer.'

We do not know if Halyna managed to return.

Victor, aged between 40 and 45, was a businessman in Mariupol. However, he left Mariupol for Kyiv because his business was linked with Donetsk and Crimea, and it became impossible to transfer goods. But the main reason was the war:

Honestly, if I was in the government, I would pay benefits to those people who still have not fled from Mariupol as it is almost a war zone if you talk about its suburbs that sometimes are under shelling and people have to sleep in basements. It is terrible.

Still, for many thousands of people, Mariupol was the last resort to escape from hostilities in the east. Olexander, a man of between 40 and 45 years, moved to Mariupol from Avdiivka in 2017. At that time, Avdiivka was in a non-government-controlled area of Donetsk oblast. In February 2022, Avdiivka was among the first places to be attacked as soon as the Russian government recognized the Donetsk People's Republic. Olexander used to be a builder and a factory worker. In 2015, the house in Avdiivka where he lived with his partner and children was bombed, so they had to move to his grandmother's home. As he described their life there in Avdiivka:

> First, we could go to the allotment, at least, even if there was some shelling. But in the summer of 2016, things became worse. There is an industrial zone nearby, bullets whistle above your head. It became difficult to do any gardening as they can start shooting. And it became dangerous to take children to kindergarten. In winter, it used to be silent during the day, but at 5 p.m. when it is time to pick up kids from the kindergarten, they could start a skirmish as if on purpose.

As a result, the family had to move to Mariupol in 2017. Olexander spent several months looking for a job but could not find one. Still, he hoped to settle in a new city as he and his family were feeling safe.

We could not connect with most of our participants since, as following our ethical review we could not trace them back unless we knew them before. We do not know if they have returned home. All we know is that Russian strikes in 2022 killed and wounded many civilians in all the cities and towns where our research participants lived. '*Only stopping the war can help to overcome this situation*', the words of one of the IDPs in 2017 are as topical as ever.

Acknowledgments

Thanks to all the internally displaced people who took part in the study and gave generously of their time. Special thanks to Professor Mikheieva and Dr Mariia Kolokolova for their collaboration. The interviews were taken within the project 'Ukraine's hidden tragedy: understanding the outcomes of population displacement from the country's war-torn regions' (grant AH/P008305/1) funded by the Arts and Humanities Research Council UK with the Partnership for Conflict, Crime and Security Research.

References

Hromadske (2018) 'Ukraine's "occupied territories" draft law sent for president's signature', 8 February, available at: https://hromadske.ua/en/posts/ukraines-occupied-territories-draft-law-sent-for-presidents-signature?tag=draft-law.

IOM (2022) *Ukraine internal displacement report: general population survey: round 10 (27 October 2022),* International Organization for Migration report, available at: https://displacement.iom.int/reports/ukraine-internal-displacement-report-general-population-survey-round-10-17-27-october-2022.

Kuznetsova, I. and O. Mikheieva (2020) 'Forced displacement from Ukraine's war-torn territories: intersectionality and power geometry', *Nationalities Papers,* 48 (4): 690–706, doi: 10.1017/nps.2020.34.

UNHCR (2022) 'Ukraine situation flash update #34', 4 November, available at: https://data.unhcr.org/en/documents/details/96593.

Legal and Economic Integration of Refugees: What Works?

Ceren Ozgen, Matthew Cole
and Hiromi Yumoto

Globally, the number of forcibly displaced individuals fleeing human rights violations, persecution and armed conflict stood at more than 80 million in 2020 (UNHCR 2021). In Europe alone the number of refugees seeking protection reached 6.6 million, which was partly driven by an influx of individuals fleeing the Syrian conflict after 2014. The current crisis in Ukraine looks set to significantly increase European refugee numbers with potentially several millions seeking sanctuary in 2022 alone.

While refugees will have often experienced physical and mental trauma domestically and while in transit, other challenges are likely to face them on their arrival in the host country. For example, language difficulties, disrupted education and work, cultural differences and discrimination can all adversely affect what few opportunities might be available to them. A variety of studies indicate that the resultant lack of integration may threaten social cohesion, and worsen economic segregation.

Despite the importance of refugee integration, and the problems caused by its absence, we currently have limited knowledge and understanding of how it may be influenced. In part, this may be because integration is a concept with multiple dimensions, although perhaps the two most tangible of these are the legal and economic ones. The former refers to the acquisition of citizenship (namely naturalization), through which refugees obtain a full range of rights, including the ability to have their voices heard through the electoral process.[1] Indeed, in the absence of legal integration,

---

1. While there are weaker forms of legal integration, for example permanent residency, only naturalization provides an individual with the full set of rights possessed by an indigenous citizen.

the inability of refugees to vote may deepen their problems or amplify xenophobia due to their limited visibility to policymakers and to their neighbours. Economic integration refers to the participation of refugees within the host country's labour markets. Without it, refugees will be dependent on welfare systems and will tend to be economically and socially marginalized. An understanding of how to strengthen refugee integration is therefore vital for policy makers seeking social cohesion and economic prosperity.

What evidence do we have so far?

While studies on the naturalization of refugees are rare, there is one in the USA that shows that individual characteristics and residential locations substantially alter naturalization outcomes (Mossaad et al. 2018). For instance, a refugee's level of education, length of residence in the USA, and country of origin are all significant predictors of naturalization.

In terms of economic integration, it is well documented that refugees fare worse than other immigrants and natives in employment rates, incomes, and quality of occupations. Indeed, across the European Union the unemployment rate of refugees has been found to be 22 per cent higher than that of other migrants with similar characteristics, and this difference lasts for more than a decade after migration (Fasani et al. 2022). Other studies point to the role played by host country policies or programmes in influencing economic integration. For instance, restrictions on how much work refugees can undertake and policies to enforce geographical dispersal can significantly damage a refugee's economic prospects (Fasani et al. 2021). By contrast, however, the provision of local language training can boost earnings (Arendt et al. 2020).

Despite the above, there is still little written on refugee naturalization, particularly in Europe, and on the extent to which civic integration training benefits economic integration. This absence of reliable evidence means that policymakers have limited guidance on how to design efficient asylum and integration programmes for the millions of refugees in Europe.

Our research on legal and economic integration

To address the gaps in our understanding of refugee integration, our recent research examines what factors influence legal and economic integration.

We focus on the Netherlands, a country that has received large numbers of asylum seekers since 2014, and one that operates a comprehensive civic integration programme.

Upon arrival, all asylum seekers in the Netherlands must obtain an asylum residence permit, after which they are randomly dispersed into social housing across the country and obliged to pass the civic integration exam. Once this exam has been passed, and the refugees have resided in the Netherlands for five years, they are eligible to apply for naturalization.

Since 2013, the civic integration exam has consisted of two standard components – Dutch language skills and knowledge of Dutch society. In 2015, an additional component, known as the ONA, was added to assess and develop a refugee's understanding of the Dutch labour market. To meet the ONA requirements, refugees need to search for jobs, identify their qualifications or skills, prepare a CV, and undertake mock interviews.

In this context, we are able to examine how refugees' individual characteristics, and the residential locations to which they are sent, affect the likelihood of them gaining legal integration. We also explore the role of government policy and whether toughening the integration programme by including a dedicated labour market component has improved their chances of economic integration.

More specifically, using rich administrative data on all refugees in the Netherlands over the period 2014–2020, we examine two measures of legal integration – whether an individual passed the civic integration exam, and whether full naturalization occurred. We then explored to what extent a refugee's demographic characteristics, such as education acquired in the Netherlands and in the country of origin, the duration of the asylum application, and health conditions, influence these outcomes. The roles played by the characteristics of the municipality in which a refugee resides, such as unemployment rates, levels of urbanization (which vary widely across the Netherlands, see Figure 1 on the following page) and the share of co-nationals are also examined. To determine the effects of the policy, we compare a refugee's likelihood of employment, number of hours worked, and hourly wages, after completing both the standard integration exam, and the strengthened exam with the ONA component.

Figure 1: Level of urbanization of municipalities

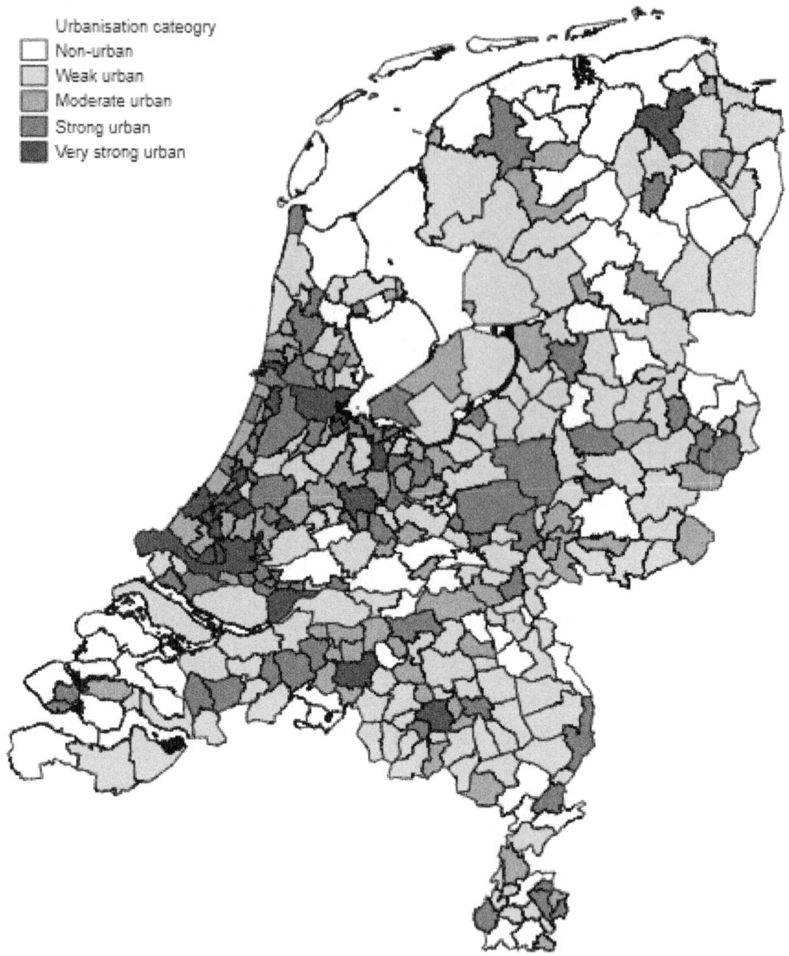

Source: CBS (2019) and StatLine (2022). According to CBS, urbanization categories are defined into five groups: very strong (2500 and over/km²); strong (1500 to 2500/km²); moderate (1000 to 1500/km²); weak (500 to 1000/km²); and non-urban (less than 500/km²).

What do we find?

A range of factors reduce the likelihood of both forms of legal integration, including a lengthy asylum application process, and physical or mental illness. For example, for an average refugee who faces approximately four-and-a-half months of waiting time, an additional month of waiting for an asylum decision reduces the probability of passing the exam and being naturalized by 1.2 per cent and 0.9 per cent respectively. The likelihood of gaining citizenship is further affected by the unemployment rate of the municipality in which a refugee resides. By contrast, both forms of legal integration are positively associated with being in work, receiving education in the Netherlands and, to some extent, the level of urbanization. Refugees with a Dutch higher education have an 84 per cent chance of passing the integration exam compared with 63 per cent for those who have not.

The standard integration exam increases the likelihood of being employed and the number of hours worked, with the ONA component providing an additional boost to a migrant's chances of finding a job. While passing the standard exam increases the likelihood of securing a job by 3.6 per cent, the ONA adds to this an additional 6.0 per cent. Furthermore, the positive impact of the ONA on employment increases over time, reaching 6.2 per cent after fifteen months. Nevertheless, we find a striking result: none of the civic integration components improve the *quality* of work in terms of hourly wages or number of hours worked.

When looking at differences between refugees, those from Syria are more likely to pass the integration exam and to benefit most from the ONA. They are 7.7 per cent more likely to pass the exam than refugees from other countries, of whom an average of 63.6 per cent passed, and 10.2 per cent more likely to find a job after passing the ONA. This could be explained by the relatively higher levels of education among refugees from Syria.

Our findings raise a number of policy implications. First, boosting the employment and educational prospects of refugees is likely to improve legal integration rates significantly. Second, the physical and mental health of refugees is perhaps a neglected deterrent to integration, suggesting a clear need to raise awareness of, and access to, appropriate healthcare services for refugees. Third, the duration of the asylum application process has a clear adverse effect on the likelihood of legal integration, suggesting that additional resourcing of the asylum process may yield wider benefits. Similarly, differences in legal integration outcomes between residential locations indicate that randomly dispersing refugees may not be an ideal policy from the point of view of integration. Instead, targeting refugee dispersal towards areas with low unemployment, high levels of urbanization, and high numbers of other co-ethnics is likely to prove beneficial. Finally, civic integration requirements, including dedicated labour-market training, clearly benefit economic integration. This may be a policy that other host countries could consider implementing. However, while such policies increase the likelihood of employment they seem to yield no benefits in terms of hours worked or hourly wages. This suggests that other factors, such as a lack of skills or training, or labour market discrimination, continue to limit the refugees' employment prospects.

These policy implications should provide some ammunition to policy makers who wish to overcome populist opposition to further investment in the asylum process. Any policies that can reduce the obstacles to refugee integration are likely to be of significant long-term benefit to host countries. Only with legal and economic integration can refugees fully contribute to host country economies, participate in their societies, and engage with and be heard by politicians and policy makers.

References

Arendt, J. N., I. Bolvig, M. Foged, L. Hasager and G. Peri (2020) 'Language training and refugees' integration', NBER working paper 26834, doi 10.3386/w26834.

CBS (Statistics Netherlands) (2019) 'Wijk- en buurtkaart', available at: https://www.cbs.nl/nl-nl/dossier/nederland-regionaal/geografische-data/wijk-en-buurtkaart-2019.

Fasani, F., T. Frattini and L. Minale (2021) 'Lift the ban? initial employment restrictions and refugee labour market outcomes', *Journal of the European Economic Association*, 19 (5): 2803–54.

Fasani, F., T. Frattini and L. Minale (2022) '(The struggle for) refugee integration into the labour market: evidence from Europe', *Journal of Economic Geography*, 22 (2): 351–93.

Mossaad, N., J. Ferwerda, D. Lawrence, J. M. Weinstein and J. Hainmueller (2018) 'Determinants of refugee naturalization in the United States', *Proceedings of the National Academy of Sciences*, 115 (37): 9175–80.

StatLine (2022) CBS (Statistics Netherlands) database, available at: https://opendata.cbs.nl/#/CBS/nl/.

UNHCR (2021) 'Global trends: forced displacement in 2020', available at: https://www.unrefugees.org.uk/wp-content/uploads/Global-Trends-2020.pdf.

Responding to Disasters in Superdiverse Contexts

Szymon Parzniewski

Increasingly, disastrous events in the world are highlighting the inequalities, and social and cultural divisions hampering the effectiveness of responses to disasters. In 2005, Hurricane Katrina triggered an increase in critical engagements with structures of social inequality, including racism (Brunsma et al. 2010). Disasters, like Hurricane Ilma in Florida in 2017, have shown that undocumented migrants are more vulnerable than the general population because fears about their legal status and the possibility of being detained and deported prevent them from evacuating. While disaster scholars argue about the role of 'what', 'where', 'when', 'why' and 'for whom' in their disaster prevention strategies and responses, migration scholars mirror these concerns and show that ensuring access to services for mobile populations has become increasingly challenging for policy and practice. Various old and new forms of diversity, the complexity associated with increasing human mobility, cultural and linguistic diversity, and precarious legal statuses, all affect people's resilience to hazards and their ability to cope with disasters. Some features of superdiversity, such as the arrival of large numbers of small groups of migrants from diverse destinations, or fluid community membership, push public servants and practitioners into reconsidering their methods of service-provision, community engagement and city-level planning (Phillimore and Sigona 2020). Superdiversification poses a range of practical challenges that are applicable to migrants' needs in the context of disasters, in particular in relation to communication and the provision of information. In this piece, I reflect on how superdiversity complicates disaster responses under two themes.

One way of understanding attempts to improve disaster responses is through contemplating the role of the 'other'. Intra-ethnic differences and distinctions have been a driving factor in superdiversity enquiry (Vertovec

2007). However, 'othering' as a process is far from clear in societies shaped by new patterns of superdiversity, or those facing 'emergent diversifications', such as Japan. Emerging research on the role of superdiversity in shaping organizations, activities, human relationships and mentalities is helping to build more inclusive landscapes of disaster responses in which people can identify with a range of social locations and engage in meaningful public participation (Marlowe et al. 2018). To understand better the potential role of 'othering' in disaster responses, one needs to bear in mind different areas of critical engagement. Little effort has been made to explore often conflicting migrant identities and then to determine which one's voice carries the most weight in a specific disaster situation. Identities are sometimes challenged and re-examined in response to tragic events. For instance, the response to the 2017 Grenfell Tower fire represented a microcosm of London's superdiversity, and generated new forms of activism, belonging and place identity (Waine and Chapman 2022). Disasters can determine how we dispose of some of the negative connotations of difference that shape the life of local communities and effectively limit the potential for conflict. Further research is required into the social 'othering' that potentially shapes the efforts of disaster planners and responders – for instance, collecting critical evidence of the cross-racial use of intra-ethnic 'othering' (Rosbrook-Thompson and Armstrong 2022) to minimize disparities in government responses and improve service provision in superdiverse populations.

Another way of seeing contemporary challenges to disaster responses is through the (potentially changing) role of 'community-centred' or 'community-based' approaches. Looking at 'community' through a superdiversity lens points to the fluidity of the concept in its temporal and spatial dimensions. The idea of 'imagined communities' originates in Anderson's 1983 book *Imagined Communities* (Anderson 1991). Nations and communities engage in imagining simply because even members of the smallest nation cannot see or know all its other members. Similar notions occur during disasters, when a supporting community often extends across ethnic, national or religious divisions, including the transnational migrants' entrepreneurial response to the Covid-19 pandemic.

There are different ways in which superdiverse communities can go about dealing with complex challenges through exploring competing views, ideas and shaping their desired futures. The imagining and reimagining of what constitutes a 'community' in a disaster context has been shaped in recent years by a wide range of factors, particularly in the context of localized place-making. Exogenous factors that originate externally can include the nature of interaction with other communities (leading to potential rivalry, merging or fragmentation of two or more communities); and the level of support a community receives locally or from the outside, as well as the level of support it offers to others. Endogenous factors that originate internally can include cultural, historical or other roots of a community within the local area; the nature of identification with the local culture of the country of origin (or both) by its individual members; and increases or decreases in the number of community members within a relatively short period.

Based on the two themes mentioned above, superdiversity is already creating or going to create a complex social context for a range of disaster situations and therefore it is important to understand its impact on migrant as well as non-migrant populations. Generating a better understanding about disaster response under the conditions of superdiversity points to new realities that must be accommodated at different levels.

References

Anderson, B. (1991 [1983]) *Imagined communities: reflections on the origins and spread of nationalism*, Verso.

Brunsma, D., D. Overfelt, S. J. Picou (2010) *The sociology of Katrina: perspectives on a modern catastrophe*, Rowman & Littlefield.

Marlowe, J., A. Neef, C. R. Tevaga and C. Tevaga (2018) 'A new guiding framework for engaging diverse populations in disaster risk reduction: reach, relevance, receptiveness, and relationships', *International Journal of Disaster Risk Science*, 9: 507–18, doi: 10.1007/s13753-018-0193-6.

Phillimore, J., N. Sigona and K. Tonkiss (eds) (2020) *Superdiversity, policy and governance in Europe: multi-scalar perspectives*, Policy Press.

Rosbrook-Thompson, J. and G. Armstrong (2022) 'Respectability and boundary making on a superdiverse housing estate: the cross-racial deployment of intra-ethnic stereotypes', *British Journal of Sociology*, 73 (2): 259–72.

Vertovec, S. (2007) 'Super-diversity and its implications', *Ethnic and Racial Studies*, 30 (6): 1024–54.

Waine, H. and M. Chapman (2022) 'Place as social identity: an analysis of the spatial enactments of community loss and activism within the built environment surrounding Grenfell Tower', *Identities*, 29 (3): 263–81.

Gender and Forced Displacement: Ukrainian Women Refugees in Poland

Sandra Pertek

The war in Ukraine has led to an unprecedented number of forced displacements, primarily of women and children, with the men remaining to defend their country. Since the onset of war on 24 February 2022, an estimated seven million people have undergone difficult journeys to neighbouring countries to escape the violence in Ukraine. In addition, a further seven million remain displaced internally (IOM 2022), and thirteen million are unable to leave because of the security risks, the destruction of roads and a lack of information on where to seek safety (UNHCR 2023).

More than 5.8 million people from Ukraine have crossed into Poland, and of these 1,353,338 have already contacted the national protection scheme (UNHCR 2022). An urgent and comprehensive protection response is needed from Poland to accommodate the specific needs of refugees, and to help them settle into their new environment. Given that most Ukrainian refugees in Poland are women with children, gender sensitivity is essential to a humanitarian response. Local and context-specific terminologies are required to enhance protection and inclusion in response to the displacement emergency from Ukraine. Therefore, my aim here is to pinpoint the challenges associated with integrating gender sensitive approaches into Poland's responses to forced displacement. After outlining the key concepts of gender and forced migration, I shall show what a gender-sensitive response to refugees in Poland should look like, as well as make some policy recommendations.

Women in forced displacement

Women from different backgrounds experience conflict and migration differently, and face a range of different gender-specific vulnerabilities

(Freedman 2007). Since, as Freedman explains, these women are often primary caregivers with restricted access to economic resources, they may be restrained from fleeing, or be highly dependent on smugglers and traffickers. The experiences of displaced women seeking sanctuary 'are framed by overlapping identity markers such as gender, age, religion, and sexual orientation, and structures such as patriarchy, xenophobia, and homophobia' (Fiddian-Qasmiyeh 2014: 406). Many are subjected to violence not only during the conflict itself, but also along the migration routes and even in places of refuge (Pertek and Phillimore 2022). To enable practitioners and policymakers to employ a gender-sensitive lens in their responses to the forced displacements means paying attention to the changing gender roles of Ukrainian women, as well as to their access to resources.

It also means identifying the specific needs of women based on an analysis of their multiple, diverse and intersecting identities, and the social expectations associated with being a woman. However, as Crenshaw (1991) reminds us through evoking intersectionality theory, gender never comes on its own but intersects with race, age, ability, ethnicity, religion and other characteristics that shape people's life experiences. For example, older women have unique accommodation needs, women with disabilities require additional support to access services, women of working age require childcare to access work, while adolescent girls need adequate learning opportunities. An intersectional perspective enables us to undertake a whole-person approach to understanding the effects of war and displacement on women of different social groups in order to support their specific needs and those of the most vulnerable groups.

Gender sensitivity and refugee response in Poland

While the Polish people showed great solidarity with the Ukrainians arriving in their country, and the Polish government opened its borders to the neighbouring state, there was a notable absence of gender-sensitive measures with which to address the specific needs of refugee women of different ages, ethnicities and abilities. For multiple reasons, promoting gender sensitivity presents its own challenges. First, this is the first major humanitarian emergency that Poland has faced without preliminary planning and preparedness since the Second World War. The large scale of the crisis has clearly stretched the capacities of the existing public systems and services, whose response to the humanitarian needs of the new arrivals has, to say the least, been rather chaotic and ad hoc. Second, since structural inequalities and power hierarchies shape the way in which aid is distributed, the more vulnerable groups, which are harder to reach and/or more at risk of abuse, are often excluded. The volunteer-run grassroots initiatives usually lack coordination and adequate safeguards and this exposes the refugees to numerous protection concerns. To mitigate such risks and to ensure that the specific needs of women and other vulnerable groups are met, gender sensitivity should be mainstreamed across the sectors, and at the local and national levels of welfare and humanitarian delivery.

In response to the escalating crisis, numerous international organizations and INGOs initiated emergency operations in Poland. Naturally, they brought with them a range of humanitarian standards and terminologies, including the gender jargon typically used to integrate gender sensitivities into emergency responses. Yet, gender, as a term, is rather uneasily transferable to the Polish language. As a social construct and in terms of its relevance to designing and implementing emergency responses, the concept of gender needs to be better understood by the local and national organizations and authorities that support refugees. To promote gender and refugee sensitivity in the Polish context, I shall now consider the value of integrating the protection and inclusion of refugees into the displacement response.

Making it work: integrating protection and inclusion in refugee response

What would a gender-sensitive response look like in Poland? What would it mean for Poland to address the needs of Ukrainian women in a gender sensitive way?

First, gender sensitivity in the context of a feminized displacement emergency would mean raising awareness of how war, flight and displacement affect Ukrainian women from different social backgrounds differently. This means taking their pre-war socio-economic conditions into consideration when attending to their varying needs and vulnerabilities.

Second, service providers and policy makers should be trained to identify the different needs of refugee women of different ages and abilities in their services, policies and programmes. For example, as in many other displacement crises, the disruption in Ukraine has led to changing intra-household dynamics, family relations and structures. This often thrusts on women the sole responsibility to provide for their children, mothers, mothers-in-law and other relatives during the journey and in the places of refuge. The added economic strain that this brings increases the risk of exploitation for the survival of their families. In turn, public initiatives should mitigate the particular vulnerabilities to which women from single households are exposed.

Third, given the stigma and limited understanding of what 'gender integration' means in a displacement emergency, a gender-sensitive response in Poland would mean adapting relevant terminologies and tools to a local context and language and developing relevant capacities. Local communities and authorities should be made aware of the concepts and principles behind gender sensitivity.

The use of protective, inclusive and gender-sensitive language could help obviate a potential attitudinal 'gender' backlash at an individual and societal level, for such backlashes are frequently driven by multiple systems of oppression, including heteropatriarchy, sexism, racism and xenophobia. An anti-feminist backlash, in particular, could threaten the security of Ukrainian women and other forced migrants of various backgrounds staying in Poland.

The needs of and disparities between different genders, ages, abilities and racial groups are inadequately considered. For example, refugees of various racial backgrounds trying to cross the eastern Poland–Belarus border to seek refuge are subjected to gender insensitive and anti-migrant rhetoric and policies. Inclusive protection programmes with adapted assistance are needed to ensure a people-centred refugee response and to build on the capacities of the marginalized people regardless of their nationality.

Promoting protection and inclusion in humanitarian emergencies goes beyond ensuring dignity, access, participation and safety for all those affected by the crisis. It also means accounting for the unique gender roles, access to resources and short- and long-term gender needs of refugees. For instance, a gender, protection and inclusion lens calls for interventions to ensure that all Ukrainian women have good enough access to decent work, sufficient aid, safe housing, health services, education and welfare to be able to settle in host communities and protect themselves from the risks of exploitation. While voluntary grassroots and bottom-up initiatives have frequently filled important gaps in aid provision, further systemic solutions are needed across sectors to enable refugees to move to other cities where they may be more likely to meet their basic needs, including sustainable housing, work and integration.

Moreover, a recent SEREDA CEE study showed that Ukrainian women in the new Polish contexts are exposed to various risks as they navigate new environments while rebuilding their lives under the impact of traumatizing memories of war (Pertek et al. 2022). With language barriers and limited awareness of rights and where to access support, refugees remain vulnerable to increased gender-based violence and exploitation. Those who are still unregistered or without important documentation are especially vulnerable. For example, women billeted with private hosts are at an increased risk of mistreatment and sexual exploitation if they are unable to pay increased rents due to unemployment and/or lack of childcare. A gender-sensitive refugee response thus must also minimize economic vulnerability and dependency by securing safe housing, work and legal support and awareness raising about risks of abuse at different levels and across sectors. For instance, reception points need to be sensitized about the risks of refugee exploitation by 'pseudo volunteers' offering assistance.

Way forward

Although a gender backlash in a humanitarian setting is counterproductive and detrimental to the well-being of refugee women, it can be avoided with appropriate adaptations and capacity building, and with a sensitive use of gender terminologies.

References

Crenshaw, K. (1991) 'Mapping the margins: intersectionality, identity politics, and violence against women of color', *Stanford Law Review*, 43 (6): 1241–99, doi: 10.2307/1229039.

Fiddian-Qasmiyeh, E. (2014) 'Gender and forced migration', in E. Fiddian-Qasmiyeh, G. Loescher, K. Long and N. Sigona (eds) *The Oxford handbook of refugee and forced migration studies*, Oxford University Press, doi: 10.1093/oxfordhb/9780199652433.001.0001.

Freedman, J. (2007) *Gendering the international asylum and refugee debate*, Palgrave Macmillan.

IOM (2022) *Ukraine internal displacement report: general population survey: round 10 (27 October 2022)*, available at: https://displacement.iom.int/reports/ukraine-internal-displacement-report-general-population-survey-round-10-17-27-october-2022.

Pertek, S., I. Kuznetsova and M. Kot (2022) '"Not a single safe place": the Ukrainian refugees at risk: violence, trafficking and exploitation: findings from Poland and Ukraine', research report, University of Birmingham. Available at: https://www.birmingham.ac.uk/Documents/college-social-sciences/social-policy/iris/2022/sereda-cee.pdf.

Pertek, S. and J. Phillimore (2022) '"Nobody helped me": forced migration and sexual and gender-based violence: findings from the SEREDA project', research report, University of Birmingham.

UNHCR (2022) 'Ukraine refugee situation', web resource, available at: https://data.unhcr.org/en/situations/ukraine.

UNHCR (2023) 'Internally displaced persons (IDP) – UNHCR Ukraine', available at: https://www.unhcr.org/ua/en/internally-displaced-persons.

Internal Displacement in Nigeria: Evidence from Lagos and Abuja

Jamila Wakawa Zanna, Samuel Adejoh
and Surindar Dhesi

Despite populist Western discourses about the so-called 'refugee crisis', most of the world's refugees are internally displaced people (IDPs) who have fled from their homes to other parts of their own country to escape from wars, violence or climate change. In 2021, there were an estimated 53.2 million internally displaced people (IDPs) in the world (IDMC 2022a) as opposed 27.1 million refugees living outside the borders of their own countries (UNHCR 2022). Some 37.1 per cent of IDPs are in sub-Saharan Africa, where 14.1 million people have been forced to flee from their homes. In Nigeria alone, the Boko Haram insurgency, non-state armed groups, as well as criminal and communal violence have led to mass population displacements, which, by December 2021, had resulted in 3.2 million officially-registered IDPs (IDMC 2022b), most of whom were enduring substandard conditions, such as insufficient food, inadequate access to healthcare facilities and unsatisfactory housing. This figure reflects the largest population of IDPs in Africa and a record high for the country. However, the data only cover those who live in refugee camps; there is little known about the numbers living in urban areas, or about the stressors in their everyday lives.

Our focus is on the well-being and environmental conditions of IDPs living in two urban areas of Nigeria – Ibeju Lekki in Lagos State, where people displaced from the Chibok region currently live in informal settlements; and Abuja, where displaced women are living in informal camps. Both studies are based on semi-structured interviews – 32 in Lagos in 2020 (Adejoh et al. 2022) and 34 in Abuja in 2022. Our findings revealed that IDPs living in Lagos and those who live in camps in Abuja face many challenges accessing shelter, food, employment, formal education for their children and affordable healthcare.

Living conditions

Many of the displaced people we interviewed actively decided to find their own place within local communities, such as in the Ibeju Lekki district of Lagos, instead of moving to an IDP camp. Several factors influenced their decision: first, the participants said they wanted their children to have a sense of belonging to a family and a home (even temporary) and to live a 'normal' life; second, some reported safety concerns associated with camps; others mentioned expectations of support; and finally, life in a city was considered to provide more opportunities for work. In the case of Abuja, some IDPs hoped that the location would facilitate support from the government. As one of the participants (P., a female in Abuja) said, 'we came here thinking that there will be more support, since it is the seat of government, and in the hope that our situation would be better.' However, for many, these expectations were not met. IDPs mostly cope through the support their own social networks and opportunities to work. As L (a female in Abuja) put it: 'government has neglected us as migrants. No job opportunities, no education for children and no food support. Those of us that didn't migrate have better lives than us.'

We identified the serious impact of adverse living conditions and lack of resources on the IDPs' well-being. Their temporary accommodation often lacks safe cooking facilities, the waste management of their toilets is poor and there is overcrowding (see Figure 1). The situation is exacerbated in urban camps and elsewhere because of the lack of affordable and safe electricity. One of the research participants, M, a young female in Abuja, noted that 'even if we rent the house (communal living), they refuse us access to the toilets. They assume we will transmit infections and diseases by using it so there is stigmatization.' IDI, a male in Lagos, said that 'here I'm living in one room and we are living with a multitude of people in the same house. There must be a challenge. I feel it somehow.'

The barriers IDPs face in obtaining energy, clean water, adequate shelter and sanitation, which combine to make their living conditions injurious to their health, exacerbate their problems. For example, a lack of electricity forces them to cook on open fires, which increases air pollution and that, in turn, leads to respiratory diseases among vulnerable groups. In addition, the use of naked flames in overcrowded and poorly constructed shelters increases the risk of fire (see Figure 2). O, a female in Abuja, said 'we use firewood to cook. We gather wood from the forest and cook with it. ... There is a lot of smoke but there is nothing we can do about that.'

Figure 1: Bathing and toilet facilities in Abuja's New Kuchigoro IDP settlement

K, a female in Abuja, said:

> I fear electrocution from the electricity pole and wires that cross over our veranda. On several occasions, the wires (electric cables) will drop to floor. One time, we were on the veranda having a chat with my neighbour and the wire dropped on her. We were only lucky that day because it wasn't our shift to get electricity.

Figure 2: showing open fire used for cooking in close proximity to homes and flammable materials in Abuja

Women in protracted displacement

Although Nigeria is a multi-ethnic and multicultural country, regardless of their status, to varying degrees women share specific experiences, for example, patriarchal practices like being limited to domestic roles, or being economically dependent on men. These factors are worse in displacement situations and have an impact on the women's socio-economic development. In addition, displacement affects women, men, girls, and boys in different and gendered ways (Ajayi 2020; Lennard 2016).

Safety is a significant concern and because of the perceived dangers within and around their informal settlements – drug abuse, prostitution and illicit activities have been reported on various sites – it is deterring IDPs from seeking work. In addition, the women we interviewed felt afraid that their children would be influenced by the culture and norms of the city, which differed from those in their home areas. Burglaries and cases of gender-based violence in the settlements have been reported by some of our interviewees. For example, I, a male in Lagos said:

> I see many things about this community, if you continue to live here, it will not favour you. ... So, there are challenges. This community is not the good that you want to remain. Anything that happens, they will begin to molest you. They will say that he is a Hausa man. But I am not a Hausa man ... I am from Chibok. ... So, any small thing, they want to fight; they want to cause problem. And if you make any move ... the community will fall on you. We are facing challenges with them here.

Our research revealed that IDPs often move in search of accessible energy sources, which includes men travelling far from their families to find work, thus increasing the women's vulnerability. Furthermore, frequent movements rupture social networks and create additional barriers to the children's education.

Most of the women IDPs we interviewed had little formal education. Before their displacement, many of them had worked on farms with their families, and it is difficult to navigate a complex informal economy without social networks and local knowledge. Their marginalization exacerbates their already alien situation, which is then further worsened by daily stressors such as lacking basic needs and poor environmental health conditions (Simpson 2018). The paucity of employment opportunities, loss of the social networks that would otherwise provide childcare, and difficulties in enrolling and keeping their children at school, coupled with a lack of safety on the streets, meant that many IDP women spend much of their time at home. As R, a young woman in Abuja, pointed out:

> I did not look for a job. You know if you do not have education, it is not necessary that someone will employ you. Everything is with knowledge. Also, I have small children and I will not be able to leave them to go to work, because there is no one to take care of them. ... To get a job, you must know somebody. And, who do I know?

Finally, our research highlights the unequal responsibility for care carried out by displaced women, compared with their male counterparts, for with the limited resources at their disposal, they take full responsibility for looking after children and the elderly. This burden, along with name calling and 'labelling', has aggravated their feelings of marginalization and exacerbated relations with the host communities, thus adding to their feelings of not belonging. As M, a woman in Abuja, put it, 'we are faced with the most challenges, women must cater for the children if the husbands cannot find something for the day. The women are left to fend for themselves.'

Conclusion

We have found that IDPs living in urban areas, both in camps and informal settlements, face living conditions that present a significant risk to their physical and mental health. Support is patchy and ad hoc, so vulnerable communities, particularly women, are exposed to serious hazards on an everyday basis. Further support is needed for IDPs to escape the hardship we have documented. There is a need for government, and humanitarian and development partners, to include the voices of all IDPs in their strategic plans for drafting environmental health policies and monitoring and implementing various initiatives. For the effective and sustainable delivery of services to alleviate the soaring human suffering and restore the lives and dignity of the displaced, it is essential for these actors to coordinate their efforts. Without timely and appropriate assistance both at local and national levels and in policy and practice there seems little hope of a brighter future for the children of IDPs in Lagos and Abuja.

Acknowledgements

The research in Lagos has been supported by the Academy of Medical Sciences GCRF networking grant, project 'Mental Health and Well-Being of forced displaced persons in African cities' led by Irina Kuznetsova. The research in Abuja was funded by the Petroleum Technology Development Fund Nigeria (Jamila Zanna).

References

Adejoh, S. O., I. Kuznetsova and S. Dhesi (2022) 'Internally displaced people in Lagos: environmental health conditions and access to healthcare in the context of COVID-19', *Critical Public Health*, 32 (5): 759–64, doi: 10.1080/09581 596.2022.2096427.

Ajayi, T. F. (2020) 'Women, internal displacement, and the Boko Haram conflict: broadening the debate', *African Security*, 13 (2): 171–194, doi: 10.1080/ 19392206.2020.1731110.

IDMC (2022a) *Global report on internal displacement 2022: children and youth in internal displacement*, Internal Displacement Monitoring Centre, available at: https://www.internal-displacement.org/sites/default/files/publications/docu ments/IDMC_GRID_2022_LR.pdf.

IDMC (2022b) 'Nigeria: country profile', webpage, available at: www.internal-displacement.org/countries/nigeria.

Lennard, J. (ed.) (2016) *Global report on internal displacement*, Internal Displacement Monitoring Centre.

Simpson, R. (2018) 'Peace education and psychosocial support for social cohesion, *Forced Migration Review*, (57): 38–9, available at: www.fmreview.org/ syria2018/simpson-r.

UNHCR (2022) *Global trends: forced displacement in 2021*, United Nations High Commissioner for Refugees, available at: https://www.unhcr.org/62a9d1494/ global-trends-report-2021.

Futures Denied: Temporalities of Citizenship and the Naturalization of Syrians in Turkey

Paladia Ziss

What citizenship *is* has been hotly debated – is it membership in a political community, a legal status, the performance of rights claims and belonging, a tool of power that naturalizes the violence of borders, or all of the above (Bloemraad and Sheares 2017)? There is general agreement, though, on what citizenship is *not* – it is not a guarantee to rights and resources granted by states. For example, legal citizens are often racialized or ethnic minorities denied full rights, while non-citizens like migrants, or wealthy residents, may make claims to membership and belonging without demanding legal status.

Citizenship is, therefore, always a site of struggle, one aspect of which is related to time: Who is in or who is out, and what rights people have, is often shaped by implicit imaginations of an eternal past of a bounded and unchanging nation (Bhabha 1994), or by imperial and colonial histories (Isin 2017). Citizenship is also about struggles of who will or will not be part of a political community in the future. A state may promise legal citizenship to individuals who invest and are considered useful for the future. By contrast, marginalized and irregularized people may be kept docile through promises of a better life that may never be achieved with or without legal status (McNevin 2020).

In this piece, I want to zoom in on an example of how these promises and future orientations may play out in practice – the recent naturalization of a small number of Syrian refugees in Turkey. Drawing on parts of my PhD research I outline how Syrians who have been naturalized experience this process in both positive and negative ways. I argue that citizenship holds a promise of a better life in the future but creates other forms of exclusion and discrimination in the present, including closing down specific future pathways and potentialities that comes along with being a refugee in Turkey.

Naturalization of Syrian refugees in Turkey

In Turkey, struggles over citizenship are closely intertwined with contested imaginations of the Turkish nation. Simply put, for much of the twentieth century the Kemalist and militarist state actively worked to produce masculine, 'Western-oriented', ethnically Turkish, and Sunni Muslim citizens, notions that women, Kurds and religious minorities have long contested. Under the authoritarian governance of President Erdoğan, the state is promoting pan-Islamist understandings of Turkish citizenship that are no less exclusionary (Yilmaz 2021). Who can become a Turkish citizen and who has access to rights and state resources is shaped by these different meanings and contestations.

The almost four million Syrian refugees in Turkey who have fled from the civil war in Syria since 2011 are caught in a crossfire of struggles over rights, resources and belonging. Most Syrian refugees are registered with a temporary protection (TP) card, which provides them with a one-year, renewable residency and some access to education and healthcare, but restricts their mobility and legal employment, and offers no regular pathway to permanent residence or citizenship. Yet, following a decision by President Erdoğan in 2016, about 200,000 Syrians have been granted discretionary citizenship. This was based on a vague idea of who could 'contribute to Turkey', for example as teachers or engineers. In practice, Syrians under TP were invited via SMS to submit an application to the Directorate for Migration Management. Then, after an indeterminate wait and security checks, some receive a Turkish ID card (*kimlik*) while others are rejected for unknown reasons. The whole issue of citizenship for Syrians is highly controversial and most non-Syrian citizens of Turkey seem to be against granting citizenship to Syrians (Akçapar and Şimşek 2018). How did Syrians who had become naturalized citizens of Turkey view the benefits and pitfalls of getting Turkish citizenship?

Promise No 1: citizenship as mobility in the state territory

TP-registered Syrians are required to live in their province of registration. If they want to leave it, they have to get a travel permit, which is often denied.

More problematically, most work can be found in urban provinces, such as Istanbul and Izmir, which have stopped registering any Syrians at all. This leaves those in search of a livelihood irregularized and vulnerable to being rounded up and deported, either to the province of their registration or, arbitrarily, back to war-torn Syria.

For my interlocutors, getting citizenship enabled them to move freely between provinces and, if they had the money, even to take holidays abroad. They felt safer since becoming Turkish citizens because they were less exposed to the threat of deportation, to which most other Syrians were exposed. However, just as citizenship promised freedom of movement for them as individuals, they became more aware of the injustices that other Syrians faced. For example, Adam told me that when he got Turkish citizenship he wanted to bring his family to live with him, but because they were Syrians with a TP identity card, he could not. He said:

> The citizenship ID is just a piece of plastic. You are from Germany, if you have citizenship there, you can bring your family to live with you. ... Here in Turkey, my family lives in [another province], I can't even bring my family to live with me in *the same country*.

Citizenship created a vision of a future in which safe freedom of movement was possible. However, it also closed off the possibility of sharing this freedom with one's loved ones, making it impossible to meet and *live with* family beyond intermittent visits. Making a future with one's family was a promise that citizenship created, but not one that was kept.

Promise No 2: citizenship as access to material resources

In welfare states, citizenship often promises better access to resources and social rights, at least compared with non-citizens. The Syrians with Turkish citizenship in my study recognized the material benefits of getting citizenship, but also saw disadvantages. Since those with a TP identity card can generally only work irregularly in Turkey, once they became citizens, well-qualified Syrians were able to access better jobs. Some also appreciated the access it gave them to social insurance, unemployment benefits, healthcare and pensions. However, these material benefits were limited to higher-class Syrians. Lower-class Syrians reported *becoming poorer* after receiving Turkish citizenship. For example, Ghazal and her family used to live in the east of Turkey and supplemented the family's income with the *kızılaykart*, a humanitarian cash card issued by the Turkish Red Crescent, from which they could pay rent and utility bills. When they were invited to apply for Turkish citizenship, they accepted, for they wanted to benefit from the economic opportunities of legally living and working in Istanbul. However, she and her husband were unable to find well-paid formal employment. As Turkish citizens, they also lost their right to cash assistance. As a result, Ghazal's son, who was 16 at the time, had to drop out of school and start working informally to plug the gap in the family's budget. Thus, while Turkish citizenship promised better material conditions through some welfare provisions, this promise was unequally kept, for it coincided with a dire economic situation in Turkey.

Promise No 3: citizenship as future belonging to society

Several people told me that they had hoped that being fully-fledged legal members of the Turkish state would bring them a better future. Judy, for example, a teacher and former accountant, had hoped that naturalization 'would change my life' and end workplace discrimination. However, this promise failed to materialize. Syrians with Turkish citizenship continued to face discrimination, both *as Syrians* and *as Syrians who were now Turkish*. Officials, house owners or employers would identify their Syrian origin via their names, place of birth, or appearance. Once identified as 'Syrian', most told me they were unable to get the jobs or flats for which they had applied. For example, Tania, who had been born in Damascus, was having difficulty registering with an electricity provider when the clerk in charge told her that 'you will never be one of us'. This feeling of being excluded despite formally being part of the citizenry created a severe sense of helplessness. As Tania said: 'I'm stuck'. I was told that other Syrians with TP identities could at least try to leave Turkey to seek asylum elsewhere through resettlement and irregular migration. While Turkish citizenship offered the possibility of permanently remaining in Turkey, this permanence was not self-chosen and created a sense of enforced immobility.

Conclusion

Syrians who became naturalized citizens of Turkey saw some advantages in terms of mobility and material benefits compared with the poverty, insecure legal status, and risk of deportation threatening their Syrian counterparts with a TP identity. However, citizenship was also perceived as a promise for a better future that had not, or not yet, materialized. As Hepworth (2014: 116) argued, 'the experience of (non-)citizenship in the present is modulated by the potential inclusion in the political community or eventual removal from that territory.' What my respondents experienced as injustices and discrimination in everyday life *as Syrians*, whether citizens of Turkey or not, took place within a politically contested terrain over what this potential inclusion in the political community of Turkey meant. In the context of Erdoğan's Islamist authoritarianism, economic crisis, and deep political divisions, the Syrian citizens of Turkey felt that, however uncertain the country's future, there was no future for them there either.

References

Akçapar, S. K. and D. Şimşek (2018) 'The politics of Syrian refugees in Turkey: a question of inclusion and exclusion through citizenship', *Social Inclusion*, 6 (1): 176–87, doi: 10.17645/si.v6i1.1323.

Bhabha, H. K. (1994) 'DissemiNation: time, narrative and the margins of the modern nation', in H. K. Bhabha, *The Location of Culture*, Routledge, 199–244.

Bloemraad, I. and A. Sheares (2017) 'Understanding membership in a world of global migration: (how) does citizenship matter?', *International Migration Review*, 51 (4): 823–67, doi: 10.1111/imre.12354.

Hepworth, K. (2014) 'Topologies of citizenship', in E. Isin and P. Nyers (eds) *Routledge handbook of global citizenship studies*, Routledge, 110–18, doi: 10.4324/9780203102015.

Isin, E. (2017) 'Citizenship studies and the Middle East', in R. Meijer and N. Butenschøn (eds) *The crisis of citizenship in the Arab world*, Brill, 511–34, doi: 10.1163/9789004340985_021.

McNevin, A. (2020) 'Time and the figure of the citizen', *International Journal of Politics, Culture, and Society*, 33 (4): 545–59, doi: 10.1007/s10767-020-09358-4.

Yilmaz, I. (2021) *Creating the desired citizen: ideology, state and Islam in Turkey*, Cambridge University Press, doi: 10.1017/9781108961295.

Community Involvement in Refugee Resettlement: Sharing Social Capital

Natasha Nicholls

Community sponsorship (CS) enables groups of volunteers to provide resettlement support to a refugee family within the local community. Groups agree with the Home Office that they will provide accommodation for one year and resettlement support for two. Initially conceived to welcome those affected by the Syrian crisis, the scheme has since been extended to include refugees from other conflicts. Prior to gaining approval from the Home Office, groups must secure family accommodation, raise £9000 and provide a full resettlement plan. Since its inception in 2016, almost a thousand refugees have been resettled by groups around the UK (RESET 2022).

In this short piece, I explore the relationships formed between volunteers and refugees over a two-year period. Putnam's theory of social capital is used to explain how the social networks of CS volunteers provide families with resources to aid their resettlement in the UK. Provided that Home Office guidelines are met, groups are able to shape how their support is offered. Volunteers are generous with their time and resources and, in many cases, strong relationships are formed between families and volunteers. However, the social capital shared with families inevitably varies, as groups have different networks from which to draw support.

Social capital derives from social connections and networks (Putnam 2002), which play a vital role in helping refugees access essential resources (Cheung and Phillimore 2014). Describing his theory of social capital, Putnam (2002) differentiated between three different types – bonding, bridging, and linking. Bonding takes place between similar social groups, while bridging refers to connections made between different groups. Linking takes place outside social networks, often with a formal institution such as a government body. Being rooted in a local community, building relationships and sharing social capital is essential to the success of CS. As one volunteer (Kathleen) explained:

> I think the beauty of community sponsorship is that the people supporting that programme are all doing it because they want to do it. And the people are at the core of that ... and I think having that gives them extra strength, community-based support. Because, you know, you cannot plonk somebody somewhere and expect them to get on with it.

Over the two-year resettlement period, many volunteers develop close relationships with the family, describing them as friends or extended members of their own family. Groups are expected to provide accommodation, English language support and assistance with finding school places and healthcare. However, many volunteers provide considerably more social, financial and practical support. For example, housing costs should be covered by the universal credit received by the family, but some groups augment this support by using group finances to contribute to the family's rent. Other volunteers provide regular childcare, help families to go on holiday, or offer financial support for driving lessons and career development. One volunteer even bubbled with a family during the second Covid lockdown to provide support because they had recently welcomed a new baby.

Volunteers provide bridging social capital to the families. They are often well-known in their community and have volunteered previously. Many have links with other organizations locally and make use of their connections to offer help to their sponsored family. In some cases, links between volunteers and their wider community initially helped groups to find a house. For some family members, being introduced to the wider social network of volunteers helped them find volunteering opportunities and paid employment.

Existing social connections between volunteers and others in the local community have also been useful for raising additional financial support. One volunteer explained how the chair of her group would request extra support from his friends if their group required more finance. There are also examples of community members outside the group offering support once they become aware of a family's arrival. In one group, an individual local to the area took weekly Arabic lessons so that he could converse with the family and then took them on regular days out to show them the local area. In another group, the friend of a volunteer was able to provide a family member with a musical instrument and free lessons.

CS volunteers also provide linking social capital by supporting families to contact the local council, Home Office, or local MPs. Volunteers offer practical ways to link families with additional support, such as accompanying them to their appointments with the job centre, healthcare providers or solicitors. Many families left behind members of their extended family when they were resettled in the UK and at least one volunteer spent considerable time petitioning the local MP and immigration minister about the possibility of family reunion, even after the two-year period of formal resettlement support had ended.

CS enables and empowers volunteers to share their social capital with refugee families, to locate social and economic opportunities and to link them to institutions that can offer further support. Volunteers from communities with large social networks, such as religious institutions, generally have few problems raising funds to support a family, doing so through donations or other fundraising activities. However, some volunteers, often within the same geographical area, felt pressured to provide the same high level of support that other groups were able to offer. One urban volunteer complained about struggling to support a CS family given the high rents in the city compared with those in a nearby rural area. She compared her groups experience with another urban group, whose CS family benefitted from reduced rent because their landlord was a friend of the group. In some cases, the same was true of employment opportunities. Another volunteer explained how her group was able to support the father of the family with finding a job, because one of the group's volunteers had links with a local building company. In a contrasting experience, another volunteer was frustrated that her rural group struggled to help the father of the family find employment, because they lacked the social links to help him find work locally within his area of experience.

Sponsoring refugees, whether privately or communally, is gaining traction globally as a viable solution to the refugee crisis. Social relationships are key to CS and the scheme enables volunteers to share their social capital with a refugee family. By providing bridging links within their own networks, volunteers can help families find paid or voluntary work, as well as opportunities to form social relationships. However, not all CS experiences are equal. In some cases, despite the group's best intentions, volunteers can struggle to help families to access employment and long-term housing. In situations where groups have exhausted their own support networks, further help, particularly regarding employment and accommodation, would arguably require more support from the government or local council in order to ensure the longevity of the scheme.

References

Cheung, S. Y. and J. Phillimore (2014) 'Refugees, social capital, and labour market integration in the UK', *Sociology*, 48 (3): 518–36.

RESET (2022) 'Community sponsorship: end of year review', available at: https://resetuk.org/news-and-campaigns/news/community-sponsorship-end-of-year-review.

Putnam, R. (ed.) (2002) *Democracies in flux: the evolution of social capital in contemporary society*, Oxford University Press.

Patchwork Community Sponsorship Scheme: Challenges and Innovations during the Pandemic

Marisol Reyes

Note: Patches were curated with images from Annie Spratt available on the free royalty images website Unsplash: https://unsplash.com/s/photos/patchwork; https://unsplash.com/photos/kDT-gRJanKw.

The community sponsorship scheme (CSS) was introduced to the UK in July 2016 to enable community groups to support the resettlement of refugee families. The community sponsorship approach relies heavily on the provision of face-to-face support to enable refugees to settle, thrive and integrate in the UK. Such support is provided by volunteers, most of whom are retired or semi-retired and aged over fifty. With the advent of the pandemic and the introduction of social distancing and lockdown measures in March 2020, community sponsorship groups were challenged to offer support to refugees in new ways, with some volunteers and refugees needing to shield and many services moving to remote provision.

Having previously undertaken an independent evaluation of the UK's community sponsorship scheme and identified the importance of the intensive support offered in person by volunteers to refugees, our research team led by Professor Jenny Phillimore identified a knowledge gap in the strategies adopted to meet refugee needs under pandemic conditions. To fill this gap, we undertook a series of interviews between January and March 2021 to explore the experience of CSS volunteers during that time.

My role in the study was to reach out to the volunteers welcoming a newly-arrived family, explore the challenges they faced, and see how they addressed them. When I interviewed these people it felt as if I were stitching together a big quilt of stories with differently shaped fabrics. A patchwork involves sewing pieces of fabric together to create a larger design, so I made an electronic patchwork of brief quotes reflecting the powerful testimonies of the volunteers' experiences of supporting newly-arrived refugees. I was particularly impressed by how the volunteers devised new ways of support-ing, such as implementing virtual forms of communication to keep group members in touch with the families they were sponsoring. The shift to digital methods meant that some volunteers had to acquire new skills, and this also helped the refugees cross the digital divide.

The lengthy pandemic restrictions had an impact on both wellbeing and integration. Participants identified increased levels of isolation, distress and anxiety in several refugee families. To ameliorate the hardships of lockdown and mental health problems, the volunteers organized creative activities, encouraged their charges to try new hobbies, organized online social events, and invited the refugees to take part in outdoor walks.

I hope that this patchwork evokes the rich array of narrative possibilities emerging from the UK community sponsorship scheme.

Meeting Refugee Entrepreneurs

Monder Ram

As an academic with a keen interest in migration and enterprise, I was keen to learn more about the Somali community in Leicester, where I worked between 1999 and 2013. Accompanied by an interpreter, I visited a Somali grocer in the St Matthews area of Leicester. Leicester was proving a popular destination for Somalis in the 2000s – we were interested in refugees who had arrived directly to the UK or having first acquired citizenship elsewhere (often in the Netherlands or Scandinavia). Many settled in the St Matthews area and started businesses. Customers were popping in and out as we entered the rather unexceptional grocery store to conduct our study's first interview in the summer of 2006.

The owner beckoned us over and suggested we talk upstairs. As we ascended the stairs, I noticed five or six men chatting away in an adjacent room. I learned a lot during the interview, particularly about the creative ways family and friends pulled together to get the business going, and how they managed amid the toxic discourse on migration engulfing the UK at that time. When the interview came to an end, I asked, 'who are the men in the other room?' 'They are local people from the community' came the reply. 'Why are they here?' I enquired. 'They come here because they have got nowhere else to go. Here is where they come to be together, to find about local schools, doctors, jobs.'

Returning to the office, I wondered how this business would fare against the prevailing enterprise policy (and academic) orthodoxy at the time, which eulogized 'growth' firms, identifying these elusive ill-defined entities as the key to job creation and economic development. This innocuous little store would surely have been erased from the prevailing preoccupations of local policy-makers intent on supporting 'growth' firms. With this erasure would come the neglect of such businesses as a resource for building social capital for individuals detached from other networks; and the elision of the prosaic yet profound ways in which the store fulfilled an

210

important role neglected by formal institutions and state agencies – namely building community, promoting social inclusion and facilitating integration. My colleagues and I (Jones et al. 2019; Ram et al. 2022a; Villares-Varela 2022), and others (Hall 2021), have documented the much-overlooked contribution that this kind of business makes to the economy and social wellbeing. The pandemic brought this to the fore as local shop-keepers provided a lifeline for many marginalized communities.

The Iraqi shopkeeper we interviewed for a study a few years later in the 'superdiverse' area of Sparkhill, Birmingham, tells a different story, this time about how a business started out of desperation can grow into a thriving concern. He had fled the Saddam Hussein regime, but not before acquiring a PhD in chemical engineering and a prestigious job in industry. Like so many well-qualified migrants we have studied (Jones et al. 2019; Ram et al. 2022a), he was locked out of the labour market through discrimination.

He set up a wholesale food business that grew quickly to employ twenty people from the local community. What is interesting about it – again not an isolated case – is the innovative way in which the entrepreneur spotted an opportunity to develop a new market, focusing on specialist foods, which was not being catered for. By drawing on his diasporic links in the Middle East, he had set up a local firm that relied on ties from elsewhere in the world to create a new way of doing business. This transnationalism, this international agility, is a specific feature of migrant businesses, and it marks them out from other firms.

The policy community ignored our internationally-connected migrant entrepreneur, as it did his St Matthews' counterpart and many others. The continued absence of such stories in contemporary discourses on enterprise policy is particularly baffling given the grandiose statements about 'global Britain', frenzied attempts to make new trade deals, and inducements to entrepreneurs to pursue the path of international trade.

The importance of these meetings with migrant entrepreneurs in many of our streets in the Midlands was brought to the fore in a recently published study I undertook with several of my colleagues at the Centre for Research in Ethnic Minority Entrepreneurship (CREME) (Ram et al. 2022a). A rare example of longitudinal research involving 34 owners of refugee businesses interviewed in 2010, and again in 2018, showed considerable variations in the performances of these firms, with many not only surviving but also achieving quite dramatic growth. Our findings complicate the blinkered views of those who do not fully recognize or appreciate the contribution of refugee businesses to many parts of the UK.

The capacity of refugee entrepreneurs to withstand the cumulative impact of austerity, Brexit and a toxic media discourse is noteworthy. Starting their ventures with meagre resources, few contacts and little or no business support, these refugees have made their way by combining their entrepreneurial skills with sheer tenacity. Their performance is even more impressive given that most of them started up as small retail operations in migrant-dominated areas characterized by considerable deprivation.

A minority of firms claimed to be struggling and had not progressed beyond the difficult trading position they reported in 2010. They survived by working inordinately long hours and by drawing on the (often unpaid) support of family and friends. In sharp contrast, we found a handful of businesses with multi-site outlets, turning over millions of pounds and growing vigorously. These ambitious entrepreneurs hold significant financial capital, use inventive marketing strategies, and draw on community labour to meet fluctuating consumer demand. Surprisingly, many used external expertise and business support intermediaries to help them expand.

For the majority, growth of a more modest kind was a more common experience, with its magnitude and form varying from firm to firm according to the mix of entrepreneurial skills, market niche, and access to resources (notably, financial capital). A common development strategy was to add on new and sometimes surprising activities to the core business. An entrepreneur we interviewed in 2010 had started as a grocer, but then added a hairdressing salon and coffee shop to his premises in response to the demand from his local community. This kind of 'patchworking' or 'bricolage' approach to survival and developing an enterprise was common, and a phenomenon we noted in an earlier study of newly-arrived migrants (Villares-Varela et al. 2018).

Many entrepreneurs received support from local businesses, communities or professionals from refugee or migrant backgrounds, which was vital to their survival and growth. One owner emphasized the importance of collaboration and said that he was constantly 'sharing intelligence' with other firms. He actively 'markets the business to the local migrant community' and has diversified his operations to incorporate a butcher's shop within a mini-market. He gets 'regular' advice from a business adviser, his accountant and a 'loyal network of business associates'. He is one of several respondents who have migrated to Britain from their initial country of asylum with the express intention of starting a business.

It is clear then that the firms we studied, like the dynamic migrant-dominated streets we see in cities across the UK, are supported by local, organic networks that academics and policy makers often overlook. Dr Suzanne Hall (2021) refers to this as a 'migrant infrastructure of care' – it comprises established mutual support and assistance between employers, professionals, local institutions, and communities. This key ingredient is vital to the survival and growth of refugee entrepreneurs.

Though impressive and surprising, the precarious circumstances of refugee entrepreneurs – even those who had grown – should not be under-stated. The multiple pressures of hypercompetitive markets, austerity, and social discrimination were unrelenting. Many would have never embarked on their entrepreneurial journey had they been able to secure work commensurate with their qualifications. Nonetheless, our study has wider implications for the community supporting businesses.

Refugee businesses, which are often concentrated in specific streets and city spaces, contribute a significant amount of economic and social value to the community. Many refugee-owned shops and cafes act as social hubs, or meeting places for a mix of native and migrant customers. Readily dismissed as no more than a set of routine commercial transactions, it is easy to overlook how this type of business activity can build social bridges. The conventional orthodoxy of 'growth' firms remains stubbornly impervious to the social value of refugee entrepreneurs.

Proactive civil and business agencies like the Entrepreneurial Refugee Network, Ashley Community Housing, and Citizens UK, have developed promising initiatives to support refugee entrepreneurs; and these merit attention in wider policy debates on 'levelling up' and 'inclusive growth'. In a recent intervention (Ram et al. 2022b), CREME collaborated with community-based intermediaries and 'mainstream' agencies on an initiative to promote productivity in firms like those in the present study. The dynamism, resourcefulness and creativity of refugee entrepreneurs could be of great benefit to policymakers looking for ways to 'build back better'.

References

Hall, S. (2021) *The migrant's paradox: street livelihoods and marginal citizenship in Britain*, University of Minnesota Press.

Jones, T., M. Ram and M. Villares-Varela (2019) 'Diversity, economic development and new migrant entrepreneurs', *Urban Studies*, 56 (5): 960–76.

Ram, M., T. Jones, S. Doldor, M. Villares-Varela and H. Li (2022a) 'What happens to refugee-origin entrepreneurs? Combining mixed embeddedness and strategy perspectives in a longitudinal study', *Ethnic and Racial Studies*, 45, (16): 1–27, doi: 10.1080/01419870.2021.1991970.

Ram, M., I. McCarthy, A. Green and J. Scully (2022b) 'Towards a more inclusive human resource community: engaging ethnic minority microbusinesses in human resource development programmes targeted at more productive methods of operating', *Human Resource Management Journal*, 32 (3): 540–54, doi: 10.1111/1748-8583.12416.

Villares-Varela, M., M. Ram and T. Jones (2018) 'Bricolage as survival, growth and transformation: the role of patch-working in the social agency of migrant entrepreneurs', *Work, Employment and Society*, 32 (5), 942–62.

Villares-Varela, M., M. Ram and T. Jones (2022) 'Thwarted or facilitated? The entrepreneurial aspirations and capabilities of new migrants in the UK', *Sociology*, Early View, 1–19, doi: 10.1177/00380385221083865.

Birmingham's Muslims: Problematized Communities in a Superdiverse City

Chris Allen

In January 2015, Steve Emerson – a so-called 'terrorism expert' – appeared on Fox News and claimed that Birmingham was 'totally Muslim', a city so dangerous that 'non-Muslims just simply do not go in' to it (cited in Allen 2017). While Emerson's claims are as farcical as they are unfounded – he later apologized for his comments – they are indicative of how some people perceive and understand the city's Muslims. Despite being a significant and well-established constituent part of the superdiverse tapestry that is today's Birmingham, the city's Muslims have been regularly and routinely 'problematized' for more than a decade. Not only has this had a detrimental effect on Muslims and non-Muslims alike, but it has also shaped, informed and given credence to contemporary Islamophobia.

Birmingham's Muslims in context

The city is home to the largest number of Muslims in the UK outside London. While new census data will yield a more accurate figure, recent estimates suggest their number to be approximately 301,000, which is 27 per cent of the city's total population (Allen 2021). Birmingham's Muslims are, like the city itself, superdiverse. Encompassing what might best be termed 'old' and 'new' Muslims, many of the former arrived in the city from the Indian sub-continent and East Africa in the decades following the Second World War. While the majority are of Pakistani heritage, they are far from homogeneous and include Punjabis, Sindhis, Blauchis, Pashtuns and Mirpuris who form the majority. Birmingham's 'new' Muslims came to the city in recent decades from a much broader range of geographical locations, including eastern Europe, West Africa and the Middle East. This has led to the growth of Somali, Kurdish, Iraqi and Iranian communities in different parts of the city. There are also growing numbers of white and black converts to Islam (Allen 2017).

The majority of the city's Muslims (71.7 per cent) live in Birmingham's seven most deprived wards – Washwood Heath (16,847), Sparkbrook (19,372), Bordesley Green (18,629), Springfield (13,461), Lozells and East Handsworth (10,853), and Nechells (8822). Of these, Bordesley Green, Washwood Heath and Nechells are in the top 1 per cent of the country's most deprived super output areas (Allen 2021). Accordingly, many of the city's Muslims experience high levels of unemployment, poor health and educational under-achievement. This has ramifications for the future, not only in relation to housing and employment, but also, given the disproportionately young demographic of the city's Muslims – around half are aged 25 or younger – in terms of education (Allen 2021). At present, Muslims account for more than 80 per cent of the school-age population in some areas, increasing to 86 per cent of all children aged between five and fifteen in Washwood Heath (Allen 2017). Maybe it is no surprise that Washwood Heath was one of the wards most affected by Operation Trojan Horse, the name given to a series of unfounded allegations about a planned 'takeover' of state schools by Muslims 'extremists' in the city, and considered in more detail below.

Decades of problematization

According to Isakjee (2013), the problematization of Birmingham's Muslims began when, following the 7/7 terror attacks in London, the UK government identified the city as a preventing violent extremism (PVE) pathfinder location. As the forerunner to Prevent – the UK government's controversial and much criticized counter-extremism strategy (Allen 2017) – the aims of the PVE pathfinder were to target certain Muslim communities and then encourage them to identify with being a desirable part of British society. Then, added to those objectives was the need for Muslims to reject and actively condemn violent extremism. Thus, underpinning the PVE pathfinder was the inference that Birmingham's Muslims were already 'problematic' – 'problematic' in that violent extremist activity was known to be evident among Birmingham's Muslims, especially among those who were young.

The scrutiny placed on the city's Muslims intensified in 2010 with Project Champion (Isakjee and Allen 2013), an ill-conceived counter-terrorism initiative that saw more than 250 CCTV and automated number plate recognition cameras being installed in 'rings' around two of the city's most densely-populated Muslim areas. Not only were Muslims living in those areas misled about the purpose of the cameras – the residents were told that the cameras were for crime reduction only – but an independent review by Thames Valley Police (Thornton 2010) showed how, as a means of getting the go-ahead for the initiative, democratic structures and elected representatives were bypassed to secure the funding. By the time the cameras were dismantled shortly after the publication of the independent review, trust between the city's Muslims and its governing institutions had rapidly eroded: the streets and areas where many of Birmingham's Muslims lived and called home were now feeling – to them at least – problematized and securitized.

Similar feelings arose in 2014, with allegations that Muslim 'extremists' were plotting to take over twenty of the city's state-funded schools. Despite West Midlands Police quickly claiming that the allegations were false, they nonetheless prompted the largest investigation into the education sector in British history. Despite no evidence of a plot being uncovered, the allegations intensified the amount of scrutiny placed on Birmingham's Muslims and the suspicions of others in the city towards them. Amid claims of entryism, the controversy escalated fears of cultural clashes and further takeovers of public spaces and institutions (Holmwood and O'Toole 2018). Accordingly, Birmingham's Muslims were seen to pose a very real threat to institutions in the city and the country more widely.

Birmingham's Muslims were most recently problematized after the 2017 terror attack in Westminster. Despite taking place in London, details soon began to emerge that the perpetrator, Khalid Masood, was a Muslim who at the time had been living in the city. In an instant, the world's media turned its focus on Birmingham, especially its Muslims. Again coming under intense scrutiny, a Belgian news reporter called Birmingham the 'global centre of jihadism' and described it as 'the new Molenbeek', the Brussels suburb where police raided a number of houses in March 2016 following the terror attacks in Paris four months earlier. In the UK, one national newspaper referred to Birmingham as a 'hotbed' of Islamist-inspired extremist activity; another said it was a 'breeding ground for British-born terror' (Allen 2017).

It was the *Daily Mail*, however, that ran the headline, 'So how DID Birmingham become the jihadi capital of Britain?' (emphasis as per original headline). The newspaper went on to claim that within a few miles of where Masood had lived, 26 of the country's 269 'jihadis' had been 'produced' (Allen 2017). Despite the emphasis on Birmingham's Muslims, however, the reality was that Masood had only lived there for about a year prior to the attack and, as confirmed by Neil Basu, deputy assistant commissioner of the Metropolitan Police and senior national coordinator of UK Counter-Terrorism Policing at the time, Masood had acted alone. Masood also had no links with any known extremist networks in Birmingham (Allen 2017), with any of Birmingham's Muslim communities, or with any of the city's mosques. Nonetheless, the focus on security matters that drew attention to the city's Muslims not only added to their problematization, but also went some way towards codifying them as internal 'enemy others', which posed a threat to the city as well as to the people living in it.

Problematizing Muslims, normalizing Islamophobia

Existing research shows that the increasing normalization and acceptance of Islamophobia legitimizes the notion that Muslims are problematic and threatening, but also that they belong to a homogeneous and undifferentiated group of 'others' (Allen 2020), who are liable to be threatening, dangerous, violent and more. Once such thinking becomes embedded in the society it ends up being taken for granted and seen as common sense. Thus, in the context of Birmingham, it is common sense to be suspicious and mistrusting of the city's Muslims. As research in the wake of Project Champion and Operation Trojan Horse illustrated, more and more people in the city came to believe there is 'no smoke without fire' (Allen 2021).

While some Muslims in Birmingham tried to address their ongoing problematization, for many others, the cumulative messages conveyed by the PVE Pathfinder, Project Champion, Operation Trojan Horse and the 'jihadi capital of the world' label merely caused weariness. At the very least these messages aroused suspicion and increased scrutiny, but at most they provoked Islamophobic bigotry and hate. Consequently, Birmingham's Muslims feel less well integrated than previously; there are greater tensions between the different Islamic communities and, most worryingly, more of them have experienced, or fear that they will experience, Islamophobia and anti-Muslim hatred (Allen 2021). While Emerson may have alleged that Birmingham is a city that non-Muslims just do not enter, the reality is that Birmingham is now a city where some of its Muslims no longer feel they belong, despite it being where they were born, grew up and continue to live.

References

Allen, C. (2017) *Birmingham, Muslims and Islam: an overview in socio-economic context*, University of Birmingham.

Allen, C. (2020) *Reconfiguring Islamophobia: a radical rethinking of a contested concept*, Palgrave Macmillan.

Allen, C. (2021) 'Young, Brummie and Muslim in the problematised city: investigating identity and belonging among Muslim youth in Birmingham, England', *Journal of Social Inclusion*, 12 (1): 23–36.

Holmwood, J. and T. O'Toole (2018) *Countering extremism in British schools? The truth about the Birmingham Trojan Horse affair*, Policy Press.

Isakjee, A. (2013) *Tainted citizens: the securitised identities of young Muslim men in Birmingham*, Doctoral dissertation, University of Birmingham.

Isakjee, A. and C. Allen (2013) '"A catastrophic lack of inquisitiveness": a critical study of the impact and narrative of the Project Champion surveillance project in Birmingham', *Ethnicities*, 13 (6): 751–70. doi: 10.1177/1468796813492.

Thornton, S. (2010) *Project Champion Review*, Thames Valley Police.

Moving Difference and Brazilians in London: Colonial Legacies Shaping the Global Present

Angelo Martins Jr

The following is my fieldwork note of a conversation with Marcos, a middle-class, albeit dark-skinned, Brazilian living in London.

It is not really 'globalization' as they say, not everyone can go wherever they want. Besides courage, you need to have a visa, money, come from the right country, have the right passport, speak the language. ... And they have put all 'migrants' inside the 'same bag'. If you do not come from England, Europe or other rich countries, you are an immigrant. For them, an immigrant is a poor worker, a criminal, illegal and everything you see every day on TV here. 'The problem' is either a person of black descent, which for them will always be an immigrant, or it is a foreigner. And the fact that I am black, I feel it a little more. Racial prejudice in Brazil exists and it is strong, but it is different. It changes a lot in Brazil whether you are poor or not, if you have studied or not, whether you live in the favelas or not. There is racism, but we have greater fluidity. I am dark skinned, but I was adopted by a white family; I went to university; I lived in a middle-class neighbourhood in São Paulo, which kind of diluted my situation there. But here it is more literal: you are either white or not. ... We have to be careful; I often find myself having prejudices here too. Because there is too much hate against the immigrant, the black, the Muslim and we end up simulating what they say. We try to do the same thing as the English, but we are not English. It happens a lot to us here, you are out of Brazil, you are an immigrant, you do not want to be seen as an immigrant, but you are Brazilian. We need

220

to watch ourselves constantly to fit in. Many Brazilians will have this experience for the first time, becoming 'a problem', even those who have money and already spoke English. In the end, they are not Europeans, even if you have European grandparents and a European passport.

The freedom to move from place to place is a privilege in today's world, so ideas about human mobility and human difference are necessarily intertwined. When white people from the Global North move around the world they are typically imagined to be tourists, gap-year students, business travellers, or expatriates, whereas black and brown people from the Global South are thought of as 'migrants'. Their migrancy – the fact that they have moved – is taken to define them, and they are also frequently represented as homogeneous groups. Academics, policymakers, politicians and journalists often speak of 'South Asian migrants' or 'asylum-seekers' as if they constituted one, undifferentiated group of people.

Much has been said about the link between a tendency to homogenize 'migrants' and racist stereotyping by anti-migrant thinkers – for example, 'they' are all criminals and rapists. However, among those who hold a more positive view of migration, it can be associated with more exoticizing stereotypes. In migration scholarship this has sometimes translated into assumptions about 'migrant communities' as bound together by a shared experience of movement or common homeland, acting in solidarity to support one another in the country of destination.

As a Brazilian working and then studying in London, I was surprised that the academic literature emphasizing commonality and solidarity among migrants did not speak to my own experience. This observation prompted me to conduct research on Brazilians in London, on which my book *Moving Difference* (2020) is based. The research involved ethnographic and interview research with men and women who, while all 'Brazilian migrants in London', differed in terms of the regions of Brazil from which they came, their socio-economic and educational backgrounds, and their racialized identities. Their differences moved with them, shaping not only their reasons for migrating and how they navigate the different levels of opportunity and constraint, but also how they see and interact with each other in London. However, Britain has its own social and political hierarchies and, in London, my research participants found themselves not only lumped together as 'Brazilians' but also lumped in with Global South 'migrants' in general.

Moving geographically ruptured the racial privilege of many of my lighter skinned and white middle-class Brazilian research participants, who had never previously felt it possible that *they* would be seen as a devalued inferior other, as a 'social problem'. For them, being positioned as a 'migrant' implied the possibility of experiencing classed, 'racial' and social degradation. Now they had to negotiate their position on two matrices of difference – one 'here' in Britain and one 'there' in Brazil. While some reflected critically on these hierarchies and expressed political solidarity with other migrants, many responded by seeking to distance themselves from stigmatized identities 'here' and stressing their superior position 'there'. They were not the *real* 'migrants', they told me, not poor, uneducated, low skilled, 'illegal', promiscuous, or criminal like the other Brazilians in London. They did not wish to live among the 'Brazilian community' in areas of London where *real* migrants live but rather in areas where there are just 'beautiful [in other words white] people speaking English on the street', where 'everything is clean and you do not see rubbish on the floor, or a bunch of ugly, smelly people who make you feel you are in Africa, not in Europe'.

Moving Difference describes how Brazilians in London negotiate and recreate difference in terms of class, region, gender, 'race', 'culture' and documental status. It examines the linked histories and social imaginaries of 'race' and degradation that allow us to make sense of the very visceral racial, classed, gendered and regional disgust my Brazilian research participants (especially the white, lighter-skinned middle-class ones) expressed when speaking of their co-nationals and of other migrants and their 'spaces'. Although their disgust is expressed 'here', in London, the feeling has its origins in the colonial presence of Europeans and enslaved Africans 'there', in Brazil – a past that has historically shaped Brazilian projects of 'race' and nation as well as continuing to inflect the lives of Brazilians in London today.

After abolition in 1888, Brazil, influenced by eugenic racial assumptions, embarked on a whitening project to incentivize European immigration as a way of 'civilizing' the new nation by 'improving' its mixed 'blood'. This new population of European (and Japanese) migrants was concentrated almost entirely in the south and south-east of Brazil, regions that, since independence, had acquired the central position in the national economy, especially with the production of coffee and, later, industrialization. At the same time, without access to land or any form of state compensation, an entire class of black and 'mixed' people – the former slaves and their descendants – as well as lighter-skinned poor Brazilians (often from the Northeast Region) have been marginalized both in the configuration of urban spaces and in the labour market, dealing with daily exclusion, discrimination, degradation and state violence.

Living as 'sub-citizens' in the poor urban peripheries and/or slums of the southern cities, members of the middle class and elite use them as a cheap, precarious labour force to undertake the most 'unqualified' activities – 'dirty' and 'heavy' jobs for the men and domestic and sexual labour for the women. They are socially imagined as repulsive bodies, blamed for Brazil's supposed failure to become more developed, modern or civilized, and often executed on the streets by the police. As a way of dealing with such historical exclusion, Brazilians constantly negotiate racism through hierarchies of colour, hair type and class positioning as they attempt to distance themselves from any residual trace of blackness or poverty that might identify them as a 'degraded body'.

Today, Brazil's colonial and racial histories play an important part both in generating the desire to travel and determining whether and how journeys are undertaken. While many Brazilians believe that moving to London will allow them to achieve the material and cultural ideals of a 'modern' Western lifestyle that is impossible to attain in 'not fully modern' Brazil, the lighter-skinned descendants of European participants in Brazil's whitening project enjoy greater freedom of movement in Europe and so find it easier to realize their ambition to move to London. Once in the UK, however, they find themselves realigned in the constellation of ideas about race, modernity and human worth in such a way as to stand precariously close to those who are socially imagined as disgusting, degraded, and uncivilized. Meanwhile, the darker-skinned or black working-class Brazilians who do manage to move to London come to realize that their physical mobility (previously imagined as a straightforward marker of progress and privilege) also carries the threat of social and racial immobility: they might be fixed 'here' in ways that they are not rigidly contained 'there'.

Taking the configuration of the social world as a continuum of connections, ambivalences and paradoxes, *Moving Difference* offers a lens through which to see how the global mobile present is connected to the global legacies of the colonial past. The lives of Brazilians in London shed light on how 'here' and 'there', 'present' and 'past', are always entwined – creating and recreating racialized inequalities and difference, including unequal access to the privilege of mobility.

Reference

Martins Jr, A. (2020) *Moving difference: Brazilians in London*, Routledge.

Insecurity and Abundance: Food and Belonging in a Hostile Environment

Andy Jolly

Chauvinist welfare policies that restrict access to social security benefits and other welfare provisions can make it difficult for households to consume enough food for an active, healthy life. In the UK, successive governments have famously pursued policies to create a 'hostile environment' for those with an irregular migration status, and most temporary migrants to the UK are subject to the no recourse to public funds (NRPF) rule, which removes the right to claim a whole range of social security benefits. In addition, the UK government prevents those with an irregular migration status from taking up paid employment. As a result, children in households subject to immigration control are at particular risk of food insecurity. At its extreme, this means that perhaps as many as 95 per cent of undocumented migrant children live in households with low or very low food security (Jolly and Thompson 2022). In practical terms, food insecurity means that household members experience reduced food intake and disrupted eating patterns because of limited resources to buy food.

However, this description obscures a more complex situation around food and the social contexts in which it is purchased, prepared and consumed, as encapsulated by the above image. The photograph was taken as part of a photo-elicitation exercise with undocumented children, in which the participants were encouraged to take photographs of their lives based on the theme of food. To explore food insecurity in undocumented migrant households in Birmingham for my PhD study at IRiS, I used a mixed-method approach that combined Delphi methods, household-food insecurity questionnaires, semi-structured interviews and visual methods.

Fahmida, a twelve-year-old Pakistani girl living in a household in Birmingham with an irregular migration status and a high level of food insecurity as measured by the widely used USDA Household Food Security Survey Module, took the photograph. The image depicts an inviting and colourful bowl of fresh vegetables, seeds, herbs and spices ready for cooking, and confounds one's basic expectations of the everyday life and eating habits of a food-insecure household. As such, it both contextualizes and complicates the stark numerical data, hinting at a more nuanced understanding of life as an undocumented migrant and specifically of how migrant children experience food poverty and insecurity. The context of this image can perhaps be understood in three interrelated ways.

First, the image shows the significance of food as a marker of identity in diasporic communities, for it is not only a source of nutrition but also has broader importance and value. Food and food choices provide a link with pre-migration identities, particularly for the more senior members of the household, and the ability to cook food using familiar ingredients provides an evocative link with 'home' – it creates a multi-sensory experience involving smells, colours, textures and even sounds.

Second, the image can be viewed as an example of how young people with an irregular migration status exercise political agency and resist the categories applied to them (Lind 2016). Although she was living in a household that scored very highly on the most widely used measure of food insecurity, the image with which Fahmida chose to represent her experience of food was a homely and inviting example of fresh food. She used her agency to resist a framing of passive victimhood, and instead expressed her pride in the food her family produced and consumed. The photo gave Fahmida an opportunity to exercise choice in how she wished to be represented and she chose a celebratory image of abundance and identity rather than a shame-producing image of poverty and want. As such, the photo is perhaps a small act of resistance to popular representations of young people experiencing food insecurity as mere victims or objects of pity.

Finally, and perhaps most significantly, the image highlights a seemingly perplexing paradox. This is that a family experiencing high levels of food insecurity also had times of plenty when they could access and prepare fresh home-cooked food. Even a family that had suffered hunger over the previous year could experience times when food was more plentiful. What emerged from the photo-elicitation exercise was thus more nuanced and complicated than the stark findings of the food security measure alone. While the latter focused on deficits, the photograph allowed for more atypical but significant experiences to be recorded.

More fundamentally, the food insecurity/abundance paradox is perhaps best explained in the context of a cultural understanding of food that places value on sharing and mutual support. Although a household may often experience food insecurity, at other times opportunities to share food with friends, family and co-ethnic neighbours will arise. These social, participatory and collaborative understandings of food and the role it plays were made possible not only by the persistence of pre-migration relational food practices and networks, but also by the firmly-rooted nature of migrant communities in Britain. Fahmida attended a local school with a large circle of friends, and the family was well networked within the local area, including links to both formal and informal support organizations. The family also belonged to a longstanding Pakistani community in Birmingham dating back to migration to the city from Mirpur in the 1960s.[1] The 145,000 people of Pakistani heritage in Birmingham make it the local authority with the largest Pakistani population in the UK (Arian 2022).

1. Following the Pakistani government's construction of the Mangla Dam in the Mirpur area of Azad Jammu and Kashmir in 1965, many residents of the nearly three hundred submerged villages and towns resettled in the UK, predominantly in London, the West Midlands and West Yorkshire.

Fahmida's experience resonates with McNevin's (2013) understanding of 'ambivalence', which describes the migrants' claims to rights, as well as their agency or political activity, in the contexts in which they live, even when they lack formal citizenship status. However, Fahmida had a perspective that went beyond ambivalence, for it actively embraced her identity. She was unashamed of her irregular immigration status and saw no inherent tension between the British government's hostility and her loyalty to her friends, neighbours, community and, by extension, the country in which they all lived. Indeed, other participants explicitly identified with an everyday Britishness that was at odds with their formal legal status and that contradicted binary ideas of citizenship and identity.

In contrast to the 'othering' that Fahmida experienced as an undocumented migrant, she could point to examples of food sharing and informal support mechanisms. These everyday networks of mutual aid were an exercise in what Bailey (2012) describes as 'belonging and agency in everyday life' where members exercise agency and self-determination through practical support, despite the hostile and abject environments in which they live.

Interwoven into the informal networks of mutual help that sustain these families are the groups and organizations that form part of a broader supportive environment, but these are not for the most part run by undocumented migrants. This ecosystem of organizations is extensive, for at the time of the photo-elicitation exercise, twenty-two organizations were working with undocumented migrant families in Birmingham. Although most are smaller charities, community organizations, and faith groups, some are large national or international NGOs.

In contrast to the hostile response of the UK government, these networks, both informal and formal, act as *hospitable environments* of mutual aid and solidarity that provide a refuge in which people can exist and, in some cases, thrive. These hospitable environments encourage children, especially those either born in or having long resided in the UK, to feel a sense of belonging that is independent of the formal legal measures of citizenship. These 'hospitable' environments, which the families inhabit alongside the more 'hostile' one, are based on kinship, solidarity, a sense of place, and political affinity rather than on their legal status, and are underpinned by faith groups, voluntary organizations, friends and supporters rather than state services.

References

Arian, M. (2022) *Pakistani community health profile*, Birmingham City Council. Available at: https://www.birmingham.gov.uk/downloads/file/23779/pakistani_community_health_profile_report.

Bailey, O. G. (2012) 'Migrant African women: tales of agency and belonging', *Ethnic and Racial Studies*, 35 (5): 850–67, doi: 10.1080/01419870.2011.628037.

Jolly, A. and J. L. Thompson (2022) 'Risk of food insecurity in undocumented migrant households in Birmingham, UK', *Journal of Public Health*, 1–6, doi: 10.1093/pubmed/fdab408.

Lind, J. (2016) 'The duality of children's political agency in deportability', *Politics*, 37 (3): 288–301, doi: 10.1177/0263395716665391.

McNevin, A. (2013) 'Ambivalence and citizenship: theorising the political claims of irregular migrants', *Millennium*, 41 (2): 182–200, doi: 10.1177/0305829812463473.

The Surbanization of Superdiversity in Flanders: its Spread, Speed and Scale of Superdiversification

Dirk Geldof[1]

Superdiversity has been studied at the level of global cities, such as London, and many studies have been done on specific neighbourhoods within such cities. However, can we also use the superdiversity lens to analyse countries or regions, including large areas with low levels of diversity? This is what we explored when developing an 'Atlas of Superdiversity' for the Flemish authorities (Geldof and Vanhaeren 2022; Vandekerckhove et al. 2022). Most atlases offer static maps. Applying the superdiversity lens challenged us to look at population dynamics to analyse and map the spread, speed and scale of the processes of superdiversification and to develop dynamic typologies of neighbourhoods at their scale and speed of diversification.

Speed, spread and scale of superdiversification

Superdiversity is a lens through which to understand the migration-driven processes of demographic and social change (Geldof 2016; Vertovec 2007). Meissner and Vertovec (2015) distinguished between the spread, speed and scale of superdiversification. Its speed is the rate at which neighbourhoods or municipalities become more diverse. The scale of superdiversity reflects the proportion of residents from migratory backgrounds and the complexity of the population, and provides an eye for processes of scaling up. Spread is about the spatial dispersion across cities and municipalities. The multidimensional combination of the speed, scale and spread of the process of superdiversification results in a growing complexity of the population.

1. Special thanks to Roxanne Vanhaeren (Atelier Romain) for data analyses and the production of the maps.

In an atlas of superdiversity in Flanders (Belgium) we analysed and visualized these processes, based on the official population data and datasets of housing and neighbourhood characteristics for the period 1990–2020 (Geldof and Vanhaeren 2022; Vandekerckhove et al. 2022).

Flanders as a colourful patchwork quilt

Never before have so many people with roots in migration, from so many different countries of origin and with so many different backgrounds, lived together in Flemish towns and municipalities. The whole of Flanders is becoming more diverse, but the speed, scale and spread are very different, with specific patterns of spatial settlement between – but also within – cities and municipalities.

In 1990, it was mainly the larger cities in Flanders and the historical coal-mining regions of central Limburg that had high levels of diversity, but from then onwards, we see a gradual spread, with an increase in diversity in cities such as Leuven and Mechelen. In the twenty-first century, the speed and spread of diversification has accelerated, with a further spread and upscaling in other cities and regions such as Ronse, Aalst and South Limburg.

Today, even more than in the twentieth century, urban areas can be recognized by the high proportion of inhabitants from migrant backgrounds. Cities such as Brussels, Antwerp, Genk and Vilvoorde have developed into majority–minority cities, in which at least half the population is of non-Belgian origin. The Brussels Metropolitan Region is one of the most superdiverse cities in the world and it became a majority–minority city at the turn of the century. Today, no less than three out of four (75 per cent) of the inhabitants are of foreign origin (including the birth nationality of the parents).

More different nationalities of origin

Behind this upscaling, these areas are undergoing a process of diversification in which the numbers of countries of origin, religious backgrounds, languages spoken, different migration histories, and lengths of stay are all increasing. Between 1990 and 2020, the number of different nationalities living in all Flemish municipalities increased. In 2020, places with a lower proportion of inhabitants of non-Belgian origin were also experiencing a

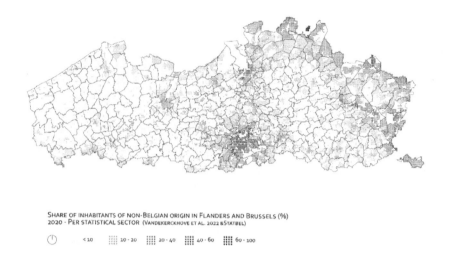

SHARE OF INHABITANTS OF NON-BELGIAN ORIGIN IN FLANDERS AND BRUSSELS (%)
2020 - PER STATISTICAL SECTOR (VANDEKERCKHOVE ET AL. 2022 &STATBEL)

◷   < 10   ▦ 10 - 20   ▦ 20 - 40   ▦ 40 - 60   ▦ 60 - 100

greater diversity of countries of origin. All cities house residents from more than 100 different countries of origin; in the Brussels Region and Antwerp this figure is more than 170 for the city as a whole, and up to 114 in the smaller statistical sectors within these cities.

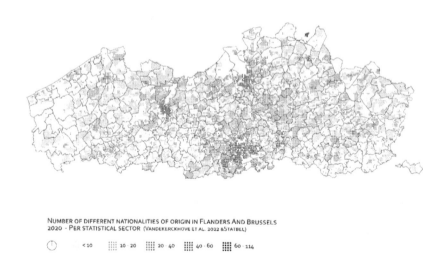

NUMBER OF DIFFERENT NATIONALITIES OF ORIGIN IN FLANDERS AND BRUSSELS
2020 - PER STATISTICAL SECTOR (VANDEKERCKHOVE ET AL. 2022 &STATBEL)

◷   < 10   ▦ 10 - 20   ▦ 20 - 40   ▦ 40 - 60   ▦ 60 - 114

Age and demographic dynamics

Increasing superdiversity is related not only to new migration, but also to demographic and spatial developments. Flanders will become more diverse in the next decade, not only because of new migration, but also because of the age composition of the current population. People in the oldest age groups are mainly of Belgian origin, so this group will become smaller through mortality. Conversely, a much larger proportion of the inhabitants with a migrant background consist of children and young people than in the rest of the population. The majority of children in almost all the main Flemish cities today have roots in migration. In the next two decades, these diverse younger age groups will grow into a superdiverse working-age population: they are the families and parents of tomorrow.

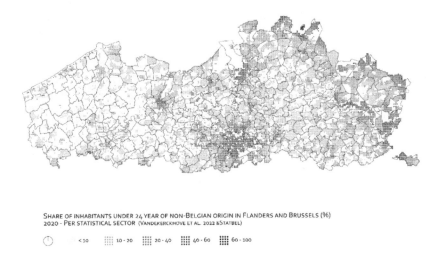

SHARE OF INHABITANTS UNDER 24 YEAR OF NON-BELGIAN ORIGIN IN FLANDERS AND BRUSSELS (%)
2020 - PER STATISTICAL SECTOR (VANDEKERCKHOVE ET AL. 2022 &STATBEL)

○   <10   ▦ 10 - 20   ▦ 20 - 40   ▦ 40 - 60   ▦ 60 - 100

A typology of (super)diverse neighbourhoods

What dynamic patterns can we recognize in this spatial and demographic process of superdiversification? On the basis of a cluster analysis with 39 population indicators (with the share and profile of inhabitants according to origin and nationalities of origin), we constructed a typology of super-diversity in Flanders to analyse the changes in its spread, speed and scale over the past three decades.

Large parts of Flanders remain areas with limited diversity (<10 per cent of the inhabitants) or limited levels of diversity (10–15 per cent). The border regions represent a specific type of diversity – a high presence of Dutch nationals in municipalities along the Dutch border and, more recently, a high presence of French nationals in municipalities along the French border. However, the scale of superdiversity remains limited here: it mainly concerns migration from the neighbouring country.

233

Superdiversity in the twenty-first century increases further in areas where people of non-Belgian origin have been living for decades – the Limburg mining region, large cities such as Brussels, Antwerp and Ghent, and smaller towns, such as Vilvoorde, Lokeren or Zele, which had been characterized in the past by their pockets of industry.

A recent process of fanning out is a spread to areas that were previously less diverse, but that have clearly scaled up over the past two decades.

- A first form is the diversification of less diverse neighbourhoods *within superdiverse cities* and around the former Limburg mining area.
- A second form is the recent *suburbanization of superdiversity*. This is most pronounced around the Brussels Capital Region. In the eastern periphery of Brussels, mainly people of EU or OECD origin settle, often linked to the international institutions in Brussels. The western periphery of Brussels is characterized by a suburbanization of people of non-EU origin, driven by both upward social mobility and processes of gentrification and pressure at the bottom of the Brussels housing market. Patterns of dispersal and suburbanization are also emerging around cities such as Antwerp and Ghent, and around the former mining communities in Limburg.
- A final form of dispersal goes to smaller cities that had undergone a certain amount of industrialization in the past, but are now affected by deindustrialization. They are characterized by an ageing population and the availability of older and cheaper dwellings. Examples are Boom, with a past in the brick industry, or the Dender region, which was historically known for its textiles (Ninove) and match industry (Geraardsbergen).

Finally, we analysed the correlation between the typologies of super-diversity and the spatial and social characteristics of neighbourhoods. This included housing characteristics (for example, rented or owner-occupied, type of house, or presence of a garden), neighbourhood characteristics (such as green public spaces, access to services, or availability of transport) and specific facilities such as places of worship or the presence of offices for making financial transfers abroad. The housing market largely determined the spread, speed and scale of the superdiversification – what types of houses and apartments were available where and at what prices? We found a close connection between unequal socio-economic positions and unequal spatial distribution. Who can afford to live where? Also, disposable incomes and the supply of housing are more important in determining the spatial distribution of superdiversity than either ethnic or cultural elements.

Methodological reflections

Belgium and Flanders have only become societies of immigration since the Second World War, so the normalization of superdiversity is still quite controversial. Diversity is no longer solely about minorities, as it was in the twentieth century, but is becoming a contested characteristic of ever larger parts of contemporary Belgian society (Geldof 2016, 2018). The last three decades of superdiversification are documented and examined in a rather unusual way in the atlas on superdiversity in Flanders (Vandekerckhove et al. 2022).

Nevertheless, this atlas raises some methodological problems. The first is that focusing on nationality of origin as a starting point risks under-exposing the importance of the complex combinations of origin, gender, socio-economic position, language and other characteristics. In other words, the atlas does not yet fully recognize people's multiple identities (Geldof 2022). Further research is needed to look beyond the ethnic lens and to visualize and map the growing diversity while also paying attention to family structures, the increase of mixed families, differences between first, second and third generation, and people's socio-economic positions.

A second problem concerns how the measurement methods and categories remain tenable over time. Currently, we are operationalizing origin by combining four parameters – current nationality, birth nationality, and birth nationality of each parent. When both second- and third-generation migrants are born in Belgium, their children 'disappear' from the statistics: they are Belgians with two Belgian-born parents. Only when the nationality of origin of a future parent is still non-Belgian (usually because of a more recent migration), the next generation remains visible in the statistics as residents of non-Belgian origin. However, just as Richard Alba (2020) was suspicious of the measurement methods used on the American census, so too must we consider what distortions we could be introducing through our measurement methods.

A third problem surrounds the risk of underestimating the impact of the relocation movements of autochthonous Belgian citizens. Neighbourhoods not only become more diverse because of the mobility of people from a migrant background, but they are also affected by the removals of autochthonous Belgians. The emergence of majority–minority cities is inextricably linked to the white urban flight and suburbanization of the past half century. While the atlas on superdiversity in Flanders documents and analyses the processes of superdiversification in a dynamic way for an entire region, it only takes us one step closer to a better understanding of population dynamics and their spatial impact over time.

References

Alba, R. (2020) *The great demographic illusion: majority, minority, and the expanding American mainstream*, Princeton University Press.

Geldof, D. (2016) *Superdiversity in the heart of Europe: how migration changes our society*, Acco.

Geldof, D. (2018) 'Superdiversity as a lens to understand complexities', in A. Creese and A. Blackledge (eds) *The Routledge handbook of language and superdiversity: an interdisciplinary perspective*, Routledge, 43–56.

Geldof, D. (2022) 'Identity politics in contexts of superdiversity: from single to multiple identities?', in F. Meissner, N. Sigona and S. Vertovec (eds) *The Oxford handbook of superdiversity*, Oxford University Press, doi: 10.1093/oxfordhb/9780197544938.013.33.

Geldof, D. and R. Vanhaeren (2022) 'De overgang naar een superdiverse samenleving', in D. Geldof, K. Van Acker, G. Loosveldt and K. Emmery (eds) *Gezinnen na migratie: Hulpverlening en gezinsbeleid in een superdiverse samenleving*, Garant, 25–41.

Meissner, F. and S. Vertovec (2015) 'Comparing super-diversity', *Ethnic and Racial Studies*, 38 (4): 541–55, doi: 10.1080/01419870.2015.980295.

Vandekerckhove B., D. Geldof, P. De Decker, R. Vanhaeren, W. Van Damme, M. Van Hulle, E. Schillebeeckx and R. Balcaen (2022) 'Atlas Superdiversiteit: Vlaanderen. Toekomst-verkenningen: ruimtelijke verkenning van een superdiverse samenleving', uitgevoerd in opdracht van Departement Omgeving, available at: https://omgeving.vlaanderen.be/atlas-superdiversiteit.

Vertovec, S. (2007) 'Super-diversity and its implications', *Ethnic and Racial Studies*, 30 (6): 1024–54.

Dignity and Self-worth in Precarious Economic Situations: Irregular Domestic Workers in Geneva

Loïc Pignolo

While sitting in her living room, Claudia tells me about her life as an irregular domestic worker.[1] She became quite emotional as she described her first steps in Geneva society from arriving there illegally in the early 1990s to getting various jobs cleaning, or caring for children and the elderly. Strong in her memory is the disconcerting experience of having worked for employers whose attitudes towards her differed so greatly. Some were kind, offering her tea and biscuits during working hours, whereas others were inflexible, demanding and unfair. She recalls being dismissed one day for eating her employer's biscuits without permission:

> I was fired because I ate a box of biscuits. ... What happened is that the lady was counting the biscuits she had left. And then she came and maybe looked at how many biscuits there were left and then she said to me, 'You ate that.' 'Oh yes, sorry, but I was hungry' and all that. 'You're not allowed to eat that. So if you eat that, what can I expect from you? Eat something else afterwards? No. Get out now.' So, there is a lot of ... I don't know. Maybe slavery with white gloves.

When asked about what she meant by 'slavery with white gloves', she explained that it was a situation very similar to slavery, although not

1. This chapter has been written as part of a research visit to the Institute for Research into Superdiversity (IRiS) at the University of Birmingham. I would like to thank Professor Nando Sigona warmly for his precious help and comments on an earlier draft.

formally. Due to the employment dynamics, employers could do whatever they wanted, ranging from unfair treatment and dismissals without warning to kind, respectful treatment.

Given what has been written about paid domestic work over the last few decades, Claudia's experiences came as no surprise. Indeed, these kinds of working conditions are highlighted in numerous studies on paid domestic work (Hondagneu-Sotelo 2007; Rollins 1985). These issues arise partly because paid domestic work is often informal, so takes place outside the formal regulations governing the sector (Hondagneu-Sotelo 2007), but also because domestic workers are often irregular migrants. This offers employers clear advantages because it enables them to impose working conditions on their employees without having to comply with any formal obligations. Whether intentional or not, this imbalance in the power relationship has several, often negative, consequences for the employee. Low pay, long working hours, hard physical labour, extra hours, fear of losing a job (thus being forced to work hard without complaining or taking breaks), and demeaning treatment are common experiences that domestic employees have to endure (Hondagneu-Sotelo 2007; Rollins 1985).

Demeaning treatment may take the form of rituals of deference or 'maternalism'[2] (Rollins 1985), which some employers use to emphasize a worker's inferiority and thus to boost their own self-esteem and sense of moral worth (Rollins 1985). Demeaning treatment may also involve lack of consideration for domestic workers' dignity and needs (Hondagneu-Sotelo 2007). Due to these precarious conditions, domestic workers often have resentment[3] (Rollins 1985: 243–51), even hatred or envy.

Echoing Claudia's comments, the domestic workers to whom I spoke during my PhD fieldwork, and who had lived or were still living in an irregularized situation, emphasized this reality. They felt powerless and exploited by some of their employers, who offered working conditions regarded as precarious and demeaning. Working long hours for low pay, often without paid holidays, led them to feel as if some, if not all employers, saw them as slaves or robots. Dismissals without notice, especially in conjunction with unpaid wages, seemed the worst experience. Although all my interviewees experienced poor treatment from their employers, they

---

2. In other words, rituals that treat an employee as a 'child'.
3. Rollins (1985) uses the French word *ressentiment*.

also felt that it was difficult to contest their working conditions, one reason being job insecurity. Indeed, they feared that challenging their employers would lose them their jobs, especially if they had few hours of work and/or needed to earn enough to provide for their children. Another reason was the fear of being arrested or deported should they lodge complaints with the police about their employer's abuse of power. Both reasons are linked to the vulnerability irregular migrants face at work because they do not have legal status (Bloch et al. 2014). While the domestic workers with whom I spoke did not report many experiences of deference or 'maternalism' (Rollins 1985), they nevertheless reported suffering from this vulnerability. In particular, their precarious working conditions created a sense of injustice and a threat to their dignity and moral worth. At times, their suffering was accentuated by the difficulty of leaving Switzerland, especially when it meant they could not see their families back home. Moreover, they felt this sense of unfairness even more acutely when they considered the legitimacy and utility of their economic activities for receiving societies such as Switzerland

Willen (2019) noted how irregularization undermines the dignity of those affected by it, and that irregular migrants exercise agency in their attempts to maintain or regain their dignity. For the remainder of this text, I shall address two coping strategies that the domestic workers I met used to build positive images of themselves, despite feeling as if they had been thrust into insecure, precarious, and unjust economic situations. As Rollins (1985) noted, such coping strategies were ways of protecting themselves from threats to their personal dignity. One strategy was to focus on the positive economic benefits of participating in Geneva's domestic economy, such as the prospect of building a better life than in their country of origin, or of offering better life chances to their children. As one interviewee said, 'I earn a lot of money compared with the Philippines, more money than a manager in the Philippines.' Hondagneu-Sotelo (2007) explained how the wages that domestic workers earned helped them to build a positive sense of self, despite the multiple difficulties they faced. A similar narrative would arise when domestic workers had to accept jobs with particularly precarious conditions, especially at the beginning of their career in this market, in which case they considered the situation as better than nothing, or as a temporary step before better opportunities came along.

In addition to focusing on the positive economic benefits, domestic workers also managed to find satisfaction and social recognition through the work itself. Indeed, regardless of the working conditions, housework, or looking after children and elderly people, are regarded as intrinsically 'good' and 'honest' activities. Although, given their qualifications, some were aware of experiencing a loss in social status, being a domestic worker was not perceived as something of which to be ashamed. Moreover, domestic work was also experienced as rewarding. Whether through developing efficient cleaning skills, creating emotional bonds with children or the elderly, or more generally putting 'love' and 'care' into their duties, the domestic workers I encountered were able to find satisfaction in their work. Also, building positive and close relationships with employers was seen as a way of gaining dignity. Hondagneu-Sotelo (2007) noted that domestic workers saw personalistic relationships with their employers as a way to protect themselves from indignities and to be more respected, although it did not alter the power imbalance, or necessarily improve their working conditions. In my case study, I found that developing those kinds of relationships, which, among other things, involved intimate discussions, exchanging gifts, and shared moments such as having tea, coffee or meals together, made domestic workers feel valued and 'part of the family'. Some workers thus saw having good relations with their employers as more important than other things, such as a good salary.

These two types of coping strategies – focusing on the positive economic benefits, and finding satisfaction and social recognition in practice – highlight what kinds of agency irregular migrants can exercise over threats to their morality and dignity. If, as Sigona (2012) shows, irregular migrants are able to demonstrate agency 'in the ways they shape and adapt daily routines and mundane social interactions to changing circumstances, precarious livelihoods, and the protracted and concrete possibility of being deported' (Sigona 2012: 51), I would add that they can also exercise agency over how they shape their moral understanding of what they experience, and in their efforts to maintain their dignity. These strategies shed light on the deep impact that irregularization has on the mode of being-in-the world (Willen 2019) of irregular migrants, especially on their moral experience of the economy.

References

Bloch, A., N. Sigona and Z. Roger (2014) *Sans papiers: the social and economic lives of young undocumented migrants*, Pluto Press.

Hondagneu-Sotelo, P. (2007) *Doméstica: immigrant workers cleaning and caring in the shadows of affluence*, University of California Press.

Rollins, J. (1985) *Between women: domestics and their employers*, Temple University Press.

Sigona, N. (2012) '"I have too much baggage": the impacts of legal status on the social worlds of irregular migrants', *Social Anthropology*, 20 (1): 50–65.

Willen, S. S. (2019) *Fighting for dignity: migrant lives at Israel's margins*, University of Pennsylvania Press.

Immediate Descendants of Immigrants as Mediators of Cultural Plurality

Annavittoria Sarli

'The voice in your head asks questions in Italian, and then you ask yourself the same questions in Punjabi. ... It is as if you were asking for another person's opinion when in fact you are asking your own.' With these words, Ushapati, a university student born in Italy to Indian migrant parents, drew my attention to the fascinating potential of people who grow up in multiple ethnocultural environments.

I decided to explore the issue further, so as to highlight the sorts of opportunities that multi-ethnic societies come with. Italy's policy and media debates refer to migration-related issues mostly using words of emergency, deviancy or alleged cultural threats and rarely acknowledging the everyday presence of ethnic minorities as permanent constituents of society (Milazzo 2021).

This public discourse reinforces the widespread perception of migrants' children as foreigners and makes it difficult for the population to accept that diversity is growing.

Italy's current citizenship law, which is mainly based on *jus sanguinis*, makes it difficult for people born in Italy to foreign parents to acquire citizenship of the country in which they have spent most of their lives (Mascitelli and De Lazzari 2016; Pesarini and Tintori 2020). The argument that a citizenship law based on *jus soli* would admit a bunch of offenders to the national community is a recurrent theme among those who oppose a legal reform that would shift the criteria for national membership from an ethnic to a civic basis.[1] In this context, an investigation into the potential

---

1. Such an argument appears, for example, in *Il Giornale* newspaper articles (Dell'Orco 2022; Rame 2017).

contributions of the immediate descendants of migrants might feed a counternarrative that would support their claims to full membership and recognition (Sarli and Phillimore 2022).

Focusing on people's potential was easier than expected. The interviews and focus groups I conducted with sixty university students of migrant descent – which turned into insightful and deeply touching conversations – very often revealed strengths that may result from growing up at the crossroads of multiple worlds.

Zahia, who had been raised in Italy by Moroccan parents, said that 'it is that diversity in which you grow up that allows you to see the world, the reality around you, not only from one perspective but from multiple ones. You always know a little more because you don't simply know just one reality but two.' Lucy, an Italian-Filipino student, added that 'being a second-generation individual gives one the opportunity to get a much more complex overview of things. In other words, you never think of things as black or white, but understand that there can be many aspects that are not entirely absolute or objective.' Belonging to different ethnocultural worlds may therefore give people critical skills and a broader view of reality while strengthening their tolerance towards ambiguity and uncertainty. Fatima, who had been born in Italy to Somali parents, said it can also foster multiperspectivity and the ability to bridge different views. As she explained, 'it often happens that two people have two diverging opinions, but I can understand what the other person means because it looks like something I already know. So, it may happen that I intervene to clarify the concept the other person cannot understand.'

Interestingly, my interlocutors often referred to their ability to act as agents of change in helping to equip the society better to deal constructively with complexity and diversity. As Coumba, an Italian student of Senegalese descent explained, 'often my classmates live a life that is certainly valuable but does not allow them to have a broader perspective on the possibility that there are different ways of living, different value systems. And, therefore, I am often instrumental in helping their understanding.' However, growing up in Italian society as the descendant of a migrant is not easy. Jiao, raised in Italy by Chinese parents, put it clearly: 'you grow some skills by having one foot in one culture and one in another, but it is also a burden that you carry with you. ... If you cannot handle the weight, you may become "a bad person".'

This daily and continuous adjustment to different cultural expectations may mean that migrants' children struggle to develop a coherent self-image:

'I realized that I was twenty-seven completely different Amals', an Italian–Tunisian student told me, 'and I asked myself "who am I then?"' This struggle becomes particularly intense in contexts, like the Italian one, in which people tend to be categorized as members of a single group and in which cultural identities are often perceived as homogeneous and unchanging. As Zrinka put it: 'it is not just about me being "Croatian or Italian", it is also about me having lived in South Africa for two years, so why can't I feel "South African" too? Why do I have to fit into people's categories?'

However, the most arduous challenge is probably that of constantly being perceived as different in a mainstream society in which membership is based on shared cultural and racial kinship. The words of Henry, an Italian-Nigerian student, speak volumes: 'I always wanted to cancel this diversity of mine ... because usually you are taught that we all have to be the same to be accepted.' Likewise, Amina expressively described what it means to be 'the other' in a social constellation in which the intergroup power dynamics tend to reproduce a separation between a good normality and a bad anomaly: 'since even I did not recognize being Moroccan as a value, as an asset, when others asked me about this part of me, I felt somehow fragile, as if they were devaluing me.' Socially constructed disparities of power and values are internalized, and cultural difference risks being perceived as something shameful or to be obliterated. This is why Sufian, an Italian-born student with Egyptian parents, argued that

> the challenge lies in knowing how to grow as a future generation, aware from the very beginning of the potential with which diversity comes. Sometimes people criticize fish for not being able to fly, you know? So, if you do not live in a setting that can value your potential, it is normal that that same potential risks making you feel guilty, whereas it should make the others feel guilty!

Why is it that some immediate descendants of migrants (please note that it is just *some* of them) are able to rid themselves of the sense of inadequacy that their surrounding environment projects onto them? Being able to share your experiences with other people who have faced similar challenges is of course crucial. Italian-born Germain, whose parents had migrated from the Ivory Coast had this to say about it:

You deny that side of yourself a little bit. Then, once you find yourself in a situation where you are in contact with people like you and see that they coexist perfectly within both cultures – and even see the value in them – you ask yourself, "but how come? I want to be like them too!".

Brigitte, an Italian-Cameroonian student, was able to give new meaning to her inner diversity thanks to some empowering relationships she had at school: 'it used to be a burden, a very heavy burden. Everything changed in high school thanks to some people, my professors, who taught me that what I was had value.'

Henry, born and raised in Italy to Ghanaian parents, learnt how to value his minority culture when he moved to England. 'Coming here I realized that in fact there are people who live a beautiful life in Ghana. There are books written by very famous authors, acclaimed all over the world. Entering the English world really changed my mentality, because in Italy information on interculturality is limited.' He then added:

One thing I have always missed in Italy was representation, I have never seen anyone at any level achieving something major who was a person of colour. So, coming here to England, at first it felt strange to go to a shop and see a black salesman, or getting on a bus and seeing a black driver, or going to a bank and seeing a black banker. Then I said: 'OK, wow, in what kind of society did I live in Italy?' Italian society does not recognize that there is diversity and that it should mirror all the people who make it – not 'foreigners' and 'Italians' but simply 'Italians'!

It is through this kind of lived experience that perceived fragilities can be turned into strengths: 'many of us have this kind of extra thing – the ability to be with other people in this world in a different way,' said Yousuf, an Italian-Moroccan student, 'because we had to learn how to be with ourselves after realizing who "ourselves" was, that is a good training!'

Omar, an Italian student of Lebanese descent, echoed the same idea when he claimed that, 'by self-reflecting, I learnt that in reality I cannot and should not erase my diversity, but I should rather enhance its value.' He went on to say that, 'I think this helps you to value the diversity of others too.' Omar's words show that through a process of meaning construction that entails an often-harrowing self-scrutiny, the immediate descendants of migrants can move from being othered to enhancing the value of 'otherness'. While this may seem like a happy-ending story, should it really be so hard?

References

Dell'Orco, D. (2022) 'Le violenze di Capodanno dimostrano la follia dello ius soli', *Il Giornale* (online), 16 January, available at: https://www.ilgiornale.it/news/politica/violenze-capodanno-dimostrano-lassurdit-dello-ius-soli-2002598.html.

Mascitelli, B. and C. De Lazzari (2016) 'Interculturalism, multiculturalism and Italianness: the case of Italy', *Journal of European Studies*, 8 (2), doi: 10.30722/anzjes.vol8.iss2.15165.

Milazzo G. (2021) *Notizie ai margini: nono rapporto Carta di Roma 2021*, Associazione Carta di Roma, available at: https://www.cartadiroma.org/wp-content/uploads/2021/12/Notizie-ai-margini.pdf.

Pesarini, A. and G. Tintori (2020) 'Mixed identities in Italy: a country in denial', in Z. Rocha and P. Aspinall (eds) *The Palgrave international handbook of mixed racial and ethnic classification*, Palgrave Macmillan, 349–65, doi: 10.1007/978-3-030-22874-3_19.

Rame S. (2017) 'Stupratori di Rimini, Gasparri alla sinistra: "Con lo ius soli sarebbero italiani"', *Il Giornale* (online), 3 September, available at: www.ilgiornale.it.

Sarli, A. and J. Phillimore (2022) 'The intercultural competence of second-generation individuals: knowledge gaps and steps forward', *International Journal of Intercultural Relations*, 88: 11–21, doi: 10.1016/j.ijintrel.2022.03.004.

Connecting Superdiversity and the Politics of Brexit[1]

Sarah Neal and Allan Cochrane

Brexit has profoundly shaped public debate and politics in the UK since 2016. Leave and remain positions have become key political identifiers and are often stronger than political-party affiliations. As we have watched the news and seen long lines of stationary lorries in Kent, or heard about healthcare and food production shortages, Brexit has never been far from the headlines or from people's everyday lives.

Widely interpreted as an anti-migrant articulation of national identity, the politics of Brexit has framed a period of social and cultural cleavage in the UK that has sharpened divisions, racialization and anti-migrant sentiments. Not surprisingly, the main analytical gaze has focused on explanations for the leave vote and what it represented. Many of these explanations are now familiar, as they variously pivot towards an emphasis on low-income, post-industrial geographies, racism and post-colonialism, or identity and cultural polarization. In the noise of seeking to explain why the leave campaign was successful, there has been less room for understanding the nature and political geographies of the remain vote.

Yet, the political geographies of the remain vote often overlapped with geographies of superdiversity. This is most obvious in London but also in other more ethnically diverse areas, which also voted for the UK to stay in the EU or had narrower leave majorities. This raises the question of how superdiversity – a social phenomenon produced by complex, fragmented migrations, mobilities and settlements – should be reconfigured and reimagined in the politics of Brexit.

1. This short article draws on our chapter in *The Oxford Handbook of Superdiversity* (Neal and Cochrane 2023).

247

Superdiversity highlights the intersectional multiplicities associated with patterns of migration to urban places in the first two decades of the twenty-first century. In this context, it has become an easy shorthand for describing ethnic demographic change. In its most intense forms, superdiversity has tended to build on a dynamic relationship between new migration groups, formations and settlements, the legacies from older migrations as well as other processes of social change such as urban regeneration and gentrification. The populations of Britain's big cities have seen significant shifts since the early 2000s. This is particularly apparent in globalized London, where, according to the 2021 Census, 46 per cent of residents identify 'with Asian, black, mixed or "other" ethnic groups, and a further 17% with white ethnic minorities' (ONS 2022). Some 37 per cent of London's population are not UK-born and only a minority of London's residents identify as 'white British', but many of the UK's other big cities also have complex, superdiverse demographic profiles. Beyond these urban centres of superdiversity new migration patterns have begun to change and dynamically reconfigure smaller cities and towns such as Milton Keynes and Peterborough, as they increasingly become part of a changing geography of migration settlement and ethnic diversity.

Rural areas of the UK, not often associated with or conceptualized as sites of migration, have also become a focus for global mobilities, EU migration and migrant labour markets (Neal et al. 2021). This new ruralism in twenty-first-century mobilities incorporates forms of superdiversity that have begun to stretch the concept beyond its urban associations. The tensions surrounding the ruralization of migration in the UK were highlighted in the 2016 referendum with the highest leave vote in the UK being in Boston, a small town in the largely rural region of Lincolnshire in the East of England. In contrast to the experience in many urban areas, in which remain voting tended to be higher in places that had experienced high levels of migration, in the case of Boston the leave vote seems to have been associated with significant EU migration, reflecting high labour demand from agri-business and food production. Rural Lincolnshire is part of the wider experience in which the UK countryside has been extensively restructured and become a significant site of labour migration and, increasingly, asylum seeker and refugee settlement. High-profile media and policy attention has been directed towards the economic impacts of Brexit for farmers, food production industries and land/environmental management. However, insufficient attention has been given to the social implications of the post-Brexit settlement for rural communities, rural-based migrants and broader configurations of rural diversity, belonging and cohesion. In a new project funded by the Leverhulme Trust (January 2023–25) Sarah and colleagues will examine what the rural referendum outcomes reflect and what the ongoing processes and social consequences of Brexit will be for these newly diverse rural communities.[2]

The implications of Boston's leave vote, as in the Midlands and Northern England's deindustrialized regions, have been widely interpreted as the place-based articulation of anti-migration, anti-superdiversity politics (Goodhart 2017). However, the macro patterns of Brexit voting obscure more complex and dynamic local processes of social and political change in the UK: even in the Midlands and North of England the pattern of referendum voting was much more uneven and uncertain than has been popularly understood. This highlights the need for a more 'grey scale' analysis of Brexit's political geography, which focuses on the different pulls in the remain/leave trends. In London, and several other big (and not so big) and more superdiverse cities in England, the majority voted to remain – Liverpool, Manchester, Bristol, Newcastle, Leeds, Cambridge, Oxford, York, Brighton. Some affluent, semi-rural suburban areas (Oxfordshire, Surrey and Sussex) voted remain but other parts of the same prosperous South East England (much of Kent and Hampshire) voted to leave. Sarah and others have argued elsewhere (Neal et al. 2021) that, despite rural areas having a higher (55 per cent) leave vote, there were rural areas and rurally located towns that voted remain (for example, Ceredigion in West Wales and Stroud in Gloucestershire, Exeter in Devon) and even in London, several of the boroughs on the outer east of the city (including Barking and Dagenham) voted leave.

What does such granularity in political geographies mean for understanding the politics of Brexit and, in particular, its relationship with superdiversity? It raises some fundamental questions about the extent to which Brexit and the leave vote can be read unproblematically as the emergence of a new English nationalism. It draws attention to the ways in which the Brexit vote showed that 'England' itself is a fundamentally contested and uncertain category,

2.   This two-year project (Living Brexit in rural Britain: migration and rural communities) is funded by the Leverhulme Trust to examine how socially differentiated rural communities experience, manage and imagine post-Brexit social relations and rural futures in England, Scotland and Wales. The members of the research team are Sarah Neal, Anna Gawlewicz (University of Glasgow), Rhys Dafydd Jones (Aberystwyth University), Jesse Heley (Aberystwyth University).

rather than being united around some clear-cut nationalist agenda. This is a point made by Virdee and McGeever (2018: 1815–16) when they argue that the multicultural realities of England will always unsettle English nationalism.

In their analysis of Brexit and its implications for understanding contemporary British politics, Sobolewska and Ford (2020) go further to suggest that the vote reflected sets of identity and cultural politics that have superseded old divisions based on class or income. It is in this context that considering the implications of superdiversity becomes a means of more closely interrogating (and questioning) broadly drawn social categories, without discounting the significance of those divisions. So, for example, among minority ethnic groups there was a significant leave vote, even if it only amounted to around 30 per cent in aggregate terms. However, there is evidence that concerns about the inequity of treatment between their own experiences and those of migrants from countries of the European Union (particularly the accession states after 2005) encouraged a leave vote, in the hope that post-Brexit Britain would allow an easier route to migration from Commonwealth countries (see Begum 2019). Meanwhile, it was in London's most superdiverse boroughs such as Hackney, Haringey and Lambeth, with their entanglements of historical and contemporary migrant settlement, multiculture and socio-economic inequalities, that the highest remain votes were recorded.

The UK's vote to leave and the politics of Brexit did not come out of nowhere. For scholars such as Michaela Benson (2020), Brexit is 'the culmination of longer histories of racism in Britain'. In much post-referendum analysis, stress has been placed on the perceived threat of migration and the need to control borders as a racialized focus influencing how people voted – and certainly that was one of the central themes highlighted by those campaigning for a leave vote. English nationalism, however, while in the ascendency remains, as we noted earlier, a 'nationalism' that is contested and contradictory and less fixed than might be expected. The danger of seeking to capture social change in the language of votes and voting behaviour is that it encourages the clustering of complex social phenomena into what seem to be stable, coherent groups (capable of being described as 'tribes' or having shared identities). The concept of superdiversity is a powerful reminder that there is an everyday politics of difference and of negotiating space that cannot readily be reduced to such divisions. While it is possible to generate political mobilizations around specific political projects (like Brexit), it is also important to recognize the extent to which other ways of thinking, other identifications, are possible and the strength of the remain vote in some of the most superdiverse urban geographies may be read as indicative of this.

While superdiversity is not in itself a theory (Vertovec 2017), using the concept as a prompt and a frame for the analysis of the political geographies of Brexit's outcomes highlight the value of new theorizations around the effects, experiences and politics of contemporary superdiverse migration flows and settlements in both older and newer multicultural geographies of the UK. The situated emphasis of superdiversity is central to its meaning and the ways in which it is used in migration studies. But, as migration and diversity continue to unfix, unsettle, refix, and resecure ideas of national identity then extending superdiversity as an anti-racist, trans- or post-national optic for making sense of nation, citizenship, exclusion and racialized inequalities is a pressing project. It pushes us to think super-diversity beyond the politics of place even as it is informed by the nuances of place-based politics and demographic and social transformations.

References

Begum, N. (2019) '"The Eastern Europeans are taking all the Asian jobs": ethnic minority support for Brexit', in P. Cowley and R. Ford (eds) *Sex, lies and politics: the secret influences that drive our political choices*, Biteback, ch. 42.

Benson M. (2020) 'Brexit and the classed politics of bordering: the British in France and European belonging', *Sociology*, 53 (3): 501–17.

Goodhart, D. (2017) *The road to somewhere: the populist revolt and the future of politics*, Hurst.

Neal S. and A. Cochrane (2023) 'Superdiversity through the lens of Brexit', in F. Meissner, N. Sigona and S. Vertovec (eds) *The Oxford handbook of superdiversity*, Cambridge University Press.

Neal S., A. Gawlewicz, J. Heley and R. D. Jones (2021) Rural Brexit? The ambivalent politics of rural community, migration and dependency, *Journal of Rural Studies*, 82: 176–83

ONS (2022) Ethnic group, England and Wales: Census 2021. Office for National Statistics. https://www.ons.gov.uk/peoplepopulationandcommunity/cultural identity/ethnicity/bulletins/ethnicgroupenglandandwales/census2021.

Sobolewska, M. and R. Ford (2020) *Brexitland: identity, diversity and the reshaping of British politics*, Cambridge University Press.

Vertovec, S. (2017) 'Mooring, migration milieus and complex explanations', *Ethnic and Racial Studies*, 40 (9): 1574–81.

Virdee, S. and B. McGeever (2018) 'Racism, crisis, Brexit', *Ethnic and Racial Studies*, 41 (10): 1802–19.

PART FOUR:
GAZES, PERSPECTIVES AND INTERVENTIONS

Superdiversity from a Governance Perspective

Maria Schiller and Peter Scholten

What type of governance questions does superdiversity evoke? As a concept that captures a social reality of increasingly complex migratory patterns and migration-related diversities, superdiversity itself neither represents a mode of governance, nor has a specific effect on governance. However, it does seem to provide a broad variety of challenges to conventional modes of governance, such as the use of social categorizations in policy, the organization of policy and delineation of responsibilities for addressing superdiversity across various areas and levels, and the development of a perspective or vision on living together in superdiverse contexts.

The aim of this chapter is to explore what challenges superdiversity poses in terms of governance, and what the implications are for modes of governance.

Superdiversity and governance

The concept of superdiversity captures the social complexity of migration and migration-related diversities (Vertovec 2007, 2021). Because of its very complexity, however, it comes with a variety of challenges in relation to governance, broadly defined. The governance of migration and migration-related diversities refers to any policies (formal and informal) that are adopted by any actor (governmental and non-governmental) on migration and migration-related diversities (whether or not explicitly framed as migration or diversity governance).

A first challenge is that superdiversity calls into question the use of categorizations in governance. Concepts such as 'ethnic groups', 'migrant', 'minorities' and many others that have played a central role in how societies have framed migration and diversity, are challenged by this added complexity. This, among other things, involves the many intersectionalities that come with superdiversity, for instance blending notions of socio-economic status, ethnicity and legal status. However, the use of such categorizations is often deeply entrenched in policy discourses and can lead to simplifications or a denial of complexity, and thus turning a blind eye to superdiversity (Scholten 2020).

Another challenge is to avoid treating migration and diversity as stand-alone topics, as they are connected to broader economic governance, social governance, climate governance, and health governance. As Dahinden (2016) convincingly demonstrated, many issues projected on migrants and on migration are not essentially connected either to being a migrant or to migration. At the same time, migration and diversity sometimes need dedicated attention and leadership. Governing the complexities of super-diversity requires prime ministers, mayors and other strategic policy-makers to take leadership and to address migration and its resulting diversification proactively (Bazurli et al. 2022).

A third challenge is that superdiversity can work out very differently in different contexts and at different points in time: it is essentially a situational phenomenon. This can put it at odds with governance approaches, which tend to be situated in national or supranational settings and are often characterized by high levels of path-dependency. In the context of the literature on the 'local turn' in migration studies (Zapata-Barrero et al. 2017), attention has been drawn to the urban and even to the neighborhood level.

A final challenge is that superdiversity scholarship provides no ready-made recipe for its governance, no political vision on how living together in superdiverse contexts should or could succeed, no goals for its governance, and no paths to follow. This ambiguity surrounding the concept makes it somewhat different from multiculturalism with its emphasis on cultural recognition and equality, or from interculturalism and its orientation towards cultural exchange and communication. The open-endedness and malleability of superdiversity means that policymakers need to produce their own responses, which suggests that their policies will be tailor-made and context-specific. It also carries the risk that its governance could go in different directions and thus also serve neoliberal agendas.

Besides delineating these governance challenges, we wish to add a meta one, namely that of taking a reflexive stance on conceiving superdiversity as a governance challenge per se. Taking inspiration from recent critiques in the literature, migration and diversity governance have often been accused of falling into the trap of 'methodological nationalism' (Wimmer and Glick-Schiller 2003), of assuming persistent national policy models (Bertossi 2011), and of demonstrating a strong commitment to societal engineering, also referred to as 'integrationism' or the 'integration nation' (Favell 2003). Another challenge to governing superdiversity could be deciding when it requires active governance and when it does not.

A (complexity) governance perspective

What does superdiversity need from a governance perspective? The literature contains interesting work on what modes of governance best fit situations characterized by high levels of complexity, such as superdiversity. For instance, Verweij and Thompson (2006) argued that coping with complex issues, such as climate change, requires a strongly situational and flexible approach, with a wide variety of actors; in other words, 'complex problems require complex solutions'. This resonates with a broader evolving literature in governance studies on how to respond to complexity (Geyer and Rihani 2012).

One aspect of complexity governance is polycentrism (Rhodes 1997), which means that governance requires the involvement of a broad range of actors, which often includes but is not limited to central government. This so-called network governance, which is a traditional feature of the shift from government to governance (Klijn and Koppenjan 2014), opposes highly state-centric approaches to migration and diversity governance, such as 'integrationism'. Also, complexity improves network governance because the networks themselves are often well situated to adapt to temporal and local circumstances.

Another aspect of complexity governance is mainstreaming, which means embedding complex topics into a broad variety of issue domains or policy areas. In other words, it is an attempt to prevent complexity denial, which arises when matters such as migration and diversity are treated as stand-alone topics. Adaptive leadership (Baltaci and Balci 2017; Uhl-Bien 2007) is another way of handling complexity. An important element here is the development of a long-term agenda tailored to the specific context, but one that is also open to learning from and reacting to emerging conditions and situations (Schiller 2016).

Finally, there is reflexivity, or at least some form of temporal and situational responsiveness in governance dynamics. Rather than relying on fixed models and target groups, reflexivity involves policymakers constantly reacting to often unforeseeable and uncontrollable social developments, changes in who is in need and/or considered deserving, and being responsive to the need for active steering in any given situation.

The politics of denying superdiversity

A perspective that embraces complexity can shed light on how governance could or should respond to superdiversity. However, that does not mean that government actors will agree to respond in a way that accommodates complexity. This may be due to a variety of reasons, such as a lack of familiarity with or understanding of the intricacies involved, or adopting a normative stance that refuses to acknowledge subtlety, such as being opposed to superdiversity, or being put under political or organizational pressure not to recognize it.

In the field of migration and diversity governance, one can see a variety of reasons why a complexity approach does not, or at least not always, take off. One of these is the persistence, for historical and political reasons, of a commitment to central control or, as Boswell (2011) described it, narratives of central societal steering. There is a firm belief that (rational) government policies are not only required to but also capable of coping with migration and diversity 'problems' – hence, the strong focus on migration and integration policies, often in the form of distinct 'national models' or in a choice of specific 'quick fixes', such as building a wall to halt migration. This often leaves little space for a more situated and flexible approach.

Another factor is that both political and public discourses on migration and integration have become heavily institutionalized and are thus difficult to alter or render more 'complex'. The concept of integration, as well as social categorizations such as 'migrants' or 'minorities', has become so embedded in how we think and speak about migration and diversity, that we cannot always recognize the limitations of our discourses. Such concepts have become constitutive of how many of the complexities we are able to see, and what we miss.

In addition, political interests and the exercise of power can sometimes interfere with the willingness or ability of certain actors to acknowledge complexity. Since discourses on minorities and migrants are also about power and belonging, they often produce and reproduce inequalities between groups. Upholding specific categorizations, and complicating or solving problems will tend to advantage some and disadvantage others, regardless of whether they adequately represent social complexity.

An inability to respond to complexity, for whatever reason, has consequences. It can create 'policy fiascoes' in which policies not only fail to meet their own objectives, but also produce inadvertent effects. This is sometimes described as 'alienation' – a form of disengagement between governance and its dynamics on the one hand, and social complexity and social dynamics on the other. One could interpret the so-called 'integration crisis' as a manifestation of alienation in which superdiversity becomes disengaged from a belief in rational societal steering and group categorizations. Likewise, the so-called 'refugee crisis' could be seen as a manifestation of the disengagement between narratives of migration control on the one hand and the emerging social complexities of migratory pathways on the other.

Conclusion

From a perspective that accommodated the complexity of superdiversity, we started out by recognizing and naming some of the challenges we were likely to encounter. These included using categorizations in the context of superdiversity; treating migration and diversity as intrinsically interlinked with other governance issues, yet requiring reconfiguration to specific places and situations; and the meta challenge of taking a reflexive approach to governing superdiversity. As we argued, there is no one size fits all approach, but recognizing complexity calls for situational, flexible, poly-centric approaches, mainstreaming responsibilities, and adaptive and reflexive leadership. The bounded rationality of policymakers, who become overwhelmed or simply resist addressing complex issues, is a major obstacle to dealing with complexity. Also, administrations can resort to hierarchical top-down ways of governing, and politics and power can stand in the way of adaptive ways of governance. That said, the perception of crises could serve as a window of opportunity for recognizing the need for more complex governance in responding to superdiversity.

References

Baltaci, A. and A. Balci (2017) 'Complexity leadership: a theoretical perspective'. *International Journal of Educational Leadership and Management*, 5 (1): 30–59.

Bazurli, R., T. Caponio and E. de Graauw (2022) 'Between a rock and a hard place: mayors, migration challenges and multilevel political dynamics', *Territory, Politics, Governance*, 10 (3): 297–305.

Bertossi, C. (2011) 'National models of integration in Europe', *American Behavioral Scientist*, 55 (12): 1561–80.

Boswell, C. (2011) 'Migration control and narratives of steering', *The British Journal of Politics & International Relations*, 13 (1): 12–25.

Dahinden, J. (2016) 'A plea for the "de-migranticization" of research on migration and integration', *Ethnic and Racial Studies*, 39 (13): 2207–25.

Favell, A. (2003) 'Integration nations: the nation-state and research on immigrants in Western Europe', *Comparative Social Research*, 22: 13–42,

Geyer, R. and S. Rihani (2012) *Complexity and public policy: a new approach to 21st century politics, policy and society*, Routledge.

Klijn, E.-H. and J. F. Koppenjan (2014) 'Complexity in governance network theory', *Complexity, Governance & Networks*, 1 (1): 61–70.

Rhodes, R. A. W. (1997) *Understanding governance: policy networks, governance, reflexivity and accountability*, Open University Press.

Schiller, M. (2016) *European cities, municipal organizations and diversity: the new politics of difference*, Palgrave Macmillan.

Scholten, P. (2020) *Mainstreaming versus alienation: a complexity perspective on the governance of migration and diversity*, Palgrave Macmillan.

Uhl-Bien, M., R. Marion and B. McKelvey (2007) 'Complexity leadership theory: shifting leadership from the industrial age to the knowledge era', *The Leadership Quarterly*, 18 (4): 298–318.

Vertovec, S. (2007) 'Super-diversity and its implications', *Ethnic and Racial Studies*, 30 (6): 1024–54.

Vertovec, S. (2021) 'The social organization of difference', *Ethnic and Racial Studies*, 44 (8): 1273–95.

Verweij, M. and M. Thompson (eds) (2006) *Clumsy solutions for a complex world: governance, politics and plural perceptions*, Palgrave Macmillan.

Wimmer, A. and N. Glick-Schiller (2003) 'Methodological nationalism, the social sciences, and the study of migration: an essay in historical epistemology', *The International Migration Review*, 37 (3): 576–610.

Zapata-Barrero, R., T. Caponio and P. Scholten (2017) 'Theorizing the "local turn" in a multi-level governance framework of analysis: a case study in immigrant policies', *International Review of Administrative Sciences*, 83 (2): 241–6.

Precarious Legal Status

Cecilia Menjívar

A range of legal categories in the USA involve precarious legal statuses, and the immigrants who hold them share a lack of security. These statuses take a variety of forms across the major categories of immigration and include temporary work permits, family-based temporary residency, temporary permits for asylum seekers, temporary protection for those waiting for their applications to be adjudicated, and all statuses that limit access to social benefits by virtue of being classified as legal sub-permanence. Excluded from this broad tent are temporary statuses that are not meant to lead to permanence, such as tourist visas and the like. Technically, immigrants with a temporary permit, such as temporary protected status, or protected under the deferred action for childhood arrivals (DACA) program (in the USA), are classified within the unauthorized (or irregular) category, which underlines the precarity of these temporary statuses. The population classified as undocumented is approximately 25 per cent of the total US immigrant population (Budman 2020). Of this 25 per cent, it is estimated that approximately 15 per cent hold a temporary status (Capps et al. 2020).

Permanent residency ('green card holders' in the USA), as its name implies, guarantees a right to reside in the country permanently. It is also intended to provide a direct path to citizenship through naturalization (Motomura 2006), with all the rights that this 'last step' in the process conferred, including the right to vote and hold certain elected positions. Any status below lawful permanent residence is believed to be precarious given the insecurity and uncertainty precarious statuses embody.

However, with the expansion of immigration enforcement under the punitive turn in immigration control around the world, more immigration categories have been enveloped under the tent of precarity. Thus, the range of precarious statuses has been expanded to include undocumented individuals, asylum seekers applying for protection, immigrants placed under state surveillance after release from detention and, increasingly, statuses that until recently were supposed to be permanent, such as (in the USA) permanent residents and naturalized citizens. Although the deportation of a lawful permanent resident and the denaturalization of a naturalized citizen technically do not result in precarity, both contribute to eroding the stability of legal statuses with significant consequences for the immigrants, their families, and communities. As such, both previously secure statuses have now fallen under the expansive reach of precarity today. And, although the focus of this essay is on the USA, this case is not alone, for immigrant-receiving countries around the world have adopted similar precarization strategies as tools of immigration control.

In the USA, efforts to destabilize permanent legal statuses, and thus increase their precarity, have accelerated in the past two decades. Commingling the immigration and criminal justice systems that informed the 1996 Illegal Immigration Reform and Immigrant Responsibility Act (IIRIRA) contributed towards eroding the stability of lawful permanent residence. This law, applied retroactively, reclassified certain offences that lawful permanent residents committed at any point in their lives into felonious and deportable crimes, even when the offence was not a serious crime when committed and even when the individual had already served a sentence. As a result, thousands of lawful permanent residents are placed in deportation proceedings each year, comprising about 10 per cent of all deportations (American Immigration Council 2010). Between 2004 and 2016, an estimated 45,808 immigrants who entered the country as lawful permanent residents were deported (or removed) (TRAC 2016). These immigrants are barred from readmission because they now have a criminal record (for example, they have been processed in the system), aggravated by any attempt at re-entry because re-entry constitutes a felonious crime.

More recently, during the Trump administration, denaturalization efforts gained momentum. A 'denaturalization task force' was created to investigate potentially fraudulent naturalization cases. Efforts to revoke naturalization are couched in a criminalization framework as the stated impetus behind them is the suspicion that certain naturalized citizens have misrepresented themselves on the application, a felony. Investigations of potential fraud or wilful concealing of information in the naturalization process were expanded in 2017. Whereas there were only 305 denaturalization cases filed between 1990 and 2017, since 2017 there were approximately 2500 cases under investigation for possible fraud (National Immigration Forum 2018).

Immigrants with precarious legal statuses beyond the undocumented category inhabit a space I call liminal legality (Menjívar 2006), which is characterized by a materially, socially, and existentially different condition from undocumented living (or permanent legality). A key component of it is the long waiting times and uncertainty embedded in these spaces. In my work, I have found that living in this condition, often for years, has a deep impact on a person's sense of self, family relationships, and contacts with institutions, and it even emerges in their artistic expressions. The effects of living with temporary legality are immediate and long term and have been found to emerge in other aspects of life too. For instance, the range of precarious statuses stratifies access to resources and social benefits, including the healthcare safety net (Van Natta et al. 2019), as undocumented immigrants are left out of the formal healthcare system but those on temporary statuses have differentiated access to it. Similar stratified access and experiences have been found in key areas of immigrant integration, including education, employment, and home ownership (Waters and Pineau 2015). Thus, precarity among immigrants with temporary statuses manifests in truncated paths to integration with long-term and multigenerational effects. For instance, they may be civically active and know when to exercise their rights, but at the same time their limited legality keeps them advancing socio-economically as they remain in lower-paid jobs and occupations that do not lead to mobility (Menjívar et al. 2022). Thus, precarity among immigrants with limited legality is remarkably enduring because it affects their children, including their US-born ones, and even their grandchildren (Menjívar 2023).

Although uncertainty and a fear of waiting characterize precarious legal statuses, especially in contexts of increased immigration enforcement and generalized punitive efforts to control immigration, living in this condition also generates a sense of hope for the future. By virtue of inhabiting in-between spaces, such immigrants can see and embrace the possibility of exercising what rights they have, which is what drives the immigrant mobilizations seeking justice.

The effects of living with precarious statuses, however, are not limited to the national territory in which the immigrants live, for the ripple effects reach their countries of origin. Their families at home also experience waiting and anxiety because their loved ones may be unable to secure more permanent statuses. A precarious status by its very nature places these immigrants at risk of deportation; thus, such immigrants live with one foot in one country and the other in the other. Consequently, they continue to send regular remittances, buy houses, and even keep savings accounts in their countries of origin because the thought of abruptly having to go back is never far from their minds. For them, it is often difficult to make long-term plans and decisions for themselves, their children, and other loved ones both in their home countries and in the country of their immigration.

References

American Immigration Council (2010) 'The ones they leave behind: deportation of lawful permanent residents harms U.S. citizen children', Immigration Policy Center, 26 April, available at: https://www.americanimmigrationcouncil.org/sites/default/files/research/Childs_Best_Interest_Fact_Sheet_042610.pdf.

Budman, A. (2020) 'Key findings about U.S. immigrants', Pew Research Center, available at: https://www.pewresearch.org/fact-tank/2020/08/20/key-findings-about-u-s-immigrants/.

Capps, R., J. Gelatt, A. G. Ruiz Soto and J. Van Hook (2020) 'Unauthorized immigrants in the United States: stable numbers, changing origins', Migration Policy Institute, available at: https://www.migrationpolicy.org/sites/default/files/publications/mpi-unauthorized-immigrants-stablenumbers-changingorigins_final.pdf.

Menjívar, C. (2006) 'Liminal legality: Salvadoran and Guatemalan immigrants' lives in the United States', *American Journal of Sociology*, 111 (4): 999–1037.

Menjívar, C. (2023). 'State categories, bureaucracies of displacement, and possibilities from the margins', *American Sociological Review*, 88 (1): 1–23.

Menjívar, C., V. Agadjanian and B. Oh (2022) 'The contradictions of liminal legality: economic attainment and civic engagement of Central American immigrants on temporary protected status', *Social Problems*, 69 (3): 678–98.

Motomura, H. (2006) *Americans in waiting: the lost story of immigration and citizenship in the United States*, Oxford University Press.

National Immigration Forum (2018) 'Fact sheet on denaturalization', 2 October, available at: https://immigrationforum.org/article/fact-sheet-on-denaturalization.

TRAC (2016) 'Historical data: Immigration and Customs Enforcement removals: ICE data through January 2016', available at: https://trac.syr.edu/phptools/immigration/removehistory/.

Van Natta, M., N. J. Burke, I. H. Yen, M. D. Fleming, C. L. Hanssmann, M. P. Rasidjan and J. K. Shim (2019) 'Stratified citizenship, stratified health: examining latinx legal status in the U.S. healthcare safety net', *Social Science & Medicine*, 220: 49–55.

Waters, M. and M. G. Pineau (eds) (2015) *The integration of immigrants into American society*, National Academy Press.

The Necropolitics of
Immigration Policing

Jonathan Xavier Inda

For the last few decades, migrants in the USA, particularly those without legal documents, have been cast as criminals who threaten the nation's wellbeing and security. Consequently, the measures employed to govern this population have been exclusionary and punitive. Initially, the US federal government sought to manage and police unauthorized migration principally through militarizing the US–Mexico border, the goal being to prevent people entering the country illicitly. This militarization accelerated under Donald Trump's presidency and continues under Joe Biden's administration. In addition to the militarization of the geopolitical border, the USA now also heavily polices the nation's interior to rid itself of putatively dangerous elements inside the country. Interior policing has sanctioned workplace raids and immigration sweeps of public places, and has empowered local law enforcement agencies to apply immigration laws. This intensified policing of the interior has resulted in the massive deportation of immigrants. To facilitate this deportation drive, the USA has developed a vast archipelago of carceral spaces in which immigrants are detained pending their removal from the national territory.

Importantly, the militarization of the border and the policing of the interior has resulted in a great deal of violence towards migrants and asylum seekers. The criminalization and denigration of migrants in official and popular circles has seemingly given state authorities and their proxies a free licence to mistreat them. These state practices amount to what can be called a necropolitics of immigration policing (see also Williams 2015). In *The History of Sexuality*, Michel Foucault (1980: 143) uses the term biopower to designate 'what brought life and its mechanisms into the realm of explicit calculations and made knowledge-power an agent of transformation of human life'. Biopower thus points to how political and other authorities have assigned themselves the duty of administering bodies and managing populations to foster individual and collective life. Foucault also suggests that there is an underside to biopower, in which 'entire populations are mobilized for the purpose of wholesale slaughter in the name of life necessity' (Foucault 1980: 137). This means that biopower not only fosters life, but also routinely does away with it in order to preserve it. The reasoning here is that the death of the other – that is, of those deemed dangerous, unfit, or diseased and thus a threat to individual and collective existence – will make life in general healthier and purer. This death does not have to be the direct or literal act of putting some-one to death. It could also be indirect death – the act of exposing to death, of multiplying for some the risk of death, or simply political death, expulsion, rejection, or exclusion. An outwardly life-affirming power, then, biopower also has an exclusionary, lethal underside. Achille Mbembe (2003) calls this underside necropolitics – a politics of death. In the USA, migration is managed in a decidedly necropolitical way.

Deadly borders

The necropolitics of immigration policing is perhaps most visible at the geopolitical border between Mexico and the USA. Customs and Border Protection (CBP) agents routinely mistreat immigrants apprehended while attempting to cross the border without documents, or who request asylum. Indeed, abuse, dehumanization, and neglect are part of the institutional culture of the CBP. Apprehended migrants are routinely denied food, water, and medical treatment. They are also often placed in overcrowded and exceedingly cold holding cells. Furthermore, children, women, and other vulnerable individuals are time and again deported to Mexico at night. Finally, migrants are subjected to pervasive verbal abuse (particularly derog-atory sexual and racial epithets), as well as to physical abuse (such as agents striking and/or kicking people in custody and using chokeholds).

Significantly, the abuses perpetrated by the US CBP have also involved deadly and lethal force. The American Civil Liberties Union of Texas estimates that 218 people, a number of them under questionable circumstances, died in encounters with the CBP between January 2010 and April 2022. These deaths included that of Anastasio Hernández Rojas. CPB agents arrested him as he was attempting to make his way back to the USA after being deported to Mexico. He was trying to rejoin his family – three children, all US citizens, and his partner. Border enforcement agents beat and tasered him to death while deporting him back to Mexico. The official narrative suggests that Anastasio became violent as he was being deported. Agents attempted to gain control of him, but he was simply too strong for them (at one point there were close to twenty agents on the scene). When they 'failed' to gain control of him, one of the agents was 'forced' to taser him. However, civilian witnesses and the trauma on Anastasio's body tell a different story. It is the story of man who was severely beaten by multiple officers and who cried out for help. There are two videos of the event: in one, you can hear Anastasio pleading for help as agents were beating him. In another, you see him immobile on the ground, surrounded by about a dozen agents, one of them repeatedly tasering him. Anastasio suffered a heart attack as a result of the assault and was later pronounced dead.

Lethal detention

The same culture of cruelty found at the geopolitical border pervades the vast immigration detention complex. Although detention is not supposed to be punitive, the reality is that its spaces feel and function like prisons. In fact, they are often worse than prisons. Immigration detention facilities tend to be less well supervised than prisons and the detainees have fewer rights than prisoners. As such, immigration detainees routinely experience abuse and neglect, perhaps most notably through their exposure to substandard medical care. Problems that plague detention facilities include inadequate initial medical screenings or examinations; a delay or failure to respond to sick call requests; inadequate mental healthcare services; the misuse of isolation; and mismanagement or denial of prescribed medications.

The type of healthcare provided to migrants in detention can be called 'minimalist medicine'. This is a type of medicine that cares little for migrant bodies, providing only enough care to minimally sustain life. The goal of detention care seems to be to nurture the lives of detainees only modestly – to give them just enough care so that they are in good enough shape to be released or deported. This 'just enough' approach to medical care in detention has disastrous consequences for detainees. Many migrants need more than just enough healthcare. Between October 2003 and October 2021, there were at least 222 deaths in Immigration and Customs Enforcement (ICE) custody. Substandard care contributed to a number of these deaths.

A case that highlights the deadly consequence of minimalist medicine is that of Moises Tino Lopez, a 23-year-old native of Guatemala. On 26

August 2016, the ICE picked him up and placed him in custody for being in the country without authorization. He was held at Hall County Corrections, a local prison in Grand Island, Nebraska, pending his removal from the USA. While in detention, he began to have seizures and, to his great misfortune, medical staff failed to provide him with proper care. He never saw a physician, received no tests to determine the cause of his seizures, and his anti-seizure medication was badly mismanaged. To top it all, through no fault of his own and despite his serious medical condition, prison staff placed him in solitary confinement where he had several more seizures, the last of which proved fatal. All alone in his cell, there was no one to witness his last seizure and intervene to save his life. Moises died on 27 September, after about a month in detention. The official cause of death was brain injury caused by a seizure-induced cardiac arrest.

An ethics of uncare

There is no doubt that immigration policing in the USA is highly necro-political. It seems to be guided by an ethics of uncare. As sociologist Evelyn Nakano Glenn (2000: 86) has noted, care is 'a practice that encompasses an ethic (caring about) and an activity (caring for)'. 'Caring about' refers to affective disposition – to hold dear, to feel concern about, attachment to, or interest in. It has to do with how people and things matter. 'Caring for' involves the practical activity of looking after, providing for, protecting, and sustaining someone or something. In the context of immigration policing, there is a dearth or absence of both affective and practical care. Indeed, it appears that the immigration system cares little about the well-being of migrants. Their lives simply do not matter. This lack of concern is reflected in the lack of practical care non-citizens receive. Indeed, instead of receiving care, migrants are subjected to violence. The consequence of this uncare – of neither caring about nor caring for – is that migrant lives are imperilled to the point of death.

References

Foucault, M. (1980) *The history of sexuality*, Vintage Books.

Glenn, E. N. (2000) 'Creating a caring society', *Contemporary Sociology*, 29 (1): 84–94.

Mbembe, A. (2003) 'Necropolitics', *Public Culture*, 15 (1): 11–40.

Williams, J. M. (2015) 'From humanitarian exceptionalism to contingent care: care and enforcement at the humanitarian border', *Political Geography*, 47: 11–20.

Governing Diversity in Italy: How Racism Affects the Institutional Approach to Migration

Guia Gilardoni

Historically, rich mixes of different people have been freely entering Italy for centuries and huge numbers of Italians have been emigrating to all corners of the earth, and still are. In the early 1990s, however, when international migration flows started to set their sights on Italy, Italians discovered that they were far more racist than they expected themselves to be.

Between 1 January 2008 and 31 December 2019, the civic association Lunaria recorded 7267 racist acts, of which 5231 were of verbal abuse, 883 of physical violence against individuals, 169 of damage to property, and 984 of discrimination (Lunaria 2020). Among the verbal attacks, 3670 consisted of discriminatory propaganda, mainly via websites, blogs, social networks, verbal declarations, and posters. In addition, there were a further 1128 threats to or verbal harassments of individuals, of which 433 were public demonstrations against migrants, asylum seekers and refugees. The most worrying data refer to the 883 cases of physical violence against individuals and the 169 cases of property damage directed at people from a migrant background. Significantly, more than 2600 of the reported cases of discrimination and racism were carried out by institutions. Also, given that discrimination and racism tend to be under reported, these data should be considered as the tip of the iceberg.

While this is all happening, the anti-racism side of the landscape is weak (Human Rights Watch 2011). With the exception of the Black Lives Matter movement, which in Italy gave voice to a usually unheard community, there is a general absence of institutional strategies for containing racism, which is on the whole never considered. The available data on racial harassment are partial and not systematically collected.

The increasing racism, which is also occurring at an institutional level and which is responsible for the lack of any official anti-racist policy, may partially lie in Italy's history of nationhood building. As a relatively recently-created nation-state (1861), it was mainly implemented during the fascist period, when Mussolini was attempting to foster a strong sense of Italian nationalism in what was still a very ethnically divided land. Through his charismatic personality and finely honed political and communicative skills, Mussolini was able to found a nation on the idea of race through a process of auto-racialization – not unlike the nationalisms of other European countries that had strong ethnic, biological, and racial under-pinnings (Padovan 2006). The process also coincided with Italy's colonial period, which, though shorter than that of other Europeans states, was a crucial time for constructing an Italian imagined community (Anderson 2006). Thus, after centuries of deeply-rooted localisms, Italian national identity was successfully validated through the distinction they were able to make between themselves and the black people the colonials were encoun-tering in the Horn of Africa.

Gaia Giuliani and Cristina Lombardi-Diop (2013) analysed the entanglement between racism and sexism in Italian culture by exploring the construction of a female Italian's racial identity as a white woman. The gradual inclusion of darker-skinned women from South Italy into the ideal of a white Italian woman was implemented through the visual and discur-sive contrast with the subaltern black women of colonial East Africa, who were arbitrarily turned into a symbol of primitive lasciviousness and sexual availability. The racism that black women suffer in Italy today derives from this historical past in which the woman becomes an object, a fetish, a foreign body undeserving of respect (Obasuyi 2020). The encounter with African natives allowed Italians to build a common sense of belonging, to start seeing themselves as united as a people. The historically rooted ethnic differences and divisions between North and South Italy, were overcome by accentuating the contrast with the Africans of East Africa.

During the fascist era, Mussolini enhanced Italian nationhood by proclaiming Italians an Arian race. The National Fascist Party's first and second *Libro del Fascista* (Book of the Fascist), published in 1939 and 1940, are important historical sources on the racist education of Italian people. Used as teaching materials, these two little books, especially the second one, are the compendium of the perfect racist. Italians are here defined as belonging to the Arian race and, in the chapter headed 'What do I need to know about race' (PNF 1940: 77), there is an interesting question and answer section:

Q. Which race do you belong to?
A. I belong to the Arian race.
Q. Why do you affirm to be Arian?
A. Because the Italian race is Arian.
Q. Are races all equal?
A. There are physical and spiritual differences between races.
Q. What is the mission of the Arian race?
A. Arian race has a mission to civilize the world, and make it constantly move forward.
Q. What are the highest expressions of world civilization?
A. The highest expressions of world civilization are due to the Arian race.

For at least four years, every Italian school used such books to teach children that racism was a self-evident reality. The new Italian generation of the early 1940s was taught to conceive of themselves as superior to first Africans in the colonies and immediately after that to the Jews.

The foundations of today's racism were laid during the colonial and fascist period through tropes that still resonate today, such as the portrayal in the media of migrants as invaders, and the need to defend Italy's identity, culture, and traditions. Since the first essential defence of the identity of a particular group is to prevent the marriages or mixing of people of different origins, it is still common in mainstream thinking to find it difficult to recognize someone with a black skin as Italian.

After the end of the fascist era, the term 'race' was banned from the Italian lexicon, but racism did not disappear. Instead, it adopted more subtle, politically correct forms based on culture and religion rather than biology, for example cultural racism, or so-called racism without races (Back and Solomos 2000; Fredrickson 2002; Martiniello 2013; Siebert 2003). The anti-migrant political discourse, which fuels so much political propaganda, evolved on these bases.

The first time a political party in Italy focused on security/immigration was when Silvio Berlusconi's party joined forces with Lega Nord to fight the 2008 election. This started a process of openly criminalizing migrants, which later evolved into criminalizing all those who supported migrants, but the centre-left coalition failed to put forward an alternative vision; in fact, it had sometimes adopted similar positions, albeit with different tones (Human Rights Watch 2011).

Matteo Salvini's extremely successful and rarely contested slogan, 'Italians first', which brings to mind Donald Trump's 'America first', is clearly rooted in the colonial past when a sense of superiority, along with the power to dominate and exploit, were the main ingredients of nation-hood. Mussolini himself clarified the importance of racism to the colonial challenge when, on 18 September 1938, he roused the crowd at a mass event in Trieste, stating that:

> The Jewish problem is ... only one aspect of this phenomenon. ... The racial problem did not suddenly burst out of nowhere. ... It [exists only] in relation to imperial conquest; because history teaches us that empires are conquered by arms, but are held by prestige. And for prestige it is necessary to have a clear, severe racial consciousness, that establishes not only the differences, but also very clear superiorities.

This is crucial to any recognition or understanding of racism in Italy today, where prestige is still considered to be very important. This could perhaps go some way towards explaining the negative attitude of Italians towards migrants, but it mostly explains the subtle institutional racism that is clearly informing the national migration policy.

As Clelia Bartoli (2012: 61) highlighted,

> when Italy became a country of immigration, the legislation adopted to regulate the new phenomenon was not primarily intended to allow newcomers to participate as equals. On the contrary, legis-lation and policies have built the minority of the migrant through a hierarchical set of legal statuses regulating access to services and rights. This comes from the colonial past, which indeed was brief but strongly significative.

A hidden historical continuity is at the base of the current institutional racism. This is evident in that the state and its institutions govern diversity with a set of laws, rules and bureaucratic procedures that produce civic stratification and inequality in the migrant population. This historical continuity is less hidden in the recent election of Giorgia Meloni who, in September 2022, became the first woman to be elected as prime minister of Italy. The victory of Fratelli d'Italia, which is an openly racist political party explicitly linked to Mussolini's fascism, makes even more problematic the institutional racism that permits the political legitimization of racism discourses and practices in Italy.

References

Anderson, B. (2006) *Imagined communities: reflections on the origin and spread of nationalism*, Verso.

Back L. and J. Solomos (eds) (2000) *Theories of race and racism: a reader*, Routledge.

Bartoli, C. (2012) *Razzisti per legge: l'Italia che discrimina*, Roma-Bari.

Fredrickson, G. M. (2002) *Breve storia del razzismo*, Donzelli.

Giuliani, G. and C. Lombardi-Diop (2013) *Bianco e nero: storia dell'identità razziale degli italiani*, Mondadori.

Human Rights Watch (2011) *Everyday intolerance: racist and xenophobic violence in Italy*, Human Rights Watch.

Lunaria (eds) (2020) 'Cronache di ordinario razzismo: quinto libro bianco sul razzismo in Italia', Associazione di Promozione Sociale Lunaria, Roma, available at: https://www.cronachediordinariorazzismo.org/quinto-libro-bianco.

Martiniello, M. (2013) *Penser l'ethnicité: identité, culture et relations sociales*, Presses Universitaires de Liège.

Obasuyi, O. Q. D. (2020) *Corpi estranei: il razzismo rimosso che appiattisce la diversita*, People.

Padovan, D. (2006) 'Le scienze sociali e la costruzione dello spazio pubblico: il caso del razzismo fascista', *Rassegna Italiana di Sociologia*, 2, 225–68.

PNF (Partito Nazionale Fascista) (1940) *Il secondo libro del fascista*, PNF.

Siebert, R. (2003) *Il razzismo: il riconoscimento negato*, Carocci.

Civil Society's Role for Inclusion in Conditions of Socio-Economic Vulnerability and Diversity

Gabriella Elgenius

Civil society is increasingly recognized for its role in aiding integration or inclusion, particularly in locations where it can mitigate disadvantage and vulnerability. My research with colleagues in seven socio-economically vulnerable and diverse areas in Sweden and England shows that, despite claims to the contrary, civil society contributes to key dimensions of integration, such as education, employment, language skills, health, social care, and political participation. Research on civil society relies on evolving conceptualizations and a combination of mixed quantitative and qualitative methodologies, to enable the analysis of both broad patterns and in-depth case studies. Seven case-study neighbourhoods were selected in Sweden and England. Administrative and registration data have been analysed and micro-mapping techniques used in combination with interviews with civil-society actors, stakeholders and users. Thus, a mixed methods approach allows us to work with and compare findings from different datasets. In so doing, we approach civil-society action from a holistic eco-system approach to gauge the width and breath of action from a local neighbourhood perspective with a focus on grassroots, informal activity as well as formal action (see links to the research projects websites below.)

Much scholarship has focused on interactions between residents in superdiverse neighbourhoods (Wessendorf 2014), but less attention has been paid to the width and breath of civil society, its many organizations, associations, informal groups, initiatives, foundations and social enterprises that contribute in various ways to local not-for-profit activities (Elgenius et al. 2022). There is no consensus on what the contested concept of integration means, on who should integrate or be the focus of integration policies, or on who should be responsible for its implementation (Saggar and Sommerville 2012). In the absence of an agreed definition and normative undertones, I shall refer to integration as a process of inclusion, of becoming an accepted part of society (Penninx and Garcés-Mascareñas 2016), and will emphasize civil society's role in mitigating socio-economic vulnerability and reducing social distance.

The integration indicators framework (Ager and Strang 2008; Ndofor-Tah et al. 2019; Phillimore et al. 2021) outlines domains and corresponding indicators normatively associated with integration or inclusion. The relevant domains are markers and means, social connections and facilitators, and they rest on a foundation of rights and responsibilities. Facilitators of integration refer to indicators such as language, culture, digital skills, safety and stability. Social connections identify indicators such as social bonds, bridges, and links that help form the networks that promote inclusion within and between groups. The 'markers of integration' are also means of achieving inclusion through access to education, health, housing, leisure, social care, and work. This framework also provides an analytical handle with which to understand civil society's contributions in socio-economically vulnerable and diverse areas. Our findings show that formal and informal initiatives in civil society respond to *all* domains through local networks and holistic ways of working to overcome barriers and local vulnerabilities. Thus, civil society action for and by local populations fills gaps traditionally supported by the welfare state, and mitigates disadvantages. At times of welfare cuts, it will compensate for a shrinking welfare state by, for instance, tackling local disadvantage, alleviating shortfalls in the education system, resisting stigmatization and racism and/or advocating policy change.

Changes in migration patterns to Europe in recent decades have transformed many neighbourhoods in which civil-society organizations operate and arrange activities. And, arguably, these changes supersede previous experiences of diversity (Meissner and Vertovec 2015). Superdiversity is thus a useful concept in that it allows us to reflect on the evolving demographic complexities and socio-economic vulnerabilities within which civil society operates. A focus on the intersections of different factors – such as age, class, gender, nationality, religion, divergent experiences of the labour market, and social rights associated with migration status and length of residence – introduces a much-needed emphasis on existing inequalities and power relations associated with migration. The interconnected nature of such categorizations and how they interact and multiply within structural systems of disadvantage, discrimination or exclusion, can therefore also be analysed. Superdiversity extends the intersectional approach by incorporating migration-driven factors such as immigration status, length of residence, mobility and transnationalism. These multiple characteristics of superdiverse neighbourhoods are central to the theoretical framework and empirical design because they also play out in civil-society activities. Providers and residents rely heavily on the support and networks that civil society provides to address complex problems in a holistic way (Phillimore et al. 2018) and, more recently, to work with civil-society organizations and social enterprises during the pandemic (Elgenius et al. 2022).

Superdiversity is also a useful lens through which to select and sample case studies, be they cities, neighbourhoods, organizations, actors or activities. Crucially, it helps to move away from framing social relations between 'ethnic' groups, or distinguishing between minorities and majority 'host' populations (Grzymala-Kazlowska and Phillimore 2018), neither of which is useful in or relevant to superdiverse conditions. There are several challenges to the ethnicity terminology, a few of which are discussed below.

First, it is misleading to imagine any population in the static singular, as exemplified by the terminology 'minority', or 'majority', or the assumed relationship between two 'groups'. True, the minority–majority distinction can highlight hierarchies in relation to claims of belonging to the nation, such as majority gate-keeping and claims to 'indigeneity' and the impact of such claims on 'migrant' populations (Elgenius and Garner 2021). Yet, given the existence of socio-economic inequalities, as well as different migration statuses and lengths of residence, these binaries overlook population complexity and heterogeneity.

Second, the minority–majority distinction makes little sense in superdiverse neighbourhoods, where the so called 'majority' is often absent (Pemberton and Phillimore 2018).

Third, an emphasis on 'ethnicity', as with cultural difference, obscures experiences of socio-economic disadvantage, insecure employment or working conditions, and educational and health inequalities. Ethnonational categorizations offer only a partial picture of the civil society and its social connections – bonds, bridges, and links – and the socio-economic conditions that provide a key premise for civil society activity. Thus, a shift from emphasizing cultural difference to social distance is needed. Social distance constitutes a barrier to all forms of mobility, impeded by socio-economic disadvantage, unequal opportunities on the labour market, the lack of a voice, stigmatization, racism, and legal and spatial constraints (Everyday Integration 2022). A political climate increasingly defined by anti-migrant rhetoric, resentment and the exaggeration of ethnic differences and 'integration challenges', framed as problems, alongside a nostalgic rhetoric about the nation (Elgenius and Rydgren 2019, 2022) will also enforce social distance.

Fourth, civil-society action in superdiverse neighbourhoods coalesces around several factors, such as gender, place, and commitment to the local neighbourhood, rather than to 'ethnicity'.

Ethno-national terminology is also the source of heated debates on the links between civil society, diversity, and integration. Discussions on the nature of the social capital produced by civil society have traditionally been framed as either ethnic bonding within groups or ethnic bridging between minority and majority groups. The argument is that diversity undermines civil action and capital by lowering trust and preventing integration, whereas ethnic bridges promote integration (Putnam 2007). Such claims have been forcefully disputed on the grounds that distinctions are made regardless of local conditions, demographic complexity and levels of deprivation. Identifying bonding and bridging organizations or activities simplifies the complexity of social connections built around a range of identities. Whereas it has been claimed that bonding capital prevents integration in the political discourse, evidence shows that it can provide useful resources that contribute towards platforms for building bridges and links (Elgenius 2017a, 2017b; Heath and Demireva 2014). Instead, having no networks impede integration and inclusion (Wessendorf and Phillimore 2018).

On the theme of heated debates, deprived and/or diverse areas are also talked about as 'civil-society deserts', or as being 'resource poor' (BRÅ 2018; see discussion by Mohan 2015 about these claims). These designations apply to the few official organizations listed in administrative registers that have comparatively high levels of unemployment. There are several challenges to consider here, including those raised above in relation to the critique of the ethnicity terminology. In addition, civil societies mobilize in many ways, and grey zones of local activity include not only the numerous different organizations that engage in civil-society activities such as traditional not-for-profit organizations but also foundations, social enterprises and initiatives of a more informal nature that contribute but remain unnoticed

(Elgenius 2017a; Elgenius et al. 2022). Informal activities and actors are overlooked despite the research showing plenty of informal action in superdiverse areas (Soteri-Proctor and Alcock 2012).

To illustrate how uneasily civil-society action lends itself to simplifications, below I cite one of many examples of a grassroots initiative that started out as a private scheme to support homework. This initiative, formed alongside an evolving trajectory of insights, mobilizations and collaborations, shows how multidirectional and multidimensional forms of inclusion might look. It started out as an informal attempt to provide homework support for a few families and a small group of local children, but grew through social bonds as well as bridges and links to other groups, local civil-society actors and stakeholders.

The close connections between activities that promote education, health, social care and leisure are blurred in this process. What may have started in one part of the neighbourhood as a homework club for children soon spread to other parts, before a decision was made to respond to requests from adults preparing for various degrees. Through parental and local cooperation, this network was able to build on its original activities to arrange leisure events during school holidays, put on health and safety seminars for parents, and promote parental and local alliances between residents and stakeholders.

From the point of view of the facilitators of inclusion, this homework club also helped to promote linguistic, cultural, and digital skills. Starting out as an informal grassroots initiative, it came to provide homework support to hundreds of children, yet, in the absence of qualitative fieldwork and micro-mapping, it would have been overlooked in the official administrative data. Its social connections may have started by building on existing bonds and a mix of local and linguistic ties, but they soon built bridges that linked them to local actors, stakeholders and the authorities.

This is just one manifestation of the limitations of using ethnic categorizations of social capital to describe cases of bonding, bridging, linking and mixing. Ignoring the complexity and local nature of social connections, as well as the sheer variety of organizations, is especially risky in conditions of socio-economic vulnerability and superdiversity, given that regulatory frameworks may be less well known and grassroots initiatives more likely to operate informally and below the radar. In addition, the rhetoric around non-participation does not consider the racism and discrimination that have been found to have an impact on funding opportunities and to favour mainstream organizations (Piper 2018).

Thus, given the failures of the welfare state, civil-society action needs to be understood within a framework of local conditions of socio-economic disadvantage, and diversification of rights associated with migration status, and thus linking civil society action to local contexts and vulnerability factors. A local neighbourhood perspective will also achieve a fuller picture of civil society's contributions to and support for different domains and indicators of inclusion. A holistic neighbourhood approach is needed to understand how civil society connects to the communities and residents it serves. In terms of research, this is only achieved through comparative, mixed methodologies, the latter building on quantitative as well as qualitative material. The analyses of administrative data contribute broad patterns, but to assess civil society's role in local neighbourhoods more fully these need to be compared and combined with qualitative fieldwork. Robust methodological designs, along with comparative and mixed methodologies, will mitigate concerns about ethno-national conceptualizations and highlight that civil-society action coalesces around several factors and commitments to the local neighbourhood, experiences of socio-economic vulnerability and inequalities, including insecure employment or working conditions, and educational and health inequalities. Moreover, the role of civil society cannot be fully assessed until we know more about the variety of formal and informal civil-society action in conditions of socio-economic vulnerability and diversity.

Research projects on civil society, integration and participation

'Empowering cities of migration: new methods for citizen involvement and socio-spatial integration', S. Pemberton, G. Elgenius, C. Falge, L. Goodson. Funded by the Swedish Research Council for Sustainable Development (FORMAS). See: https://www.gu.se/en/research/empowering-cities-of-migration-new-methods-for-citizen-involvement-and-socio-spatial-integration-empower.

'*LOCALiTIES:* the role of civil society in supporting employability in diverse areas in Sweden and the UK', G. Elgenius, M. Borkowska, J. Kawalerowicz and J. Phillimore. Funded by the Swedish Research Council for Health, Working Life and Welfare (FORTE). See: https://localitiesproject.home.blog/project/.

'Rethinking integration: a comparative mixed methods study of civil society action in vulnerable superdiverse neighbourhoods in Sweden', G. Elgenius, J. Phillimore and J. Kawalerowicz. Funded by the Swedish Research Council. See:

https://www.vr.se/english/mandates/funding-and-promoting-research/resear
ch-on-migration-and-integration/research-projects-about-migration-and-integ
ration/rethinking-integration-a-comparative-mixed-methods-study-of-civil-so
ciety-action-in-vulnerable-superdiverse-neighbourhoods-in-sweden.html.

References

Ager, A. and A. Strang (2008) 'Understanding integration: a conceptual framework', *Journal of Refugee Studies*, 21 (2): 166–91.

BRÅ (The Swedish National Council for Crime Prevention) (2018) *Utvecklingen i socialt utsatta områden i urban miljö 2006–17*, Brottsförebygganderådet.

Elgenius, G. (2017a) 'Ethnic bonding and homing desires: the Polish diaspora and civil society making', in K. Jacobsson and E. Korolczuk (eds) *Civil society revisited: lessons from Poland*, Berghahn Books, 257–85.

Elgenius, G. (2017b) 'Socio-political integration through diaspora organisations and civil society initiatives', in A. Heath (ed.) *'If you could do one thing?' Ten local actions to promote social integration*, The British Academy, 66–75.

Elgenius, G. and S. Garner (2021) 'Gate-keeping the nation: discursive claims, counter-claims and racialized logics of whiteness', *Ethnic and Racial Studies*, 44 (16): 215–35, doi: 10.1080/01419870.2021.1943483.

Elgenius, G., J. Phillimore, M. Borkowska and J. Kawalerowicz (2022) 'Problematising concepts and methods for civil society research in superdiverse neighbourhoods', *Voluntary Sector Review*, Early View, 1–18, doi: 10.1332/204080521X16539125679789.

Elgenius, G and J. Rydgren (2019) 'Frames of nostalgia and belonging: the resurgence of ethno-nationalism in Sweden', *European Societies*, 21 (4); 583–602, doi: 10.1080/14616696.2018.1494297.

Elgenius, G. and J. Rydgren (2022) 'Nationalism and the politics of nostalgia', *Sociological Forum*, Early View, 1–14, doi: 10.1111/socf.12836.

Everyday Integration (2022) 'The Bristol integration framework: the everyday integration project', University of Bristol and partners, available at: www.every dayintegration.org.uk.

Grzymala-Kazlowska, A. and J. Phillimore (2018) 'Introduction: rethinking integration. New perspectives on adaptation and settlement in the era of super-diversity', *Journal of Ethnic and Migration Studies*, 44 (2): 179–96, doi: 10.1080/1369183X.2017.1341706.

Heath, A. and N. Demireva (2014) 'Has multiculturalism failed in Britain?', *Ethnic and Racial Studies*, 37 (1): 161–80, doi: 10.1080/01419870.2013.808754.

Meissner, F. and S. Vertovec (2015) 'Comparing super-diversity', *Ethnic and Racial Studies*, 38 (4): 541–55.

Mohan, J. (2015) 'Charity deserts and social justice: exploring variations in the distribution of charitable organizations and their resources in England', in

B. Morvaridi (ed.) *New philanthropy and social justice: debating the conceptual and policy discourse*, Policy Press, 191–212.

Ndofor-Tah, C., A. Strang, J. Phillimore, L. Morrice, L. Michael, P. Wood and J. Simmons (2019) 'Home Office indicators of integration framework 2019', available at: https://assets.publishing.service.gov.uk/government/uploads/system/uploads/attachment_data/file/805870/home-office-indicators-of-integration-framework-2019-horr109.pdf.

Pemberton, S. and J. Phillimore (2018) 'Migrant place-making in super-diverse neighbourhoods: moving beyond ethno-national approaches', *Urban Studies*, 55 (4): 733–50.

Putnam, R. (2007) '*E pluribus unum*: diversity and community in the twenty-first century', *Scandinavian Political Studies*, 30 (2): 137–74.

Penninx, R. and B. Garcés-Mascareñas (eds) (2016) *Integration processes and policies in Europe: contexts, levels and actors*, IMISCOE research series, Springer.

Phillimore, J., L. Morrice, K. Kabe, N. Hashimoto, S. Hassan and M. Reyes (2021) 'Economic self-reliance or social relations? What works in refugee integration? Learning from resettlement programmes in Japan and the UK', *Comparative Migration Studies*, 9 (article 17): 1–19, doi: 10.1186/s40878-021-00223-7.

Piper, N. (2018) *Racism, nationalism and citizenship: ethnic minorities in Britain and Germany*, Routledge.

Saggar, S. and W. Somerville (2012) 'Building a British model of integration in an era of immigration: policy lessons for government', Migration Policy Institute project, available at: https://www.migrationpolicy.org/sites/default/files/publications/UK-countrystudy.pdf.

Soteri-Proctor, A. and P. Alcock (2012) 'Micro-mapping: what lies beneath the third sector radar?', *Voluntary Sector Review*, 3 (3): 379–98.

Wessendorf, S. (2014) *Commonplace diversity: social relations in a super-diverse context*, Springer.

Wessendorf, S. and J. Phillimore (2019) 'New migrants' social integration, embedding and emplacement in superdiverse contexts', *Sociology*, 53 (1): 123–38, doi: 10.1177/0038038518771843.

Seeking Refuge in Spain: Transiting the Asylum System and Falling into Irregularity

Gracia Moreno-Amador[1]

From the mid-1990s and into the first decade of the 2000s, Spain was processing about 5,500 asylum applications a year. However, with the sudden rise in the arrival of refugees in Europe in 2015 this figure steadily increased from 14,887 in 2015, to 31,740 in 2017 and then to 118,446 in 2019. Despite Covid-19 and its impact on mobility, Spain has continued to receive high numbers of applications – 88,826 in 2020 and 65,482 in 2021. Most asylum seekers come from Latin America, notably Colombia, El Salvador, Honduras, Nicaragua and Venezuela; North Africa, notably Algeria, Mali and Morocco, or from Palestine, Syria and Ukraine (Ministry of the Interior 2015–21). In the last three years Spain has moved from receiving the fewest number of asylum applications among the European countries to being top of the list along with Germany and France (Eurostat 2021).

Although refugees in Spain can access and examine their asylum records, this fails to translate into actually extending their protection. Refugee status offers the highest level of protection. Unlike other forms of protection, such as those granted on humanitarian grounds or on a temporary basis, the holders of refugee status are guaranteed permanent residence, as well as the right to work and to unimpeded mobility. The main differences are related to the recognition, durability and revocability of a person's rights. Protection granted on humanitarian grounds is temporary, usually for a year but extendable if necessary. In other words, these rights are fragile, precarious

---

1. Thanks to Soufian Marouan; Maha Marouan, Pennsylvania State University; and the IRiS Anthology Editorial Team for their generous contributions during the editing process.

and temporary. Despite the existence of various protective categories, at least 74 per cent of applicants moving through the asylum system fall into an irregular administrative category (Ministry of the Interior 1995–21).

The increase in asylum applications has been the most notable change, along with the attendant adjustments to the Spanish asylum system, which include expanding the state reception system. However, once the applications have been examined, the share of asylum decisions that grant refugee status has remained low for almost thirty years. Although this has created a funnelling effect, it has not fundamentally altered the nature of the asylum system. My aim here is to cast light on the selection process and how this effects the Spanish asylum system in terms of both asylum policies and their impact on asylum seekers in Spain.

Widening access to and identification of 'asylum seekers'

As mentioned above, the shift in the Spanish asylum system from 2015 onwards coincided with the so-called 'refugee crisis', namely the large-scale arrival of refugees in Europe. While Spain was less popular as a destination country than places like Greece and Italy, the European migration agenda and the attempt to provide a joint political response through the now infamous quota system clearly shaped its migration agenda. At the same time, Spain introduced a series of administrative changes, including the response of regional and local administrations, as well as mobilizations and campaigns by civil society who wanted to welcome refugees and push for a change in the national policy response to the new migration challenges. These changes were framed by the regulation of the asylum law (Law 12/2009), as opposed to the previous asylum law (Law 9/1994), that had incorporated an 'inadmissibility procedure'. This procedure established an asylum screening stage before asylum seekers could be recognized as such and thus be able to apply for asylum (Garcés-Mascareñas and Moreno-Amador 2022). The previous asylum law (Law 9/1994), the inadmissibility procedure was applied to individuals seeking asylum both in 'the territory' and 'at the border'. However, with the 2009 change in the asylum law, the inadmissibility procedure was only maintained at the border. This means that the Spanish authorities could now consider the asylum applications of people who had crossed the borders and were applying within Spanish territory (López-Sala and Moreno-Amador 2020).

Between 1995, when the asylum law came into force, and 2009, when it was revised, around 60 per cent of applications were deemed inadmissible, as shown in Figure 1 (Ministry of the Interior 1995–2009). Some of the main reasons for inadmissibility were that the application contained no grounds for refugee status; that the facts, data or allegations were implausible or currently invalid; or that the applicant had been recognized as a refugee in a third state or came from a third state that could have provided the requisite protection. The high likelihood of being deemed inadmissible and, subsequently, the high percentage of rejection rates, possibly deterred future applicants. As a result, refugees may have declined to consider asylum as a right. Nevertheless, asylum policies cannot be understood separately from broader migration policies. Although Spain did not see itself as a country of asylum, it was recognized as a country of immigration (Garcés-Mascareñas 2019). The numbers of migrants in Spain far exceed those of asylum seekers. This is because there had been a strong demand for foreign labour, especially in the 2000s when around four million migrants arrived in the country. Consequently, the law on foreigners was geared towards opening up alternative channels of entry and of acquiring residential status.

Figure 1: Evolution of asylum applicants, 1995–2021

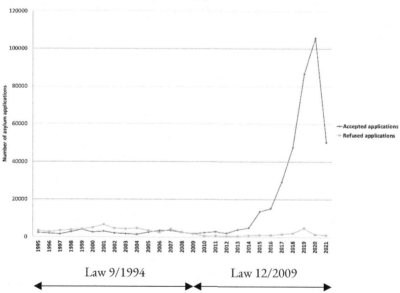

Source: Own elaboration based on data from the Ministry of the Interior (1995–2021).

Transit through the asylum system and subsequent denial of refugee status

Identification under the ambiguous legal category of 'asylum seeker' or, to put it differently, the status of waiting to be recognized as a refugee, has guaranteed the principle of non-refoulement, which is a cornerstone of the 1951 Geneva Convention. Apart from the partial recognition of some fundamental rights, rejections of asylum cases have remained high in recent years, as is evident from the following graph (Figure 2). Between 1995 and 2021, only about 2.5 per cent of the applicants were granted refugee status, around 4 per cent were accorded subsidiary protection status and 19 per cent have been given the right to remain for humanitarian reasons (Ministry of the Interior 1995–2021). In summary, despite access to the initial procedure, the vast majority of applicants eventually failed to obtain the protection they sought in the final phase.

Figure 2: Decisions on asylum applications (in percentage), 1995–2021

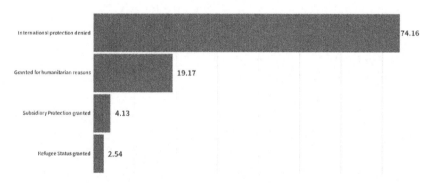

Source: Own elaboration based on data from the Ministry of the Interior (1995–2021).

The reduction in the number of individuals granted international protection – refugee status and subsidiary protection – has persisted over time. Alongside this, however, other subcategories of protection have gained recognition, including protection on humanitarian grounds, which applies mainly to Venezuelans, and more recently in 2022, temporary protection in the case of Ukrainians. First, this has resulted in the fragmentation of the refugee category into other fragile, precarious and temporary legal categories. Second, it has showed how asylum management produced selection, discrimination and recognition (or not) depending on the country of origin, which responds, to a greater extent, to the interests of the destination country rather than to the reasons why some people are being forced to flee their countries of origin. Moreover, these protection statuses have been conditioned by revocability or subject to a cancellable period. Thus, applicants who obtain this type of protection are also sooner or later liable to find themselves in an irregular administrative situation.

Also, people who pass through the asylum system and whose asylum decisions are rejected become migrants in an irregular administrative situation based on the law of aliens (Law 4/2000). They are transferred from the asylum system to the alien system. In other words, these former asylum seekers become 'rejected' refugees and thus 'illegal'. This means losing their residence rights, along with any work permit they might have had and the termination of their labour contract. It also carries an increased risk of detention and the possibility of deportation in the event of police checks on the streets.

The paradoxes of the asylum system and its effects

Refugee status in Spain has become an exception 'for the chosen few'. Although this is also happening in European countries other than Spain, it is based on the premise that a right to asylum is best defended when access to it is restricted (Fassin and Kobelinsky 2012). This has several implications.

First, under the 1951 Geneva Convention the concept of refugee status retains its validity and legitimacy. The institution of asylum is represented as a safeguard and guarantor of the right to refuge, and democratic Western countries regard themselves as standard-bearers in the fight for human rights. Paradoxically, most people are excluded from such protection and treated as illegitimate and undeserving. The ongoing separation between those who do and do not deserve institutional recognition is at the heart of the asylum system, which selects, divides, hierarchizes, excludes or includes refugees in a differential manner.

Second, the combination of inclusionary and exclusionary practices cast light on the inconsistent nature of the asylum policies. Firstly, the claimants are frequently granted partial and temporary rights and access to the social services and assistance. Subsequently, when their applications fail, aspirant asylum seekers suddenly find themselves in a precarious position and vulnerable to deportation, or at least until they manage to regularize their status in Spain. It should be noted that these people often have to wait for an inordinately long time before a final decision on their asylum application is made. These lengthening waiting periods produce enough 'computational' time in which to lay the groundwork for legal stability or subsequent potential regularization. The 'waiting time' in the asylum procedure is thus turned into a preliminary step towards obtaining legal status, rather than what the asylum system should have guaranteed from the outset – the fulfilment of the right to asylum, protection and safety.

Finally, a rejection of their applications by the state authorities implies not only non-recognition of their rights but also the negation of their personal stories and lived experiences. This type of institutional violence, whether direct or indirect, sometimes leads to the revictimization of those who have been through the asylum system and gone on to tell their life stories. In effect, the system itself projects and reproduces a false representation – one that stigmatizes and depoliticizes the actions, struggles and resistance of exiled political subjects who have fled from persecution and violence in their countries of origin.

References

Eurostat (2021) 'Asylum and first-time asylum applicants by citizenship, age and sex, annual aggregated data (rounded)', available at: https://ec.europa.eu/eurostat/web/products-datasets/-/tps00191.

Fassin, D. and C. Kobelinsky (2012) 'How asylum claims are adjudicated: the institution as a moral agent', *Revue française de sociologie*, 4 (4): 444–72.

Garcés-Mascareñas, B. (2019) 'To be or not to be: deficiencies in the Spanish reception system', *Notes Internacionals*, CIDOB, 214: 1–5.

Garcés-Mascareñas, B. and G. Moreno-Amador (2022) 'Multilevel policymaking of refugee reception policies in Spain', in *The multilevel governance of refugee reception policies in Europe*, Routledge.

López-Sala, A. and G. Moreno-Amador (2020) 'Seeking protection at the gates of Europe: refugees, labeling and dissuasion practices at the southern Spanish borders', *Estudios Fronterizos*, 21: 1–20.

Ministry of the Interior (various dates) 'Statistics', ministry website: available at: https://www.interior.gob.es/opencms/en/archivos-y-documentacion/.

Japan's Immigration: Policy and Challenge

Gracia Liu-Farrer

After losing its colonies in the Second World War, Japan tried to redefine itself as a mono-ethnic nation. In fact, until the late 1980s when its economic growth created an acute labour shortage, it refused to accept foreign workers. Although its immigrant population has increased rapidly since the late 1980s, Japan maintains a discourse of not being an immigration country (Roberts 2018). Here, I shall give an overview of the characteristics of and changes to Japan's immigration policy in the three decades between 1989, when it revised its Immigration Control and Refugee Recognition Act (ICRRA), and the beginning of the Covid pandemic. I discuss the challenges that Japan faces as an immigrant country without an official immigration and integration policy.

Japan saw a rapid increase in resident foreign nationals between 1989 and 2019 (Figure 1), as well as a dramatic shift in the national origins of these immigrants (Figure 2). Its main foreign resident populations are from China, Korea, Vietnam, the Philippines, and Brazil. Over the last three decades, the number of Korean immigrants, most of whom were migrants or their descendants from the colonial period, declined through naturalization or death, while the other nationalities were primarily students, or labour and marriage migrants who arrived in Japan after the late 1980s.

The increasing population of foreign residents and their specific national backgrounds are outcomes of Japan's descent and skill-based immigration policy. Descent-based selection is reflected in the creation of long-term residency visas through the 1989 Immigration Control and Refugee Recognition Act (ICRRA). This visa is granted to the descendants of Japanese nationals (up to the third generation) and their families, legal guardians of children of Japanese nationals, or other individuals considered eligible by the Ministry of Justice

288

Figure 1: Foreign residents population trend (1989–2018)

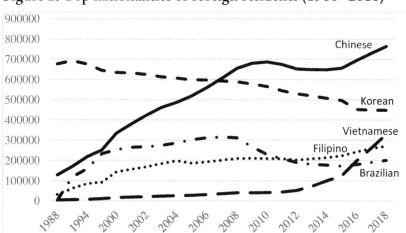

Data sources: MOJ (2007, 2008–2019).

Figure 2: Top nationalities of foreign residents (1988–2018)

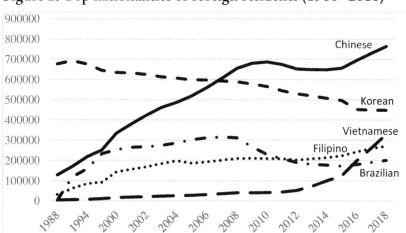

Data sources: MOJ (2007, 2008–2019).

(MOJ 2020). This visa is the main channel through which hundreds of thousands of immigrants from Latin American countries, especially from Brazil and Peru, have come. Although a visa category intended to allow co-ethnic individuals to resettle in Japan, it proved attractive to both Japanese businesses and ethnic Japanese in South America, and this resulted in a rapid increase of ethnic Japanese-Brazilian and Japanese-Peruvian migrants. Most of these Brazilians and Peruvians worked in the manufacturing sector as temporary manual labour. When the 2008 financial crisis closed many such workplaces, a large number of Brazilian and Peruvian migrants were repatriated, causing a dip in the population trend. However, the population gradually recovered. The flexibility of the legal status of long-term residents and their desire to make quick money, resulted in a pattern of circular migration among Nikkei Brazilians (Sasaki 2013).

The 1989 ICRRA also marked the beginning of skill-based labour migration into Japan. The 1980 ICRRA created fourteen employment visa categories. Thirteen of these are designed to promote the immigration of technical, professional, and business migrants, including engineers, investor/business managers, intra-firm transfers, specialists in humanities/international services, and professors. In 2012, the Ministry of Justice proposed a point system for highly-skilled workers (*kōdojinzai pointo*) in which individuals are given points according to their level of education, employment situations, research outputs and salaries. In 2015, the new visa category of highly-skilled professional (*kōdosenmonshoku*) was established to differentiate between those who meet the point requirement and those who do not. People who qualify as highly-skilled professionals enjoy privileges such as a shortened residence requirement for permanent residency. Since many of the skilled migrants working in Japan were initially international students, and the Chinese have been the largest foreign student population in Japan, the majority of highly-skilled professionals have been Chinese.

While welcoming highly skilled foreign workers, Japan's immigration policy restricts the immigration of so-called low-skilled labour, and instead appropriated and expanded some of the non-employment visa categories to import such labour. One such 'side door', noted above, is the long-term resident status through which many Brazilians became employed in Japanese manufacturing. Among other 'side doors' are the international student visa and the trainee and technical intern programme.

'International student', a status granted to those who enter Japan to pursue education, has been used as a channel to bring in labour to staff the service and manufacturing industries (Liu-Farrer and Tran 2019). Since 1983, when Japan instituted its plan to accept 100,000 international students, waves of international students of various nationalities have arrived in Japan, making the student visa one of the most accessible entry categories. In 2008, the Japanese government embarked on a more ambitious plan to recruit 300,000 international students by 2020. Between 1984 and 2018, Japan accepted more than 1.3 million overseas students, mostly from neighbouring Asian countries (Liu-Farrer 2020). Because a student visa permits off-campus work during the school year and can be changed to a work visa when a student finds professional employment, international education has become a channel through which to import low-wage labour during school years and skilled professionals thereafter. In the three decades, China has sent the largest number of students to Japan. Recently, Vietnamese students have been increasing rapidly.

Another channel for importing a large amount of de facto migrant labour is the category of trainee and technical interns. Although supposedly a professional programme, the Technical Intern Training Program (TITP) has been used as a channel through which to import cheap labour into Japan. Until 2010, the people brought in via this programme were not considered workers and not protected by labour law. However, when the US State Department accused the programme of human trafficking, the Japanese government agreed to recognize technical interns as workers after a short training session. In October 2018, employers around Japan reported having 1,460,463 foreign nationals on their payrolls. Among them, 21.1 per cent were technical interns, and another 21 per cent international students (MHLW 2019). In other words, more than 40 per cent of the foreign workers in Japan were restricted from entering as migrant workers but nonetheless allowed to participate in the labour market.

In spring 2019, Japan's unemployment rate dropped to 2.4 per cent and the country faced the most severe labour shortages in its post-war history. Moreover, the types of labour in demand – regular manual work and service positions – were precisely those that Japan's migration policy had sought to restrict, but that technical interns and students could not fill. Technical interns, although important to Japan's manufacturing, construction, fishing, and agricultural sectors, are not allowed to change jobs or apply for other types of visas, so have no legal entitlement to remain in Japan once their tenure terminates, which is five years at the most. Students, too, can only work part time. If they succeed in finding employment after graduating, they are likely to enter the white-collar labour market. If not, they must return to their home countries or risk becoming undocumented migrants. Labour shortages in many industries are predicted to worsen as Japan's population continues to shrink, especially in rural areas. Such realities have forced the Japanese government to admit that it needs to import foreign manual and service workers (Oishi 2020), so new policy measures were adopted in the second half of the 2010s. In 2015, different types of foreign workers, such as domestic helpers, were granted permission to work in so-called National Strategic Special Zones (*Tokku*), including Osaka, Kanagawa and Tokyo, but their numbers have remained small.

In December 2018, the Japanese Diet passed amendments to ICRRA to create the new visa category of 'Specified Skilled Worker' (SSW) to accept workers in fourteen industries, from agriculture to care services. SSW has two tiers. SSW1 represents 'a middle-skilled category', which requires a minimum of three years of work experience and equivalent skills, and SSW2 is considered equivalent to high-skilled workers. Although this policy marks a break from Japan's previous immigration stance that shuns the import of manual labour, SSW visas remain rigid and restrictive. First, the quota for each category, which totals 345,000, is fixed at a 2018 calculation of labour shortages in different industrial sectors. Second, the government places strict controls over labour. Employers have to report on labour conditions on a quarterly basis; workers are not allowed to bring their families with them; and they cannot extend their stay beyond five years, unless they succeed in attaining SSW2 status. An SSW2 visa, however, is at present only open to two of the fourteen categories of workers and, as of April 2022, only one person had been granted this status. Therefore, under the current policy, the majority of the workers, even when they are employed full time and gain skills, will be unable to continue working in Japan after five years. In short, the SSW is still mostly a temporary guestworker scheme. While there is discussion about expanding the SSW2 categories, by the autumn of 2022 the policy had not changed.

In short, since the late 1980s, Japan has seen changes in its immigration policy and a huge increase in its immigrant population. Yet, its immigration policy remains restrictive and selective. Above all, it sees immigrants primarily as workers, not as long-term residents who will become integral to Japanese society. In other words, Japan has not changed its no-immigration discourse. This denial of the reality has much to do with Japan's post-war effort to refashion itself as an ethno-nationalist nation and to see immigration and immigrants as posing a potential threat not only to its social order but also to this identity (Liu-Farrer 2020).

Japan is currently at a crossroads. The global pandemic has hardly reduced its labour demands; the country's population has kept declining;

and it will increasingly depend on immigrants to sustain its economic and social roles. Avoiding the discourse of immigration does not make the reality of immigration disappear. Adhering to an ethno-nationalist identity will only alienate generations of immigrants to come. Japan has a vast cultural repertoire to draw on for its immigration project. It has historically demonstrated its ability to absorb different cultures and then indigenize and reinvent them. It practices religious plurality and cultural hybridity, and at the same time preserves community cohesion and civility in public life. These are the reasons why many foreigners are drawn to Japan in the first place and are comfortable living there. What Japan needs now is to utilize such cultural tools and to have a vision of itself other than an ethno-nationalist one.

References

Liu-Farrer, G. (2020) *Immigrant Japan: mobility and belonging in an ethno-nationalist society*, Cornell University Press.

Liu-Farrer, G. and A. H. Tran (2019) 'Bridging the institutional gaps: international education as a migration industry', *International Migration*, 57 (3): 235–49, doi: 10.1111/imig.12543.

MHLW (Ministry of Health, Labour and Welfare) (2019) *Ippan shokugyō shōkai jōkyō (heisei 31 nen 4 gatsu bun) ni tsuite [Situations regarding ordinary job introduction (April 2019)]*, available at: https://www.mhlw.go.jp/stf/houdou/0000212893_00017.html.

MOJ (Ministry of Justice) (2007) 'A summary of registered foreigners', available at: https://www.moj.go.jp (in Japanese).

MOJ (Ministry of Justice) (2008–2019) 'Statistics of foreign residents', available at https://www.moj.go.jp (in Japanese).

MOJ (Ministry of Justice) (2020) 'Immigration Control and Refugee Recognition Act', (English translation), available at: https://www.cas.go.jp/jp/seisaku/hourei/data/icrra.pdf.

Oishi, N. (2020) 'Skilled or unskilled? The reconfiguration of migration policies in Japan', *Journal of Ethnic and Migration Studies*, 47 (10): 2252–69.

Roberts, G. S. (2018) 'An immigration policy by any other name: semantics of immigration to Japan', *Social Science Japan Journal*, 21 (1): 89–102, doi: 10.1093/ssjj/jyx033.

Sasaki K. (2013) 'To return or not to return the changing meaning of mobility among Japanese Brazilians, 1908–2010', in B. Xiang, B. S. A. Yeoh and M. Toyota (eds) *Return: nationalizing transnational mobility in Asia*, Duke University Press, 21–38.

Digital Immigration Status: From Logics of Inscription to Logics of Control

Kuba Jablonowski

Immigration status governs access to land and resources, and demarcates the lines of economic, social, and political inclusion. In modern societies, it is determined by the state through what Sarah Horton (2020) calls a practice of 'bureaucratic inscription'. First, a decision is issued to grant status to an individual, or to deny it. Second, relevant documents are issued to evidence this status. To borrow another phrase from Horton, these documents become the all-important 'paper trails' that govern an individual's life and, in a wider perspective, provide distinct 'moments of visibility to a field of power' exercised by states over populations when immigration status is inscribed or denied (Horton 2020: 3). But what happens when such practices of bureaucratic inscription go digital?

My intervention starts with this question to reflect on the wider role of technology in border management and speculate on its future trajectories. I argue here that this change in the mode of inscription of immigration status – the shift from paper documents to digital solutions – reconfigures its socio-political function in border regimes. The specific impacts of digitization depend to a great degree on exactly how digital status is designed and configured. In general, however, the digitization of status transforms border management from practices of inscription, where status can be granted and then evidenced with a document, towards practices of control where, even if granted, status is a provisional arrangement of code and data. Digital status may remain inaccessible to its holder and, instead, require authorization each time it needs to be evidenced. Given that the process of authorization is a further opportunity for the state to capture and record data, such dynamics of control unfold at three different scales. First, control is exercised at the microscale of an individual person as access to status is authorized or denied during status checks. Second, there are mesoscale effects as digital transformation changes operations of border bureaucracies – from increased involvement of private enterprises to mundane impacts on caseworking cultures. Finally, control is also exercised at the macroscale of a society, as data harvested through status checks are then used to inform the wider apparatus of immigration control.

Let me illustrate this with a British example. Digitization of immigration status in the UK unfolded in the shadow of the 2016 referendum on the country's membership of the European Union (EU). This referendum determined that Britain would leave the bloc in a process called Brexit. The UK government had an established digital strategy before the referendum, and technology had filtered into its border management for decades. However, the process of leaving the EU added urgency and significance to the digital transformation of immigration control. In a relatively short time frame, the UK needed to develop a means of regulating and administering the statuses of millions of people who lived in the country under the EU's free movement laws, as these laws were about to be repelled through Brexit. To handle this challenge, the UK Home Office created a new, digital-only immigration status and a new, digital-by-default application process called the EU Settlement Scheme (EUSS). With some minor exceptions, all those who lived in the UK under EU free movement had to apply to the EUSS by June 2021, or they would lose their status.

Digital status granted under the EUSS can only be evidenced online, using several websites dedicated to right to work checks, right to rent checks, and to viewing or proving status for other purposes. There is no off-line alternative. An online, digital transaction needs to be carried out with the system for each status check. The status holder needs to input access credentials: their biographic information and identity document number. The system then deploys algorithmic logics to match access credentials provided by the user with records dispersed across the system's databases, and to determine the most relevant record to display as their current immigration status (Foster 2021). This digital infrastructure became fully operational in July 2021. By April 2022, with little consultation or scrutiny, it was extended to other forms of immigration leave in the UK. All status holders, even those with valid residence cards, must now use websites to prove their status online.

In administrative terms, the EUSS proved to be a capable system. It issued over six million decisions by the end of December 2021, including more than five million grants of status and hundreds of thousands of refusals and rejections (Home Office 2022). Its application interface, that is the front end of the EUSS, was described as 'simple and straightforward' by the Home Office (2018: 2). In contrast, the back end of the system is complex. It is comprised of several databases and algorithmic logics that determine which personal data and what immigration status is displayed during a check, given that many applicants have more than one status recorded. One person can have multiple statuses for several reasons. For example, applicants who were initially refused but then granted status on repeat application will have two separate outcomes – that is, status decisions – on their record. Applicants first granted limited and then indefinite leave to remain will have more than one status recorded too. Overall, hundreds of thousands of people already have more than one status in databases that comprise the EUSS, and this number is growing. In such cases, the system does not simply display status during the online check. Rather, its algorithmic logic must first determine what status to display. And when the logic goes wrong, the status holder is locked out of the status they hold. Many such glitches were identified and publicized since digital status went live.

Whether it functions correctly or not, this new technology displays a novel logic of control that gradually dislocates the prior logic of inscription. Traditional forms of documenting status, as explained above, grant it to an individual and thus categorize this individual as a specific type of migrant. Early research on the impacts of digitization on bordering suggested that technology may further enable and entrench these established practices of bureaucratic inscription. When biometric authentication systems proliferated in the 2000s, Louise Amoore (2006: 348) argued that digital technology allowed rescaling the border to the level of an individual as their body becomes 'inscribed with multiple encoded boundaries of access' through biometrics. However, the case of digital status implemented in the UK shows different impacts. First, access to status is guarded by the online authorization system instead of being encoded in the representation of the body itself. Second, status checking transactions serve to capture and record further data – this time on status checkers. After the system went live, a freedom of information request revealed that it captures the name, or the company name, of the status checker as well as information about the type or purpose of the check. According to the Home Office (2021), these records document whether 'the third party carried out a check … should the record later be needed' to evidence compliance with their statutory duty of delegated border control as an employer, a landlord, a bank, and so on.

Online checks, therefore, have at least two functions. First, they authorize access. The ongoing requirement to evidence status online points to the microscale of the logic of control that operates at a level of an individual person, who is allowed or denied access to the status they already hold. Second, they generate records. The ongoing capture of third-party data during checks implies significant macroscale effects as the system learns information not just about status holders, but multiple other socio-economic actors who interact with them.

With digital status, the Home Office created a device to control immigration status instead of merely inscribing it, and to capture vast amounts of data on status checkers in addition to data on status holders. This conjures up the image of the deep border, which 'learns representations from data' (Amoore 2022: 2) through machine learning to produce and govern clusters of population with particular risk-assessed attributes. We do not yet know what the Home Office does with all the data captured through status checking transactions. However, categorization and surveillance of individual status holders is not the stated purpose here and the focus is on ensuring the compliance of status checkers instead.

When she articulated the notion of the deep border, Amoore revised her earlier argument on biometrics as a logic of inscription and showed how data are used to compute the border in real time as 'a line of best fit' (Amoore 2022: 8). Digital immigration status, as implemented in Britain after Brexit, certainly displays similar characteristics: it is generated during the check rather than inscribed when the decision is issued, and every instance of data processing results in further data generation. The end results are yet uncertain, and it is not even clear if there can be end results in a system that relies on the ongoing acquisition and processing of data. The underlying logics of control, however, are clear for us to see.

References

Amoore, L. (2006) 'Biometric borders: governing mobilities in the war on terror', *Political Geography*, 25 (3): 336–51, doi: 10.1016/j.polgeo.2006.02.001.

Amoore, L. (2022) 'The deep border', *Political Geography*, Early View, doi: 10.1016/j.polgeo.2021.102547.

Foster, K. (2021) 'Reply from Home Office about identification of individuals across multiple applications', letter, 20 December, DECS reference: MIN/0198690/21, available at: https://the3million.org.uk/library.

Horton, S. B. (2020) 'Paper trails: migrants, bureaucratic inscription, and legal recognition', in S. B. Horton and J. Heyman (eds) *Paper trails: migrants, documents, and legal insecurity*, Duke University Press, 1–26.

Home Office (2018) *EU Settlement Scheme: statement of intent*, 21 June, available at: https://assets.publishing.service.gov.uk/government/uploads/system/uploads/attachment_data/file/718237/EU_Settlement_Scheme_SOI_June_2018.pdf.

Home Office (2021) 'Information collected through the EUSS View and Prove service', 23 November, available at: https://www.whatdotheyknow.com/request/information_collected_through_th.

Home Office (2022) *EU Settlement Scheme quarterly statistics*, December 2021, 24 February, available at: https://www.gov.uk/government/statistics/eu-settlement-scheme-quarterly-statistics-december-2021/eu-settlement-scheme-quarterly-statistics-december-2021.

Points-Based System 2.0

Colin Yeo

Politicians regularly and repeatedly call for the introduction of a points-based immigration system. It has become something of a mantra. During the Brexit referendum in 2016, the leave campaign promised to introduce a 'genuine Australian-style points-based immigration system' (Gove et al. 2016). Boris Johnson followed suit, and in his first speech in parliament as leader of the Conservative Party in 2019 he pledged to introduce a new 'Australian-style points-based system' (Johnson 2019). Johnson's loyal home secretary, Priti Patel, duly trumpeted the introduction of what she gamely but inaccurately describes as a points-based system. As with every single commitment Boris Johnson ever made to anyone but himself, the reality is that he failed to keep it.

The idea of a points-based system has come to serve as a substitute for an actual immigration policy: it seems to be the points that matter, not the criteria on which those points would be awarded or the anticipated outcomes. But it is particularly vexing for those of us familiar with the pre-existing Australian-style points-based system introduced by a Labour government in 2008. For all its faults, of which there were many, it was a genuine attempt at an identifiable immigration policy.

This system was preceded by a White Paper in 2006 promising that the new system would be better at identifying and attracting the migrants who had the 'most to contribute', would be 'more efficient, transparent and objective' and would improve compliance and reduce scope for abuse (Home Office 2006). The system would be based on objective criteria, easier to understand, quicker and simpler for employers and educational institutions and more straightforward to administer. None of this was to come to pass: the system turned out to be complex, bureaucratic, and expensive. But the underlying idea had been to facilitate the migration of types of migrants considered to be desirable, particularly workers and students.

The era of Theresa May – first as home secretary then as prime minister – saw a gradual dismantling of Labour's original points-based system, in substance if not in styling. It was formally still called a 'points-based system' but after the abolition of the highly skilled individual route in 2011 all of the criteria were mandatory; there were no alternative routes to obtaining the different visa types by scoring some points from some criteria but not others. That remains the case today: Priti Patel's so-called points-based system 2.0 is in reality nothing of the sort.

The reality is that ministers and civil servants at the Home Office had cooled on the idea of evaluating migrants on the basis of objective points-based criteria. This was clear from the December 2018 immigration White Paper, issued in what turned out to be the dying days of a Theresa May's premiership (Home Office 2018). The immigration system would no longer be a 'points-based' one but rather a 'skills-based' one. There had turned out to be two key, related problems with objective decisions. First, civil servants found it very hard to craft objective criteria that led to their intended outcomes. The second related issue was that an objective and transparent system left little room for negative discretion to be exercised. For both these reasons, visas were being granted to the 'wrong' migrants, at least as far as ministers and civil servants were concerned.

However, setting aside the obsession with the Australian points-based styling, we can see a publicly stated immigration policy emerging in parallel with an unstated and diametrically opposed de facto policy. Essentially, government policy has been stated to be to reduce economic migration, particularly low-skilled or low-paid migration, in the expectation that British businesses will adapt by offering higher wages and better conditions to recruit resident rather than foreign workers. Johnson (2021) said that he intended to move on from 'the same old broken model with low wages, low growth, low skills and low productivity, all of it enabled and assisted by uncontrolled immigration'. Businesses should desist from using immigration as 'an excuse for failure to invest in people, in skills and in the equipment, the facilities, the machinery they need to do their jobs'. Instead, Johnson said, his ambition was to move towards 'a high-wage, high-skill, high-productivity and yes, thereby low-tax economy'. Paul Scully, the minister for the labour market, was more explicit and direct, stating that, instead of relying on labour from abroad, businesses should be 'looking at how to make employment more attractive, including through wage increases and offering training' (Witherow 2021). Around the same time, an anonymous government source was quoted by the BBC as saying that, to move to a high-wage, high-skilled economy, 'businesses should invest in their workforce and improve pay and conditions' (Wells 2021).

In reality, the Johnson government pursued a very different policy. The end of free movement of workers from the European Union undoubtedly made it harder for British businesses to recruit from Europe. However, the government has somewhat simplified recruitment of skilled workers, has enabled a potentially significant number of Hong Kong residents and Ukrainian refugees to relocate to the UK through new visa routes and has repeatedly introduced supposedly temporary visas for workers when there have been labour shortages. By March 2022, more than 113,000 applications had been granted under the Hong Kong visa scheme launched in January 2021. At the time of writing, it remained to be seen whether this figure would stay constant over time, was artificially high because of initial demand, which would later fade, or was artificially low because of travel restrictions during the pandemic. Research by Migration Observatory suggested that in early 2021 a total of 186,000 eligible Hong Kong residents planned to come and a further 932,000 were considering it.

The impact of the Ukrainian refugee crisis is hard to judge. By July 2022, more than 100,000 Ukrainian refugees had arrived in the UK and been granted permission to stay and to work for three years. Whether or to what extent these refugees will enter the labour market is unclear. Some are thought already to have returned to Ukraine. Many are women with children and their language and other labour market motivation and skills are unknown.

Meanwhile, in 2021 the government expanded to 30,000 places the visa scheme for agricultural workers. The announcement was accompanied by an implicit threat to reduce visa numbers over time, 'with a view towards helping the sector transition to a future state based on automated technologies and a motivated domestic workforce'. The latest news is that the Truss government plans to expand the scheme still further, to 40,000 places. In late 2021, in response to shortages of lorry drivers and resulting panic buying of petrol, a scheme for up to 5000 foreign lorry drivers was announced. At the same time, as a reaction to reports of potential shortages of turkeys for Christmas, a scheme for up to 5500 poultry workers was also unveiled. A government spokesperson said that this was 'a time-limited once-only provision which recognizes the extraordinary set of circumstances facing the

UK food supply chain'. It was swiftly followed by a separate, emergency, visa-free scheme for up to 300 HGV fuel drivers, as long as they held an EU licence to drive HGV fuel tankers and would leave the UK by 31 March 2022. A fortnight later, in response to reports of mass destruction of pigs because of a shortage of abattoir workers, a scheme for up to 800 pork butchers was announced. Again, this was presented as a short-term measure, with the government explicitly stating it 'expects the pork sector to encourage better training offers, career options and wage increases to ensure that the sector draws on the large domestic labour pool in the UK'.

There may be more going on here than first meets the eye, though. The various visa announcements might be more about managing headlines than the economy. The terms on which the visas were offered were unattractive, and it was reported in November 2021 that only nine of the HGV driver visas had actually been taken up.

Maybe the government will at some point stop introducing supposedly temporary visa schemes in response to labour shortages. Past form suggests otherwise, as does the increasingly urgent problem of rising inflation. Public statements from the top of government that employers should increase wages seem unlikely to be repeated. It seems likely that the Truss government will continue the pragmatic policy of creating and expanding visa routes in response to pressure from industry and employers. A points-based policy this most certainly is not.

References

Gove M., B. Johnson, P. Patel and G. Stuart (2016) 'Restoring public trust in immigration policy – a points-based non-discriminatory immigration system', Vote Leave, 1 June.

Home Office (2006) 'A points-based system: Making migration work for Britain', Home Office, CM 6741, March.

Home Office (2018) 'The UK's future skills-based immigration system', CM 9722, December.

Johnson B. (2019) House of Commons debate, vol. 663, col. 1458, 25 July.

Johnson B. (2021) 'Speech to Conservative Party conference', 6 October.

Wells, I. (2021) 'No more visa schemes for businesses, say government sources', BBC News, 29 September.

Witherow, T. (2021) '"Stop moaning and pay Brits more": ministers tell firms complaining about shortage of foreign workers to increase wages for UK employees instead', *Daily Mail*, 13 September.

The EUSS and the Digitalization of Everyday Bordering: The Case of Roma People in the UK

Marie Godin and Mihai Calin Bica[1]

The EU Settlement Scheme (EUSS) was officially launched on 29 March 2019 and is based on the EU–UK Withdrawal Agreement, which followed the UK's EU referendum. It was designed to give a new immigration status to EU citizens (and their non-EU family members) by 31 December 2020. As of 1 July 2021, the new post-Brexit immigration system rules came into force, meaning that EU citizens are now required to prove their immigration status in the UK to continue enjoying the same rights. Roma people faced many issues with the EUSS from the very beginning of its implementation because of its entirely digital nature – from its digital application to its digital proof of status.

Since the Brexit referendum, the migrant organization Roma Support Group (RSG),[2] established in 1998, has focused on many issues that have affected the lives of Roma people in the UK. These include informing Roma migrants about the EUSS and digital-only status, supporting them during the different stages of the procedure (with people applying for pre-settled and settled status), monitoring and following up on the application process, and raising awareness of the challenges that Roma people face when they have to interact with public authorities, charities, and parliamentarians. Similarly, the3million, a partisan grassroots organization of EU citizens in the UK, formed after the 2016 referendum to protect the rights

1. This research was funded by the BA/Leverhulme Small Research Grant scheme (COV19/200330: Refugee-led initiatives at the time of COVID-19: exploring new forms of digital information, assistance and livelihood – PI: Dr Marie Godin). Contact: Marie.Godin@qeh.ox.ac.uk.
2. https://www.romasupportgroup.org.uk/about-us.html.

of people who have made the UK their home, has also raised concerns about the digital-only proof of immigration status with a campaign entitled *#DeniedMyBackup. EU citizens must not be guinea pigs* 🐭 *for a new digital-only UK immigration status. We need physical backup of our right to live and work in the UK* 📇 *for when digital does not work* ⊖ (the3million 2021). This campaign raised awareness of the risks such a system entailed, including creating new barriers to opportunity and wellbeing for many EU citizens, making a clear case for physical proof of EU citizens' rights to work and live in the UK as a safety net if the digital fails.[3] The RSG also joined the campaign online, as with this tweet posted on 15 October 2020 stating that 'the EUSS and its "digital only status" is a real threat for many Roma community members such as Nicoleta.'[4] In April 2021, the3million asked for a judicial review of the government's policy to give digital-only proof of immigration status to millions of EU citizens. The case is known as *R (The 3million Ltd) v Secretary of State for the Home Department [2021] EWHC 1159 (Admin).* The main argument put forward in the case is the discriminatory nature of the scheme for groups on the grounds of disability, age and race (which included 66,000 Roma people).[5] However, at the time, the High Court refused to permit a judicial review challenge of the policy as it had not yet come into effect and was thus 'premature'.

As Tomlinson et al. (2022) argued, this situation presents the possibility of a digital version of the Windrush scandal. It is in this context that our research, which documents the discriminatory impacts of the digital-only status on the lives of EU Roma citizens living in London and their coping strategies took place. While there has been a lot written about the obstacles Roma people face in accessing the EUSS, less is known about how it has been affecting people on a daily basis since it became effective in July 2021.

From a hostile environment to a digital hostile environment

According to Yuval-Davis et al. (2019: 233), the term 'technologies of everyday bordering' refers to expanding the 'hostile environment' through

---

3. https://www.crowdfunder.co.uk/p/denied-my-backup.
4. https://twitter.com/RomaSupport/status/1316726449265676289.
5. https://www.lauradevine.com/news/digital-only-immigration-status/.

extending bordering processes more deeply into everyday life, sub-contracting and extending border-guard roles to employees of private and public organizations including banks, the Driving and Vehicle Licensing Agency (DVLA), hospitals as well as private landlords so that irregular migrants would find it harder to find work and accommodation or to access healthcare and education.

If at first the hostile environment was only targeting irregular migrants, it soon proceeded to envelop a broader category of citizens, including EU migrants. These bordering practices are now taking place every day and everywhere, both online and offline, undermining a naturalized sense of entitlement to citizenship, especially for those who are vulnerable and racialized (Yuval-Davis et al. 2019: 240).

While discussions of digital exclusion were previously framed around access to technology, literacy, or being on the wrong side of the digital divide, a more nuanced understanding of what digital exclusion means in relation to intersectional vulnerabilities has emerged over the last few years (Tsatsou 2022). In addition, there are complex connections between online and offline inequalities; the latter can produce online inequalities and, conversely, the digital space can itself reinforce social inequalities. These dynamics between the offline and online world often produce digital vicious cycles. In the UK, while the digitalization of public services (NHS, employment, education) since the Covid-19 shock has accelerated the marginalization of vulnerable people (Fu et al. 2022), the digitalization of the immigration system has also played a major role.

In November 2018, when the RSG was supporting Roma people registering for the EUSS during the trial period (also known as Private Beta 2), the data showed that only 3 per cent of those who took part in the registration process were independently able to complete an online appli-cation (Godin and Calin Bica 2019). More recently, during the Covid-19 lockdown, the RSG observed that only 20 per cent of the Roma families it was helping had an IT device such as a tablet or laptop (RSG 2020). Many families have at least one smartphone in their household, but its usage is limited to phone calls and basic social media activities. Based on the RSG's experiences of assisting Roma people with the EUSS, a lack of English literacy and digital skills also plays a huge role in excluding people from being able to check their immigration status online and get their 'share code' to prove their status to employers and/or landlords when asked to do so (RSG 2022).

To allow EU citizens to familiarize themselves with the new digital immigration system, the Home Office implemented a transitional phase, a 'grace period' lasting until 30 June 2021, during which they could use their passport or national identity cards to prove their immigration status in the UK. Despite this, Roma people were given insufficient time to move 'safely' from using physical documents to accessing and sharing their immigration status information online, having just received either pre- or settled status when the pandemic hit (RSG 2022). The impact on vulnerable groups such as the Roma of both the pandemic and the digitalization of public services has been coined in the literature on undocumented migrants as the 'double lockdown' (Bastick and Mallet-Garcia 2022). The digital-only immigration status, as part of the hostile digital environment, has often accentuated the 'double burden of exclusion', a combination of both digital and social exclusion.

Coping with the UK's hostile digital environment

Our research, which was based on a mixed-methods approach (survey, focus groups and interviews), showed the impact of a digital immigration status on Roma people's daily lives with respect to seeking employment, crossing borders, trying to access social benefits, or simply applying for a driving licence. The lack of awareness among those with a pre-settled status about when they would need to update their situation is also worrying. In this context, the Roma community developed three coping strategies to limit the discriminatory nature of the new immigration system – (1) avoiding the system; (2) recreating a sense of 'security'; and (3) relying on others' good or bad will.

Avoiding the system: self-exclusion

One feature of the EUSS that is unfamiliar to many people is the need for the holders of a (pre)-settled status to update their digital account every time their personal details changed. IT difficulties arise when an applicant's circumstances change, such as acquiring a new telephone number, email address, or passport/ID number. A huge number of cases arise over various authorities conducting sporadic checks on people's statuses. The constant fear of these repetitive online checks resulting in expulsion can lead people to avoid interacting with the system. The Joint Council for the Welfare of Immigrants (JCWI) recently published a document called 'Resisting the digital hostile environment', which stated that 'a digital-only status that provides migrants with no physical documentation risks allowing the Home Office to "switch off" a person's status and entitlement to services when it decides – rightly or wrongly – that a person no longer has the right to be in the UK' (JCWI 2021). Simply, to avoid data glitches, some prefer not to deal with the system at all. This produces a chain of social reactions, such as avoiding using social services, undertaking illegal work, or being exploited by rogue landlords. As other studies on undocumented migrants (Bastick and Mallet-Garcia 2022) show, digital exclusion can be self-reinforcing. However, not only migrants avoid using the system, but so too do other social actors who are unfamiliar with the new digital bordering system and find the digital environment too threatening. Some mentioned that EU Roma citizens were failing to get formal jobs because of the requirements that a digital residency status imposed on them and the checks with which their prospective employers needed to comply. Therefore, a lack of knowledge about how the system works penalizes Roma workers who are being barred from certain jobs. Consequently, there is a growing informal economy comprised of people who are unable to prove 'their right to have rights' (Arendt 1958), particularly in the construction sector, but also in agriculture, factories, and car washes.

Recreating a sense of 'security': misusing the system

One effect of the digitization of the immigration system is the removal of physical evidence (in the form of a biometric residence permit, or a permanent residence card) through the introduction of a digital-only immigration status. However, people who either distrust the system, and/or have difficulty accessing it, often keep a hard copy of the Home Office letter informing them of its decision about their (pre)-settled status, or a printed version of a share code. Applicants are notified by an automatically generated email when the EUSS status is granted. As a result, many Roma people have used this message as proof of status when it is just a notification. The share code is by its nature temporary (valid for ninety days), and is not a substitute for an ID document. Yet, it is not uncommon to hear of people printing all these documents as alternative

ID documents to reassure themselves in case they are asked about their status in the UK or at the border. Giddens's (1991) concept of 'ontological security' is relevant in this context. This refers to a 'person's fundamental sense of safety in the world and includes a basic trust of other people'. Obtaining this trust is 'necessary in order for a person to maintain a sense of psychological well-being and avoid existential anxiety' (Giddens 1991: 37). With the digital-only immigration scheme, people cannot predict what will happen when they interact with their bank, their landlord, public services, their employer and/or the police. Being perceived as a new migrant on a daily basis creates not only ontological insecurities but also a sense of not belonging to a place in which, in some cases, they have lived for more than twenty years.

Relying on 'others': becoming dependent

By failing to provide people with alternative ways of proving their immigration status, the system creates the very conditions that make them dependent on others. This obviously puts pressure on the public services and voluntary organizations like the RSG to provide support, but migrants – and in this case Roma people – also sometimes opt to consult informal third parties. Some of these are genuine, but others charge for what often amount to poor quality, exploitative services. The exploitation can take different forms, but it can last for a long time because those providing the service retain access to people's UK Visas and Immigration (UKVI) accounts, thereby forcing them to rely on their services for longer than they might have envisaged. Finally, since Roma people are more likely to have trouble accessing and managing their digital status, they will also be more likely to have difficulty securing their immigration status once their pre-settled status expires and, hence, their increasing reliance on others (neighbours and friends, but also ill-intentioned people) (Mellana 2020; RSG 2022). By March 2020, the RSG has assisted more than a thousand Roma community members with submitting their EUSS applications, and found that 62 per cent of them were granted pre-settled status, compared with the national average of 41 per cent (RSG 2020). Overall, there is a lack of awareness surrounding digital-only immigration, with people often not knowing who can ask for their 'share code', under what circumstances, and for what purposes, and thereby risking abuses and multiple dependencies.

Conclusion

The Home Office sold the digital-only status as being 'quicker, more secure and cost-effective to enable those granted status under the EUSS to access and share evidence of their immigration status using an online service.'[6] However, as discussed, the opposite is often happening for some groups of EU citizens, including members of the Roma community; it often takes them longer to gain their status; the overall process makes them feel more insecure; and their costs can be higher because they often need to depend on other people's goodwill. It can be argued that, overall, the EUSS scheme, and its digital-only status, has become a tool for systematic exclusion that legitimates discrimination and fosters fear and mistrust. Our findings show that few in the Roma community use technology to address their vulnerabilities, which a hostile digital environment is exacerbating.

Low levels of digital literacy, lack of connectivity and poor infrastructure in the Roma community create barriers not only to securing and managing their immigration status but also to accessing basic public services. The expanding 'digitization of everyday bordering practices', along with a distinct lack of public support for Roma people since the pandemic, heightens their exposure to digital and social exclusion. The unpredictability of everyday bordering practices makes Roma people feel as if they have just arrived in the country, and need to remain vigilant if they are to be able to prove 'their right to have rights'.

Because digitalizing the immigration statuses of EU citizens forms part of a broader project of data infrastructural development in immigration administration (Tomlinson et al. 2022: 318), more research is needed to identify how a digital-only immigration status can increase inequalities and social exclusion. More than ever, it is time for researchers and those involved in protecting vulnerable populations in an increasingly hostile digitized world to work collectively not only to gather evidence about the damage and discriminatory impact of a digital-only immigration system on people's daily lives but also to help develop innovative solutions that take into consideration the intersectional experiences of the EUSS.

---

6. Home Office Policy equality statement: EU Settlement Scheme (December 2020) para 78. Available at: https://www.gov.uk/government/publications/eu-settlement-scheme-policy-equality-statement/policy-equality-statement-eu-settlement-scheme.

References

Arendt, A. (1958) *The origin of totalitarianism*, second enlarged edition, World Publishing Company.

Bastick, Z. and M. Mallet-Garci (2022) 'Double lockdown: the effects of digital exclusion on undocumented immigrants during the COVID-19 pandemic', *New Media & Society*, 24 (2): 365–38.

Fu, L., A. Lindenmeyer, J. Phillimore and L. Lessard-Phillips (2022) 'Vulnerable migrants' access to healthcare in the early stages of the COVID-19 pandemic in the UK', *Public Health*, 203: 36–42.

Giddens, A. (1991) *Modernity and self-identity: self and society in the late modern age*, Stanford University Press.

Godin, M. and M. Calin Bica (2019) '"It took 2 hours and one third didn't get through": piloting the settled status application with Roma migrants', *Eurochildren Blog opinion*, 21 January, available at: https://eurochildren.info/2019/01/21/it-took-2-hours-and-one-third-didnt-get-through-piloting-the-settled-status.

JCWI (The Joint Council for the Welfare of Immigrants) (2021) 'Resisting the digital hostile environment', briefing report, August, available at: https://www.jcwi.org.uk/briefing-resisting-the-digital-hostile-environment.

Mellana, C. (2020) 'Digital status handle with care', *New Europeans UK*, available at: https://neweuropeans.uk/wp-content/uploads/2021/02/Digital-Status-Handle-with-care-report-NEUK.pdf.

RSG (Roma Support Group) (2020) 'Statement on the impact of EU Settlement Scheme digital-only status on the Roma community in the UK', available at: https://www.romasupportgroup.org.uk/uploads/9/3/6/8/93687016/statement_on_the_impact_of_the_eu_settlement_scheme_digital_only_status_on_roma_communities_in_the_uk_final_oct_2020.pdf.

RSG (Roma Support Group) (2022) 'Roma communities in the UK: EU Settlement Scheme and post grace period situation', briefing paper, March.

the3million (2021) 'Fixing the digital status: a proposal for a safe and simple proof of rights', available at: https://the3million.org.uk/sites/default/files/files/t3m-SecurePrintedEUSS.pdf.

Tomlinson J., J. Maxwell and A. Welsh (2022) 'Discrimination in digital immigration status', *Legal Studies*, 42: 315–34.

Tsatsou, P. (2022) 'Vulnerable people's digital inclusion: intersectionality patterns and associated lessons', *Information, Communication & Society*, 25 (10): 1475–94.

Yuval-Davis, Y., G. Wemyss and K. Cassidy (2019) *Bordering*, Polity Press.

The Resurgence of Resistance: Celebrating Solidarity at a Time of Hopelessness

Victoria Canning

When it comes to asylum-related issues, opportunities to celebrate anything are few and far between. For migrants subjected to border harms, as well as researchers, practitioners and activists intervening over its infliction, it is increasingly difficult to feel positive. Each day seems to bring new demeaning mechanisms for undermining the autonomy and dignity of migrants. During interviews in 2017, one torture rehabilitation director in Denmark remarked that, 'they're testing this unfortunately, a social experiment, how far they can get with their whip', while a barrister in England questioned the rationale of government agendas, asking 'even if you accept the premise that migration is a problem and needs to be reduced, why don't you wait to see what the last set of bad laws did before you bring in the next of the bad laws?'

Five years later, both remarks are more pertinent than ever. In the UK, the Nationality and Borders Act marks the dissolution of the Refugee Convention as we know it. In Denmark, the 'social experiment' mentioned above has meant developing more than 144 restrictions since 2015, and implementing a 'no ghettos' law, which entails capping non-Western neighbourhoods at 50 per cent in low-income areas. Moreover, Denmark was the first country in the EU to push for the Rwanda deal, which would outsource borders, and this was even before the controversial moves now unfolding in the UK. In Sweden, anti-migrant sentiment has led to the 'Temporary Law' of 2016, which restricts permanent residence permits for people seeking asylum and their families, and thus leaves many people in a perpetual state of temporariness (see Canning 2019a for more in-depth information on these examples and others).

Indeed, in the ten years in which IRiS has been intervening in migration-related issues, Europe and many other parts of the world have borne witness to increasingly vitriolic attacks on the rights of refugees, and EU and non-EU migrants more broadly. On the grand stage of border harms sits the avoidable travesty of more than 24,260 deaths in the Mediterranean since 2014 alone (IOM 2022), each death facilitated by the push of conflict, persecution and poverty, and enabled by a concrete shift to securitization over EU humanitarianism (Bhatia and Canning 2021). IRiS, like Migration Mobilities Bristol, and Oxford Border Criminologies, among others, has been at the forefront of documenting the reality of these changes and the impacts of the extension of endemic border violence.

Bureaucratized banality and everyday forms of degradation

While grandiose attempts to use Kafkaesque deterrence have characterized some policies, these are not necessarily implementable. One example, which drew international criticism, was Denmark's controversial jewellery law proclaiming the power to confiscate cash and jewellery over the value of 1340 euros – an unwelcome echo of not-too-distant histories in Europe, but in reality of little significance. Instead, it is often the more insidious border incidents that go unnoticed, so remain hidden and unrecognized.

On the banal, everyday front, border harms are often less quantifiable or noticeable. They can fade into the wallpaper of controls that surround people seeking asylum across Europe. My research, which has mostly focused on Britain, Denmark and Sweden – until recently considered beacons of human rights – reveals increasing restrictions being imposed on the rights of migrants generally and on people seeking asylum in particular. This is often in the form of banal bureaucratic exercises – lengthy asylum processes that reduce autonomy through imposing restrictions on migrants furthering their education or seeking work; the spectre of detention or deportation hanging over their heads whenever the post arrives; the sense of precarity felt by residents of asylum centres or other housing facilities occasioned by the knowledge that any wrongdoings– however minor – might lead to a complaint being made to the migration authorities. Systems that force migrants into financial dependency on the state by removing their right to work, while simultaneously providing insufficient means to survive comfortably without depending on foodbanks or charity, obviously exacerbate their poverty. Indeed, one of the greatest challenges that organizations face when attempting to attract support for their cause is not advertising or information, but the fact that people cannot afford the bus fares to get to them. For women, in particular, the intersectional implications of this can be having to depend economically on men with whom they would rather not be in a relationship, violence, or coercive control.

While at first sight these examples might seem relatively trivial, for those 'stuck' in these systems, the everyday nature of such banal controls can be highly detrimental to their mental health and, in some case, even lead to suicide. In fact, that 107 people living in Home Office asylum housing in the UK have died since 2016, and at least seventeen of these were through suicide (Purkiss et al. 2022), does not come as a shock. Creating a zemiological lens, or in other words employing the disciplinary study of social harm, allows us to recognize that inflicting harm on people is avoidable and if something is recognizable it can be more effectively resisted.

These overlooked experiences have formed the two key ideas on which I have focused for the last fifteen years. The first is to recognize the infliction of so-called 'border harms' as deliberate. By identifying these as typologies and dimensions, and drawing on zemiology to do so (Canning and Tombs 2021), it becomes easier to recognize structural patterns in the acts of violence that are manifested as harms in the lives of individuals. These harms can be physical, emotional, psychological, relational, temporal, and spatial, or they can be to one's sense of autonomy. The second is to recognize and state that the degradation is inflicted by design (Canning 2019b). By shifting our focus to the deliberate nature of border controls and the harms they inflict, we can collectively move away from seeing discourses of 'hostility' as the almost unintended by-products of the job (such as working in a 'hostile environment') and instead emphasize the deliberate ways in which asylum systems (and migration controls more broadly) are scaffolded to build in and embed harms and structural violence.

What can we celebrate collectively, and is there space for hope?

As intimated at the beginning of this contribution, the activism and research surrounding border survival seem to be presenting an ever more challenging landscape. Every new restriction comes with the challenge of navigating nuanced resistance, and a constant barrage of stories of mounting rights abuses. Only weeks before writing this, more than 200 people died in the Mediterranean, and at least 23 were killed attempting to enter the Spanish enclave of Melilla in Morocco (Al Jazeera 2022). Then, at the same time, came the exposé on deaths in Home Office accommodation.

At around the same time, I was recovering from vicarious trauma and compassion fatigue – nobody tells you about the guilt associated with those. After fifteen years, the sense of hopelessness accompanying the nuanced and seemingly endless forms of border violence had simply become too much. Emerging from this, on re-engaging with activist colleagues I detected a clear demographic expansion in the number of voices protesting against the state and corporate harms being inflicted on refugees. Meetings about immigrant detentions draw people from all walks of life. Grassroots, migrant-led activism has transformed the landscape of some pockets of resistance nationally and internationally, as have the voices of people who have survived detention and exposed the endemic nature of confinement and offshore detention practices (Boochani and Tofighian 2021). For the first time in my memory, discussions on abolition (not just *reform*) were being met with far less resistance than before. Lawyers sidelined as 'activists' or 'radicals', but actually just doing their jobs well, are now better organized and more responsive than ever before. In short, there is a wider sense that violent border tactics have gone rogue, and the result has been increased and organized resistance. The previously invisible is surfacing.

Going forward, it is important to consolidate two things. The first is to recognize that the problematic practices of harming people are just that – harm infliction. While there is no immediate end to the elaborate (often costly) schemes that states invent to weaken migrant rights, the banal, everyday harm that undermines people's autonomy, dignity and sense of self remains. As with the recent deaths of people seeking asylum in Britain, while individually such matters may seem minor, together they invoke every type of bureaucratic violence (Abdelhady et al. 2020), and the consequences of this can have catastrophic effects on people's health and wellbeing.

Second, as governmental agendas to deter and demean continue to overstep national and international legal remits, it is important to recognize that they are an integral part of the historical and contemporary scaffolding that supports the structures that have allowed states (and their corporate allies) to get as far as they have. As responses to the Rwanda deal played out in the UK, depending on the political leaning of the source, the media would regularly refer to a 'new era' in either bordering Britain, rights erosion, or Tory hostilities.

These may be new strategies with new legalistic consequences, but they are not the markers of a 'new era'. They are the extensions of pre-existing xenophobia, racism, privatization, securitization, outsourcing, and border violence. They are the result of more than a hundred years of aggressive policies gradually reducing border management to degradation by design, worsened in the past decade as the foundations for politicizing migration – laid predominantly in the late 1980s – have come to fruition. They are part of a continuum. For the sake of accountability for those complicit in the endemic harms they have created, and for the sake of the dignity of those at the receiving end of them, that continuum should be recognized.

So, it is here that I shall end with something to celebrate: so long as everyday resistance mounts, there can be possibilities of change, and thus glimmers of hope. Centres like IRiS document, scrutinize and intervene in border violence and harms to ensure that those accountable for them cannot deny their part. This exposure is a further opportunity to work in solidarity, and one in which migrant-led grassroots organizations, lawyers, NGOs, and the medical professions can effectively engage. That is the value of rigorous, critical research, resistance to harm, and the power of collective intervention.

References

Abdelhady, D., N. Gren and M. Joormann (2020) *Refugees and the violence of welfare bureaucracies in northern Europe*, Manchester University Press.

Al Jazeera (2022) 'Rights groups call for probe into deaths during Melilla crossing', 25 June, available at: https://www.aljazeera.com/news/2022/6/25/rights-groups-urge-probe-into-deaths-o.

Bhatia, M. and V. Canning (2021) *Stealing time: migration, temporality and state violence*, Palgrave Macmillan.

Boochani, B. and O. Tofighian (2021) *The weaponisation of time: indefinite detention as torture*, in M. Bhatia, and V. Canning (eds) *Stealing time: migration, temporality and state violence*, Palgrave Macmillan, 65–83.

Canning, V. (2019a) 'Reimagining refugee rights: addressing asylum harms in Britain, Denmark and Sweden', Migration Mobilities Bristol.

Canning, V. (2019b) Degradation by design: women seeking asylum in northern Europe, *Race & Class*, 61 (1): 46–63.

Canning, V. and S. Tombs (2021) *From social harm to zemiology*, Routledge.

IOM (International Organisation for Migration) (2022) '24,263 missing migrants in Mediterranean since 2014', Missing Migrants Project, available at https://missingmigrants.iom.int/region/mediterranean.

Purkiss, J., A. Walawalker, M. Gidda, E. Rose and M. Townsend (2022) 'Revealed: dozens of vulnerable asylum seekers have died in Home Office housing since 2020', *The Guardian*, 25 June, available at: https://www.theguardian.com/uk-news/2022/jun/25/asylum-seekers-deaths-home-office-housing-data.

Birmingham's Anti-racist Future

Asif Afridi

The Birmingham charity brap believes that sometime in the future, racism – as we experience it now, in all its guises – will no longer exist. We do not believe this is a whimsical notion. On the scale of human history, racism is a relatively new phenomenon. This is not to say that humans did not find other ways to discriminate against each other before, but the creation of false biological categories and their use to demonize one group of people, while elevating the status of another, was not one of them.

We cannot change our futures unless we accept the possibility of change, unless we imagine a future in which working actively towards anti-racism will bring us closer to an anti-racist reality. These, in our view, are dreams worth pursuing. Racism is a disease. It destroys lives. Its outcomes are embedded in the outcomes people experience in cities like Birmingham. For instance, in 2019 African Caribbean pupils were three times more likely to experience fixed-term exclusions than the Birmingham average (DfE 2020). For decades, employment rates in the city for people from mixed ethnic, Black or Pakistani/Bangladeshi backgrounds have remained significantly lower than they have for people from white backgrounds (University of Birmingham et al. 2020).

One of the worst consequences of our society's belief that racism is inevitable is the transmission of racist ideologies to young people. Our society is built on the notion that we gift each generation something better. However, the evidence tells us that not only do we pass on our racist beliefs to young people, but that children begin to notice false racial hierarchies around the age of three (Katz and Kofkin 1997). For cities like Birmingham, this is a disaster.

Our perpetuation in the belief of different 'races' can also shape the types of change we believe are desirable and possible. It can mean that we believe that different outcomes experienced by racialized groups are deserved. It can mean that we believe that 'difference', and the better representation of ethnic minority groups in positions of power, is all that is required to address systemic racism. Yet, building an anti-racist city requires more than this. It requires us to think outside the racial frameworks that shape our world – to imagine something different.

Building an anti-racist future is something each citizen deserves. Living free of this form of discrimination is as fundamental as any ambition we have for a society that is committed to principles of social justice. We need a route map for fundamental change. We need to create a future that is not dealing with the consequences and outcomes of a discriminatory society – but instead is addressing how we take racism off the table.

Building an anti-racist city: what does the evidence tell us?

In 2021, brap undertook a large-scale review of what has worked or not worked in tackling racism at a 'place-based' level. We examined evaluations and academic studies to understand the impact of previous place-based strategies in the UK (such as the UK Neighbourhood Renewal Strategy and New Deal for Communities in the 1990s). We also looked at international examples and interviewed people who have been involved in successful place-based work to tackle racism and promote inclusion.

In the past, programme or community-level initiatives have tended to make little difference and, at best, have led to only minimal adjustments. In fact, there is clear evidence that the approaches used to tackle racism in previous neighbourhood regeneration and place-based schemes failed to bring about any significant long-term change. They may address the short-term needs of some people from black and minoritized ethnic backgrounds who can engage with an initiative, but are unlikely to tackle the 'systemic', institutional nature of racism and the way it operates within particular neighbourhoods, towns and cities.

In short, the design and delivery of place-based activities do not generally incorporate a proper anti-racist approach, one that would notice and challenge both 'overt' and 'covert' racial stereotypes and assumptions, and this includes changing the actual design of the equity initiatives. 'Race' is seen as a construct that is restricting progress for all of us, and we need to engage in more ambitious place-based action if we are to challenge and eradicate systemic racism in cities like Birmingham. In brap we identified eight key design principles for future place-based initiatives (see Figure 1).

318

Figure. 1: Design principles for place-based initiatives

Systemic focus	• Combining a spatially based and people-based approach. • Involving communities as partners to support collaborative learning and systems change. • Responding to root causes of structural discrimination.
Long-term and well-resourced	• Ambition and commitment to achieve impact at a scale commensurate with the problem. • Long-term, multi-agency approach. Investment in building capacity and community leadership of traditionally marginalized groups.
Inclusive engagement practice	• Flexible and emergent engagement opportunities. • Investment in targeted engagement practice. • Community-defined boundaries for place-based action.
Power building	• Strong governance and anti-racist accountability mechanisms. • Addressing internal power dynamics that can limit voice of marginalized groups. • Supporting influencing activities to challenge systemic inequality in a place.
Partnerships and relationship building	• Developing shared understanding of anti-racism • Working at multiple levels to achieve change. • Building trusting relationships between funders and a place (high funding security and predictability; opportunities to learn together and challenge each other).
Equalities practice of coordinators	• Reviewing impact and developing skills and knowledge. • Good understanding of anti-racism and ability to engage various stakeholders in discussing inequality in a place. • Understanding how systems of sexism, ageism, racism, etc. operate at both community level and within partner organizations.
Framing and narrative building	• Connecting place-based action to well-evidenced analysis of structural causes of discrimination in a place. • Strategic communication and framing of anti-racist messages to help build support for place-based action across a range of partners/communities
Evaluation	• Investment in high-quality data disaggregated by protected characteristic. • Using experimental long-term methods to test the impact of different strategies on anti-racist goals. • Monitoring changes in beliefs, capacity, agency and behaviour of partners to assess systems-level change.

Dreaming into a better future

While evidence exists about how to design successful place-based initiatives to tackle racism, we are also acutely aware that creating a city free from racism is new territory – it is something that we have not known in our world for the hundreds of years since the concept of 'race' was created to support slavery, capitalism and colonization. We will need to 'dream' together to imagine how this future might look. Nobody has all the answers to how to create this type of world in our city – we will need to be kind to each other, to listen to each other, and to support each other if we are to create it now for future generations.

The process we use to create an anti-racist city is critical. In cities like Birmingham, the white leaders in our city have for too long outsourced responsibility for tackling racism to those who face it, yet given them insufficient power or resources to change things. Unless power is shared with those without a voice, and unless the journey is democratic and driven by people from a range of walks of life, it is unlikely to succeed. If we fail to focus on building relationships between a wide constituency of people – including those who face racism in the city, as well as white-presenting leaders with power in key institutions, then it is unlikely to succeed.

Key features of a successful place-based scheme to tackle racism are long-term investment in and support for community development, and building the power of those who face marginalization and racism. In recent years, brap has sought to support this type of engagement and power-building initiative by working with a range of school pupils, young people, teachers, as well as voluntary and public-sector organizations to explore this ambition further. Many, encouraged by wider global movements like Black Lives Matter, have begun to envisage an anti-racist future for Birmingham.

Our conversations with communities, especially young people, to map their dreams for an anti-racist Birmingham, has resulted in a road map for the future of the city. You can see those dreams for the future in Figure 2. Over the coming months and years, we will be working with partners across the city to bring this blueprint for the future to life. We will be calling on the city's institutions to make a commitment to anti-racism. We will encourage and support them to be accountable for the racial harm they may already have caused in the city. We will be creating opportunities for those affected by racism (including those marginalized within minoritized ethnic groups) to share their voices in ways that feel inclusive and empowering. We will also be calling on white people to take more owner-ship of the city's anti-racist agenda. They need to recognize their responsi-bility as leaders to support the anti-racism cause and not assign the task to racism's victims.

In 2022, a range of organizations stand ready to take the next steps to build this anti-racist future that many of us imagine. We are seeing glimmers of hope and pockets of activity across different communities and organiz-ations in the city. Our challenge now is to build on them, to nurture and support them.

If you would like to find out more or to join us in this movement for change, please contact us at: https://www.antiracistfutures.org/.

Figure 2: Blueprint for an anti-racist city in Birmingham

Figure 2: Blueprint for an anti-racist city in Birmingham

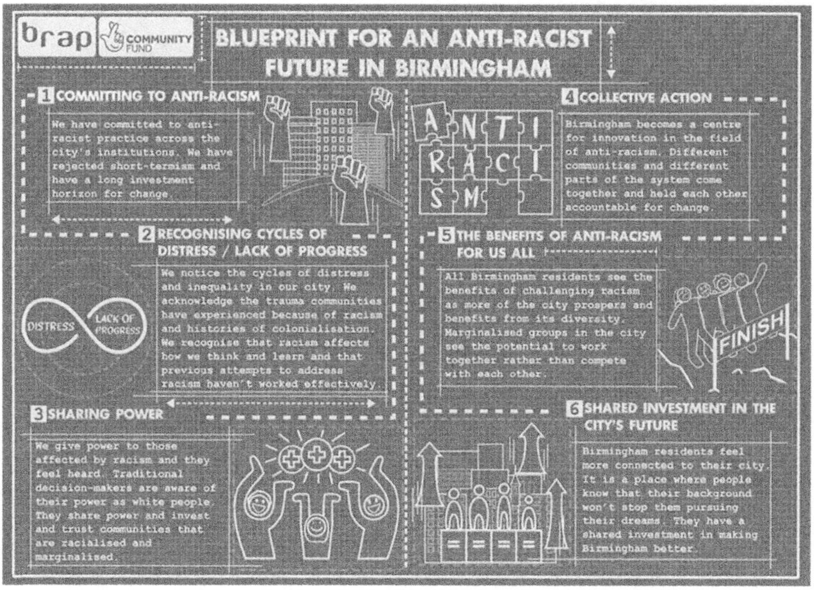

References

brap (2022) *Promoting inclusion, tackling discrimination through place-based action*, Local Trust.

DfE (2020) *Permanent and fixed-period exclusions in England: 2018 to 2019*, Department for Education.

Katz, P. A. and J. A. Kofkin, (1997). 'Race, gender, and young children', in S. S. Luthar, J. A. Burack, D. Cicchetti and J. R. Weisz (eds) *Developmental psychopathology: perspectives on adjustment, risk, and disorder*, Cambridge University Press, 51–74.

University of Birmingham, Research England, West Midlands Growth Company (2020) *Birmingham economic review 2020*, Greater Birmingham Chambers of Commerce.

Why a Trauma-informed Partnership Approach to Women's Asylum Claims and Support is Essential

Sarah Taal

The Baobab Women's Project is an organization led by refugee and migrant women in the West Midlands to improve the handling of the gender aspects of women's asylum claims. It draws on the findings of a University of Birmingham project on sexual and gender-based violence (SGBV) against refugees from displacement to arrival (see SEREDA 2022). A quick glance into how the Home Office assesses a woman's need for protection suggests that it could better guide her through the process of seeking asylum by adopting a trauma-informed partnership approach.

Home Office interviewing and decision-making

The interviewing techniques and decision-making mechanisms of the Home Office are meant to be gender sensitive and responsive to the needs of asylum claimants. However, the system is almost always confusing and the process often takes an inordinately long time. In its caseworker guidance on asylum interviews (HO 2022), the Home Office should provide a positive, secure space in which people seeking protection feel comfortable enough to disclose sensitive information about their experiences. They should be allowed their dignity, treated with respect, and where a vulnerability is identified, steered towards appropriate support (HO 2022: 8/9).

Yohanna, from Eritrea, came to the UK in 2016 and claimed asylum within days of her arrival. She had no passport and entered the country over land. She knew nobody in the UK, and her only information about how the system operated came from smugglers and others seeking sanctuary. She knew it was unsafe for her to remain in Eritrea, but had difficulty explaining why via her interpreter. The Home Office official treated her in an accusatory and angry manner. The interpreter spoke in a different dialect from her and told her not to mention rape in her country because it would give their people a bad name. Although she wanted to answer the interviewer's questions correctly, she became confused by the rate at which they came, panicked and gave some incorrect information. The interview took a long time, and she was not allowed any breaks. She had received no legal advice before the interview.

Fatima flew to the UK from Iraq on a fiancé visa in 2018, so only claimed asylum after her relationship with her fiancé broke down and she became destitute. At this point, she was taken in by the Birmingham Community Hosting (BIRCH) Network, received support from Women's Aid and Baobab, and had access to a legal adviser before her interview. She became very upset during her substantive interview. The Home Office had already received a letter detailing her mental distress and trauma, and a Baobab advocate had asked that they treat her as a vulnerable woman. The Baobab advocate was called in during the interview and, after a discussion with the interviewer, it was agreed that Fatima needed to see a doctor before continuing.

Yohanna was refused protection and called uncredible, but Fatima was granted refugee status. As these contrasting cases show, it is important how women are interviewed, for if they receive care and understanding, they feel better able to talk; and having advice before the interview can help them understand the need to give as many details as they can, even if they find it painful or shameful to do so. Good legal advice, specialist women's advocacy and a proficient interpreter are all imperative.

Asylum support applications and terminations

When people claim asylum, they are granted support if they are destitute; the procedure for deciding whether to grant it is rigorous. In terms of offering appropriate accommodation to vulnerable people, the Home Office should consider individual cases and offer something suitable. Its guidance states that people who have been tortured, raped or subjected to other serious forms of violence can be recognized as vulnerable persons with 'special needs' if there is a professional evaluation to document their claims (Asylum Support 2014: 21.1.2).

Olu from Nigeria, came to the UK in 2018 and, in 2019, both claimed asylum and entered the National Referral Mechanism (NRM) for trafficking survivors. She backed up her claim with a letter of support from her GP, as well as one from an advocate about her accommodation needs. She was granted refuge accommodation, counselling and a 1-1 caseworker from Women's Aid during the NRM process; she later moved to dispersed asylum accommodation near her psychological support. She was able to process her past experiences of SGBV in a safe and supportive environment. She had a community around her and felt able to manage her feelings when navigating the system.

Selam came to the UK from Ethiopia and claimed asylum in 2021; she had been trafficked but was neither identified as a survivor nor processed through the NRM. She was given initial accommodation and then dispersed to Birmingham. She had various health difficulties, including back pain, limited mobility and post-traumatic stress disorder (PTSD) following torture. She was unwell in both the initial and the dispersed accommodation. She was put in an upstairs room and could not get downstairs to use the bathroom or go outside to buy food. In fact, she became extremely ill and wanted to die. After being admitted to hospital, then discharged, she was given a downstairs room and her health gradually improved, although mental flashbacks and nightmares continued to plague her.

Dispersal accommodation is often difficult to negotiate. Women who submit fresh claims after having been in the UK for some time have usually established their own local networks of support. Therefore, if they are undergoing hospital or psychological treatment, the Home Office can grant them local accommodation. Sara from Ethiopia, a survivor of both trafficking and SGBV, who was both undergoing counselling and in physical pain, was given local accommodation mainly because she was able to supply letters from her hospital, doctor and support worker that elucidated her needs. Hana from Eritrea, however, also a survivor of trafficking and SGBV, was sent to a city outside her area mainly because she had not accessed GP care or counselling. Needless to say, Sara's health stabilized, whereas Hana's deteriorated. Whether women have supporting documentation often depends on who they meet, and who might have sent medical reports on their behalf to the Home Office for consideration.

Unless they have children, women refused protection are evicted from their asylum support and left destitute. When Maya, who was without friends to help her, was refused protection and made homeless, she accessed a night shelter after being raped by a man who had been offering to help her. Fahima engaged in survival sex to eat and put a roof over her head. This is a common story among refugee women (Dudhia 2020). It goes without saying that it is unsafe for women who have been subjected to SGBV to be evicted and forced into precarious situations to stay alive.

Women are sometimes wrongfully evicted from the places in which they are staying, which can cause them great distress. Chloe had already submitted a claim for protection, so when the Home Office sent her an eviction letter, she launched an appeal against it. The Home Office then withdrew the eviction, stating that it had not received her recent claim and giving her another email to send it to. Although she re-sent her claim to the revised email address, her accommodation provider still came to the property to enforce the eviction order, and threatened to call the police if she refused to move. It was only after the formal intervention of a third party that she was advised that she could stay. As a documented survivor of torture who had been traumatized by a system refusing to protect her, having to worry about being made homeless on top of her ongoing concerns about whether her claim would be accepted was taking a heavy toll on her health. However, Chloe has now been granted humanitarian protection.

What type of support is provided has a huge effect on a woman's ability to navigate her way through and engage with the asylum system without too much distress. When women have suitable accommodation, the backing of a community and a network of supporters, they feel up to doing what is required to regularize their situation, such as attending interviews and securing advice from their solicitors. When placed in inappropriate accommodation they become ill and fight just to survive.

The granting of asylum status, refusals, psychological help and trauma-informed care

Whether or not women are granted asylum status has a lot to do with the quality of the care and advise they receive throughout their asylum journey, and whether they can access safe accommodation near supportive networks.

Since being a refugee is inevitably associated with having experienced traumatic situations, all applicants for asylum should be offered access to psychological services. This is especially important in the light of the finding that the very act of having to recount their painful experiences to the representatives of various agencies, such as the Home Office, voluntary organizations, the NHS, and counsellors, rekindles rather than alleviates the trauma. Women find it shameful to discuss some of their experiences and, during their sessions at Baobab, frequently complain of suffering from flashbacks and headaches as a result. Their distress is particularly great when officials dismiss or disbelieve their accounts. Against Violence and Abuse, a UK-based charity geared towards ending gender-based violence and abuse, has been doing helpful work in this respect (see AVA 2018). More training needs to be available to all people who work with refugees so that they can provide gender and trauma-informed care.

In and of itself a trauma-informed approach is not enough; the techniques and methods that the practitioners use must also be trauma informed. If the right psychological help and care is provided from the start of the asylum process, the refugees emerging from the process will be more empowered and better able to engage in life after their asylum status has been secured.

References

AVA (Against Violence and Abuse) (2018) Charity website, available at: https://avaproject.org.uk.

Asylum Support (2014) 'Policy bulletin instruction', UK Visas and Immigration, available at: https://www.gov.uk/government/publications/asylum-support-instructions-policy-bulletins.

HO (2022) 'Home Office asylum interview guidance: version 9', available at: https://assets.publishing.service.gov.uk/government/uploads/system/uploads/attachment_data/file/1083449/Asylum_interview.pdf.

SEREDA (2022) SEREDA Project webpage, Institute for Research into Superdiversity, University of Birmingham, available at: https://www.birmingham.ac.uk/research/superdiversity-institute/sereda/index.aspx.

Dudhia P. (2020) '"Will I ever be safe?" Asylum-seeking women made destitute in the UK', Women for Refugee Women report, available at: www.refugeewomen.co.uk/wp-content/uploads/2020/02/WRW-Will-I-ever-be-safe-web.pdf.

We are All from Somewhere

Sabir Zazai

As I write, more than a hundred million people (UNHCR 2022) across the world are experiencing displacement. We live in an increasingly unstable world, where the speed and scale of forced migration is outpacing solutions.

Behind each one of these figures is a person just like you and me, a person with loved ones, with hopes and dreams for the future, someone who wants to live in a safe environment. Life as a refugee is never easy and for people who have not experienced displacement it can be difficult to imagine

Imagine having to leave your home and everything you love with no notice. Imagine having to take a dangerous journey in your search for safety. Imagine having to negotiate your way through a complex legal system. And then imagine adjusting to life in a strange country. For a hundred million men, women and children displaced around the world, this is a daily reality.

I can say this with some authority because I had to experience life as a displaced person at a very young age. I, along with my family, first became internally displaced when a terrible civil conflict broke out between the various factions of mujahideen leaders after the fall of the communist regime in Afghanistan. We remained internally displaced for many years, counting the days, weeks and months before being able to make a peaceful return to our family home in Kabul, but things only got worse.

My own experience taught me that, unless life becomes unbearable, not everyone wants to cross an international border. Today, there are 6.9 million people displaced by conflict in Syria and 3.6 million by the war in Yemen. The number of people living in internal displacement around the world reached a record 53.2 million at the end of 2021 (UNHCR 2022).

A key challenge in responding to forced migration is that we often fail even to try to understand its root causes. When people are forced to move, to become refugees, to leave everything behind, it is because they are having to contend with injustices, inequalities, and human rights violations – inequalities in the right to be safe and protected, to be who you are, to think what you think, to say what you say, to be healthy, and to ensure that your children can go to school. Inequalities and injustices are at the very heart of forced migration and until we recognize that we shall never be able to address the reasons why people move in the first place.

The responses we have seen to global displacements from so many leaders and states can best be described as superficial, and lacking in moral leadership and compassion. Not even 1 per cent of refugees are resettled each year. Because of an absence of coherence, leadership and international collaboration, people end up enduring further suffering and injustices while internally displaced, without prospects of either returning to rebuild their homes, or safe routes to seek protection elsewhere.

In many Western countries, including the UK, this commitment to offer sanctuary to those seeking protection has been under growing attack and, in recent years, an attack turbocharged by the rise of populist national-ism from Australia to Hungary, from Trump's USA to here in the UK. For too long we have relied on governments to 'do the right thing' when it comes to refugee protection and integration. They rarely do.

Here in the UK, the current frontline in this onslaught is the Nationality and Borders Act (2022), sometimes dubbed the 'Anti Refugee Bill', which received royal assent in the Queen's Speech in May that year. Quite simply, this is the biggest threat to refugee rights we have seen in the UK for decades. Drawing much from the Australian conservative playbook on making extreme calls on refugees the norm, this act drives a coach and horses through Britain's fundamental commitment to providing asylum for those fleeing persecution and war. In fact, it is so extreme that the UN refugee body took the unusual step of condemning the proposed UK law on the grounds that it would contravene international law (UNHCR 2021).

Major elements of the new Nationality and Borders Act came into force on 27 June 2022. The act enshrines two classes of refugees based not on *why* they came (what forced them to flee their home) but on *how* they came (for example, if they were forced to come by 'irregular' routes such as in lorries or boats – as I did). Under the new law, the government is empowered to rule that people forced to reach the UK via whichever route they possibly could would not have their asylum claims heard, no matter how valid their case, and to expel them to another country.

The new laws give the UK government powers to expel people seeking asylum 'offshore' to a country with which they have no connection and before their claim for asylum has been given a fair hearing in the UK. This would be similar to the controversial, expensive and failed approach Australia uses but only worse because people will be asked to claim asylum elsewhere. While the government does not yet have the agreements or infrastructure it needs to put this into practice, apart from the widely criticized Rwanda plan (Home Office 2022), the powers in the act would enable it to move to it in future. The new law could also criminalize people helping asylum seekers reach the UK – not just people smugglers, but refugees themselves or others providing help, such as those rescuing people at risk of drowning; even potentially the Royal National Lifeboat Institution (RNLI).

The UK government has already shifted to housing asylum seekers in out-of-town institutional settings, such as army barracks, rather than in flats or houses in the community, where they would be able to integrate and start rebuilding their lives. This is despite the disastrous recent experience of the government putting people in segregated institutions condemned by the High Court for their appalling conditions and preventable Covid outbreaks (High Court 2021). The UK government says that people should seek asylum through so called 'safe and legal routes'. First, there is no illegal way to seek asylum. Second, these new laws introduced by the Nationality and Borders Act offer no new safe routes to sanctuary. On the contrary, the new laws fail to set any clear global target for resettling refugees in the UK through international resettlement programmes. Together With Refugees, a collective of more than 500 organizations calling for a fairer and more humane asylum system, is calling on the government to commit to a clear target to resettle at least 10,000 refugees a year through internationally-agreed programmes and to allow for better family reunion rules so that those with family members in the UK could be easily reunited. Sadly, the new act has no such provisions.

We are going through one of the most critical times in the UK's history of asylum and immigration policy. The war in Ukraine and the events of August 2021 in Afghanistan should have been enough of a reminder of how life can change for people in a split second. The war in Ukraine also reminded us of the upswell of public generosity with people opening their hearts and doors to welcome people fleeing this dreadful conflict. Instead of harnessing this moment of public goodwill, the UK government is embarking on an inhumane and costly anti-refugee regime that will make life difficult for people seeking sanctuary and it will leave an indelible stain on the UK's reputation.

This is the moment for us to mobilize from the bottom up, in our families and communities. We are the ones able to make a difference. The ripple effects of our behaviour and actions have huge potential, however small they may seem. We must remind the government that these divisive laws are not made in our name. They divide our diverse communities by instilling fear and anxiety in our society at a time when we need to work together for a better future and a more welcoming society for everybody.

There are many humane alternatives to these plans, all based on years of peer-reviewed academic research (Solomon and Betts 2022). Trading refugees, or shutting the door on people fleeing conflicts, violence and human rights violations, are not solutions and they are certainly not in line with our traditions, our ambitions for a global Britain, or a cause for good. The truth is that migration makes us stronger. When we welcome people from across the world, our communities are deeply enrichened by the contributions and experiences of those who make their homes in them. The path the UK government is trying to forge is one that will deprive us all of so much. At this perilous moment, we must stand together and speak loudly and proudly about the ways in which migration has enriched our lives.

We are all from somewhere. Migration will continue to be an important part of our history and offering people sanctuary is one of our most fundamental values as a place of welcome. It is not where we have come from or how we have arrived here but it is where we go as a society that really matters and, sadly, where we are heading right now is not looking good.

References

High Court (2021) 'Napier Barracks judgment', Neutral citation number: [2021] EWHC 1489 (Admin), 3 June, available at: https://www.judiciary.uk/wp-content/uploads/2022/07/Napier-Barracks-judgment.pdf.

Home Office (2022) 'Memorandum of understanding between the UK and Rwanda', 14 April, available at: https://www.gov.uk/government/publications/memorandum-of-understanding-mou-between-the-uk-and-rwanda.

Nationality and Borders Act (2022) UK government legislation, available at: https://www.legislation.gov.uk/ukpga/2022/36/contents/enacted.

Solomon, E. and A. Betts (2022) 'Asylum plan ignores viable alternatives', *The Times*, 19 April, available at: https://www.thetimes.co.uk/article/asylum-plan-ignores-viable-alternatives-jmk28jscr.

UNHCR (2021) 'UK asylum bill would break international law, damaging refugees and global co-operation', press release, 23 September, available at: https://www.unhcr.org/uk/news/press/2021/9/614c163f4/unhcr-uk-asylum-bill-would-break-international-law-damaging-refugees-and.html.

UNHCR (2022) *Global trends: forced displacement in 2021*, United Nations High Commissioner for Refugees, available at: https://www.unhcr.org/62a9d1494/global-trends-report-2021.

Breaking News:
How we Helped Change the Story

Nazek Ramadan

As migrants living in the UK in 2010, we felt as if we were under attack. We had been attacked before, but in that year's election, for which migration was presented to the public as one of the country's top three concerns, was a tipping point. The public debate about immigration was ubiquitous in that election year: politicians looking for electoral gain were demonizing us, scapegoating us for shortcomings for which we were not responsible and for issues that had nothing to do with us, yet the media completely ignored us. Everyone was talking about us, but not *with* us. Our voices were not heard in the news or read in magazines and newspapers. Our own research into the coverage of migration in the media showed that only 15 per cent of the stories on migration had quoted a migrant (Crawley et al. 2016). Our faces were anonymous. We were not people with a life story, or with likes and dislikes: we were an issue, a number, something to be managed and contained.

Some of us had had enough and were not going to remain silent for any longer: that year a small group of us, mainly migrants and refugees but also some highly committed activists and media experts, came together and set up Migrant Voice with a view to making our voices heard. We started with a specific objective in mind, which was to bring migrants like ourselves to the forefront of the stories about us. We wanted to tell our own stories and engage in the debate that was currently taking place about us, albeit without us. We had a broader goal: we wanted to improve the ways in which migrants, asylum seekers and refugees were being depicted in society. Cognizant of the important role the media plays in shaping public opinion, we realized that it is easy for news stories to fit migrants into certain categories; as we found in our 2020 report (Migrant Voice 2020a), these stories often reduce migrants to being either a threat, a victim, or a hero. Given that it appears to be more difficult to portray migrants as the multi-faceted humans we are, from the beginning we knew that we, as migrants, needed to learn how to engage with and influence the media.

We began by training migrants in media skills, and this involved creating spaces in which to build positive relationships between them and journalists. As migrants, our goal was to challenge the discrimination and negative rhetoric directed towards us in the media, amplify our voices, and pass on our new skills and knowledge to the wider community.

For a number of years, we wrote, edited and published a newspaper, also called *Migrant Voice* (Migrant Voice 2015), which gave us an opportunity to ensure that the articles, interviews, editorials, photography, and so forth reflected our voices. Eventually, in an attempt to reach more people, we came to a strategic decision to channel our work through the mainstream media, so discontinued our newspaper. Even so, one of our recent projects involved the publication in 2020 of *Beyond*, a migrant-led e-magazine that celebrated Black History Month. In an opening message to *Beyond*, one of our members wrote: 'some of us, like myself, had no previous media experience and struggled with even the most basic technology, yet here I am writing a welcome message in an online magazine!'

Our 'Meet a Migrant' initiative brought migrants and journalists together in a room in which they could start engaging in face-to-face conversations. These meetings led to high-profile media appearances and the development of a media toolkit (Migrant Voice 2020b), which was later used to train Migrant Voice 'ambassadors' to identify and pitch stories from within their communities, and to give them the skills and confidence they needed to do so.

Through our training programme, which includes our signature 'Media Lab' sessions, hundreds of migrants have been taught how to develop, pitch, and write a story, as well as to use their own words and images to create videos, photographs and podcasts. Many of these sessions are hosted by professional journalists and editors. In 2019 alone, we trained and mentored 500 members on how to tell their stories. Of these, 150 appeared in the media and a further 150 were able to speak directly to policymakers about the issues affecting them. This contributed towards migrants acquiring more equality in political spaces. Migrants, who rarely inhabit such spaces, were able to share their experiences and perspectives directly with the MPs and take part in discussions as equal partners. These MPs now consult us about migration issues, seek our perspectives, submit questions on our behalf, and attend our meetings. We feel proud of having been able to persuade the media to pay significantly more attention in their news stories to migrant voices and perspectives. Their reports now feature migrants far more prominently and their voices are more nuanced than ever before; in some of the media outlets with which we have worked, journalists now contact us to ask us what stories and issues we think are missing from the coverage.

From its inception, we used Migrant Voice to call for changes to policy, but over the years came to realize that we would have to step up our campaigning work if were to introduce the changes we needed. We can now use our media stories to raise awareness as part of our campaigns and speak directly to policymakers. Our work expanded over time and we now regularly speak on the media, on public platforms, in communities, on the streets and in cultural settings to create positive changes in the society towards countering xenophobia, forging new ties, running campaigns, strengthening communities, influencing policy, and delivering justice.

In our 'Meet the Editors' initiative, we offer informed, fair analysis of news reports on migrants and migration, and introduce various media outlets to contacts from within our communities (the driving force behind all newsrooms). This has enabled us to move from being a serial pitcher of individual stories to becoming a trusted source on previously unreported events, a provider of new readers and, most importantly, an informed adviser on migration issues. This has led to successful collaborations with editorial rooms and an increase in more accurate, nuanced and diverse depictions of migrants' experiences. At last, we can start to recognize ourselves and our voices in the reports.

Twelve years on from when we set up, the media landscape has changed significantly. While its mainstream outlets remain extremely influential, the exponential rise in the use of social media has meant that it is no longer unusual in the news to hear directly from the migrants, refugees and asylum seekers themselves. They are now increasingly speaking about their negative experiences of the immigration system, their marginalization and exclusion, and their wish to bring about positive changes that will build solidarity in the society.

Since migration continues to be an important and highly contentious topic of debate in the UK. we must continue to ensure that the voices of our members remain centre stage, so that they can exert a positive influence on the media, public opinion, and government policies on migration. Our long-term aim is to build Britain into a society in which migrants and refugees have full equality, a society in which they are heard, respected, have rights, and are embraced as equal members of the community.

We are not there yet. Migrants are operating in a hostile environment – and one that is socially, politically and economically deliberately fostered as such. People who come here are scapegoated as 'spongers' (Goodfellow 2019); their rights are curtailed;[1] they are punished with extortionate and ever-increasing visa fees (Migrant Voice 2022); and their families are cruelly divided (Reunite Families UK 2022). They are mistrusted and bureaucratically harried.[2] And, although their voices are heard more than in the past, they are still not listened to enough. Our work continues.

References

Crawley, H., S. McMahon and K. Jones (2016) 'Victims and villains: migrant voices in the British media', Coventry: Centre for Trust, Peace and Social Relations, Coventry University, available at: https://www.migrantvoice.org/design2020/img/upload/3._Victims_and_Villains_Digital-2-Feb_2016_1.pdf.

Goodfellow, M. (2019) *Hostile environment: how immigrants became scapegoats*, Verso.

Migrant Voice (2015) 'MV newspaper 2015', webpage, available at: www.migrantvoice.org/work/research_and_campaigns/mv-newspaper-2015.

Migrant Voice (2020a) 'UK media coverage of migration during the first Covid-19 lockdown', report, December, available at https://www.migrantvoice.org/img/upload/Migrant_Voice_Media_Monitoring_Report-December_2020.pdf.

Migrant Voice (2020b) 'Making headlines: getting migrant voices into the media: a toolkit', available at https://www.migrantvoice.org/design2020/img/upload/5._Migrant_Voice_media_toolkit-2018_.pdf.

Migrant Voice (2022) 'Destroying hopes, dreams and lives: how the UK visa costs and process system impact migrants' lives', April, available at: www.migrantvoice.org/img/upload/Visa_fees_report_-_digital_final_to_upload.pdf.

Reunite Families UK (2022) 'Two pager summary of the immigration rules as they impact spouses and families', available at: https://www.reunitefamiliesuk.co.uk/wp-content/uploads/2022/07/reuniteonepager-converted.pdf.

1. For example, many migrants and their British children have no access to state support. See https://nrpfnetwork.org.uk/.
2. For example, migrants have to pass 'right to rent' and 'right to work' checks before they can rent a property or become employed.

A New Era of Acceptance: Immigration Attitudes after Brexit

Heather Rolfe

For many, the vote to leave the EU was seen as proof of a growth in negative attitudes to immigration. In 2016, public concern about it was high, and had been on the increase since the start of the decade (Blinder and Richards 2022). Concern about immigration peaked in 2015, with the British Election Survey finding that 71 per cent of people agreed that 'too many people have been let into this country'; by 2017, this had fallen to 66 per cent and then, by 2019, had dropped further to 53 per cent. On immigration for work, trends are similar: the latest British Social Attitudes survey found that 50 per cent of the public believe that immigration is good for our economy, compared with 21 per cent in 2011 (NatCen 2022).

People have become more concerned about other policy issues. Our 2012 British Future polling on hopes and fears found that almost one in four people were worried about immigration, but a repeat of this poll in 2022 found that their concerns about prices, bills and pressure on the health service loomed larger. Older people, who have traditionally been the most concerned about immigration, are now more worried about the future of our planet (Ballinger et al. 2022). Some of the concerns that have displaced those about migration may be more enduring than others, for example those centred on the cost of living. However, it is not just that other issues now eclipse people's worries about immigration, but that, in a dramatic turnaround since 2015, people are more likely to see the impact of immigration as positive rather than negative. This indicates that the public now thinks differently about its impact, not just that it is less contentious. As Figure 1 shows, in 2015, 41 per cent of people believed the impact of immigration to be negative (scoring 0–4 on the impact of migration), and just under a third saw it as positive (scoring 6–10). By

2022, this had reversed, with 41 per cent believing the impact of immigration to be positive, and under a third to be negative. The proportion seeing its impact as neutral (recording a score of 5) has remained constant at around one in six people.

Figure 1: Has migration had a positive or negative impact on Britain?

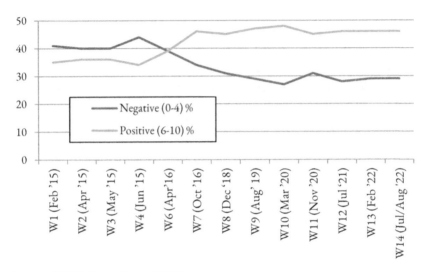

Source: British Future/Ipsos (2022).

Migration for work is now considered necessary

In 2012, concerns about migrants taking jobs from British workers were widespread, partly fuelled by statements from politicians and media coverage based on spurious evidence from campaigning organizations, for example Migration Watch (Migration Observatory 2012). These concerns have subsided over the years: while in 2012 two-thirds of the public thought that immigration had a negative impact on the availability of jobs, this fell to only a quarter in 2022, with only 9 per cent seeing its impact as 'very negative' (Ballinger et al. 2022).

Our British Future/Ipsos biannual immigration attitudes tracker finds that people are now much more likely to see immigration as necessary for employers and the economy. A large majority of people now believe that employers should be allowed to recruit from overseas to job vacancies that cannot be filled within the UK, at all levels of skill (Rolfe et al. 2021).

Figure 2: Under what circumstances should employers be allowed to recruit people from outside the UK?

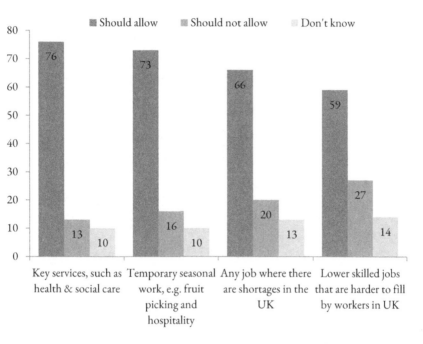

Source: British Future/Ipsos (2022), sample size: 3206.

Roughly three-quarters of the public supports overseas recruitment for positions in key services, such as health and social care (76 per cent). A similarly high proportion of the public supports the use of migrant labour for seasonal work, such as fruit picking and hospitality (73 per cent). These two policies are more strongly supported by older than younger people, with more than 80 per cent of those aged 55 in favour of these options. Perhaps more surprising is that two-thirds of people support recruitment of migrants to any job for which there are labour shortages, and well over half support recruitment of people from overseas for the low-skilled jobs that are harder to fill from within the UK.

Most people also believe that migrants have a role to play in recovery. In another about-turn since 2012, 53 per cent of people believe that migrants' skills and labour are necessary to achieve this aim. In 2012, a similar proportion believed that immigration would damage economic recovery by taking jobs from British workers (Ballinger et al. 2022).

Figure 3: Are migrants' skills good or bad for economic recovery?

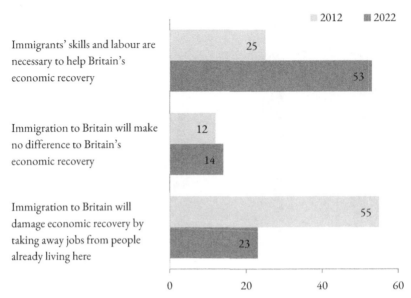

Source: Ballinger et al. (2022: 14), based on a Focaldata survey sample of 2,006.

It is not just about the economy

The shift in attitudes goes beyond the economic impact of migration. Between 2012 and 2021, the public changed its mind about the impact of immigration on certain aspects of UK life, with the biggest shift involving the NHS: our 'Jubilee Britain' research found that more than half the public (53 per cent) sees the impact of migration on the NHS as positive and 25 per cent as negative (16 per cent as 'slightly' and 9 per cent as 'very' negative). Back in 2012, more than four in ten (45 per cent) saw migration as having a negative impact, and only a third saw it as positive (Ballinger et al. 2022).

People are now also much less concerned about the impact of migration on schools, with roughly equal proportions of the public concerned about its impact, believing that it has no impact at all, or seeing its impact as positive (Ballinger et al. 2022). While people worried about non-English speaking migrants lowering standards, their fears were proved unfounded and children have integrated well (Geay et al. 2013; Strand et al. 2015). Yet, our Jubilee Britain research found that migration anxieties still surrounded other areas of life in the UK, particular over housing and crime.

Why have attitudes changed?

A number of factors are likely to be responsible for the change in attitudes towards immigration. The UK has experienced considerable economic and social change in recent years: Brexit and Covid-19 have impacted on people's lives in unexpected ways. Our British Future/Ipsos biannual immigration attitudes tracker has found that one in five people (21 per cent) now say they have become more positive about immigration since the referendum. This is not necessarily a reliable indicator of attitude shifts, since some will have become more positive without acknowledging it. However, the reasons given suggest that certain key influences have affected the public's thinking.

Figure 4: Why have people who have changed their minds become more positive about immigration since the EU referendum?

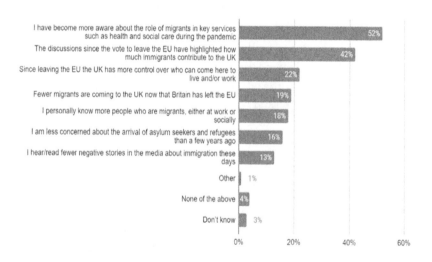

Source: British Future/Ipsos (2022), sample size: 3206.

More than half attribute their change of view to a greater awareness of the role of migrants in key services, such as health and social care, during the pandemic. This factor had particularly influenced the thinking of people in the older age groups, with two-thirds of people aged over 45 stating this as a reason for their more positive attitude towards migrants. This is likely to reflect social contact with the sector's workforce as well as health concerns. Changing attitudes to migrant workers are likely to

341

reflect people's experiences of life during the pandemic. Media coverage and personal experiences shone a light on migrants' role in key sectors such as health and social care, delivery, food and drink production, and agriculture. Labour shortages during the recovery phase, as well as from the effects of Brexit, may well have played a further part in these attitude shifts. Other reasons for changes in attitudes, as reported by the public, include greater control over entry than existed under free movement and, for some, reduced immigration (although net migration has increased in recent years).

It is good to talk

Almost half the public thinks we talk too little about immigration and two-thirds of those with the most negative views are more likely to believe this. The saying, 'it is good to talk', especially applies to immigration. Our regular attitudes tracker survey found the second most common reason given by those who had changed their attitudes was discussions about immigration since 2016 (Rolfe et al. 2022). These discussions are likely to have been wide-ranging, going beyond Brexit and the economy to the impacts of immigration on schools, the health services and on communities in general. Talking helps people to listen to others, as well as giving them a say, so we must keep on talking.

'Contribution' and 'control' as twin principles

Research has highlighted the role of key principles in public attitudes to immigration. Those that resonate most with the public are 'contribution' and 'control'. Contribution refers to the expectation that migrants will 'put in before they take out', through taxation, national insurance and social mixing. 'Control' refers to rules and procedures for entry to the UK, to weed out those intending to commit crime or live off the state. Some leave voters saw free movement as enabling those with such malevolent intentions. Reducing numbers was, for many, of secondary concern.

Experiences of Brexit and Covid-19 have reinforced these values: the end of free movement has helped to address the concerns of those who wanted more control over immigration. Living through the pandemic has highlighted to many the social and economic contributions of migrants, especially in certain key sectors.

Is the future positive?

While talking has set some people in a more positive direction, it is also likely that their greater familiarity with migration, and contact with migrants at work and in the community, has also played an important part in changing their views. Attracted by job opportunities, migrants from Poland and other central and eastern Europe countries settled all over the UK. The most recent large group of migrants, from Hong Kong, is similarly dispersed throughout the country, including towns and suburbs with relatively few migrants (Rolfe and Chan 2022). More British people are now likely to see migrants less as outsiders and more as colleagues and neighbours with different backgrounds. Day-to-day contact will have helped normalize immigration for many British people who have previously experienced immigration second hand, including through the media. Perhaps as a reflection of their greater familiarity with migrants, as well as empathy for those who arrive in the UK under difficult circumstances, there is considerable public interest in welcoming newcomers from abroad.

As Figure 5 shows, this includes helping migrants learn English, activities organized by schools, and participating in social events designed to make contact with refugees. The survey does not specify the origin or circumstances of the new arrivals, so people will have been indicating their general support and not only that tied to a particular programme. At the same time, the public is much more divided on appropriate policy responses to asylum seekers and refugees than it is towards work or student migration (Rolfe et al. 2022).

While the post-Brexit future for immigration attitudes looks positive, feelings about people migrating to this country for work could change should circumstances become more difficult for British families. While people might feel fairly relaxed about migrant fruit-pickers and care workers coming here, and support the aim of attracting highly skilled talent to Britain, they will expect to benefit from the promises made for jobs and skills in the levelling-up White Paper (DLUHC 2022). The government and regions will need to strike the right balance between attracting talent to fill labour market gaps, and ensuring that local people, especially the younger ones, have the skills and opportunities that they will need to prosper.

Figure 5: Interest in taking part in activities to welcome migrants or refugees

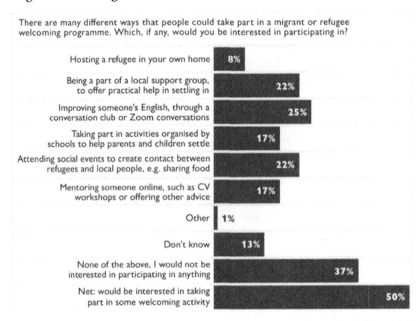

There are many different ways that people could take part in a migrant or refugee welcoming programme. Which, if any, would you be interested in participating in?

Activity	%
Hosting a refugee in your own home	8%
Being a part of a local support group, to offer practical help in settling in	22%
Improving someone's English, through a conversation club or Zoom conversations	25%
Taking part in activities organised by schools to help parents and children settle	17%
Attending social events to create contact between refugees and local people, e.g. sharing food	22%
Mentoring someone online, such as CV workshops or offering other advice	17%
Other	1%
Don't know	13%
None of the above, I would not be interested in participating in anything	37%
Net: would be interested in taking part in some welcoming activity	50%

Source: Welcoming Committee (2022) using research by ICM Unlimited for British Future/Welcoming Committee, 25–28 March, with a sample size of 2,012.

References

Blinder, S. and L. Richards (2022) 'UK public opinion toward immigration: overall attitudes and level of concern', briefing document, The Migration Observatory at the University of Oxford, 20 January, available at: https://migration observatory.ox.ac.uk/resources/briefings/uk-public-opinion-toward-immigra tion-overall-attitudes-and-level-of-concern/.

Ballinger, S., S. Katwala and H. Rolfe (2022) *Jubilee Britain: after a decade of upheaval, where are we going now?*, British Future, available at: https://www.britishfuture.org/publication/jubilee-britain/.

DLUHC (Department for Levelling Up, Housing and Communities) (2022) 'Levelling up the United Kingdom', government policy paper, available at: www.gov.uk/government/publications/levelling-up-the-united-kingdom.

Geay, C., S. McNally and S. Telhaj (2013) 'Non-native Speakers of English in the Classroom: What Are the Effects on Pupil Performance?', *The Economic Journal*, 123 (570): F281–F307, doi: 10.1111/ecoj.12054.

Ipsos (2022) *Attitudes towards immigration*, Immigration tracker 2015–2022, available at: https://www.ipsos.com/en-uk/immigration-tracker-october-2022.

Migration Observatory (2012) 'Migrant workers: taking our jobs – or not?', webpage, available at: https://migrationobservatory.ox.ac.uk/resources/commentaries/migrant-workers-taking-our-jobs-or-not/.

NatCen (National Centre for Social Research) (2022) 'Broken Britain? Public attitudes in an era of crisis', British Social Attitudes reports, available at: https://www.bsa.natcen.ac.uk.

Rolfe, H., S. Ballinger and S. Katwala (2021) *Immigration: a changing debate*, British Future, available at: https://www.britishfuture.org/publication/immigration-a-changing-debate/.

Rolfe, H., S. Ballinger and S. Katwala (2022) *Shifting views: tracking attitudes to immigration in 2022*, British Future, available at: https://www.britishfuture.org/publications/.

Rolfe, H. and P. Chan (2022) 'Settling in: Hong Kongers and their new lives in the UK', Welcoming Committee for Hong Kongers/British Future, available at: https://www.welcomehk.org/research/settling-in-report.

Strand, S., L. Malmberg and J. Hall (2015) 'English as an Additional Language (EAL) and educational achievement in England: an analysis of the National Pupil Database', Department of Education, University of Oxford, January, available at: https://www.naldic.org.uk/Resources/NALDIC/Research%20and%20Information/Documents/eal-and-educational-achievement-prof-s-strand.pdf.

Welcoming Committee (The Welcoming Committee for Hong Kongers) (2022) 'Britons welcome Hong Kongers as figures show UK issues over 110,000 BN(O) visas', available at: https://www.welcomehk.org/news/britons-welcome-hong-kongers-as-figures-show-uk-issues-over-110000-bno-visas.

Printed in Great Britain
by Amazon